Women in the West

SERIES EDITORS

Sandra L. Myres
University of Texas at Arlington

Elliott West
University of Arkansas

Julie Roy Jeffrey
Goucher College

Other titles in the *Women in the West* series are:

A STRANGER
IN HER
NATIVE
LAND

Crayon drawing of Alice Fletcher
by E. H. Miller, 1888.
(Peabody Museum, Harvard University)

Joan Mark

A Stranger in Her Native Land

ALICE FLETCHER

AND THE AMERICAN INDIANS

University of Nebraska Press

LINCOLN AND LONDON

The paper in this book
meets the minimum requirements
of American National Standard
for Information Sciences—Permanence of Paper
for Printed Library Materials,
ANSI Z39.48–1984.

Library of Congress Cataloging-in-Publication Data
Mark, Joan T., 1937–
A stranger in her native land.
(Women in the West)
"Bibliography of works by Alice Fletcher
and Francis La Flesche": p.
Bibliography: p.
Includes index.
1. Fletcher, Alice C.
(Alice Cunningham), 1838–1923.
2. La Flesche, Francis, d. 1932.
3. Indianists—United States—Biography.
4. Anthropologists—United States—Biography.
I. Title.   II. Series.
E57.F54M37   1988
973'.0497
87-30201
ISBN 0-8032-3128-8 (alk. paper)
ISBN 0-8032-8156-0 (pbk.)

To my mother

FOREST MOSIER TE PASKE

and to the memory of my father

HENRY J. TE PASKE

Contents

Contents

x

PART 4

Abroad and at Home

Illustrations

Preface

"Well-nigh all anthropology is personal history."
—Alice C. Fletcher, quoting Frank Hamilton Cushing, in a
memorial tribute.

I discovered Alice Fletcher fifteen years ago when I came across several hundred of her letters to F. W. Putnam, the curator of the Peabody Museum of Archaeology and Ethnology at Harvard. The letters began in 1878 with terse, formal requests for information. They soon swelled to long confidential accounts of her adventures as, with Putnam's encouragement, Alice Fletcher at the age of forty-three turned herself into an anthropologist. She left her friends in New York and New England and traveled west, to Dakota Territory to go camping with the Sioux, to Nebraska where she lived with the Omahas, and to Idaho where she lived among the Nez Perces. She sent collections of artifacts back to the Peabody Museum and then descriptions of Plains Indians religious ceremonies and a monograph on Omaha Indian music.

My initial interest in Alice Fletcher was as a member of a lost generation in American anthropology, a little-known group of remarkable pioneers, mostly men but including several women, who between 1880 and 1900 shaped the study of anthropology more or less as it continues in the United States. I thought then (and still think) that this group had been ignored in scholarship partly because of a deeply ingrained academic preference for European rather than American intellectual forebears. Anthropologists would rather trace their lineage back to Marcel Mauss or Claude Lévi-Strauss than to Frank Hamilton Cushing, to Franz Boas rather than to F. W. Putnam. Alice Fletcher was a member of that lost, overlooked generation. My first concern in an earlier book, *Four Anthropologists* (1980), was to try to set that record straight. Alice Fletcher was one of the four, the only woman, and I treated her no differently than the men. Her sex seemed to me irrelevant, her path to anthropology no more tortuous, her difficulties in the field no greater, her subjects of study no different, than those of her male colleagues.

But as I finished that book and turned to a full-scale biography of Alice Fletcher, my sex-blind position became increasingly untenable. On the one hand I felt the gentle prodding of my feminist friends, who urged me to look at what I had been ignoring. What about, for example, the extensive female support system that Alice Fletcher created for herself? Why was all that support necessary if Alice Fletcher's career moved along as smoothly as did the careers of her male colleagues? On the other hand, and finally overwhelmingly, I began to find that the more I worked on Alice Fletcher in traditional, sex-blind terms, the less I understood her. There seemed to be not one Alice Fletcher but six or seven, as I uncovered caches of correspondence in archives around the country. The Alice Fletcher who wrote plaintively to Phoebe Hearst and sentimentally to Isabel Barrows could turn into a martinet on the Omaha Reservation. The Alice Fletcher who presented herself to F. W. Putnam as a dedicated and cautious empirical scientist, scarcely betraying to him her political interests, became a stubborn, unyielding ideologue with her colleagues in the Indian rights movement. How was I to reconcile these various selves? How did Alice Fletcher herself hold it all together? Was there any central core in her life?

My difficulties were increased by the extraordinary unevenness of the resources available for a biography of Alice Fletcher. Alice Fletcher kept voluminous records of her professional years, the last forty years of her life. These papers, together with those of Francis La Flesche, the young Omaha Indian man who lived with Alice Fletcher as her son, are in the National Anthropological Archives at the Smithsonian. But Alice Fletcher destroyed everything pertaining to the first forty years of her life. What I have been able to learn about Alice Fletcher's early years I have had to piece together from extremely meager sources. Under these circumstances, to attempt a psychoanalytic interpretation of Alice Fletcher's character would be not only impossible but ludicrous.

But, as Gertrude Stein knew, there are other avenues into character besides psychoanalysis or psychology. In *The Making of Ameri-*

cans Stein wrote, "All men and all women, if they keep on in their living come to the repeating that makes it clear to anyone who listens to them then the real nature of them."[1] And again, "I began to get enormously interested in hearing how everybody said the same thing over and over again with infinite variations but over and over again until finally if you listened with great intensity you could hear it rise and fall and tell all that there was inside them."[2]

Taking a clue from Gertrude Stein, I began to listen with great intensity to Alice Fletcher's "repeatings." One of the words she used over and over again in writing of herself is *struggle*, as in "terrible struggle" or "the worst struggle of my life." Nearly always the struggle was against male power or male authority used wrongfully, or it was against the Victorian gender constructs that set limits on what she as a woman could do. She chose a strong word, one that means "to contend or fight violently with." Alice Fletcher did not flinch from recognizing the threat of violence that underlay male power in even the supposedly gentlest and most civilized of battle-fields: the home, the professions, the universities. She recognized the harm that was done her when she was denied due recognition. With no place to vent her anger and her feelings of helplessness she turned them on herself and took to her bed, sometimes for weeks at a time, in what today would probably be diagnosed as depression. Over and over again Alice Fletcher found herself struggling against male power, male authority, and male prerogatives, against the limits her society imposed on her because she was a woman. It was a battle she refused to give up. By the testimony of her actions and her repeated words, this "struggle" can be seen to be a central motif in her life.

As I worked on this book I came to see Alice Fletcher's sex not as irrelevant to her professional activities but as the single most significant factor in explaining the course of her career. Out of the vast amount of excellent recent feminist scholarship, I have cited here, for the most part, only those works to which I specifically refer, but behind these lies a mother lode, the work of a generation of scholars in women's history who have transformed our historical understanding in ways so profound that it will not soon be undone.

The second of Alice Fletcher's "repeatings" that provides a key to understanding her is her statement that she was "alone in the world."

She used this phrase so often that it was as if she pointed to it as the second central emotional theme in her life, a theme that takes us beyond gender constructs to a more generalized American condition. Alice Fletcher understood her aloneness, her rootlessness, to be a direct result of her familial situation, but she used it also as a metaphor for a psychological state of being, her own and gradually that of others too. "We are all immigrants," she told an audience in 1888. In 1915 she wrote, "Living with my Indian friends I found I was a stranger in my native land."[3] She realized that the loneliness she experienced so deeply was not hers alone, that it was common in the American immigrant experience of having moved across and conquered a land but not yet having learned to be a part of it. The American Indians had been here at least ten, perhaps twenty thousand years, time to develop a sense of the sacred geography of America, of nature and their place in it. The Euro-Americans had not. Although they might have been in America for two or three or even, as in Alice Fletcher's case, for nine generations, many still felt uprooted, restless, alone, and lonely.

I have not explicitly interpreted Alice Fletcher according to the tenets of any particular psychological scheme. My understanding of her, however, has been shaped by the theories of Harry Stack Sullivan, to which I was introduced more than twenty years ago by Sullivan's biographer, Helen Swick Perry, when I went to interview her for my dissertation on the influence of Freud on American cultural anthropology. At first glance, Sullivanian psychiatry seems even more bizarrely inappropriate for the data on Alice Fletcher than does orthodox Freudianism. Sullivan worked primarily with very sick male adolescents, mostly schizophrenics, and he pioneered in creating for them small hospital wards where they could interact with carefully chosen staff. He studied the importance of close pre-adolescent friendships, childhood "chums," an approach that is of no use in seeking to understand Alice Fletcher, for we know virtually nothing about those years in her life. But what makes Sullivan appropriate as an interpretive theorist for Alice Fletcher is that he too experienced the aloneness, the isolation, the uprootedness of American life. His response was a therapeutic method in which he tried to help his patients to deal with the dilemmas of their daily lives, to solve present problems and get on with the business of living rather than to trace every problem back to childhood. Where Sullivan is particularly helpful is in his theory of the developing self. In Sullivan's view there is no established self that moves relatively intact and inviolate from infancy through adulthood. Rather, he saw the self as constantly changing in reponse to the "interpersonal relations" in which it is engaged. Sullivan went so far as to suggest that "every human being has as many personalities as he has interpersonal relations."[4]

Sullivan's formulation helped me to see that the different selves that Alice Fletcher seemed to be were not simply roles she played nor adaptive postures crafted to help her get what she needed. She actually was, as each of us is, a slightly different person in each human encounter, a human self not only responding to different people in different ways but also responding to the same person differently, depending on what has happened since the last encounter. Sullivan's theory gives primacy to the ongoing relations between a self and the "significant others" (his term) with whom that self interacts. What this suggests to a biographer is that in the telling of a life, the interactions with other people, the incidents of daily life, are the very essence of the story. Alice Fletcher not only revealed herself in her interactions with others but also, through those interactions, became Alice Fletcher.

If one significant intellectual influence on this book was Harry Stack Sullivan, another was Gertrude Stein. Stein, one of the great literary modernists of the twentieth century, is not usually thought of as a biographer. Yet, in the early years of her career in particular, she was intensely interested in character and in telling lives. Embedded in some of her best-known work, in *Three Lives*, *The Autobiography of Alice B. Toklas*, *The Making of Americans*, and *Everybody's Autobiography*, is a set of ideas that I found nearly revolutionary as a guide to biography, that most atheoretical of genres.

Stein's contribution to biographical theory was fourfold. First, she suggested that the path to understanding another person is not through psychological theory but simply through listening, that people reveal themselves in their "repeatings." Second, she anticipated Sullivan's emphasis on interpersonal relations in her recognition that people define themselves primarily in relation to other people. Third, she debunked the necessity of finding an "important" subject, implying by example that any life if intensely examined will turn out to be worth telling and that any life is worth as much as any other. Every life has value, for its own sake and for the task that Stein assigned to herself for a number of years: "a beginning of the way of knowing the complete history of each one who ever is or was or will be living . . . the winning of so much wisdom."[5] Finally, just as Stein levels persons and our judgments of their importance, so she flattens time. Every moment in a life is as significant as every other moment and reveals as much about that life. What Stein offers a biographer by example is the freedom to choose moments, to use many or few, to break up chronology or adhere to it rigorously.

Harry Stack Sullivan and Gertrude Stein are the shadowy presences behind these pages. If what follows seems to be anecdotal, monochromatic, and without dramatic structuring to key denouements at critical moments, it is at least deliberately so. I have tried to write this story of a life in a way that is congruent with my understanding of how life is lived, an understanding that has been immeasurably shaped by their ideas.

Two comments are perhaps in order about my relation to Alice Fletcher as a subject. When I began writing this biography I identified with her and idealized her. Inevitably, as I learned more and began to see her mistakes and blind spots, I found myself embarrassed by her and very critical of her. As I neared the end and began the process of separation from her, the highs and lows evened out. My feelings about her became more balanced and even, I hope, objective. I write of this because I suspect that it is common among biographers and is worth sharing. I experienced too that change in understanding that age brings. As I grew older, I understood her differently. These phenomena point to the fact that biography is the result of a happenstance interaction of one human life with another, as a limited body of data on one person is interpreted by another person at a particular time and place in the writer's own living.

Many friends and colleagues have found materials, sent references, and shared ideas and information with me. They include David Aberle, Joan Cindy Amatniek, Robert Cogan, Michael Coleman, Paula Fleming, Ralph W. Dexter, Pozzi Escot, Gary Sue Goodman, Jesse Green, Margaret Harris, Joy Harvey, Dennis Hastings, Curtis M.

Hinsley, Jr., Emlyn Hodge, Frederick E. Hoxie, Dell Hymes, Ira Jacknis, Edith Kaufman, Sally Gregory Kohlstedt, Marjorie F. Lambert, Dorothy Sara Lee, John Lindahl, Lea McChesney, Donald McVicker, Allen C. and Eleanor D. Morrill, Carl Nagin, Gregory Palmer, Hewitt Pantaleoni, Ross Parmenter, Helen Swick Perry, Robin Ridington, Margaret W. Rossiter, Jane R. Smiley, William C. Sturtevant, Douglas Schwartz, Thomas Vennum, and Stephen Williams. On the Omaha Reservation Dennis Hastings, Edward Cline, Elmer Blackbird, Alfred Gilpin, Mark Merrick, Nathan Merrick, and Paul E. Brill discussed tribal affairs and Omaha history with me, and in nearby Walthill, Nebraska, Marguerite Diddock Langenberg, grandniece of Francis La Flesche, shared with me her memories of the La Flesche family. An "Author's Query" in the book review section of the *Sunday New York Times* brought me into contact with a collateral relative of Alice Fletcher's, Barbara Horsky. I am grateful for her warm interest in this project. The manuscript was read by Joy Harvey, Margaret Rossiter, and Edward Mark, all of whom made excellent suggestions.

Access to unpublished materials and permission to quote from them as requested have been granted by the American Philosophical Society; the Bancroft Library at the University of California, Berkeley; the Beinicke Library, Yale University; the Idaho State Historical Society; the Hampton University Archives; the Quaker Collection at Haverford College; the Harvard University Archives; the Houghton Library at Harvard University; the Library of Congress; the Historical Collections, Museum of New Mexico; the Maria Mitchell Library, Nantucket, Massachusetts; the Massachusetts Historical Society; the National Anthropological Archives, Smithsonian Institution; the National Archives; the Nebraska State Historical Society; the New York Historical Society; the New York Public Library; the Peabody Museum of Archaeology and Ethnology, Harvard University; the Presbyterian Historical Society, Philadelphia; the Rush Rhees Library, University of Rochester; the Schlesinger Library, Radcliffe College; the Sophia Smith Collection, Smith College; and the Southwest Museum.

I began this book as a Fellow at the Charles Warren Center for the Study of American History at Harvard and finished it while a guest of the Rockefeller Foundation at the Bellagio Study and Conference Center. Meanwhile my ongoing professional home has been the Peabody Museum of Archaeology and Ethnology at Harvard. I am grateful to all of these institutions, their officers and staffs, for support and encouragement. My research during 1979–80 and 1985–86 was supported by grants from the National Science Foundation, which I gratefully acknowledge.

Only those who know Edward Mark can begin to appreciate how much he has been a sustaining force throughout this work.

PART 1

Growing Up
in Victorian America

One

Early Years:
"The terrible story"

ALICE Cunningham Fletcher was born in 1838 in Cuba, the place itself a sign of her father's despairing sense that time was running out on him and a harbinger of the rootlessness that she would feel for much of her life. His death, when she was an infant, would become one of the definitive events in her life.

Thomas Gilman Fletcher had been a rising young lawyer in New York City until he fell ill of "consumption brought on by over-exertion."[1] Born in 1801 in Alstead, New Hampshire, he was an eighth-generation descendant of the Robert Fletcher who had come to America from England in 1635. His father, Peter Fletcher, ran a tavern and country store in New Ipswich, New Hampshire, carried on a blacksmithing business, did some farming, and was known for his remarkable business ability. A family genealogist described the Fletchers as "all members of Congregational churches and support-ers of good works of benevolence and reform."[2]

Thomas Fletcher graduated from Dartmouth College in 1824, studied law with Charles H. Ruggles, and then entered a law practice in New York City. He married Almira Barnes of Berlin, Connecticut, and they had two sons, Frank Hopkins Fletcher, born in 1831, and another who died in infancy. Almira Fletcher died in 1835, and shortly thereafter Thomas Fletcher became ill. He spent the next two winters in the Caribbean, at St. Croix and Cuba, returning every summer to New York. On June 8, 1837, Thomas Fletcher married a woman from Boston, thirty-year-old Lucia Adeline Jenks,[3] and in October they sailed for Cuba. Alice Cunningham Fletcher was born there on March 15, 1838. She was named Alice for her mother's mother and Cunningham for her mother's girlhood friend,[4] poignant reminders that Lucia Adeline Jenks Fletcher gave birth in a strange country hundreds of miles away from family and friends, with only her new and very ill husband and his seven-year-old son as kin at her side.

3

Alice Fletcher described her mother as a "highly educated lady of Boston."[5] Like her husband, Lucia Adeline Jenks could trace her ancestors back to the early years of the American colonies. In the late 1620s bog iron was discovered near Lynn, Massachusetts, and a company was formed in London to build an iron foundry there. Joseph Jenks, a middle-aged widower and skilled iron worker, was one of a group of half a dozen men sent to the Massachusetts Bay Colony in 1643 to operate the works. Within a few years he was joined by his young son, Joseph. Four generations later the Jenks family was still in the iron business in Massachusetts. Francis Jenks (1770–1812), Alice Fletcher's maternal grandfather, was the proprietor of a blacksmith and bellows shop in Boston. He and his wife, Alice Nye, had five children, of whom the youngest was Lucia Adeline.[6]

Lucia, Thomas, and their two children returned to New York in the summer of 1838. Thomas's health had not improved in Cuba, and he was now so ill that he could scarcely walk.[7] The family boarded in a farmhouse in Morristown, New Jersey, where Thomas died in November 1839 at the age of thirty-eight, leaving his widow with a nine-year-old stepson and Alice, aged twenty months.

The widowed Mrs. Fletcher had no family home to return to. Her husband's father had retired and followed his younger son to the Midwest. Her own father, Francis Jenks, had died when she was five years old. Lucia Adeline Fletcher, choosing to stay around New York, moved to Brooklyn, which in the 1840s was New York's newest suburb. While German and Irish immigrants were moving into the eastern and northern sections of the city, wealthy Yankee merchants settled in the Brooklyn Heights area, with its magnificent view of the New York harbor and a ferry that went directly to Wall Street. Lucia Adeline Fletcher settled in Brooklyn Heights as well. There she enrolled eight-year-old Alice in a pioneering educational venture, the Brooklyn Female Academy.

The academy was founded in 1846, after fifteen prominent Brooklyn citizens gathered to discuss a common problem. The problem was their daughters, more specifically, the education of their daughters, of whom William S. Packer, one of the leaders of the group, had eight. How could these young girls, many of them quick and eager to learn, get an education comparable to that being offered young men in the best colleges in the country? Packer discussed the question with Seth Low, whose grandson would later be president of Columbia University, and with others. They agreed that what was needed was not only a collegiate institution but also a preparatory and a primary school, so that their daughters could have a steady, solid, and cumulative course of learning. With capital stock of thirty-five thousand dollars, raised by selling shares at one hundred dollars each, they founded an institution on Joralemon Street in Brooklyn Heights which they named the Brooklyn Female Academy. The venture was an immediate success, in both educational and financial terms. The enrollment at the end of the first year was 686 students, and the corporation was soon paying dividends of 6 percent to its investors.[8]

The school burned to the ground on January 1, 1853, but was immediately rebuilt and renamed the Packer Collegiate Institute, after Mrs. William S. Packer gave a large gift for the new building. A year later, to match what was available for girls, the Brooklyn Collegiate and Polytechnic Institute for boys was founded. These two schools attracted others, and by the end of the century Brooklyn, "the city of churches," was also renowned for its educational institutions.[9]

The original faculty of the Brooklyn Female Academy consisted of nineteen women and four men, almost half of whom, along with the president, Dr. Alonzo Crittenden, had been wooed away from the Albany Female Seminary, founded in 1814. Crittenden was famous as an innovative educator. He disapproved of memory drill, favoring instead original compositions and oral examinations. The intent of the school was to "afford to young ladies the same facilities for acquiring a good English and Classical education that are provided for young men at the best collegiate institutions in the country."[10] The education provided may well have been better than that available in most of the tradition-bound men's colleges. The girls studied Latin, but also geography, history, arithmetic, natural history, and natural philosophy. The school was particularly proud of its emphasis on scientific training. The advertising circular for the school boasted of "new and extensive Apparatus for experiments in Chemistry and Natural Philosophy, with a Cabinet of Minerals and of Shells, with Globes, Maps and Charts, and with appropriate drawings and illustrations in Natural History, Geography, and Astronomy."[11] Their scientific equipment included a six inch Fitz telescope, which was of research quality, and a large horizonal orrery for tracing the movement of the planets, made by noted instrument maker Thomas Barlow of Kentucky.[12] The natural science professor, Alonzo Gray, was a graduate of Amherst College and Andover Theological Seminary, had taught science at Phillips Academy and at Marietta College, and had written popular texts on chemistry, geology, natural philosophy, and agriculture. The circular also promised regular instruction in vocal music and Friday afternoon exercises at which selected compositions were read before an audience of faculty, students, and parents. Tuition was five dollars a quarter for primary students, with rates rising to fifteen dollars for those in the Collegiate Department.

The name Alice C. Fletcher of Brooklyn, New York, appears in the list of Primary Department students in the circular of the Brooklyn Female Academy printed in 1847. It does not appear again in the very scanty records that are extant from the early years of the school. Alice Fletcher herself in her later years made only the barest of references to her early schooling. In a brief biography prepared in 1890 when she was appointed Thaw Fellow at the Peabody Museum at Harvard, she wrote that she had attended "the best schools."[13] In 1892, in an address to the fourth graduating class at the Carlisle Indian school, she recalled her own graduation day. "I remember how the world looked, how wide it was, how little I seemed to have to do with it except to enter into it and enjoy myself and escape the restraints of the school, and I thought how different it is with you for you have harder problems to face."[14] Did she stay on beyond the primary grades and graduate from Packer? It seems likely, for she continued to live in Brooklyn and Packer would have been "the best school" available. It seems likely also for the more intangible but convincing reason that for the rest of her life she so exactly represented those values that the Brooklyn Female Academy/Packer Collegiate Institute was designed to inculcate in young women.

Although the Brooklyn Female Academy offered young women an education equal to that given young men, it did not intend that its daughters would graduate to demand equal professional opportunities with men and disrupt the social order. Crittenden was training women to be homemakers and a few to be teachers, and he stressed the cultivation of character and taste as much as that of intellect.

Packer students were given a sense that they were scions of an energetic elite in American society, daughters of the first families of Brooklyn and elsewhere—for Packer soon had many boarding students—natural leaders of intellect, character, and taste who set the goals and cultural standards in their communities and who founded institutions for what they perceived to be the common good. The leading citizens of Brooklyn were not interested in universal education for everyone but in superior education for their own sons and daughters. Their sons were then to take their "natural" places as leaders in businesses and the professions. Their daughters were to take their places as leaders of cultured society and upholders of its values. All of her life, Alice Fletcher believed in and worked for equal educational opportunities for men and women but always within the carefully circumscribed bounds of the given social order.

Alice Fletcher had other qualities in keeping with the rigorous education offered at Packer: an interest in natural science, the practiced ease and confidence with which she could sing or speak before large audiences, and the thoroughness with which she did everything she undertook. Serving as a base for this training, of course, was what she inherited from her parents or learned from them at home. Alice Fletcher can have had little memory of her father, but he was recalled often in family traditions as a good musician and fine flute player. And there were other memories of him. In 1912 when she was in her seventies, Alice Fletcher spoke at a centennial celebration of Dickens's birth. She said,

> One of my earliest remembrances connected with the name of Dickens is of an afternoon when my grandmother sat beside the pretty Chippendale work-table arranging the lace on one of her caps, for in those days, old ladies wore caps, she and my mother were in a reminiscent mood and were recalling the mirthful evenings when my father read aloud from Pickwick and they "laughed until they cried." The jingling name "Pickwick" caught my childish ear, but "Dickens" puzzled me. I had heard the word as an expletive and had been told that it was "naughty" and I must not use it. Why my parents and my grandmother should enjoy talking about this forbidden word, I could not make out, but I concluded that I had discovered another of the contradictions peculiar to the actions of grown up folk.[15]

Alice Fletcher once joked that her mother, "who never misspelled a word looked upon my failings in that respect with a sort of wonder. I think she sometimes suspected that her daughter was a changeling."[16] These quick glimpses of her mother and grandmother suggest a loving, happy family situation, but there is one contrary bit of evidence. In the only other comment she left about her youth, Alice Fletcher wrote that as a child she was not allowed to read fiction, except once when she was resting after a painful illness. Then the ban was removed, and she was able to discover Pickwick and all the rest of Dickens for herself.[17] This ban on fiction suggests a new arbiter of moral standards in the household, and indeed there was one. Alice Fletcher's mother had married again, a man from Maine five years younger than herself named Oliver C. Gardiner.

The first glimpse of this new family comes from the 1850 census for the Third Ward in Brooklyn, New York. The Gardiner household consists of Oliver C. Gardiner, age 38, "Editor"; Lucy A., age 43; Alice C. Fletcher, age 12, who "attends school"; Francis H. Fletcher, age 19, whose occupation is "clerk"; Alice James (surely Alice Jenks, the grandmother, her name misunderstood by the census taker), age 78; and two females born in Ireland, Mary Gume and the oddly named Howard Coulery, ages 16 and 18, the family's maids. Brooklyn City Directories for these years show the Oliver C. Gardiner residence at 128 Hicks Street in 1847. In 1851 the family moved a few blocks away to 127 Henry Street and two years later moved four doors up the street to 135 Henry Street. These are pleasant, tree-shaded streets in Brooklyn Heights lined with four-story row houses. The Packer Collegiate Institute on Joralemon Street was only a few blocks away. In 1857 Oliver Gardiner moved his family across Joralemon Street to a four-story row house at 174 Clinton Street, only two blocks from the Packer Institute. Alice Fletcher was nineteen at the time of the last move.

Here there is a long, discreet historical silence. The next public record of Alice Fletcher is in 1872, when she was present at a meeting of Sorosis, the New York woman's club. In her collected papers, there is nothing from these years apart from cartes de visite showing her in Munich, Germany, a very earnest and soberly dressed young woman on a European tour. Alice Fletcher herself wrote of these years only that she attended "the best schools," then taught in pri-

Alice Fletcher as a young woman.
(National Anthropological Archives,
Smithsonian Institution)

vate schools and studied history and literature. She implied that her life between her twelfth year, the year of the 1850 census, and her thirty-fourth year, when we can begin to trace her activities in New York, was so uneventful that she could sum it up in a sentence or two. In fact it was so traumatic that she chose to expunge it.

The missing link, and a key to Alice Fletcher's life, has been found in the unpublished diary of Caroline H. Dall, a Washington feminist and writer who was sixteen years older than Fletcher. Caroline Healey Dall met Alice Fletcher at a meeting of the American Social Science Association at Saratoga, New York, in September 1881 and immediately took a personal interest in her. On January 11, 1885, Dall, who had by this time become Alice Fletcher's friend and confidant, went to visit Fletcher in her rooms at the Temple Hotel in Washington. That night Dall wrote in her diary:

> Sun. Jan. 11, 1885   lunched with Nettie [daughter-in-law] and played with the children until it was time to go to Alice Fletcher from whom I heard for the first time the terrible story of her life. Those who see her and love her now recognising a most noble port.[sic] can hardly imagine how beautiful she must have been when with troops of lovers and friends she was the pet of gay society in Brooklyn. Pursued by a stepfather's fiendish malice, which never spared one who served her, she had a tough fight for life. Protected at first by her guardian Edwin Hoyt, who would have married her had *she* consented, she finally became governess to a Mr. Conant's daughters. He paid her a large salary for many years, and she ought to have been independent at his death, but bad investments came near to ruin her. It was for her bread that she first sought employment at the Peabody Museum and as a lecturer.
>
> . . . like myself she has been betrayed by the stupidity of her friends. When she went to Mrs. D. Storrs asking for protection against her base stepfather, Mrs. Storrs being her only near blood relation, Mrs. Storrs told the story to the girls in her class at school and it was due to the loving devotion of one, that she was not ruined by the tale.[18]

Alice Fletcher's near total silence about the first half of her life is here explained. She had had to struggle against the "fiendish malice" of a "base" stepfather. From Dall's description it is possible to infer

that Fletcher may have been the unwilling recipient of sexual overtures, perhaps even a victim of sexual abuse. She apparently had an
authoritarian stepfather whose high moral tone in public masked
his private behavior; an absent, helpless, distracted, or disbelieving
mother; a guardian who wanted to marry her himself; and a relative,
a female cousin, who "betrayed" her through "stupidity."

There are other possible explanations. The stepfather may have
been trying to arrange a marriage or find a job for Alice which would
free him from having to support her or which might serve his business or social interests. He may simply have been a stern discipli-
narian, intent on curbing her social life in ways that she considered
arbitrary and unfair, although such an action scarcely qualifies as
what Caroline Dall called "the terrible story." Whatever the exact
situation, the facts are that Alice Fletcher fled or was driven from
her home and was taken in by another family.

Where Alice Fletcher's mother was throughout this crisis is a mystery. She is not to be found in Brooklyn death records, searched
from 1850 through 1895, and the Fletcher family genealogy, published in 1881, implies that she was still alive at that date. Alice
Fletcher's steady silence about her mother—she never mentions her
apart from the brief recollections already quoted here—suggests
that her mother was somehow implicated in the crisis, that she did
not, or could not, defend her daughter.

Nor had her mother's family been any help. The Mrs. Storrs in
question was Alice's cousin, Mary Jenks Storrs, the daughter of Francis Jenks, Jr., a Unitarian clergyman in Boston. Born in 1824, Mary
Jenks married Richard Salter Storrs, a young Congregationalist clergyman, in 1845. The next year they moved to Brooklyn, and he
began his long, prominent ministry at the conservative Church of
the Pilgrims in Brooklyn Heights. At the time Alice turned to her for
help, Mary Jenks Storrs was a well-connected Brooklyn matron in
her early thirties with three small daughters of her own.[19] She apparently did not believe her cousin's story.

Alice Fletcher may have watched with bemusement some twenty
years later when Richard Salter Storrs led the campaign to bring the
wildly popular Henry Ward Beecher, minister at the rival Plymouth
Church in Brooklyn Heights, to trial for adultery.[20] A comparison of
the public reaction to this case with Mrs. Storrs's response to Alice

Fletcher's plea for help twenty years before is an implicit comment on Victorian sexual morality and the accepted bounds of credibility, discourse, and action. Adultery was titillating, easy to credit, and even easier to talk about. All summer long in 1874 Brooklynites and Beecher-followers across the country read about the trial and discussed at length the guilt or innocence of Henry Ward Beecher and Mrs. Tilton. The tyranny of a stepfather, on the other hand, was considered a private intrafamily matter and even close relatives would not intervene.

Who was the Oliver Cromwell Gardiner who pursued his stepdaughter with "fiendish malice?" In 1843 Gardiner, then living in New Jersey, wrote to the well-known educator Horace Mann in Massachusetts asking for Mann's reports as secretary of the Massachusetts Board of Education and describing himself as much interested in the teaching of youth. Sometime later a mutual acquaintance, E. M. Shurston, wrote to Horace Mann, desiring to dissociate himself from "Mr. O. C. Gardiner" and warning Mann about the latter's "peculiarities."[21] Gardiner gave as a forwarding address for himself in 1843 the New York firm of Jenks and Palmer, which suggests that he may have met Lucia Adeline Jenks Fletcher through members of the Jenks family whom he happened to know. In 1848, describing himself as "late associate editor of the Democratic Review," Gardiner wrote an impassioned history of the free soil movement called *The Great Issue*.[22] Later he is described in Brooklyn city directories variously as "merchant" (in 1851), "lawyer" (in 1852, 1853, and 1855), and "broker" (in 1857), with an office on Wall Street.

The man who helped Alice Fletcher was Claudius Buchanan Conant, a wealthy hardware merchant who lived in Brooklyn between 1850 and 1860. Conant was born in New York City in 1819. He married Eliza Ann Ayers in 1836, and eventually they had ten children.[23] Conant moved his growing family to Brooklyn Heights in 1850, living first at 84 Cranberry Street, then at 179 Adams Street, and in 1854 moving to 42 Pierrepont, just around the corner from Alice Fletcher's residence at 135 Henry Street. Pierrepont Street was a main thoroughfare leading directly to the East River, a grander street than the cross streets of Hicks, Henry, and Clinton where the Gardiners lived, with larger, more elegant row houses, some of stone rather than brick. There the Conants stayed until they left the city in 1860, taking Alice Fletcher with them. They settled in Madison, New Jersey.

Alice Fletcher was a year younger than Conant's eldest daughter, Elizabeth Anne. They likely were classmates at the Packer Institute, and it was perhaps Elizabeth Anne's "loving devotion" that saved Alice from "ruin" at school and brought her plight to Conant's attention. Conant was still young himself, only eighteen when his first child was born and in his mid-thirties at the time he met Alice Fletcher.

Conant hired Alice Fletcher as a governess for his younger daughters Ida and Sara, who were seven and eight years younger than she. If she were around eighteen when she joined the Conant household, they would have been ten and eleven, and they became her lifelong friends and substitute family. Claudius Conant continued to support Alice Fletcher with a "large salary" even when her services as a governess were no longer necessary, and he set her up to be financially independent.

Although Alice Fletcher had been rescued, the "tough fight" left its scars. Included among these must be her "flirtatious ways," which Caroline Dall was later to observe and note with disapproval. Alice Fletcher was of medium height, with a slender figure and long, chestnut-colored hair, of which she was very proud. She was quick to laugh, sweet tempered, and often merry. It is not hard to imagine, as Caroline Dall did, a thoughtful, vivacious, and pretty child growing up into a beautiful and very appealing young woman, but growing up in a household where her every act was watched by a dour, tyrannical stepfather. The coquettish ways she learned so well may have been a desperate child's attempt to win sympathy and some measure of fair treatment.

Underneath the flirtatiousness was an avoidance of any form of physical sexuality. Alice Fletcher never married. But she yearned for male companionship, a home, and a warm, loving family life such as she had caught a glimpse of as a small child when she listened to her mother's and grandmother's recollections of her father. She worked out a way to have a version of these things for herself, but she was never able to put aside her abiding and despondent sense that she was, and would always be, alone in the world. This theme appears over and over in her diaries and journals. It is the one theme that remains constant throughout all her changing versions of her life.

Both Alice Fletcher's flirtatiousness and her sense of aloneness were related to her early awareness of male power in her society, which she would experience and struggle against all her life. But her attitude was ambiguous, for male power was, as she well knew, the power to help as well as to hurt. She had been despicably treated by one man, her stepfather, but generously rescued by another, Mr. Conant. All her life Alice Fletcher looked to men for help, although the help she got often came from women. The women she tended to take for granted. It was the power that men had that she respected—and wanted for herself.

Another of Alice Fletcher's characteristics shaped by her childhood experiences was her tendency to relate to other people either as a dependent child or as a mother. She had difficulty dealing with people as equals. Alice was not close to her half-brother, who was seven years older than she, and there were no other children in the family. She grew up virtually as an only child, with no siblings from whom she could learn the give and take of different opinions and equal rights. In the Conant family, for all their kindness to her, she was not one of the large number of siblings but was set apart in the special role of governess, a parent substitute.

More significant, she grew up in the Gardiner household needing to be constantly atuned to the overwhelming and authoritarian paternal presence, a presence flattering in its intensity and frightening in its demands and implications. She could have had little time or emotional energy left for normal peer relations.[24] Alice Fletcher tended to view herself as set apart, special but wicked, prone to faults, and most deserving of praise when she completed some difficult, assigned task. This was the child's role she was to play over and over again for the rest of her life, with her feminist associates, her scientific mentors, her supportive woman friends. The other role in which she was comfortable was that of a mother, bringing aid and giving instructions, firmly directing other people's lives. There were even times when she suddenly assumed this role toward a person like F. W. Putnam, her scientific mentor, to whom she had just been playing daughter. It was the role she later consistently played with the Indians. These two alternate, but incomplete, stances toward other people were the roles she had learned at home.

What Alice Fletcher never learned was how to compromise. On the contrary, she grew up in a situation in which her refusal to compromise had been what saved her. Afterward, she tended to see the human world in sharply contrasting terms. People were right or wrong, worthy or unworthy, sometimes simply good or bad. She had never had a chance, in a childish world of equals, to learn from opponents or to learn that it is sometimes necessary to give a little in order to get along together. She never saw that it was possible for right-thinking people to come to different conclusions. It was a problem that, unrecognized by her, plagued her all her life.

The fight left scars, but it also left Alice Fletcher with an inner strength which was to sustain her for the rest of her life, carrying her to the top of her profession and into the highest social, political, and scientific circles in the country. She learned early that what would become of her was up to her. She saw that either she could give in when pressed by hostile forces or she could arm herself as best she could and keep on fighting. Alice Fletcher chose to fight. She might falter and even occasionally flee, but she would not waver from a course she had set for herself, once she had decided it was right. The roots of this toughness—some would see it as stubbornness—lay deep in her childhood.

The terrible struggle in which her mother had been no help also left Alice Fletcher with a strong will to identify with her father, although she had scarcely known him. All her life she cherished a small locket he had given her which contained a picture of him and a lock of his hair along with the first curl cut from her own small head.[25] She clung to bits of lore about him—his business ability, his drive and desire to succeed, his liking for Dickens, his love of music and his skill as a musician—and she developed those qualities in herself. She treasured her name, "Fletcher," and took her identification from it: she was a gallant archer who aimed her arrows high. Unlike many professional women, she did not have a supportive, encouraging father. In effect, however, she did, for she created one for herself out of shreds of legend and memory and out of her need to identify with him. Alone in the world, she created an image of her father to stand beside her and, thus bolstered, went forth to face whatever lay in store.

Two

Woman's Clubs; or, "What Shall We Do with Our Daughters?"

ALICE Fletcher's years as a governess came to an end around 1870, when she was in her early thirties. With Claudius Conant, her former employer, still paying her a substantial salary, she took rooms at 25 Stuyvesant Street on Manhattan and set out to explore the cultural life of New York City.

One early glimpse we have of Alice Fletcher is at a concert in Brooklyn in 1873. Sidney Lanier, a young southern lawyer, had come to the North to try to make a name for himself as a poet and flute player, and he gave a series of small concerts in Brooklyn before moving on to the greater challenge of New York. Lanier included in the program two of his own flute compositions, "Blackbirds" and "Swamp-Robin," based on birdsongs in his native Georgia. Alice Fletcher, thinking of her own lawyer father, his boyhood on a farm in New Hampshire, and his reputation as a flute player, was deeply stirred by the music. Afterward she told the startled young southerner that he must become the founder of a truly American music. "Hitherto all American compositions had been only German music done over," she told him, "but . . . these were at once America, un-German, classic, passionate, poetic, and beautiful."[1]

Sidney Lanier was so taken aback by her enthusiasm that he stood speechless. The next day, eager to make a more gracious response, he wrote her a letter of thanks, to which she replied, telling him again how much his music had meant to her. "Your flute gave me that for which I had ceased to hope, true American music, and awakened in my heart a feeling of patriotism that I never knew before." She rejoiced that when she yearned for "the Divine inspiration of music" she no longer had to "worship as it were in a foreign tongue."[2]

The earnestness, self-dramatization, and vague high-mindedness in her response is characteristic of Alice Fletcher in these years. What brought her down to earth, honed her practical skills, and set her on the path to a career was her participation in Sorosis, one of the earliest woman's clubs in the country. The club indirectly owed its founding to Charles Dickens and his successful reading tour through the United States in 1868. When the New York Press Club announced a dinner at Delmonico's in Dickens's honor but hesitated to admit women, two prominent women journalists were so incensed that they resolved to found their own organization. Jane C. "Jennie June" Croly and Sara Willis Parton ("Fanny Fern" to her literary fans) gathered several of their friends and founded Sorosis, also at Delmonico's, on April 20, 1868. The women stated simply and vaguely that their purpose was "to render women helpful to each other and useful to society."[3]

The first president of Sorosis was the poet Alice Cary. She and her sister Phoebe were famous for the Sunday evening receptions at their home on 20th Street in New York, which Alice Fletcher also frequented. Like the Cary sisters, most of the early members of Sorosis were writers or journalists, but they invited other "representative women of our metropolis and adjacent sister cities" to join, and they added prominent women scientists like Maria Mitchell and the physician Dr. Mary Putnam (later Dr. Mary Putnam Jacobi) by making them honorary members. Alice Fletcher was invited to join Sorosis in 1870 and moved swiftly into the inner circle of active members. She was elected recording secretary in 1872 and also often performed in trios or as a soloist at Sorosis meetings, where her "inimitable" renditions of Scottish songs like "Bonnie Prince Charlie" were much appreciated.[4]

Sorosis in its early years was known as much for sociability and "mutual admiration," as one reporter wryly noted, as for anything else.[5] But after four years of social meetings, business meetings where they discussed the rudeness of Macy's department store employees and resolved not to trade there anymore, and monthly evening receptions to which gentleman escorts were invited, some of the members began to get restless. In November 1872 Jennie June Croly and Dr. Mary Putnam challenged the club to see if it could accomplish something.[6]

Accomplishing something in the 1870s usually meant founding a voluntary organization, preferably a national one, for a particular purpose. This phenomenon was part of what historian Robert Wiebe has called a "search for order" among Americans in the late nineteenth century, and nowhere was it stronger than among women. The Civil War had led thousands of women to do things neither they nor anyone else had thought they could do, from running farms and businesses to nursing the wounded in hospitals to raising millions of dollars through fairs for the Sanitary Commission. One legacy of the war was a widespread feeling that there was a potential army of talented women across the land who needed only to be brought together for great things to happen. What they lacked was organization and communication. The *Woman's Journal*, founded in Boston in 1870 by Lucy Stone and Henry Blackwell, became in effect a national bulletin board for women. It carried the suffrage message, but also long columns of scattered notices about what women were doing: opening schools, running farms, starting their own businesses. To many a woman reader, these notices, like the alumnae notes in today's college magazines, may have been the most carefully perused part of the paper. Communication among women, on what was possible for women, had begun. Organization was still lacking.

Sorosis picked up the challenge. Early in 1873 Charlotte Wilbour proposed that Alice Fletcher, as the secretary of Sorosis, send out a call to "representative women" everywhere asking them to come and meet together. One hundred and fifty women answered the call, a response so encouraging that a new call was sent out on September 1, 1873, to sixteen hundred prominent women in the United States and Europe.[7] Alice Fletcher and her committee took many of the names for their mailing list from the "Notes and News" column of the *Woman's Journal*. On October 17, 1873, four hundred women gathered for a three-day meeting at the Union League Theater in

New York. There they organized the Association for the Advancement of Women (AAW).

The name was significant. The original call had been to a "congress" or "woman's parliament," but then the women decided they wanted an ongoing association. They chose to model themselves on the foremost scientific organization in the country, the American Association for the Advancement of Science, founded in 1848.

On the face of it, the two causes, advancing women and advancing science, do not seem to have much in common. Yet in the context of mid-nineteenth century American life they did. Both organizations were formed to bring their members out of isolation and into contact with like-minded people. Both wanted to cast their nets as widely as possible while at the same time allowing a small group of leaders to retain control. Both were intended to be nonpolitical. Nearly all the officers of the Association for the Advancement of Women were suffragists, but they were members of the moderate suffragist party, and they did not want their organization split or taken over by the radical wing of the suffrage movement. When Olympia Brown attacked them for avoiding the question of suffrage, they replied that their activities were intended as an addition to, not a substitute for, suffrage meetings.[8]

Two of the women knew the organizational structure of the American Association for the Advancement of Science (AAAS) firsthand. Maria Mitchell had been a member of the AAAS since 1850, when women were first invited to join. Julia Ward Howe had attended AAAS meetings as a journalist. She had no scientific inclinations herself, but as her daughters wrote, "Scientific achievement seemed to her well-nigh miraculous and roused in her an almost childlike reverence."[9]

Like the scientists, the woman leaders of the AAW planned annual meetings to be held in different cities. Like those of the scientists, their programs consisted of preselected papers, followed by discussions. The American Association for the Advancement of Science had one permanent secretary whose task was to plan and organize the annual meetings. The Association for the Advancement of Women started out with four secretaries, one of whom was Alice Fletcher. The second year, 1874, they reduced these to two, Fletcher and Frances E. Willard. Then for two years Fletcher carried the job alone. A local reporter at the Chicago meeting in 1874 described her. "Miss Fletcher, the Secretary, impresses one immediately as a remarkably wholesome, healthy, cheery woman. . . . She does her work in an earnest, practical way. It was quite amusing, on Saturday morning, to see her dump herself and her satchel . . . on the platform steps, and proceed to count out the money." [10]

Three well-known women emerged immediately as leaders in the Association for the Advancement of Women. Julia Ward Howe, author of "The Battle Hymn of the Republic," was the opening speaker at the first congress. Mary A. Livermore, a popular public lecturer and coeditor of the *Woman's Journal*, was elected president at the first congress. Maria Mitchell, world famous as the discoverer of a comet, was elected president at the second and third congresses. They were all in their mid-fifties and were among the most famous women in America in 1873, yet they were not contentedly basking in their honors, as they might well have done. Each had reached a plateau in her own life and was setting out on a new course.

Julia Ward Howe, short, red-haired, and full of sparkle, was making her final peace with a dying husband who throughout their married life had opposed her public activities. For the first twenty years of her marriage to the reformer Samuel Gridley Howe, Director of the Perkins Institute for the Blind, Julia Ward Howe, the orphaned daughter of a New York banker, had contented herself with private study and writing poetry and plays. In 1863, however, after the death of a young son, she became determined to make her voice heard. She wanted to share her ideas. She also yearned for some of the public acclaim that went to popular male preachers, lecturers, and political orators, the media stars of their day, whose performances she had been observing carefully for years. The result was struggle at home, for Dr. Howe was adamantly opposed to his wife's speaking in public, and to the resulting public attention. What Mrs. Howe talked about—her travels, her philosophical ponderings on "Doubt and Belief," her views on ethics—was less important than the fact that she talked in public at all, and in so doing gave instant respectability to a new profession for women, that of public lecturing. Although the Grimké sisters of South Carolina, Sarah and Angelina, had given public lectures for years, as had many suffrage leaders, they were all tainted with radicalism. Julia Ward Howe gave an aura of Boston respectability to this new profession, a way for a proper woman to earn her own living, and Howe did need to earn money, for her husband and her brother had between them squandered her considerable inheritance.

Julia Ward Howe was not really popular as a public speaker, however, until she took up reform topics. The irony is that she had not previously been much interested in reform. She loved languages, literature, and philosophy. She read easily in French, Italian, German, Latin, and Greek. Occasionally in conversation with a Harvard professor she would discover not only that she knew a particular work better than he did, but also that she had read it in the original language and he had not. But for "good causes," particularly those in which her husband was engaged, she cared little.

Yet by the late 1860s, a combination of guilt and slowly growing conviction propelled Julia Ward Howe into speaking for reforms of various kinds. She went reluctantly to a woman suffrage meeting in 1868 and was converted. That women should be free agents and have equal rights and equal responsibilities constituted for her, she later said, "a discovery . . . like the addition of a new continent to the map of the world."[11] From that day on, woman suffrage, a woman's peace crusade which she tried to lead singlehandedly, and woman's clubs were her main activities, and she gave to these last a reformist orientation by urging that they pursue both culture and public service. Her role in the Association for the Advancement of Women was that of high priestess of traditional New England culture turned to the reform of society.

Mary Livermore, a large, hearty woman with a booming voice, got her start in public life in Illinois during the Civil War, organizing and speaking on behalf of the Sanitary Commission and eventually coordinating the activities of four thousand women. In 1869 she founded the *Agitator*, a woman suffrage paper in Chicago, but almost immediately she decided to merge it with Lucy Stone's new Boston *Woman's Journal*. She and her clergyman husband moved to Massachusetts, where she helped to edit the united paper for two years. In 1873, when the Association for the Advancement of Women was founded, she had just resigned as coeditor in order to set out on a full-time career as a public lecturer. Her agent, James Redpath of Redpath's Lyceum Bureau, promised her that if she would let him make all her engagements and would avoid those "two vexed questions," woman suffrage and temperance, he would make her a rich woman within twenty years. Mary Livermore ignored his advice and became spectacularly successful anyway.

Mary Livermore had many topics, including "Abraham Lincoln," "Co-operative Housekeeping," and "Some Eminent People Whom I Have Met," but her best known lecture was the one titled "What Shall We Do with Our Daughters?" In her autobiography, published in 1897, she estimated that she had given that lecture more than eight hundred times, from Maine to California. Although she altered it over the years, its essence remained the same. She called for physical training for girls, for sensible dress—away with "steel-clasped corsets" and "pinching French boots"—and for coeducation. She urged that every girl be trained for a trade or profession but argued also that girls receive "moral culture" and domestic training, for they were the wives and mothers of the future. Finally she argued that they should be given equal legal status with men.[12]

Mary Livermore thought it was too late to stir many middle-aged women out of their comfortable (or uncomfortable) situations. "Their positions are taken, their futures are forecast, and they are harnessed into the places they occupy, not infrequently by invisible, but omnipotent ties of love and duty," she wrote.[13] Therefore it was of "our daughters" that she spoke. The effect of this was to take the sting out of her potentially radical program, for she addressed her plea for social and legal equality for men and women not to the situation of the middle-aged men and women who sat in her audiences but to their hopes for their daughters. The ideas were radical, but the hard questions, such things as jobs, suffrage, legal equality, opening the professions, were put off for the future. All that was immediately necessary was to oppose corsets, encourage exercise, and try to provide good schooling. Meanwhile the ideas had been planted.

Mary Livermore reveled in her chosen career. "Neither school, college, nor university could have given me the education I have received in the lecture field," she claimed.[14] She relished the business consultations with her agent and local committees, the days of reading in libraries and of writing in her study, but most of all the adventures and mishaps of life on the road: mistaken luggage, makeshift transportation, strange traveling companions, and always new audiences. When Alice Fletcher set out a few years later on a career as a public lecturer, her inspiration was clearly Mary A. Livermore.

If Julia Ward Howe represented genteel culture with a reformist impulse and Mary A. Livermore public lecturing, Maria Mitchell showed Alice Fletcher that there was yet another possibility for a woman, a career as a scientist. Maria Mitchell was much less eager to be on a public platform than were Julia Ward Howe and Mary Livermore, but conviction propelled her. A sturdy, plainspoken woman of Nantucket Quaker descent, she had become world famous in 1847 when she discovered a comet. She moved from being librarian at the Nantucket Atheneum to doing calculations for the *American Ephemeris and Nautical Almanac*, a practical guide for seafarers. In 1865 she was named professor of astronomy and director of the observatory at the newly founded Vassar Female College. Like many men of science in her generation, Maria Mitchell saw a life of science in almost religious terms, as a vocation, as a way of life in humble pursuit of the truth by the only method that could give the truth.

Maria Mitchell was a presence at Vassar, the best-known name on its faculty and visible proof of Matthew Vassar's conviction that women were capable of learning and teaching at the highest levels. By 1873 Mitchell had begun to turn part of her attention from astronomy to "the woman question." What positions were women capable of taking in society and what was holding them back? She regarded this, like every other problem, as a scientific question to be approached in a scientific manner. From her own observations she was convinced that women were potentially as capable as men. They even had some additional skills, such as patience and acuteness of observation, which they had acquired through long training in childcare and needlework. Mitchell knew whereof she spoke, for she herself had spent long hours mending clothes, knitting socks, and caring for her younger brothers and sisters. But women were held back, she thought, by their lack of education and by their poor work habits.[15]

When the Association for the Advancement of Women was organized, Maria Mitchell was the only one of the leaders who had a definite idea of what she wanted the group to be. Mitchell saw it as a forum that could spread her ideas about the need for better education for women, and as a group that might work together in a scientific manner toward the solution of women's problems. When she was elected president, to succeed Mary Livermore, she used her presidential address in 1875 to urge that they begin to collect statistics. When men physicians argued, as Dr. Edward H. Clarke did in his famous *Sex in Education* (1873), that women would strain their health if they tried to do college work, she wanted to be able to reply with figures on how many girls died of overstudy as compared to the number who died from aimless lives. When a Russian astronomer told her how many women were studying science in St. Petersburg, she wanted to tell him how many were studying science in Boston. When a platform orator lamented America's "useless women," she wanted to reply with statistics on working women.

Maria Mitchell set out a three-part program for how women might help one another. They should gather facts on what the actual situation was, they should encourage young women to get a good education and prepare themselves to enter the working world, and then, where necessary, they should create jobs for other women, by starting schools and business enterprises and by opening up new industrial occupations. Following her lead, the Association for the Advancement of Women in 1875 formed itself into six committees to take practical action in various areas: science, statistics, industrial training, reform, art, and education.[16]

Of the Third Congress of Women, held in Syracuse in the fall of 1875, Maria Mitchell wrote in her "Commonplace Book": "I was amazed to find that they considered me a good Presiding officer. I made my little speech boldly and fearlessly. . . . We had a remarkably harmonious and orderly meeting, no quarrel and almost no agitation. Mrs. Howe and Mrs. Livermore were both charming—no new star arose, unless it was Mrs. Doggett [Kate Doggett, a leader in the Woman's Club of Chicago]. . . . I turned for the college, when it was over, with a feeling that I was 10 years younger."[17]

The next year President Maria Mitchell spoke on the other topic dear to her, "The Need for Women in Science." Her message was twofold. Woman's special skills, their delicate perceptions and patience in doing routine work, would make them valuable as trained assistants in science, she suggested. They might also do some of the lecturing, writing of popular articles, and translating which take up so much of a scientist's time. But she also encouraged women to consider careers as scientists, and she suggested how the Association for the Advancement of Women might help them. "What a scientist most needs is leisure,—time to think," she said. "We ought to be able to give aids, in the shape of a year's residence near large libraries, museums, laboratories, or observatories."[18] It was a call, like Virginia Woolf's, for "a room of one's own."

On the surface, the Fourth Woman's Congress in 1876 was a success. Attendance was large, for the meeting coincided with the Philadelphia Centennial, the papers were good, and comments in the press were favorable. "But," exclaimed Maria Mitchell in her diary, "we didn't have a good time!" The acoustics in the meeting hall were poor. Several local Philadelphia women protested vehemently against the inclusion of woman suffrage as a topic. Worst of all was a rebellion from the floor against the proposed slate of officers for the coming year, for many of the members felt that women from the East Coast (particularly New York and Boston) had dominated the association long enough. When Maria Mitchell read, "For President, Julia Ward Howe," other names were called out from the floor. The uproar was worse when she read, "For Secretary, Alice Fletcher." As Mitchell would later write, "I am told that they charged me with carrying things with a high hand which is undoubtedly true—I was sure that I must either go under the feet of a mob, or stand firm and control by sheer force."[19]

If Maria Mitchell's sudden show of authority surprised the rank and file of the AAW out on the floor, it did not surprise the executive committee. In their meetings she had consistently been a hard-liner. She argued that they should keep the original membership policy, whereby would-be members must be proposed or endorsed by other members and accepted by the Board, as in the American Association for the Advancement of Science. At Chicago, those in charge had been "careless," and any woman who walked in the door, paid a small fee, and signed the Constitution had been able to join. "The question is," Maria Mitchell wrote in her diary, "*who* is entitled to read a paper and *who* is entitled to a place in the debate. . . . I spoke for a *tight* rule in this respect, and begged for a high-toned character in our papers, and for a *very very* high toned morality in our members. I am amused to find myself spoken of as so '*decidedly conservative.*'"[20]

Maria Mitchell pushed through the election of Julia Ward Howe and Alice Fletcher in 1876, but none of them attended the Congress the following year. Julia Ward Howe was in Europe. Maria Mitchell, first vice-president, did not want to preside again and so claimed that she was "detained by her classes at Vassar, it being a most interesting season for the astronomer."[21] This left Abby May, second vice-president, who had been a sustaining presence for Mitchell through the difficulties of the previous year, as presiding officer. Alice Fletcher's secretarial duties were handled by Alida Avery, who had been college physician at Vassar but was then living in Denver. For the next three years some satisfaction was given westerners by the election of Kate Newell Doggett of Chicago as president, but the small inner circle of the AAW kept control of the annual meetings through the Committee on Topics and Papers, which they dominated. Alice Fletcher was chairman of this committee for the 1877 Congress, Maria Mitchell was chairman for the 1878 Congress, then Alice Fletcher again for the Congresses in 1879, 1880, and 1881.[22] Alice Fletcher's title had been changed, but her position remained the same. As chairman of the key committee, rather than as secretary of the association, she continued to plan the annual congresses.

The year 1876 was crucial for the Association for the Advancement of Women. Although there were later flurries of discontent, the elitist and eastern orientation of the association was not again seriously challenged during the remaining twenty-one years of its existence. Julia Ward Howe was reelected president year after year. Maria Mitchell retreated to the Committee on Science, which she set up in 1876; its major activity was to collect statistics on women in science, through a questionnaire circulated in 1876 and 1880. Maria Mitchell tabulated the results and publicized them whenever she could.[23]

Alice Fletcher returned to the Woman's Congress in 1878 and planned the next three annual meetings. But a new era had begun in her life, a hint of which appears in the program for 1881, the last Congress she organized. One of the papers was written by an American Indian woman, Mrs. T. H. Tibbles ("Bright Eyes"), giving an inside view of the life of Indian women, and at the Congress excerpts were read from a letter on "the same subject" by Alice Fletcher "who is at present among the Indians visiting a friendly tribe."[24] The following year Fletcher sent a letter of greeting to the association; thereafter she ceased taking an active part in its meetings.

The eight years that Alice Fletcher spent in the Association for the Advancement of Women were criticial for her subsequent career. She learned how to run an organization and how to use it to attain certain ends. She learned how to present her ideas in public and how to participate in public debate. She learned how to petition public officials, as in 1878 when the association complained to Francis E. Walker, the United States commissioner of the census, that twelve million working women had been omitted from the last census. The AAW urged that women be appointed as takers of the census equally with men.[25]

More significant, what Alice Fletcher found in the Association for the Advancement of Women was the opportunity to work with, and observe closely, three of the most gifted women of her day. Julia Ward Howe, Mary Livermore, and Maria Mitchell were all intensely interested in and admiring of one another. They seemed scarcely to have noticed their earnest secretary, a generation younger at age thirty-five, other than to order her about. "Make Alice Fletcher come up and go over this with you" and "ask Alice to send me a proof" they wrote to one another.[26] Mary Livermore treated Fletcher as a personal secretary, asking her to arrange appointments in addition to performing her other duties.[27] Fletcher had, in truth, done little to merit their particular approbation. Yet they recognized her as one of their own. Julia Ward Howe, after the Second Woman's Congress, called her "a person of untiring energy, and of true executive ability."[28]

What were these skills to be used for? Alice Fletcher herself was uncertain, poised like an arrow with no target. When Phebe A. Hanaford wanted to include her in a biographical dictionary of prominent women and asked her for personal data, she was nonplussed. She did not want to make public her past, and the future was uncertain. Finally she replied, "Although I have labored by my pen, my voice, and my executive powers, for the elevation of women, and the purification of the race from the sins of drunkenness both of spirits and tobacco, yet I do not find the language of data. Your request came to me with the suddenness of the vision to Abou Ben Adham and like him I can only say from my heart, 'Write me as one who loves her fellow-women.'"[29]

Ten years later, in response to a similar request from Frances Willard and Mary Livermore for a biographical dictionary of nearly fifteen thousand prominent nineteenth century American women, Alice Fletcher again ignored her early years and even her work in the Association for the Advancement of Women, writing only of her burgeoning career in anthropology.[30]

Alice Fletcher stayed in touch with Mary Livermore and often went to visit her at Malden, outside Boston, or at the Livermores' summer home in Egypt, Massachusetts. Maria Mitchell and Julia Ward Howe she seems not to have been close to, although she did go twice to Boston in the early 1880s to speak to the Saturday Morning Club, which Julia Ward Howe had organized for her daughters and their friends.[31] Never in her papers does she mention any of these three women as having been important to her. Yet their influence on her future is unmistakable. In Mary Livermore she saw the possibility of a career in public lecturing. In Julia Ward Howe she saw the possibility of a reform-oriented career. In Maria Mitchell, as well as in younger women like Dr. Mary Putnam Jacobi, she saw the possibility of a career in science. She would herself explore each of these possibilities.

What Alice Fletcher's New York clubwoman years did not do was prepare her to consider as her equals those at the bottom of the social ladder or to respect the rights and opinions of the dispossessed. Instead she was reinforced in her conviction that society ought to be led by its "natural" leaders, those people of ability, education, and energy who knew better than others what was best for the country. Maria Mitchell saw no point in wasting scholarship money at Vassar on poor girls who were inadequately prepared and could not fully benefit from the opportunities being offered them. Julia Ward Howe wanted the Association for the Advancement of Women to be "representative, in a true and wide sense," which to her meant bringing together "the best ideas" and "the foremost writers and thinkers" and did not imply creating some kind of frontier democracy.[32] Alice Fletcher sampled the best that the social world of New York City had to offer. She moved in a world of privilege, of those who believed that they were at the top of the social ladder because they deserved to be there. She was twenty years too early for the kind of education in democracy, in cultural pluralism, and in the nature of industrial society that Jane Addams would get at Hull House in Chicago and that Lillian Wald would get on Henry Street in New York City in the 1890s.

Three

On the Lecture Circuit

I N 1878 a financial crisis propelled Alice Fletcher out of the council meetings of women's clubs and onto the public lecture platform. Two scanty bits of evidence support Caroline Dall's statement in her diary that Mr. Conant paid Alice Fletcher "a large salary for many years, and she ought to have been independent at his death, but bad investments came near to ruin her." The evidence comes from the two earliest letters that Alice Fletcher kept, which she placed, significantly, at the beginning of her professional papers. One is to Fletcher from a friend in Scotland, Mrs. Catherine Johnston, dated September 6, 1876, in which Johnston hopes that Fletcher's health, as well as that of her "father," is improving. She adds:

> If health returns to you both—after such danger—you will have courage to bear vicissitudes in business, which I fear these hard times are bringing to you, as well as to many others. . . . everywhere there has been too much haste to be rich, leading to reckless speculations and expenditure.[1]

The second letter is from "Mary S." to Fletcher. Dated December 23, 1877, it offers condolences, speaking of "him we mourn . . . who gave you the deepest, tenderest friendship." The author adds, "Your first duty, darling, is to recover your strength . . . you will find work worthy of you, I am sure." She was glad that Fletcher had taken pleasant rooms at 229 E. 23 Street, New York City, for "You would have needed too much fortitude to stay in Madison all winter with your house left unto you desolate."[2]

The letters suggest that around 1875 Alice Fletcher had returned to the Conant family home in Madison, New Jersey, to help care for Mr. Conant in what proved to be his final illness and perhaps also to be nursed herself as she recovered from an illness. Claudius B. Conant, the man who had given her "the deepest, tenderest friendship," died in Madison on November 7, 1877, at the age of fifty-eight.[3] At the same time Alice Fletcher realized that her savings and investments had been wiped out in the financial depression of the mid-1870s. She found herself once again in the dreaded situation she had been in twenty years before: alone in the world without any financial resources.

But this time she, if not the situation, was different. She was not a frightened adolescent but a competent woman in her late thirties. She had been leading a leisured life in New York City without the pressure of having to earn her own living, but she had been associating with women who did. Alice Fletcher began immediately to carve out a professional career for herself. Within a year she was actively engaged as a public lecturer.

Fletcher began tentatively, using her contacts in the Association for the Advancement of Women to arrange lectures before women's groups in New Jersey, Massachusetts, and Rhode Island. Her first topics came out of her own experience: impressions from childhood of Charles Dickens, the Passion Play at Oberammergau which she had seen on a European tour probably in her capacity as governess, and her ideas on William Blake. Then she began to do serious research and to concentrate on American history. Mary Livermore and Julia Ward Howe tended in their public speeches to be inspirational and light in tone if not in content, but Alice Fletcher's presentations were like solid college lectures. She spoke on the origin of representative government, on "Virginia," on "Both Sides of the Atlantic" (an account of the diverse European origins of many American customs), and on the influence of the Dutch in American history.

"She has a fine presence, a musical voice, and much oratorical power," wrote the *Providence* (Rhode Island) *Journal*, adding, "Her lecture showed wide research." "Her language is well-chosen, her subject well digested, and her lecture . . . delivered with an ease, grace, and modesty rarely seen," reported the *Tribune* in Cambridge, Massachusetts. The *Taunton* (Massachusetts) *Gazette* commented, "Of Miss Fletcher's lectures there is but one thing to be said: that they showed careful study, originality in arrangement and expression, and that they presented in a striking manner ideas of the utmost consequence in forming an intelligent conception of our history."[4]

Fletcher's turn to history was not a personal idiosyncrasy. She was riding a wave of interest in American history stimulated by the great Romantic historians: Bancroft, Prescott, Motley, and Parkman, writers of grand vision and stirring narratives. She was also following the lead of several Boston women, including her old friend Mary Livermore, who were turning to American history for a solution to what they perceived as an ever more pressing problem. Industrialization and immigration had given rise to a vast, miserable underclass in American cities. The newcomers spoke foreign languages and had their own churches and synagogues. They were not likely to be brought to order through the pallid teachings of the Unitarians or through the Puritan doctrines of the Congregationalists. But that they needed to be brought to order, the Boston women did not doubt. The spread of saloons, the labor unrest, and the conditions of filth and overcrowding in which many immigrants lived were proof enough. Mary Hemenway, widow of the wealthiest man in Boston, sponsored cooking and sewing classes for the children of immigrants in the Boston public schools, but this was just a first step. The newcomers needed more than good housekeeping skills. They needed to know what it meant to be an American.

The Boston women sought to find in American history a sense of mission to replace that which had bound the Puritans together. Their vision was symbolically and literally realized in 1876 when "the ladies of Boston" managed to wrest Old South Meeting House on Washington Street away from its parish committee and turn it into a center for the study of American history. The building was a famous Revolutionary War landmark, but the church members, having built a new building in the fashionable Back Bay residential area, had offered the site for development. What resulted was the first campaign for historic preservation in Boston. Nearly all the prominent Bostonians of the 1870s finally joined in, and Mary Hemenway paid most of the bills, but a *Boston Post* reporter called Mary Livermore "the woman who . . . saved Old South."[5] Like her friend, Alice Fletcher was convinced that knowledge of American history was important for "earnest and wise citizenship."[6]

Fletcher discovered, particularly as she traveled west to Ohio, Wisconsin, and Minnesota, that her most popular topics were those that had to do with ancient or prehistoric America. It was as if the geography of the country and humankind's earliest marks on it were what all Americans wanted to have in common. She prepared four lectures on ancient America: "The Ancients, Here and Elsewhere," "The Lost Peoples of America," "Ceremonies of the Moundbuilders," and "Antiquities of Coast and Cave." Within a year she had expanded these into a series of eleven "Lectures on Ancient America," illustrated with maps, watercolor drawings, and specimens. Several of the lectures were on the mound builders of the Ohio valley. Others discussed "Camps and Rock Shelters," "Antiquities of the Coast," the people of the pueblos, Archaic art from Egypt, Assyria, India, and Greece, the earliest traces of humankind, and finally, "the value of anthropological study." She gave this series of lectures in Minneapolis in the fall of 1879, sponsored by the Minnesota Academy of Science, and in Madison, Milwaukee, and Cincinnati.

The editor of the *State Journal* of Madison, Wisconsin, commented:

> No new study has so rapidly aroused a world-wide interest as American Prehistorics. Finding much where nothing was hoped for, students are as enthusiastic as Californians were in 1849.
>
> No one known to me is so capable of presenting in a popular form the lasting results of investigations that have cost a mint of money, and more of time, than Miss Alice C. Fletcher. Her drawings, illustrative of cave-strata, tools, dishes, and hand-craft processes, drawings, etc. among possible pre-Adamites, are beautifully executed. . . . Whoever listens even to one of Miss Fletcher's lectures will discover an old world without crossing the ocean, and one that has already awakened throughout Europe new curiosity concerning America.

The *Wisconsin State Journal* reported:

> With a pleasing voice and attractive manner, Miss Fletcher led her quiet and attentive audience to consider the progress of discovery in archaeology, from the first flint weapon found in England, in the

seventeenth century, to the latest conclusions reached by students of the subject. The touching story of the discovery of a basket of utensils for sewing was drawn with an artist's skill and a woman's tenderness. . . . her concluding plea [was] for the preservation of our own Wisconsin mounds and the treasuring up of their exhumed contents.

"Miss Fletcher tells a wonderful story and tells it well," added the *Cleveland Leader*.[7] By 1879 the *Woman's Journal* was identifying her as "Miss Alice C. Fletcher, the noted lecturess of New York City."[8] Alice Fletcher had stumbled onto a topic popular with the public and simultaneously of great interest to scholars and scientists: prehistoric America.

America north of Mexico at first offered little in the way of a heroic past to incoming Europeans. But as settlers moved across the Alleghenies in the nineteenth century, they began to encounter earth works (mounds and animal effigies) in the Ohio and Mississippi River valleys. These earth sculptures, platforms, and burial places could hardly be compared with the great temple cities of Mexico and South America, but some of them were remarkably interesting. One of the more spectacular was a serpent-shaped mound, 4 feet high and 1,254 feet long, laid out on a hilltop overlooking Brush Creek near Louden, in Adams County, Ohio. Altogether there were thousands of earth mounds, and they aroused much interest among amateur natural historians all over the country. Isaiah Thomas, a printer in Worcester, Massachusetts, founded the American Antiquarian Society in 1812 specifically to encourage study of the mounds. Speculation flourished as to who had built them, and partisans divided themselves into two camps, some insisting that the "mound builders" were an ancient and vanished race and others that they were merely the ancestors of present-day Indians.

Archaeology was stimulated by events in Europe: geologist Charles Lyell's arguments for the long age of the earth; Charles Darwin's theory of evolution by natural selection; and the recognition in the same year (1859) that crudely chipped stones found in undisturbed geological strata in France and England were human tools. Amateur archaeologists in the United States began to look in caves, shell heaps, mines, and cuts made in the earth for bridges and railroads, hoping to find similar signs of ancient human beings in America. It was a grass-roots movement carried on by curious people all across the country.

Alice Fletcher's "Lectures on Ancient America" struck a responsive chord. They also reflected accurately the concerns of American archaeology in 1879, when it was not yet an established profession but one carried on mostly by amateurs on weekends. She spoke on mound builders, antiquities from camps, rock shelters, and shell heaps, on comparative arts studies, and on the earliest signs of human habitation. Her information came from reading and from all the expert help she could muster. She wrote to the secretary of the Smithsonian Institution asking for copies of his appeal for valuable articles for the National Museum. "I am about leaving for the West and expect to lecture upon American Archaeology hoping to awaken a wide interest in this new line of study and thought."[9] Spencer F. Baird answered her immediately, "My dear Miss Fletcher, We shall be glad to have any Indian relics you may be able to secure for us."[10]

From Frederic W. Putnam, the energetic young director of the Peabody Museum of American Archaeology and Ethnology in Cambridge, Fletcher got an even more encouraging response. She had already met Putnam, probably at the museum where she may have gone to get information for her lectures. In September 1879 she wrote to him requesting copies of the ten annual reports that had been published by the museum. She also asked: "Will you kindly inform me what other institutions are devoted to American Archaeology and Ethnology? And also what other reports beside your own, the Smithsonian and the U. S. Govt. and the American Ass. for the Ad. of Science, contain information on these subjects?"[11]

Putnam did not reply directly to her but sent word through his secretary that if she were interested in archaeology, she might come and study at the museum. Alice Fletcher was at first frightened off by his offer. "I thank Mr. Putnam most cordially for his generous proposition," she wrote Jane Smith, "but I am simply a student, and trying to interest other [sic] to go forth and make original investigation, I hardly feel myself entitled to accept so valuable a gift."[12] On her return from her successful western lecture tour she again insisted to Putnam that she was merely "trying to do her small share to strengthen the hands of scholars by awakening a public response."[13]

But Putnam persisted. He helped Alice Fletcher join the new Archaeological Institute of America, founded by the classicist Charles Eliot Norton for professional scholars and interested lay persons, and he continued to encourage her to come round to the museum. A recurring concern of his were the widespread "absurdities and exaggerations" about the ancient peoples of America.[14] If Miss Fletcher were to continue lecturing on archaeology, he wanted to be sure that she knew what she was talking about.

Putnam's invitation was not a sudden whim. The apprentice system was the way he had been trained in natural history, by Henry Wheatland at the Essex Institute in Salem and then by Louis Agassiz, the Swiss-American naturalist at the Museum of Comparative Zoology in Cambridge, Massachusetts. As a young man Putnam had moved back and forth between Salem and Cambridge. Gradually his interests shifted from fish, birds, and mollusks to early mankind. In 1875 he was named curator of the Peabody Museum of American Archaeology and Ethnology at Harvard, founded nine years earlier as the first museum in the country to be devoted solely to archaeology and ethnology.

Putnam combined scientific rigor with an openness to contributions from all kinds of people. What mattered to Putnam was the quality of the work, not the credentials of the investigator. He was building a new science, and he needed every available worker. Alice Fletcher was only one of many seemingly unlikely persons who were brought into anthropology through Putnam. Several of them were women. Cordelia Studley was already at work in the museum on physical anthropology. Zelia Nuttall was soon to carry on her studies of Mexican antiquities and codices under Putnam's sponsorship. Erminnie Smith was encouraged by Putnam to present her studies on jade at the American Association for the Advancement of Science. There she sat in on the sessions on anthropology and decided to study the language and myths of the Iroquois Indians in her home state of New York.

Putnam set up a graduate program in anthropology at Harvard from which many students (all men in the early years) received M.A. and Ph.D. degrees. But he never pinned his hopes on these students alone. There were always others: Lucian Carr and C. C. Willoughby, his assistants at the museum; the several women whose work he encouraged and whom he treated as equals; and the young American Indians Arthur C. Parker and William Jones, who became anthropologists because of Putnam's encouragement.[15]

Alice Fletcher, with her scholarly tendencies and the example of Maria Mitchell before her, could not long resist Putnam's offer of informal tutoring, with its flattering implication that she might become a scientist in her own right. By January 1880 she was a regular visitor at the museum. She was assigned a place at Lucian Carr's worktable. As Putnam scurried in and out, Carr taught her the rudiments of archaeology. He also taught her the scientific method: how to proceed carefully, to seek out evidence, and to avoid speculation. They discussed Putnam's work in shell heaps in Maine and Massachusetts, the excavating Putnam and Charles Metz were doing in the Ohio mounds, and the "palaeoliths," or crude stone tools, that physician Charles Abbott thought he was finding in Trenton, New Jersey.

Frederic Ward Putnam was forty-one years old in 1880, one year younger than Alice Fletcher. He was in the midst of personal upheavals, for his beloved wife of fifteen years and the mother of his three children died of cancer in 1879, and his family was encouraging him to marry again, which he did in 1881.[16] He was also frantically busy. The American Association for the Advancement of Science was to meet in Boston in 1880, "the largest and most important meeting of scientists ever held in the U. S.," according to Putnam, and for the first time it was to be presided over by an anthropologist, the elderly sage of Rochester, New York, Lewis Henry Morgan, then at the end of his long career.[17] A local paper described "Professor Putnam, the Permanent Secretary of the AAAS" as a man of "strikingly distinguished appearance." He was "tall, powerfully built . . . [with a] clear-cut intellectual face; dark side-whiskers and dark hair" and "large beautiful hands." Alice Fletcher clipped this notice and kept it.[18] She watched Putnam from a distance, admiring his seeming selflessness, his tireless energy, his enthusiasm. She wanted to be useful to him as she knew she had been to Mary Livermore, Julia Ward Howe, and Maria Mitchell, and she wanted to "serve science," an expression she was often to use. During her months in Cambridge in 1880 Alice Fletcher began to feel a loyalty to Putnam which was to last for nearly twenty years.

To her public lectures Alice Fletcher began to add a commendation, somewhat idealized, of the Peabody Museum in Cambridge. She described it as "the only institution in the country devoted to

Frederic Ward Putnam.
(Peabody Museum, Harvard University)

the study of man," "a Palace of Truth" so strict in its investigations that "no doubtful article can find a place in its cases, but is set aside to be proved." She urged her audiences to support it and the archaeological investigations it carried on.[19]

Alice Fletcher invited her lecture audiences to tour the Peabody Museum, and she brought other visitors. In February 1881 she appeared with Thomas Henry Tibbles, a Nebraska journalist, and Susette ("Bright Eyes") La Flesche, a young Omaha Indian and the soon-to-be Mrs. Tibbles. These two would be the agents of a major change in Fletcher's life. She had first met them when La Flesche and Tibbles had come east in the fall of 1879 to protest the removal of the Ponca Indians from Dakota Territory to Indian Territory (present Oklahoma). The party had included Standing Bear, a Ponca chief; Susette La Flesche, his young interpreter; Francis La Flesche, her younger brother and chaperon; and Thomas Henry Tibbles, the journalist who had brought the Ponca case to public attention.

Two years before, in 1877, the Poncas had been moved to Indian Territory after it was discovered that the land assigned to them in Dakota Territory had also inadvertently been assigned to the Sioux. The Poncas went, under pressure, but they suffered so much in Indian Territory from malaria and pulmonary diseases that in the spring of 1879 Standing Bear decided to take his band back home. They were taken into custody by General George Crook when they stopped at the Omaha Agency and were detained at Fort Omaha. They might have been returned to Indian Territory had not Tibbles, assistant editor of the *Omaha Herald*, taken up the case. Tibbles may have been tipped off by General Crook himself, for Crook thought the Poncas had been treated unfairly. Tibbles helped to organize a committee of citizens in Omaha to raise money for Standing Bear's defense, and in a landmark case, Judge Elmer Dundy declared that an Indian is a person in the eyes of the law as described in the Fourteenth Amendment and therefore cannot be deprived of life, liberty, or property without due process of law. He ordered Standing Bear and his party released from jail. He and his followers were to be allowed to remain in Nebraska. But that did not settle the question of where in Nebraska they were to live or what land was legally theirs. Standing Bear and Thomas Henry Tibbles decided to bring the Poncas' plight to national attention by setting out on a speaking tour in 1879.

Standing Bear, six feet tall and regal in his chief's costume, spoke in his native language, and Susette La Flesche, whose English had been perfected in several years of study at a girls school in New Jersey, translated for him. They spoke to large audiences all across the country, but Boston, with its tradition of reform activity, took them to its heart. The mayor appointed a Ponca relief committee and named himself chairman, the governor of the state set up a special investigating committee, Henry Wadsworth Longfellow hosted a reception for them in his home, and the junior senator from Massachusetts, Henry L. Dawes, set out on his career as congressional spokesman for Indian reformers.[20] In the midst of the excitement, Alice Fletcher (who frequently visited in Boston) talked to Susette La Flesche and Tibbles about her plan to go and live among the Indians, but they put her off, not certain how serious she was or what their own plans were. Alice Fletcher scarcely noticed Susette's younger brother, Francis, who would later play such a key role in her life.

In early 1881 Susette La Flesche and Thomas Henry Tibbles returned to Boston, and Alice Fletcher approached them again. She showed them around the Peabody Museum and convinced them that she was serious and that she could stand whatever hardships might be involved. La Flesche and Tibbles returned to the Omaha Reservation and were married in June; later that summer they contacted Alice Fletcher. If she would meet them in Omaha in the fall, they would take her camping for several weeks among the Sioux Indians. After that she could travel on by herself.[21]

It was the opportunity Alice Fletcher was waiting for. What she intended to do was without precedent. Many women had lived among the Indians as teachers or missionaries or traders' wives. The formidable Matilda Stevenson had even gone to the pueblos in 1879 on a government collecting expedition commanded by her husband Colonel James Stevenson. But for a woman—or man—to go and live with Indians for scientific purposes, in order to study their way of life, was just beginning to be thought of. Lewis Henry Morgan had traveled up the Missouri River for six weeks in 1862 collecting data on kinship systems among the Indians and had spent three weeks in Colorado and New Mexico in 1878 studying Indian house types. In 1878 the linguist James Owen Dorsey settled at the Omaha Reservation to begin what would be nearly two years of field study.

Francis and Susette La Flesche in
Washington in 1879 during the
speaking tour with Standing Bear and
Thomas Henry Tibbles. (Nebraska
State Historical Society)

In 1879 another young Smithsonian scientist, Frank Hamilton Cushing, went to Zuni pueblo in New Mexico with the Stevensons and then decided to stay on for a year or two to study Zuni life. He was to remain for four and a half years, with one brief return trip to Washington. And in Germany the young geographer Franz Boas was preparing to spend the year of 1883 with the Eskimos of Baffin Island.

This idea of going to live with a so-called primitive people for an extended time and for no other purpose than ethnography, to study and describe their way of life, was new in the early 1880s. It was invented independently and nearly simultaneously by these researchers. To them we owe the whole notion of "doing field-work," that hallmark of twentieth century anthropology.

Alice Fletcher's inspiration was twofold. Late in her life she told an interviewer that she had once read about an English scholar who left his university to travel through Europe with the gypsies (probably either George Borrow, author of the well-known books *Romany Rye* and *The Zincali*, or Francis Groome, founder in the 1860s of the Gypsy Lore Society), and she had decided that she wanted someday to do the same thing among the Indians in her own country.[22] But to label such a journey "science" requires another explanation. That inspiration came from Maria Mitchell's urging that women take up observational sciences like astronomy. Alice Fletcher's genius was her recognition that ethnography could be an observational science. Although it seemed a long way from astronomy, the study of ethnography could proceed in the same way—by long periods of looking (and listening) and meticulous recording of what one saw and heard.

Underneath it all lay also an urge for adventure. Alice Fletcher was at loose ends. She was forty-three and single. She had no home, no family, no steady job, no money. No one was dependent upon her. On her western lecture trip in 1879 Alice Fletcher had tried to make contact with her father's family, the Fletchers. She wrote to his sister, her Aunt Emily in Milwaukee, asking about her father and other family members and inquiring whether they might be able to arrange a lecture or series of lectures for her. The response was disappointing. Her aunt sent a hearty welcome and the addresses of aunts and uncles in La Porte, Indiana; Racine, Wisconsin; and Clear Lake, Michigan; but she wrote that she did not remember much about Alice's father, Thomas ("you should ask a good friend rather than a sister"), and that she could not do much about arranging for lectures because people there were so busy in the fall there was "no time for anything intellectual until after Christmas."[23] Aunt Emily did not travel to Madison to hear her niece lecture, and Alice Fletcher gave up trying to strengthen family ties that did not exist. She was truly on her own.

Nothing held Alice Fletcher in the East, nor was anything at risk if she took off on a wild adventure, except ultimately her own life and health. She seized the opportunity offered her by Susette and Thomas Henry Tibbles, and thinking that she ought to have a special project, she decided to concentrate her study on the life of Indian women. She sought advice from every expert she could find: from F. W. Putnam and Lucian Carr at the Peabody Museum and from John Wesley Powell and Garrick Mallery at the Bureau of Ethnology in Washington.[24] Then she set off, armed with letters from the secretary of war and the secretary of the interior that directed the recipients to extend "proper courtesies" and assistance to Miss Fletcher. She sought to downplay as much as possible her association with Tibbles, who as a result of his agitation was "in ill odor" with the government. She wrote Lucian Carr: "I know that what I am toward is difficult, fraught with hardship to mind and body, but there is something to be learned in the line of woman's life in the social state represented by the Indians that . . . will be of value not only ethnologically but help toward the historical solution of 'the woman question' in our midst. Is it not so?" Playing on her name, as she often did when in a reflective mood, she added, "Even if you tell me that I 'aim my arrows at the Sun' I must earnestly reply I must still aim."[25]

PART 2

Mother
to the Indians

Four

"What I am toward is difficult"

IVE years after "Custer's Last Stand" at the Little Big Horn on June 25, 1876, Alice Fletcher was headed west to camp among the very people who had defeated him. She was going to visit the Sioux, the most famous Indians in North America, a people barely subdued. Her excitement, as she and Thomas and Susette Tibbles started out from Omaha, Nebraska, was palpable. On September 15, 1881, they climbed into a yellow carriage drawn by four mules provided them by General George Crook, the commander at Fort Omaha, and headed north along the Missouri River.

Omaha itself was bustling. The wife of a foreign diplomat passing through Omaha four years before had described it as a place of "wooden sidewalks and muddy roads" but with "FUTURE written all over it."[1] The streets had been laid out in squares and broad avenues, and schools, churches, and a post office were built on a grand scale. Alice Fletcher had arrived to find herself in the midst of the state fair. She spent her first afternoon at the fair, riding a horse and admiring outsize turnips and parsnips, and stayed that night with Tibbles's mother, "as gay, and eager and bright as a girl—her 80 years seeming to melt in the stir of the house."[2]

Then they headed off from the comforts of "civilization." As she and Susette Tibbles sat in the heavily laden carriage, Alice Fletcher remembered the English scholar among the gypsies and thought that she and Susette must look like gypsy women in a pedlar's wagon. It was the only connection she could make to anchor herself in this suddenly alien situation.

For two days they rode north along the swiftly flowing Missouri River. The flat bottomlands of the river channel, three to four miles wide, were edged by bluffs ranging from 50 to 150 feet high. Alice Fletcher and the Tibbleses in their wagon moved up and down between the flat river bottom and the high bluffs. From the bluffs, they could look down on the river or out over the seemingly endless rolling hills. Susette Tibbles thought the prairie was beautiful, and

Alice Fletcher would one day think so too. But on that first journey she found it desolate.

One noon they stopped for dinner at a settler's home along the river. Alice Fletcher noticed a reed organ in the parlor and tried to explain to her hostess what "ethnology" was. The woman was eager to talk, and when they rose to leave she thrust a pencil and bit of paper into Fletcher's hand. "Write your name so I can remember it," she said. "One of these days you'll be famous and I'll be able to say—I know her, she stopped at my house."[3]

Alice Fletcher had no idea where they were going. She had trusted Susette and Thomas Tibbles to take her wherever they could, and they had worked out a general plan. They would visit Susette's family on the Omaha Reservation for several days, then go north through the adjacent Winnebago Reservation to the Santee Sioux mission complex, where they could stay for several days. Standing Bear with his band of Poncas was not far away, near the mouth of the Niobrara River. From his camp they would travel straight west, halfway across the northern edge of Nebraska, to Fort Niobrara. Fletcher could spend a night at the fort and rest up from the rigors of camping. Then they would cross up north into Dakota Territory and the Great Sioux Reservation. Tibbles was not well acquainted with the Sioux, but he counted on his reputation as a defender of the Indians to open the way. They would head for the Rosebud Agency, in the heart of the lower part of the Sioux Reservation, and then, turning east, return by way of the Yankton Sioux Agency, on the east side of the Missouri River. They planned to be gone about a month.

It took two days to travel the eighty miles from Omaha to the Omaha Reservation, where they were warmly welcomed by Susette's family. Joseph La Flesche had built his family a two story frame house, but at night they sat outside around a campfire, and friends came, bringing small gifts and staying to talk. The conversation was in the Omaha language, which Susette Tibbles translated for her husband and Alice Fletcher. Fletcher absorbed what she could and made herself understood as best she could. She was interested in the Omahas' criticisms of the medical care that President Garfield was getting after the assassin's attack. The Omahas thought their procedures were better, and Joseph La Flesche talked about the Indian tradition of "the walking day," the fourth day after a wound when the injured person is forced to get up and take at least a step or two. Susette La Flesche Tibbles, sitting next to her father, gave a "racy account" of their political activities in Boston and Washington to much laughter and earnest discussion. Inevitably the talk turned to land titles and the Omahas' fears that their lands were not secure.[4]

As carefully as Alice Fletcher watched the Omahas, they watched her. Young Francis La Flesche had just taken a position in Washington as a clerk in the Indian Bureau. When he arrived home in late September for his vacation, his father's first words, as he came out to greet him, were: "Your sister has gone up to the Sioux with a white woman. They went yesterday and you have just missed them by a day. Your sister's friend is a remarkable woman; in thought and expression she is more like a man than a woman."[5] Francis immediately caught the import of his father's words—that a potentially useful force had come into the life of the La Flesche family.

At the Omaha Reservation Tibbles sent General Crook's carriage and mules back to him, and they went on with a wagon and horses provided by Joseph La Flesche. As they left the reservation, traveling north along Omaha creek, a middle-aged Omaha man came galloping up behind them on a pony. It was Wajapa, a friend of Joseph La Flesche's, who indicated with gestures that he intended to go with them. Wajapa soon became the emotional focus of Fletcher's journey. They had to communicate through Susette Tibbles, but they managed to communicate a great deal, for they were intensely interested in one another.

At first Alice Fletcher simply marveled at his otherness. Although Wajapa wore citizen's clothes, he was Omaha, unlike Joseph La Flesche and his family who were of mixed (Omaha, Ponca, and French) parentage. She transcribed a song he whistled, "a strange, wild cadence like a wood bird," and watched the way he rode ahead of the wagon, picking out the trail which was like the marks of two fingers drawn on the billowing prairie, through grass as tall as the wagon.[6] At each hill he galloped ahead to the top and then sat waiting, he and his horse silhouetted against the sky.

Wajapa, in turn, watched Fletcher furtively as she cleaned her teeth and when she undid her long hair at night. He told Susette that it was the longest hair he had ever seen and that nothing else was so beautiful on a woman. One day he confronted her directly. "I believe all the white men tell lies," he said. Through Susette she told him, "Not all white men are bad; there are some good ones." Fletcher later wrote in her journal: "There was seemingly no appeal. Two races confronted each other and mine preeminently guilty."[7]

Nearly every night around the campfire the conversation grew serious as Wajapa talked of the future struggles of the Indians. His grandfather had been a chief and his father had been the leader of a band, a place now filled by Susette's father. Two years before, Wajapa had changed to citizen's dress and sent his daughter east to Miss Reed's school in Elizabeth, New Jersey, where Susette had been a student. His friends had thought him hard-hearted, to send away a little girl, but Wajapa said: "No, I look to the future. I shall sleep easy when I die if my children are prepared to meet the struggle that is coming when they must cope with the white settlers." Alice Fletcher was impressed with his mind and character, but she commented, "He is rather restless, made so by the uncertainty of Indian tenure of land. Indians love their land as no white man realizes, and will not part from it for any cause if possible to prevent it."[8]

One night Wajapa revealed his reason for making the trip. Five years earlier, when the Omahas were on their last buffalo hunt, he had left the tribe as they neared Indian Territory and had spent two months exploring on his own. He thought the Omahas might be moved to Indian Territory, and he had wanted to see what it was like. He had not liked it. On this trip he wanted to look at land to the north, for he had decided to flee north with two wives and numerous children if the Omahas were removed.

Sometimes the mood was lighter. One day they laughingly gave each other special names. Wajapa named Fletcher Ma-she-ha-the, which Susette translated as "the motion of an eagle as he sweeps high in the air." It was a compliment, for eagle was the name of his own family and band, and Fletcher was pleased, although less so when Tibbles suggested that for short she could be called "high flyer." Susette they called "the western princess" and Tibbles became "Grey coat," for that was what he had been wearing when he got Standing Bear released from prison, his hour of triumph.

On they went, as Tibbles described it (with grudging admiration for Alice Fletcher), "through a steady series of rainstorms, broken whiffle trees [the pivoting bar to which the traces of a harness are fastened for drawing a wagon], muddy roads, balky spells of a pony, thunderstorms during our night camping, and winds which burned our ethnologist's face to a blister. But that city-bred lady stood everything without one complaint."[9]

Their first stop was the Santee Sioux mission complex. The Santee Sioux were Eastern Sioux who had been moved from Minnesota in 1863 first to Crow Creek in Dakota Territory and then to the Niobrara in Nebraska in 1866. The mission complex included three boarding schools: the Episcopalians ran one government industrial school, the Society of Friends ran another, and the American Board of Foreign Missions had a boarding school as well as a mission led by Alfred L. Riggs, a Congregational clergyman. The travelers stayed with Riggs and his wife and hurried to church in the evening "to see the Indians," who watered their horses at the creek and then filed in quietly for the service. The next day Susette and Alice visited classrooms. Fletcher listened intently as the teacher explained that Indians are not intellectually slow but are slow to show what they know. At the evening prayer meeting, the women staff members prayed earnestly, and Fletcher felt that "these are the picked and advanced Guard in the Lord's Army."[10]

Another day's travel brought them to the mouth of the Niobrara River, opposite the place where Standing Bear and his band of Poncas were camped. When Standing Bear and the other Poncas saw them coming, they came down to the opposite bank and bid them cross over to a feast. Broad and flat with patches of quicksand, the treacherous Niobrara had five streams separated by mud islands. The main channel of the river changed its bed every few hours. The brightly dressed Poncas helped Alice Fletcher and Susette and Thomas Tibbles across, using the wagon and then a boat. They were wet through to the skin when they arrived, but Fletcher was soon to confront what to her was a greater ordeal—her first Indian feast. The portions of stewed beef, soup, and bread were enormous, for it was assumed that travelers were hungry. Ponca courtesy demanded that guests be fed to satiation before any questions were asked or serious topics raised.

Finally dinner was over. A council was held, and Standing Bear and the other Poncas plied Tibbles with questions. Tibbles urged each man to stake out a claim on 160 acres, build a cabin there, and begin to farm. Alice Fletcher was introduced to the Poncas as a woman who had helped their cause in the East, and she was asked to make a speech, another Indian courtesy. She wrote in her journal: "They seemed pleased and glad a christian woman has come. The tales of oppression are pitiful. . . . They are children as faced toward us, know nothing of the power of law and organization. Their implicit faith in a white man they think friendly is very plaintive."[11] What in turn did they think of her? Thomas Henry Tibbles overheard Wajapa telling some of the Poncas: "She has come to see the Indians. She seems to be a very nice woman, but I haven't known her long enough to say for certain."[12]

When they finally left to cross the river back to their own tent on the other side, they found that a white man had stolen the boat they were using. There was nothing to do but wade across the deepest part of the river. Suddenly Buffalo Chip, a large Ponca man, turned to Fletcher and insisted that she cross on his back, so she did, clinging about his neck and bending her legs to keep them out of the water. "[I] have been carried across rapid rivers on the back of an Indian," she exulted, in a first report back to Putnam.[13]

They returned to find their camp on fire. Wajapa had been left behind to guard the tent, but he had lit a fire and then run down to the river to help them cross. While he was gone, a spark flew into the grass and within moments the camp was ablaze. They managed to save the tent but they lost much of their clothing. After the ordeal, Wajapa disappeared for several hours. The string of mishaps alarmed him, for he took them to be an ill omen, and he was angry at Standing Bear who had loaned them a horse for the rest of their journey instead of giving them one as an Indian should do when his friends are in need. Wajapa had decided to take on white ways, but it annoyed him when other Indians did the same. He talked of returning home. Not until Fletcher promised to buy him a new overcoat to replace the one lost in the fire did he agree to continue on with them. Alice Fletcher began to write more often in her journal of Wajapa's moodiness and his "unreasonableness." The moodiness she interpreted as an Indian way of getting privacy in a crowded camp. The unreasonableness she attributed to a lack of opportunity for intellectual development. Without a written language, Fletcher thought, there is nothing for the gifted mind to react upon. There is only individual observation, hearsay, superstition. "No wonder they do not progress. All is emotion," she wrote.[14]

The wrenching of the wagon was worse than usual the next day, as Wajapa drove in ill temper. Their party had gained two new members, Buffalo Chip and his wife Gaha, whose name was said to mean "grandmother." Buffalo Chip knew the Sioux language, and when he offered to accompany them he was made leader of their party. According to Tibbles, Indians never set out on even a short journey without a designated leader whose orders were to be obeyed and who was responsible for the well-being of all. Gaha brought a good Indian tent with her, large enough so that a fire could be built in the center with the smoke rising out of the top, and that became their home, the entire party sleeping in a circle inside it. Gaha also took over much of the cooking, helped drive the extra ponies, and kept their spirits up with her good humor.

On Sunday, October 2, they drove past a German settlement, scattered houses and a small village of frame buildings, each with three or four lightning rods. One of the buildings had the sign "Saloon" on it, and cartloads of hearty Germans were driving up to the door. From this village the wagon party climbed up to a divide, where they looked out over vast stretches of land ahead of them with bluffs in the distance and clouds brilliant in the setting sun. In back of them lay the fertile valley and the rapids of the Niobrara. Alice Fletcher thought it a majestic scene, but that evening as they camped two miles farther, on the banks of a creek, she was too ill to eat anything except for one of the apples packed for them by Mrs. Riggs.

Her spirits were often low. "I was very weary in mind and body. . . . How hopeless seemed the effort of living as far as my life is concerned—but one can't die, and work may be done," she wrote in her journal. At night she lay awake pondering "the desolation of life when the heart has no echo . . . the vanity and solitariness of life."[15]

Tibbles devoted a chapter of his autobiography, published after his death, to this camping trip. He wrote:

> To all intents ours was an Indian camp, with all of such a camp's normal life, except the dancing. This, too, we should have had at

times except for the constant vigilance of Wajapa, who would have none of it. If Tazhebute [Buffalo Chip] in a gleeful mood even started humming a dance tune and took a step or two, Wajapa instantly clamped down on him with sarcasm which promptly ended that impulse—to the ethnologist's hardly concealed fury.[16]

One afternoon Fletcher gave Wajapa and Buffalo Chip a lesson in writing numbers. It took them nearly an hour to learn the numbers from one to ten, and Wajapa was weary when they had finished. "Learned his first lesson in the fatigue of head work," Fletcher recorded triumphantly in her journal.[17]

It took a week to travel the 150 miles from the mouth of the Niobrara River to Fort Niobrara near Valentine, Nebraska. For much of the way they dragged through deep sand, going for days without seeing a house or any sign of life other than insects and a few birds. At the fort Fletcher presented her official letter to the commander in charge, Captain Montgomery, and she and Susette and Thomas Tibbles ate dinner with the captain and his wife. Fletcher spent the night in their home and rejoiced at being "alone" and "clean once more" as she took a warm bath. In her journal she wrote, "The strain of being day and night with a different race, always alert, ever trying to keep the peace and not offend is very wearing, particularly added to the very hard and trying mode of life." The next morning she laughed and joked with Mrs. Montgomery and promised to return her hospitality "if ever I had a home."[18]

Captain Montgomery sent them on accompanied by a Sioux scout, Thigh, and his wife. Montgomery warned Fletcher that there were marauding Indians in the neighborhood. If she saw a barefooted Indian alone with his hair cut and scant clothing, she was told to speed away as fast as possible, for he would be dangerous. "If his heart was bad . . . he would kill."[19]

It began to rain not long after they left the fort, rain that soon came down in torrents, and they decided to set up camp and wait out the storm. When Alice Fletcher suggested that they slip a rubber lining she had brought under the tent poles, Wajapa seemed to be resisting, so she chided him impulsively, "You speak to us as if we were children."[20] A change came over Wajapa's face, and he vanished. Later in a flash of lightning Tibbles saw him standing motionless about fifty yards from the tent taking the full force of the rain in his face. After two hours he reappeared, sat silently by the fire for a few moments, and then wrapped himself in a buffalo robe and immediately fell asleep. Fletcher lay contrite and despairing on her own bedding roll, pondering Indian "moodiness." "What I am toward is difficult," she had written Lucian Carr. It was proving to be more difficult than she had imagined.

Five

Camping with the Sioux

ONE more day's travel in piercing cold winds took them forty miles north to the goal of their journey, the Rosebud Agency, administrative center for the Oglala and Brule Sioux. The Rosebud Agency was a complex of wooden buildings inside a stockade set out on barren sand hills on the west bank of Rosebud Creek, ninety miles west of the Missouri River. As they approached the agency buildings, the party grew quiet and somewhat apprehensive, for they were not sure how they would be received. Thigh, the Sioux scout, and his wife moved ahead with Buffalo Chip, Gaha, and Wajapa. Buffalo Chip and Gaha had decorated their hair partings with red paint, but Wajapa resolutely wore his white man's clothing, although he knew that would mean a cool welcome and no gifts. The Tibbleses and Fletcher let their wagon fall to the rear.

A tall, impressive Indian in a blue blanket appeared, and Buffalo Chip went forward alone to greet him. It was Ausapi, an Oglala Sioux chief. He had heard that they were on their way. He bid them to come and eat.

In Ausapi's log cabin, they were served large portions of boiled jerked beef, biscuits, and coffee on a canvas spread out on the floor between two beds. Gaha, noticing Fletcher's discomfort, quietly sent word around that she would take on her plate what Fletcher could not eat. Next from different families came four more invitations to eat. Alice Fletcher and the Tibbleses begged off after the second feast, Buffalo Chip apologizing for them that white people became sick if they ate more than three times a day, but the others went. Ausapi loaned them a large tent, and in the afternoon his wife came to visit them, eager to tell them her version of the situation on the reservation.

They were soon summoned to appear before the agent, John Cook, at his desk in an inner sanctum inside a second stockade. Fletcher found him to be "a long haired, shrewd faced, uncultured man." When she made a comment about the weather, he replied, "I regulate everything here but the weather."[1] But when she showed him her official letters, he changed his tone and took them on a tour of the offices. Later Ausapi told her that no Indian except Spotted Tail had ever before been allowed inside the stockade.[2]

Six thousand seven hundred Indians, mostly Oglala and Brule Sioux, were camped on the dry hills around the Rosebud Agency. They were living on rations, which consisted of the monthly beef issue and meager amounts of flour, coffee, sugar, milk, and bacon. The situation was especially tense because the leader of the Brule Sioux, Spotted Tail, had been shot and killed just two months before by Crow Dog, a traditionalist member of his own group.

Spotted Tail had been one of the Sioux "peace chiefs." Despite the defeat of Custer at the Little Big Horn, many of the Sioux chiefs knew that in the long run their cause was hopeless. In 1877 General Crook had persuaded Spotted Tail to go north on a mission of peace, to persuade the Sioux and Cheyenne hostiles that continued resistance was useless, that they ought to put down their arms, come in to the agencies, and agree to cede the Black Hills to the United States. Spotted Tail took 250 subchiefs and headmen with him and was gone about two months. He returned with 900 people and the prediction that many more would soon follow, and many did. It was the first break in the firm ranks of the hostiles and meant the end of the Indian wars. A grateful United States government moved Spotted Tail to the area around Rosebud Creek, where he wanted to be, built him a large house, set up the Rosebud Agency, and made Spotted Tail the conduit for government funds going to the agency. But Spotted Tail soon assumed prerogatives that were not his, angering the traditionalists and leading to his death. Crow Dog's family made restitution for the shooting according to tribal custom, through gifts to the family of the dead man, which should have ended the matter. But John Cook, the agent, wanted Crow Dog brought to trial for murder. Alice Fletcher, in her week around the Rosebud Agency, moved back and forth between Ausapi's Oglala Sioux, who sympathized with Crow Dog, and Spotted Tail's Brule Sioux, who were divided among themselves, trying not to take sides in the controversy.[3]

One day the group went out to Spotted Tail's camp, where the chief's mother and son still lived. They called on White Thunder, an old chief who Fletcher thought was "not very cordial to me." He brought out his papers: a treaty concerning the Ponca band and a list of articles to be issued at the Rosebud Agency, and his wife prepared a meal of bread, "wretched stuff, heavy and poor," coffee, and dried meat boiled with pork. A pretty young girl about eighteen years old came in, the wife's sister who had been a student at the Carlisle Indian School in Pennsylvania. Fletcher learned that White Thunder wanted to make the girl his second wife, but the girl had declined. "It is rather startling and unpleasant to contemplate this woman's future. I hope she will hold out," Fletcher wrote in her notebook.[4]

After the meal White Thunder asked why they had come. Tibbles spoke warily and very generally about his desire to help them, but Wajapa, when it was his turn to make a speech, launched courageously into an argument on the Indian need for citizenship, land titles, and the right to appeal to the courts for justice on individual as well as group questions. Tibbles thought the polite "Hows" of approval were rather feeble after Wajapa spoke, but one old man was enthusiastic and promptly gave a special feast so that his friends could meet Wajapa.[5]

At Tibbles's suggestion, Alice Fletcher was invited to speak. She made a little speech, urging that when the young Sioux students returned from eastern schools these older chiefs should learn some English and some arithmetic from them, so that the Indians could "protect themselves against the white men who wish to cheat them." Swift Bear, who had joined them, listened with interest, but White Thunder sat silently and made no response when she finished speaking. Fletcher in turn sniffed to her journal: "This visit was rather uninteresting. I felt the influence of the man to be less single and noble, in some ways."[6] They hastily exchanged gifts with the women and left.

Bad as the situation was on the Sioux Reservation in 1881, it was to get worse. Crow Dog was condemned to death by the First Judicial Court of Dakota at Deadwood, but he was freed on December 17, 1883, by the United States Supreme Court, which held that the Deadwood court did not have jurisdiction over matters between two Indians. In the inflamed climate another man was killed, shot by Young Spotted Tail.[7] Consequently, in 1885 Congress passed the Major Crimes Act, which brought under the jurisdiction of United States law Indians accused of any of seven major crimes: murder, manslaughter, rape, assault with intent to kill, arson, burglary, and larceny. It was the first major legal inroad on the concept of tribal autonomy. The Sioux lost the right to govern themselves according to their own code but did not gain the United States citizen's right to appeal in court illegal actions taken against them. In 1889, threatened by starvation, they surrendered eleven million additional acres of land. Immediately their rations were cut to half of what the new treaty promised, but they had no legal recourse.[8] They had no power other than moral suasion or the now idle threat of military resistance.

It was Young Spotted Tail who arranged an Indian dance for Alice Fletcher, something she had been eager to see. At the appointed hour, Tibbles escorted his wife and Fletcher to a large tent, forty or fifty feet in diameter, lighted by a pine stick fire. As Fletcher entered the tent she was startled "by a sudden mighty beating of the drum, with such deafening yells and shouts that I feared my ears would burst." Gropingly she made her way around to the back of the tent, but there "I felt a foreignness that grew into a sense of isolation. . . . The whole scene was utterly unlike anything I had ever beheld before. I was oppressed with its strangeness." The wild drumming, "nothing but tumult and din to me," was unnerving by itself, but then came the dancers, "in full undress, save for breech-cloth, paint and feathers." The sudden appearance of the dancers—moving wildly, shaking feathers, and brandishing war clubs—and the thud of their bare feet on the ground called up before her "every picture of savages I had ever seen . . . every account of Indian atrocities I had ever heard." For several minutes Alice Fletcher suffered "an intense fright," until she came to herself and remembered that she was there of her own choice and in order to study the very dance going on around her.[9]

Tibbles was almost as uncomfortable as she was. Like Wajapa and many whites who wanted "to save the Indian race,"[10] he thought dances were an obstacle to progress. He did not want to imply approval by his presence there. He had also noticed large camp kettles of soup being prepared, and he knew they would soon be required to eat again, for the third time within four hours. But when he tried to pull the group away, Fletcher sat "as if entranced." Tibbles wrote, "After each round she would beg me. 'Let's stay for just one more. I want to study this thing.'"[11]

Finally, after about an hour and at Tibbles's insistence, they left. Gaha, waiting for them outside the tent, was amused at Fletcher's excitement and soon was telling everyone how she had had to pull the white woman away from the dancing. Later they learned that the dancers were greatly disappointed at their abrupt departure, for they were each to have been given a gift at the end of the evening.

This Sioux Indian dance, disturbing and disorienting, was the start of Alice Fletcher's lifelong interest in Indian ceremonies and music. It was also the beginning of ten days of increasing discomfort and despair, her rite of passage into a career in anthropology.[12] Although John Cook claimed to have absolute power on the Sioux reservation, the irony of the fact that he carried on his rule from inside a second stockade was not lost on Fletcher. Prodded by her official letters, Agent Cook had gone through the motions of cooperating with her, but she was not deceived. He had little to offer and could not be counted on in a crisis. The local Episcopal missionary, Mr. Cleveland, and his daughter loaned Fletcher a buffalo robe and mittens for the continuing journey but could offer little else. Thomas and Susette Tibbles were outside their known territory and were among Sioux Indians on whom they had no claim. Fletcher found herself entirely dependent upon full-blood Indians: Wajapa, Buffalo Chip and Gaha, Thigh and his wife, and the Sioux they had come to see. She had a new sense of how alien they were to her whole way of life, how alive and powerful their customs were, and how incompletely and for the most part reluctantly they had been turned toward "civilization." Her helpful suggestions had been rebuffed at White Thunder's camp, and increasingly even the purpose of her journey, to study Indian life, was being challenged by Tibbles as useless if not actually harmful.

Fletcher recoiled from her involvement in the dancing and music, feeling now an intense distaste for everything around her. She went with a disapproving eye to the monthly issuing of beef, where each Indian man, mounted on a pony in full dress with paint and feathers, waited to chase down the animal designated as his, and to an Indian funeral, where the widow and children gave away all their goods as a sign of mourning. As the group prepared to leave the Rosebud Agency, Fletcher hunted up an Indian girl who had done washing for them and became exasperated when the girl blushed and giggled and would not name a price for work that Fletcher thought had been poorly done. "The senseless laugh of the women is very trying . . . I suppose the women must laugh when the men are morose—pity they can't be shaken up together," she wrote. As she walked back over the "horrid, desolate path," Indian dogs yelping and dirty children running toward her, her disgust mounted. "Nothing can describe the lack of cleanliness and order of Rosebud Agency," she wrote, ". . . [but] how can Indians do better, hemmed in as they are at the agency deprived of their native life, . . . and not fully introduced to our ways. They are stranded between two modes of life."[13]

Wajapa and Buffalo Chip were eager to leave. They sensed the tension at the agency because of the meager rations that were being given out, and they thought their horses had already eaten too much of Ausapi's hay. While they were at the Rosebud Agency, a message had come from Sitting Bull, inviting them to visit him. He was a prisoner at Fort Randall on the Missouri, 140 miles east of the Rosebud Agency. An invitation from Sitting Bull was not to be ignored, and the group set off hurriedly.

The six days of travel through snow and rain to Fort Randall proved to be the worst part of their journey. They set off without firewood, for they intended to reach a creek with trees by nightfall, but they took a wrong fork in the road, and that night, not having reached their destination, they were "a desolate camp." Fletcher was irritated that no one had thought to bring firewood or had planned ahead in other ways for such contingencies, and she spent a "fearful night" with a nervous chill, a hard cough, and painful lungs. She hurt all over, dreamed of "wild scenes," and lay awake longing for day and singing silently to herself a hymn, "Watchman will the night soon pass?" She wrote: "It was a horrible night of suffering and torment. I thought my end might be near. The vile smell of manure being burned in the fire, the dirty dishes, the mess pot of meat and scrapings, as well, made the whole thing horrid, together with the Indian drum beating in our ears, though miles away." [14]

In the morning they burned the tent pole and the woodbox for fire. Then on they went through a world Fletcher felt was vacant. "The roads are so lonely, nothing in sight but sky and undulating ground and varied tints of grass, that a tree is quite an excitement. Have not seen any game, even a prairie chicken, not here, hardly any birds. Mr. T. said nothing could live here unless supported by the Government." [15]

Two days of travel brought them to Turtle Creek. They crossed and then hurried on, for a blizzard was threatening. The wind blew very hard, and it began to rain and hail. Every morning their tent was stiff with frost and snow. The horses were worn out, firewood continued to be in short supply, and tempers were short.

Inevitably, friction grew between Fletcher and Thomas Henry Tibbles. Tibbles was a fiery sort of man, always moving from one cause to another, portraying himself as the hero. Fletcher thought him arrogant. On his part, Tibbles became increasingly irritated with her constant note-taking and questioning through Susette of Wajapa and Buffalo Chip, for he regarded her actions as a challenge to his position as an authority on the Indians. On one cold desolate Sunday, October 24, 1881, Fletcher noted in her journal, "Mr. T. put a stop to my questions." She had been asking Buffalo Chip about the painting of faces, and as Susette interpreted for her, Tibbles broke in and said: "They paint according to their fancy, it means nothing at all. . . . I've lived twenty years among the Indians and I know and I've asked and that is all." [16]

Fletcher argued with him. If, as he said, some tribes use more black and others more red in their face paintings, then it was not merely a matter of fancy, and there must be something to be learned through questions. Her case was lost, however, for Susette would do no more interpreting without her husband's approval. Fletcher felt herself a fool for having trusted Tibbles. As she neared Fort Randall and the hope of letters, she began to think of the future. If this trip ended in failure, what more was there for her? "Today it seems as though my heart would ache itself out of my body. Why can't I die?" she wrote in her journal.[17]

But the next day she rallied, finding good in all her companions and blaming herself for her difficulties. That night it was beautiful and clear, and she walked out to a hill from which she looked out over the wide silent prairie and down at the little blue tent which was home and "as good as any home, since all life holds dear, is gone."[18]

At Fort Randall, Fletcher abruptly left the camping party and became the guest of the commander, Colonel George L. Andrews, and his wife, who was, Fletcher was delighted to learn, "a New England lady" and a cousin of the woman Professor Putnam was to marry. "She bade me tell you I had 'stayed with Emily Oliver,'" Fletcher reported to Putnam, "a lovely lady—a lovely home—a complete oasis in the midst of desolation and barbarous meagreness."[19] Fletcher enjoyed life at the fort, including an afternoon drive with "Mrs. Andrews, Mrs. Dean, and Capt. Wilson."[20] She found an article on "Our Indian Question" in the *Journal of the Military Service Institute* and pored over it, copying the figures in her journal. She learned that there were nearly 270,000 Indians in the United States, exclusive of Alaska, with the greatest number in Indian Territory, California, Nebraska, Nevada, and Oregon. Out of 380 treaties only one, that of 1855 with the Cherokees and Chickasaws, permitted the Indians to leave their reservations freely to have contact with and sell their products to whites. The article was the result of an essay contest and was a sign of the U.S. Army's increasing discontent with the role it was assigned to play in Indian affairs, which was to keep Indians inside reservations and white squatters out. All three of the winning essays argued that it was no longer possible to protect the Indians against the encroachments of the white man. "*It cannot be done*," General John Gibson wrote.[21] Alice Fletcher, who for the first time in her life had just been made keenly aware of "the Indian problem" and was looking for a solution to it, read this with great interest.

The high point of Fletcher's stay at Fort Randall was her conversations with Sitting Bull, who charmed her completely. Sitting Bull, fifty years old, was deliberate, brave, and shrewd. The leader of the

Hunkpapa Sioux, he had led the negotiations for the Treaty of Fort Laramie in 1868, insisting that the price of peace between the Sioux and the United States government was that white people keep out of Sioux territory. By that treaty the southwest quarter of Dakota Territory, including most of the Black Hills, was set aside for the exclusive use of the Sioux, and the Bozeman Trail, which was to have run through Sioux buffalo country to gold mines in Montana and Idaho, was abandoned. The Sioux in turn promised not to oppose new railroads and settlements outside their reservation.

Six years later the treaty was in shambles. In 1873 the Northern Pacific Railroad began to move illegally across the reservation. In 1874 General Custer discovered gold in the Black Hills, and fifteen thousand would-be miners moved into the area. After the battle of the Little Big Horn and the defeat of Custer, Sitting Bull and his followers fled to Canada, but they could not stay there indefinitely. In the spring of 1881 Sitting Bull was forced to return home and surrender to United States authorities. It was a bitter defeat for a proud and courageous man who was one of the last Indians to lay down his gun.

Sitting Bull and his entourage, 168 persons, were prisoners at Fort Randall. They were living in a circle of tents outside the fort and were counted every morning by the officer of the day. When Alice Fletcher, Susette and Thomas Tibbles, and Buffalo Chip, who acted as their interpreter, made their first formal visit to him, he received them with great ceremony and apologized for not being able to welcome them with gifts, explaining that the soldiers had taken all his possessions.

Sitting Bull talked to Alice Fletcher of his decision to adopt civilization. The buffalo, on which their way of life had depended, were gone. There was no choice but to turn to the world of work. For us, he said, glancing around at the middle-aged chiefs and headmen who sat in a circle inside his large tent, it is too late, but the young men can easily learn to plow and cultivate the ground as the white men do. As he was speaking, one of his wives came in with wood for the fire. She threw the sticks on the flames and then dropped to the ground beside the fire, leaning on her elbow and looking intently at Fletcher. Fletcher noted her handsome face, sparkling eyes, and the gleam of the brass bangles on her arms.[22]

Sitting Bull watched his young wife silently for several moments, and then he turned to Fletcher. Through the translator, he began to speak slowly. "You are a woman," he said. "You have come to me as a friend. Pity my women. We men owe what we have to them. They have worked for us . . . but in the new life their work is taken away. For my men I see a future; for my women I see nothing. Pity them; help them, if you can."[23] He took a ring from his finger and gave it to Alice Fletcher to remind her of his request.

Alice Fletcher was so moved that she was, for once in her life, speechless. She had come to study the lives of Indian women, hoping to find some answers to "the woman question" that plagued her own society. She was beginning to glimpse a way of life in which the woman's role was perhaps more satisfying than it was for herself and her contemporaries. Indian women had their own property—their own ponies, the tent, and family household items. The economic well-being of the family was dependent on their labor, and they were honored for it. They even had their own prestigious social clubs like Sorosis, the one Fletcher belonged to in New York. At the Rosebud Agency Ausapi's wife had taken her to a traditional Sioux woman's club meeting.

But the Indians were caught in a political and economic situation in which this way of life was doomed. Sitting Bull was asking for her help in preparing his women for something he considered less satisfactory but inevitable. She was touched by his compassion and understanding, and pleased that he assumed she had the power to help them. At the Rosebud Agency she had been rebuffed by White Thunder and laughed at for her interest in Indian dancing, but Sitting Bull took her seriously. "God help me to help them," she wrote in her journal. She gave Sitting Bull two dollars to spend for the children and cautiously gave Captain Quimby at the fort another two dollars to spend on their behalf. Then she wrote to the secretary of war, asking if Sitting Bull's children, both boys and girls, could be sent to mission schools, for he wanted them educated and taught the ways of civilization.[24]

At Fort Randall Fletcher's traveling companions left her in the care of the inspector general, who was making his rounds of the Indian agencies. She traveled on with him to the Yankton Agency and then back to the Santee Sioux Agency. The camping trip was over.

From the Santee Sioux Agency, on November 7, 1881, Alice Fletcher described her recent experiences to Putnam. "I have taken such a 'header into barbarism' as a friend of mine puts it, as I would not advise any lady to attempt," she wrote. "For over two months I have been nearly all the time living with Indians, as far as possible, like one of them. . . . The hardships and horrors of it are not to be told, but from a scientific point of view, the experience has been valuable. I have worked myself round to where the Indian stands and looked at his life and ways as he does."[25]

She had won the friendship of many people, including Sitting Bull, she told Putnam. She was going to stay on among the Santees and the Yanktons, forty miles away, and then spend a month with the Omahas. She was collecting items for the Peabody Museum, including a valuable pack that had belonged to one of the most famous of Sioux medicine men. She was settling into her new career.

Her grand plans, her naiveté, and the way her preconceptions tended to overwhelm her facts can been seen from her first public utterances about her new lifework. One night on the camping trip on their way to Fort Randall, after they had revived themselves with hot soup and a blazing fire, they told stories. When her turn came, Alice Fletcher told the story of Cinderella. Susette Tibbles said the Indians had a similar story and promised someday to tell it to her.[26] Alice Fletcher was so excited about this that she wrote of it to a friend, probably Mary Livermore. The *Woman's Journal* for December 10, 1881, then duly reported that Miss Alice Fletcher in company with Mrs. Tibbles ("Bright Eyes") was visiting the agencies on the Lower Missouri for the purpose of investigating the folktales of the North American Indians. The report noted that Miss Fletcher hoped to find evidence of a common origin in the similarity of folktales of various races. "Already she claims to have heard a story which is identical with Cinderella, and doubtless other discoveries will follow."[27]

At that early date Alice Fletcher sensed very little social organization among the Indians. She thought Wajapa and the others acted almost solely in accord with their individual whims. In an article in the *Woman's Journal* in early 1882, she reported that she had seen only one instance of cooperation among the Sioux, the making by a group of women of a tent cover from buffalo skins. "This is the only genuine touch that I have found of that power which has helped to make the white race the dominant people." The Sioux Indians were living in a social structure that had advanced little beyond savagery, she believed. "Everything was individual, and the society was only together by ties of common danger. . . . There is little care and no thought for others."[28]

It is remarkable that Alice Fletcher did not recognize the feasting, which was such a torment to her, as sharing and "thought for others," and it is remarkable too that she could think the warm hospitality the Indians had shown her was only a whim. She struggled to reconcile the reality she observed with the theory she had learned, and reality did not always win. The power of cooperation as a force in social evolution was a favorite theme of John Wesley Powell's. Alice Fletcher suggested, in line with Powell's thinking, that cooperation was the dividing line between barbarism and civilization. Since the Indians were uncivilized, she reasoned, then by definition, they did not know how to cooperate.

Later, as Fletcher learned more about Indian life, she came to believe just the opposite, that the problem for Indians was that they were *too* hemmed in by tribal rules and obligations, that there was no chance or reward for individual initiative.[29] But whichever way the Indians erred, it was they who were in error, she was convinced, for their ways were different from the white European society that she, in common with most of her white contemporaries, took to be the high point of social evolution. If she had caught a glimpse of another, perhaps more satisfying, social role for women, that perception was immediately swamped by the power of contemporary social theory and by Sitting Bull's request to her that she help smooth the path toward civilization for his family.

Six

Among the Omahas

I N the fall of 1881 the *Sioux City Journal* in Iowa reported that an unusual visitor had just been in their city. It was "a Boston lady" whom Dr. George W. Wilkinson, the new agent for the Omaha and Winnebago Indians, had found living with his charges, "nearly starved." A reporter for the *Journal* went to interview Miss A. C. Fletcher and found "a brunette, solidly built, about twenty-five years old, rather good looking, and with a directness of speech, and a way of standing silent while irrelevant conversation is going on, that probably comes from her present mode of life."

Miss Fletcher was interested in reports of mound builder remains on Broken Kettle Creek a few miles north of the city, but when she was told that a local man had made some excavations and had a theory about them, she interrupted: "I do not care for his theory. I wish to know what he found." The reporter was somewhat bemused by "this disciple of original information" who hinted that she had come from "the warlike northern tribes" and intended, after visiting the Omahas, to go next to the pueblo people of New Mexico Territory and the Flatheads of Washington Territory.[1]

The *Journal* reporter was wrong about Fletcher's age—she was forty-three, not twenty-five—but he caught her firmness and sense of purpose. He also sensed the uncertainty she was trying to hide behind her confident demeanor. Putnam had taught her that anthropology needed facts, not theory. But what kind of facts did one gather when suddenly set down in the midst of the daily life of an alien people?

Alice Fletcher looked first at that closest to her own heart: Indian family life, the role of women, and the relation between the sexes. Her intense interest in these matters suggests that one impulse behind Alice Fletcher's desire to go west and live with the Indians was a subconscious desire to explore, among a distant and foreign people and from the safe stance of scientific observer, the nature of human sexuality.

A few days after her arrival on the Omaha Reservation she wrote to Putnam's secretary that the Indians were not like their stereotype. "They are great talkers, story-tellers—fond of jokes and playful, after their fashion, in their homes. Few white families are as merry, from our standpoint of fun and pleasure."[2]

If the Indian character was not what she had expected, neither was polygamy. Joseph La Flesche, like other prosperous Omaha men, had several wives. "I know well many such families," Fletcher wrote Putnam. "Licentiousness has little or nothing to do with plurality of wives. Licentiousness involves a species of consciousness and that the Indians have not even yet." She confessed: "The family relation is very hard for a white person to understand without imposing his own heredity and trained thought upon it. I've worked hard at that and have some times succeeded in twisting [my] mind to the Indian view."[3]

Another topic on which she had to twist her mind was the ownership of land. "I have taken much pains to get at the Indian ideas of property, of the use and occupation of land. Owning it, they never dreamed of, save as they have now been taught by removals. They would as soon thought of owning air or rain," she told Putnam.[4]

And to Jane Smith, Putnam's secretary, she wrote, "It is certainly a mistake to measure a race solely by the standard of the Anglo-Saxon or Modern Western European types. . . . Often these comparitive [sic] studies keep me awake the better part of the night. I can tell you, that lying on the ground, in a tee-pee full of Indians sound asleep, and looking up thro. the opening in the centre, to the stars that come and go with the hours of the night, stimulates ethnographic reflections."[5]

But Alice Fletcher was to have little time for leisurely ethnographic reflections. The Omahas wanted her help as much as Sitting Bull did. One of the tragedies of her life is that she became caught up in politics before she had time to become an anthropologist. Her respect for the power of cultural tradition among Native Americans would come only later, after she had put politics behind her.

The Omahas were a small tribe of about 1,120 persons living in northern Nebraska on the west bank of the Missouri River. Their early home had been in the East "near a great body of water,"[6] but they had slowly moved westward. The name *Omaha* means "upstream" or "against the current" and probably dates from their arrival around 1500 at the Mississippi River near the mouth of the Ohio River, where they separated from their relatives, the Quapaws, whose name means "downstream." The Omahas continued north and west, following the Des Moines River.

Sustained contact with Europeans began in 1794 when a group of French merchants based in St. Louis set up regular trading with the Omahas. The resulting influx of European goods led to a concentration of power in the hands of a few chiefs. The contact with whites also brought smallpox. An epidemic in 1800 reduced the Omaha population from an estimated 2,800 in 1776 to 1,200 in 1802.[7]

The Omahas made treaties of friendship with the United States in 1815 and 1825 but did not relinquish any land until 1830, when they signed away claims to land in Iowa. In 1836, with several other tribes, they ceded their claim to land lying between the state of Missouri and the Missouri River. In 1854 the Omahas were persuaded to give up much of their remaining land in return for a secure reservation and the promise of protection by the United States Army from raids by the Sioux. The resulting treaty reflected the power imbalance along the frontier in the mid-nineteenth century. The Omahas ceded almost six million acres of land in return for a reservation of a mere three hundred thousand acres (an area approximately twenty-five miles long by eighteen miles wide) along the Missouri in present northeastern Nebraska. For the ceded land the Omahas were paid $25,000, less than half a cent an acre.[8]

One of the two principal chiefs of the Omahas at the time of the signing of the 1854 treaty was Joseph La Flesche, Susette La Flesche Tibbles's father. He was half-French and half-Indian, the son of a French fur trader and a Ponca Indian woman. His parents separated when Joseph was a small child, and he grew up among the Omahas. In his teens he traveled with his French father, but his greatest interest was always the customs of the Omahas. He began to associate with their old chiefs and in the 1840s was chosen by Big Elk, who had become chief of the Omahas around 1810, to be his successor.

In the early 1850s, Big Elk called the Omahas together to warn them that a "coming flood" of white people would soon reach them.[9] Joseph La Flesche had seen enough of the world while trading up and down the Missouri with Joseph La Flesche, Sr., to know that Big Elk was right. He decided that the only course for the Omahas was to take on white ways as quickly as possible. In 1854 when the Omahas moved to their reservation along the Missouri River, Joseph La Flesche helped select the site for the new Presbyterian mission and school. He and his followers built a cluster of frame houses nearby, a settlement the more conservative Omahas labeled scornfully "the village of the make-believe white men." The rest of the tribe moved to two villages of earth lodges—one, called "the village of the old folks," lying three miles west near the agency on Blackbird Creek, and the other, called "the village of the wood-eaters" because the families cut timber for a living, located to the south on a wooded bottom.[10]

Joseph La Flesche's house and shop is said to have been the first frame house built by a Plains Indian. He and others in the "Young Men's Party" laid out roads to the mission and to the landing, and they fenced in and plowed a hundred acres of good bottom land along the Missouri, divided it into individual tracts, and planted corn, wheat, and sorghum. In the winter when the river froze over, they hauled their crops on the ice to market at Sioux City, forty miles to the north. When drunkenness became a problem in the tribe, La Flesche set up a police force, outfitted them in uniforms made by his wife, and pledged them to keep order and whip any Omaha who was drunk.[11]

But Joseph La Flesche's leadership of the tribe did not go unchallenged. After twelve years he was brought down by an ambitious new agent, Robert W. Furnas, later governor of Nebraska. In the spring of 1866 Furnas took the position of trader away from Joseph La Flesche and made his life on the reservation so uncomfortable that La Flesche packed up his wives and children and left. He returned within a few months but submitted his resignation as tribal chief.[12] After that he had no formal authority in the tribe.

In the winter of 1866 when a wave of religious conversions swept over the reservation, Joseph La Flesche and his wife Mary became leaders in the small group of Christians among the Omahas. They sent their children to the mission school, and when it closed temporarily in 1869 Susette was sent to study at the Elizabeth Institute for girls in Elizabeth, New Jersey. Francis and Rosalie, the next eldest daughter, remained at home after the mission school closed, but Joseph had Francis read aloud to him to keep up Francis's English, even though, knowing French and several Indian languages but not English himself, Joseph did not understand what Francis was reading.

New threats to the well-being of the Omahas led some of them once again to rally around Joseph La Flesche. The treaty of 1854 had promised that part of the reservation would be surveyed and apportionments of land given out to Omahas who wanted permanent farms and homes. Nothing was done until 1866 when Joseph La Flesche, the agent, and the missionary, still all working together, got up a petition urging that this provision of the treaty be carried out. By 1872 the eastern portion of the reservation had been surveyed, and some 350 certificates of allotment, for 160 acres each, were issued by the Bureau of Indian Affairs to heads of families and single persons. With oxen and plows paid for with tribal money, some of the Omahas began to break up the prairie and farm their tracts of land.

But the worrisome question of the security of these land allotments remained with them. In the mid-1860s, the lower house of the Nebraska Territorial Legislature had passed an act that would have removed all Indians from the future state of Nebraska. With the threat of removal hanging over them, the Omahas made further land concessions to the federal government in 1872 and in 1874.[13] Then came the abrupt removal of the Omahas' relatives, the Poncas, to Indian Territory. The treaty guaranteeing the Poncas' reservation was suddenly worthless. The Omahas worried again whether the certificates they had been given for their farms constituted actual legal title to the land. When they consulted local lawyers, they found that they in fact did not own the land, for the allotment schedule had never offically been approved by the Congress.

The Omahas were alarmed beyond measure. Joseph La Flesche tried to get help in various ways. He sent his daughter Susette and his son Francis on the speaking trip to the East with Standing Bear and the journalist Tibbles. He talked to the ethnologist James Owen Dorsey, who was spending two years on the Omaha Reservation (1878–80) collecting texts for the Bureau of Ethnology. Many of the texts that Dorsey collected were fervent petitions from Joseph La Flesche and his friends to Tibbles and "white people in the east" asking them to help the Omahas secure title to their lands. A letter to Tibbles written August 22, 1879, was signed by eleven Omaha men; another dated December 1879 was signed by fifty-two Omahas.[14] Other Omaha letters were addressed to A. B. Meacham, founder and editor of an Indian rights newspaper, the *Council Fire*, in Washington but were intended, according to Dorsey, for the president, the secretary of the interior, and the commissioner of Indian affairs.[15] The letters were eventually published as raw material for linguistic analysis in two massive scholarly volumes: 238 letters in Degiha, the language spoken by the Omahas and Poncas, with English translations. How the Omahas felt about this use of the letters is apparent in a letter Francis La Flesche wrote to Dorsey in 1894:

"Too much of the private affairs of many of the Omahas has already been published by the Bureau of Ethnology without their consent, and I do not wish to add more."[16]

When Alice Fletcher arrived on the Omaha Reservation, Joseph La Flesche was waiting impatiently to hear if his daughter and her husband or Dorsey had been able to get them any help in Washington. When nothing much seemed to be forthcoming, he decided to call on Fletcher. Less than a week after she had moved in with the Omahas, Fletcher wrote to Jane Smith, the secretary at the Peabody Museum, "Wednesday and Sat. of this week there will be a gathering of the principle men to talk with me about their works toward Civilization, and next week I shall address as many of the Tribe as can be got together on their future efforts in that direction."[17]

The meetings were held. Then Fletcher wrote a petition to the United States Senate asking that the undersigned members of the Omaha tribe of Indians be given clear and full title to the allotments of land. Fifty-three Omaha men signed the petition, and to it Fletcher appended statistics for each signer: how much land he had under cultivation, how much livestock he owned, and how many people were dependent upon him, as well as any remarks that the signer cared to make in his own behalf.[18] Several signers hinted in their remarks that they were a minority in the tribe and that they were asking for land titles only for those who wanted them and were not trying to force them on everyone, but Joseph La Flesche in his comments went beyond the issue of land titles to argue that the Omahas also needed law, courts, and citizenship so that they could run their own affairs and insure that their rights were upheld.

On December 31, 1881, Fletcher mailed the petition to the commissioner of Indian affairs. With it she sent a cover letter explaining who she was and how she had come to learn of the Omahas' situation. She asked the commissioner to trust her interpretation of the situation. There were two parties in the tribe, she admitted, "one desirous of civilization, one that clings to the past," but those in the first group, she assured him, were "the true leaders among the people."[19]

Fletcher assured the commissioner that these Indians had "worked and practically homesteaded" their lands and that the Omahas as a tribe were "generally agricultural." The qualifying adverb suggests that she knew even at the time that the statement was more a hope than a reality. The Omahas had a mixed farming and hunting economy. Joseph La Flesche and others in his "village of make-believe white men" had begun to raise stock and cultivate grain, but most Omahas still lived as much as they could by hunting small game and white-tail deer, gathering foodstuffs, and cultivating small gardens. Like other Plains Indians, the Omahas had built a way of life around the buffalo, which they hunted annually out on the Great Plains, the short-grass plains west of the 100th meridian. But the massive slaughter by sportsmen, adventurers, and commercial hunters had exacted its price. The great buffalo herds disappeared in the 1870s, so abruptly that it seemed to have happened almost by supernatural fiat. The Omahas went on their last buffalo hunt in 1876; discouraged, they took the train home from Kansas.[20] After that they got along as best they could, hunting and trapping, cutting wood, the women working gardens and some of the men working farms.

Fletcher stayed on the Omaha Reservation through the winter, waiting with Joseph La Flesche and the others for a response from Washington. Above all it was the poverty of the Omahas that depressed her. Formerly she had thought it was good to want little, she reported to the *Woman's Journal* in February 1882, but now "I have lived with those who wanted little, and it is pitiful."[21] She had decided that it was better to want much, for wanting "implies life, brings activity, stirs the mind and makes the body subservient." In an attempt to stir the Omahas out of what she regarded as their lack of drive she started evening classes at the mission school in arithmetic, reading, and writing. The Agency copied the mission, and within a few weeks the Omahas had two prospering night schools.[22]

In early February Fletcher learned that the Omaha petition had been presented in the Senate. She wrote to the senior senator from Massachusetts, Henry L. Dawes, who was chairman of the Senate Committee on Indian Affairs, and to the secretary of the interior, asking them for support.[23] Then, impatient and increasingly feeling that her own credibility as well as that of her government was at stake, she took the train to Washington to see what she could do.

Alice Fletcher spent three months in Washington in the spring of 1882. It was the first of her many forays to the city that she would someday make her home. She called on prominent senators and officials, including John Wesley Powell, the politically powerful head of the Geological Survey and of the Bureau of Ethnology, but Fletcher's real entree into Washington society came through the wives and daughters of official Washington. She spoke on the needs of the Indians wherever she was invited, in homes and churches, and before long Harriet Hawley, the wife of Connecticut Senator Joseph R. Hawley, had set a hearing for Fletcher before the congressional committee on Indian affairs. Anna Dawes, the daughter of the Massachusetts senator, reported that "Mrs. Teller [the wife of the new secretary of the interior] thinks you are charming and have most sensible ideas," and Emily Talbot arranged to have Fletcher speak at the fall meeting of her husband's American Social Science Association "on the *means* to be used, 'schools, land, homes' to advance Indian civilization."[24]

Several of these women were active in the Woman's National Indian Treaty-Keeping and Protective Association, an organization formed in Philadelphia in 1879 by Amelia S. Quinton. They used the tactic of collecting signatures on petitions to take their case to the public and to government officials. The women collected thirteen thousand signatures the first year, fifty thousand the second, and one hundred thousand the third. But an astonishing about-face took place in 1882—virtually overnight—in the Indian rights movement. The first petitions urged that treaties with Indians be kept with "scrupulous fidelity." Then the women began to call themselves by a vaguer title, the Women's National Indian Association, and the petition that Harriet Hawley, Amelia Quinton, and others presented to President Arthur on February 21, 1882, and that Henry L. Dawes presented to the Senate, called for the keeping of treaties "unless abrogated by the will of the tribe."[25] It urged that 160 acres of land be assigned to any reservation Indian who wanted it, that schools be established on reservations, and that Indians be given the protection of the law.

The change was even more clearly signaled at the founding of the Indian Rights Association in Philadelphia in December 1882. The official invitation, issued to forty prominent "public-spirited men" in Philadelphia by John Welsh, did not mention the keeping of treaties. The men were invited to join together to help secure civil rights and education for Indians, to assist the secretary of the interior and the commissioner of Indian affairs in carrying out "the wise and just measures recommended by them in their last Report," and to help bring about the complete civilization of the Indians and their admission to citizenship.[26]

Alice Fletcher had mailed the Omaha petition to Washington on the very day of publication—December 31, 1881—of Helen Hunt Jackson's famous *A Century of Dishonor.* These two upper-middle-class eastern women, both introduced to "the Indian question" by Susette and Thomas Henry Tibbles, were to become leaders in the campaign for reform of Indian affairs, but their leadership led in different directions. Helen Hunt Jackson had met Susette and Thomas Tibbles and Standing Bear on a train when they were on their way east. She heard their story and was so angered by the actions of her government that she closeted herself in the Astor Library in New York. Several months later she emerged with her book, a flaming indictment of the federal government's treatment of the Indians. Americans had just celebrated at the 1876 Centennial in Philadelphia a century of national progress. Helen Hunt Jackson argued that it had been instead "a century of dishonor." She accused the government of reneging time and time again on its Indian treaties and of violating the Indians' human and civil rights. Jackson offered no comprehensive solution to the Indian problem, but she urged that Indians be made citizens and given land allotments when they wanted them. The heart of her position was that the Indians ought to be treated fairly and allowed to work out a way of life for themselves, a position soon taken up by the National Indian Defense Association, founded in Washington in 1885 by Dr. T. A. Bland, who also edited the Indian rights newspaper *Council Fire.*[27]

Alice Fletcher went to Washington with a different idea, and important segments of public opinion had by then moved to a position nearer hers. She was there not to attack government Indian policy but to change it. She did not criticize government officials nor did she protest the violation of treaties. She believed that treaties needed to be broken, for she believed Indians were occupying more land than they could make good use of. *A Century of Dishonor* and Helen Hunt Jackson's subsequent well-publicized attacks on Secretary of the Interior Carl Schurz were not the start of the Indian rights movement but were its culmination, after which the movement nearly collapsed. The new emphasis was on Indian needs, as these were perceived by white reformers and federal policy makers. It was a foretaste of the coming Progressive era, when experts, backed by voluntary associations, would use an increasingly powerful federal government to bring about reform.

In Washington Alice Fletcher found herself in the comfortable position of wanting for the Indians what those in charge of Indian affairs also wanted. United States–Indian relations were, in 1882, at a turning point. For 150 years government policy had been to keep whites and Indians separate, pushing ("moving") the Indians ever farther west, beyond the frontier, until suddenly there was no longer a frontier. In the late 1860s the public lands south of Kansas were designated Indian Territory, and the Osage, Kansa, Oto, and Pawnee tribes from Kansas and Nebraska and the Nez Perces from Idaho were moved there. This "solution" lasted for only ten years, for congressmen from the neighboring states of Missouri, Kansas, Texas, and Arkansas began to complain about too many Indians near their borders. Government officials were now trying to decide what to do with the Indians: there was no longer any distant place to isolate them and a "few" Indians occupied large tracts of increasingly sought-after land.

The answer to Alice Fletcher seemed to be to keep the Indians where they were but to reduce the amount of land they occupied. This could be done, but in direct violation of the treaties and at the risk of a public outcry. The other option was to work out an entirely new Indian policy, one that stressed not what was being taken from the Indians but what was being given them: 160-acre homesteads of land, citizenship and the protection of law, schools, and the opportunity to become assimilated into white "civilization." This was a policy supported even by some Indians, like Joseph La Flesche who saw it as an alternative to removal. Commissioner of Indian Affairs Ezra A. Hayt reported in 1879 a swelling chorus of such requests from "the more intelligent and best disposed Indians . . . now earnestly asking for a title in severalty to their lands."[28] In 1880 Acting Commissioner E. M. Marble thought that among reservation Indians the demand was "almost universal."[29] In 1882 Commissioner Hiram Price reported, "The correspondence in the files of this office show that very many of the Indian tribes are clamorous for the allotment of their lands in severalty."[30] All three commissioners supported bills providing for individual allotments of land to reservation Indians. From 1878 on, such bills were submitted, to the 45th, 46th, and 47th congresses. Each time they were reported favorably out of committee, but no action had been taken. The bills provided 160 acres to each head of family and 80 acres to each unmarried adult, with patents being issued for the same with the provision that for twenty-five years the land could not be sold and would be free from taxes. This provision was the result of recent experience among the Chippewas, who had been given allotments of land in 1871. Almost immediately the Chippewa reservation became, in the words of Commissioner Hayt, "infested by a class of land-sharks who do not hesitate to resort to any measure, however iniquitous, to defraud the Indians of their lands."[31] Within seven years the Chippewas had lost five-sixths of their land.

Fletcher described her activities in Washington for the Omahas as "a long, and for a time a single-handed campaign,"[32] but in fact her campaign was short and almost foreordained to succeed. The ground had been prepared for a change in Indian policy. All that was needed was for someone to write and push a particular bill through Congress, and that she did.

The technique she used was suggested to her by a Washington clerk. A bill providing for the sale of part of the Omaha Reservation had already passed one branch of Congress. Fletcher was in the office of Commissioner of Indian Affairs Price one day, wishing aloud, as she later wrote, that the bill, "which was to kill the people could instead be used to save them." She added, "But I do not know how to do it." The commissioner's assistant, a Miss Cook, looked up from her desk and said, "Amend the bill."

"What is that?" Fletcher asked. The commissioner himself, listening, picked up the idea. "Do it, do it! Get hold of the bill and do it!" So Fletcher did it, adding a provision that allotments had to be given to Indians before any land on the reservation could be sold to whites, and it was her bill, with other amendments added, that was later passed and signed.[33]

There were several other reasons for Fletcher's swift success in Washington. Part of the secret of her political effectiveness was that she was tireless and single-minded. One of her opponents, former

Senator Henry M. Rice from Minnesota, told her she was "a dreadful bulldozer." Fletcher exclaimed to Mrs. Dawes: "Wasn't that horrid! I can't help it if he does not believe in individual homes for the Indians. I wish he did that is all."[34]

Fletcher also immediately grasped how government works and how to make it work for her. She first took her case quietly and privately to the highest possible authorities and then appealed to the public, and particularly to women, for support. She stressed her unique perspective on "the Indian question": she had lived with the Indians and knew them from the inside, she had heard their cry of distress and decided to help them. "Putting aside one set of notebooks, I took up another," she wrote.[35] Fletcher presented herself as a combination of the best qualities of "scientist" and "woman"; she was objective, informed, disinterested, but at the same time she had a motherly concern to right wrongs and to help the helpless. She even exhibited a quality that nineteenth-century theorists liked to think of as peculiarly feminine: a tolerance for painstaking, tedious work, applied in this case to the gathering of statistics about Indian life, which made her an authority on the subject. Fletcher asked the officials in Washington to accept her view of what the Omahas wanted and needed. Instead of a clamor of discordant voices in a tribe asking for sometimes diametrically opposed programs, here was a single, clear, apparently sensible and informed but at the same time benevolent, female voice telling them what ought to be done. Best of all, it fit what they already wanted to do.

Both Fletcher and Omaha Agent George Wilkinson thought that secure land titles ought to be given only to those Omahas who had earned them by working their land—this would reward and enhance the prestige of "the industrious peace-loving part of the community," Fletcher told the Indian commissioner[36]—but the House Indian Affairs Committee, eager to open up some lands for white settlement, "improved" the bill by applying it to every member of the tribe. Senator Charles Manderson of Nebraska helped guide the bill through the Senate. The act, passed by Congress on August 7, 1882, declared that each Omaha man, woman, and child was to be given a portion of the tribal land, secured to him or her by a patent held in trust by the federal government for twenty-five years during which time the land could not be encumbered or sold. The act also set aside some land for allotments to children who would be born during the twenty-five years, placed the Omahas under the civil and criminal laws of the state of Nebraska, and declared that the unallotted land in the southwestern part of the reservation, some fifty thousand acres west of the right-of-way of the Sioux City and Nebraska railroad, was to be thrown open to purchase by white settlers, with the resulting funds to be held in trust for the Omahas and the interest on the amount spent annually for their benefit.

Virtually overnight, assimilation, proposed in terms of land allotments and eventual citizenship, became the accepted program for Indians among federal officials and most reformers. It was humane, it was practical, and it even seemed to be supported by the best and newest sociological theorizing, that of the anthropologist Lewis Henry Morgan.[37] In *Ancient Society* (1877), Morgan had suggested that the American Indians, like the ancient Greeks, were living in a state of Barbarism, the next step up the ladder of social evolution after Savagery. From Barbarism, with a little encouragement, the Indians could be prodded on up to Civilization. The price, of course, was that they would give up a good deal of their land, and they would give up completely their tribal form of government, their culture, their whole previous way of life. A few anthropologists, including Morgan himself, warned that such changes could not be expected to occur overnight. An alarmed Morgan sent three letters to the *Nation* in 1876 and 1878 urging that the Indians be brought into the national economy in ways that were congruent with their traditional life, as herders of cattle or workers in factories located on reservations.[38] Most reformers, however, were confident that Indians, like immigrants, would be eager to merge into the melting pot, to take on the American way of life either as homesteaders of land or as workers in jobs away from the reservation. It was what Alice Fletcher thought Sitting Bull and Joseph La Flesche and other farseeing Indians wanted, and it was what she wanted them to have.

In Washington, working for the Omahas, Alice Fletcher conferred often with young Francis (Frank) La Flesche, Joseph La Flesche's son. One evening, in May 1882 shortly before she was to leave, Frank Hamilton Cushing, the government ethnologist just back from the pueblo of Zuni, came with a Zuni friend to call on her and Francis La Flesche at her hotel. Francis La Flesche was short for a

Dakotan, but he was heavily built, and he looked gigantic, Fletcher noticed, next to the small, slender, Spanish-looking Zuni, who was elegant in a red turban, blue woolen shirt, velvet knee breeches, buckskin leggings and moccasins, and an abundance of beads, turquoise, and silver jewelry.

The Zuni man greeted Fletcher by clasping her hand and drawing it near first her mouth and then his own. The four seated themselves and began a conversation which Fletcher recorded almost verbatim. Through Cushing, who interpreted for them, Francis La Flesche, after asking the Zuni if his people hunted elk, launched into an account of how the Omahas hunted, how they talked to the horses to make them swift and brave and painted the horses with a powder made of the seeds of a sweet-smelling grass that the buffalo liked. This aroused the Zuni's interest, and he began to talk of his people's hunting practices.

Next they turned to their tribal kin affiliations. The Zuni said he was a member of the Eagle gens, to which Fletcher replied that she had been given a name by the Eagle gens among the Omahas. "Frank will tell you the name. It sounds sweeter from an Indian than from any one else," she added. "I listen," said the Zuni.

"We call her 'Ma-she-ha-the,'" Frank replied. The Zuni man repeated the name several times, smiling and bowing at Fletcher. She added: "My English name brings me near too . . . Fletcher, meaning the one who makes the arrow. The eagle feather kept the arrow company, you know." She explained that her forefathers had come from across the ocean and that they were brave and strong men and women.

"Yes, that must be true," the Zuni man said. "It takes a brave strong mind to do as you have done—to be able to live with us, to love us . . . not to be troubled and turned back because our clothes are poor and often soiled, to not be troubled at our living, to be willing to leave the many things that are here and come to us that have few things."

They continued the kin discussion, Francis La Flesche saying that he "was an Elk." The Zuni replied: "Certainly he is an Elk. All the men are known by the animals through whom the gods speak."

Then they turned to a current topic, the warfare between the Zunis and the Apaches. They talked until midnight. When they parted,

Alice Fletcher told the Zuni that someday he must meet Francis's father.[39]

Alice Fletcher and Francis La Flesche were already an ethnographic team in Washington in the spring of 1882, he asking questions to get the conversation started, she swiftly taking notes. They were to be just such a team, with only occasional interruptions, for the next thirty years.

Seven

Indian Religious Ceremonies on the Great Plains

AFTER three months in Washington, Alice Fletcher was confident that the Omaha bill would pass, and she hurried back to the Great Sioux Reservation for the summer dances. She was mesmerized by the dances. They were at once tedious but transfixing, strange and repulsive but overpowering, chaste but with unmistakable undertones of eroticism. Through her study of these sacred dances she would become a full-fledged anthropologist.

One of Alice Fletcher's new political friends was Captain Richard Henry Pratt, the head of the Carlisle Indian School in Pennsylvania. Pratt asked her to accompany the thirty-eight Carlisle students returning to their homes around the Rosebud and Pine Ridge agencies in the Sioux Reservation. The children, mostly teenagers, had an emotional reunion with their parents, who had not seen them for three years, at Chamberlain on the Missouri River. From there they all traveled on together. Captain Pratt put Fletcher on his payroll for the summer at fifty dollars a month, "a mere pittance but the best I can do." In return she was to gather up more Indian students for Carlisle and the Hampton Institute in Virginia and accompany them east in the fall.[1]

Fletcher went first to Pine Ridge Agency for what was being heralded as the last great Sun Dance of the Sioux. The agent at Pine Ridge, Valentine McGillycuddy, was opposed to "the heathenish annual ceremony"[2] and had issued a proclamation announcing that after 1882 he would no longer permit it. Ten thousand Oglala and Brule Sioux were camped in a great ellipse three-quarters of a mile long with a single opening facing the rising sun. The white tepees were a stirring sight out across the valley, and as visitors moved nearer they saw the bright colors of the blankets and eagle-feathered warbonnets. Near the center of the ellipse stood the earth-colored medicine lodge of canvas and tree branches. A procession had gone out to cut a specially selected tree forty feet tall, which was stripped of its branches and set up in the center of the circle as the sun dance pole. Scarlet banners and two rawhide figures, a buffalo and a mounted naked Indian about eighteen inches high with an upright penis, were fastened to the pole.[3]

The Sun Dance lasted for six days. Every afternoon the temperature on the Dakota plains rose to 106 degrees. White visitors stayed at the agency but moved freely around the Indian encampment during the day. Alice Fletcher was eager to taste the dog soup, but when she saw a hairy paw poured into the cup intended for her, she smoothly handed it on to the young man standing near her who took it greedily. On the third day Agent McGillycuddy escorted his wife, Alice Fletcher, the local trader, a Methodist clergyman, and several high-ranking Army officers to front row seats where they awaited the arrival of the dancers.

When Alice Fletcher saw the rawhide figures moving in the slight breeze which provided the only relief in the hot sun, she wanted them for the Peabody Museum. McGillycuddy explained that when the figures were shot down from the pole there would be a great scramble for them, but he called over the local police chief and told him to try to get them for "a lady from the East." The police chief succeeded, but he was so embarrassed by the objects that when they were delivered to Fletcher she found that he had mutilated the male figure. At her wail of distress he produced the missing part from his pocket, and the local doctor promised to make it as good as new.[4] "The festival is certainly phallic as everything shows," Fletcher wrote to Ida Conant in describing her adventures.[5]

McGillycuddy was engaged in a struggle with Red Cloud, the chief of the Oglala Sioux. When on this ceremonial occasion Red Cloud came over to be introduced to the visitors, the clergyman began a harangue about the torture and other practices at the festival. Red Cloud listened impassively until the man had finished. Then in one of those eloquent speeches that marked the contact between Indians and white people on the frontier, he said:

> My friend, I am called Red Cloud because in my youth my young men covered the hillsides like a red cloud. As a boy I lived where the sun rises; now I live where it sets. Once I and my people were strong; now we are melting like snow on the mountains, while the whites are growing like spring grass and wherever they pass they leave behind them a trail of blood. They promise us many things but they never keep their promises.
>
> We do not torture our young men for the love of torture but to harden them to endurance, to test their ability to defend their families in time of war. We have been surrounded by enemies: to the north the Crows and Blackfeet; to the west the Shoshones; to the south the Pawnee; and, pressing on us from the east, the white man. It is necessary we should be warriors. Hence: I have spoken.[6]

Not long after this McGillycuddy deposed Red Cloud from his position as Chief. Although Red Cloud took his case to Washington and had the support of Dr. T. A. Bland, the pro-Indian activist and editor of *Council Fire*, he could not break the agent's power. McGillycuddy's wife later observed that in the 1880s there was probably no more autocratic position in the United States government than that of an Indian agent on a remote reservation, for the only authority over him was the secretary of the interior and, ultimately, the president of the United States.

Alice Fletcher returned to the circle every morning, watching the preparations for the Sun Dance itself. On the fifth day twenty-two dancers, including one woman and a twelve-year-old boy, entered with a buffalo skull and passed slowly around the circle. They danced at intervals for the rest of the day, through the night, and into the afternoon of the sixth day. Fletcher learned that there were four levels of participation in the dance, each chosen voluntarily to fulfill a vow made in sickness or trouble. Eight dancers went beyond abstinence, fasting, dancing, and giving away property, to scarification, the third level. Only one dancer, the leader, subjected himself to the torture of the Sun Dance. A stick with a rawhide rope attached was inserted into a puncture made in his chest, and the other end of the rope was attached to the pole. When a particular song was begun, he was to put an eagle-bone whistle in his mouth and while blowing it and bracing himself pull with all his might until he either tore his flesh loose or the rope was pulled loose from the pole. Fletcher took a swig of brandy "to keep from fainting it was so horrible to see."[7] The struggle went on for twenty minutes, and then the festival was over.

From the Sun Dance, Fletcher traveled forty miles with one group of Oglalas to where a father was keeping a Ghost Lodge ceremony after the death of one of his children. She also watched a day-long ceremony in which a young Oglala man acted out his vision of an elk and was accepted as a member of the Elk Society. She then went to the Santee Sioux Agency, where one of the Santee men described to her their ceremony of the Four Winds.

Many Indian ceremonies were open to outsiders by tradition and courtesy, but as Alice Fletcher pressed further she found the Indians increasingly reticent. When she begged to be allowed to write down the ritual chant used by Indian youths when they went off alone and fasted for several days waiting for a vision, she was repeatedly refused. The invariable reply was, "The white people do not understand us, they laugh at our sacred things, and they will laugh at these things which they did not know before."[8]

In the end she prevailed. She was allowed to transcribe not only the vision chant but also one of the most sacred and secret ceremonies of the Sioux. The reasons for her success are three, and they are the foundation upon which she built her spectacularly successful career as an anthropologist. She came to the Indians with a reputation as someone who had tried to help them. She was absolutely honest about who she was and what she was doing: she was a scientist who was recording facts about Indian life that would be published and read by white people. Finally, she was convinced (and convincing in her faith) that the bad treatment the Indians had received from whites came from ignorance and that better understanding would secure better treatment. As she wrote, "On these terms I obtained consent to make public many of the facts set forth in this paper; for, although a close observer, I was not a spy among my trusting friends."[9]

The secret ceremony was the Hunkpapa Sioux's White Buffalo Festival, revealed to her during a second visit to Sitting Bull's camp at Fort Randall in early August 1882. For three days she closeted herself in a tent with several elderly priests. "Guards were placed outside the tent to prevent eavesdropping," Fletcher wrote. "Throughout the camp a watchful interest, a superstitious dread prevailed, as it was known that sacred things were being revealed to me. The more conservative Indians were sure that punishment would follow the sacrilege."[10]

Midway through their sessions, one of the headmen of the camp came to Fletcher and angrily charged that evil things were happening because the priests were talking to her: one woman had nearly drowned, a child had nearly choked to death coughing. Fletcher spiritedly replied that evil things were *not* happening: the woman did not drown, the child did not die. But after this only two of the men were willing to continue. They insisted on moving farther away from the camp and would not draw any diagrams themselves but allowed Fletcher to make some and corrected her mistakes.

At the end of the third day the younger of the two priests, clad only in a loincloth, moved toward her in the tent and, fixing his eyes on her, said earnestly, "Promise me that no harm shall come to me or my people because of what we have told you." Fletcher replied, "I do not think any harm will come to you because you have talked to me." A second and then a third time he asked for this promise and she made the same answer, while the older priest sat bowed to the earth reciting a formula. "Then," as she wrote, "coming still closer and looking at me with an expression I can never forget as it showed me how profoundly sacred had been their disclosures, he said, 'Promise me by your God, that no harm shall come to me or to my people because I have spoken to you of these sacred things.'"[11]

With characteristic honesty, Alice Fletcher answered: "My friend, you ask me to promise you that which only God himself could promise. I will pray my God that no harm shall come to you or to your people because you have talked with me." Then she extended her hand, which he took, and "this strange scene came to a close."[12]

Fletcher was told that the White Buffalo ceremony had never been seen by a white person nor had a white person ever before been told of it. "They told me because I had done so much for them in their trouble," she wrote Putnam.[13]

From Sitting Bull's camp, Fletcher returned to the Omaha Reservation. She celebrated the passage of the land allotment act for the Omahas with them on August 7, 1882, and arranged for ten young Omahas (including Joseph La Flesche's daughter Lucy and her husband Noah) to attend school at Hampton Institute and for twenty-six to attend Carlisle. She then headed east with them. It was her last uninterrupted summer of research for many years.

Alice Fletcher had no permanent home, not even rooms to go to, when she returned to the East in the fall of 1882. No family was awaiting her. She had no job. She had somehow to provide not only for herself but also for the six extra students, beyond the authorized twenty, that she was bringing to Carlisle, and for that she needed to raise eighteen hundred dollars. She had a destination, the Peabody Museum in Cambridge, where Putnam had made her a Special Assistant in Ethnology, an honorific position without salary. She had several speaking engagements. In between she would stay with friends and let the course of her life move where it would.

Alice Fletcher went first to professional meetings: in late August to Montreal for the annual meeting of the American Association for the Advancement of Science, where she was elected a Fellow, and then to Saratoga for the annual meeting of the American Social Science Association. She spoke there on "The Civilization of the American Indian" and aroused so much discussion that she was put on the program again three days later. Caroline Dall, first meeting Fletcher, commented bluntly in her private journal on Fletcher's presentation. Fletcher did herself great credit "contrary to my expectations," Dall wrote. "She talks too much—enlarges on unimportant points and has naturally some coquettish ways which I do not like but I envy the woman who has saved their reservation to the Omahas."[14]

The next task was to raise-money for the six extra students. Alice Fletcher again spoke in homes and churches, this time on the need for Indian education. Two thousand people came to hear her one night at Washington Gladden's church in Springfield, Massachusetts, and contributed enough to support one boy. By the end of October she had all six provided for, and the commissioner of Indian affairs told her that the interest she had aroused in Indian education was worth many times the actual money raised.[15]

Fletcher also lobbied Congress directly for increased support for the Carlisle Indian School. One of her favorite tactics was to take parties of Washington men and women on one-day expeditions to visit the school. Caroline Dall describes one such visit, made on Tuesday, March 6, 1883. The group arose at five o'clock and took horse-drawn carriages to Carlisle in the midst of a heavy snowstorm which made the roads so bad that "many of the distinguished people were quite sick." At Carlisle they toured the classrooms and workshops and saw the four hundred children at dinner at noon. "The joy with which the shy creatures welcomed Alice was something beautiful," Dall wrote in her journal that night.[16]

The dramatic increase in federal appropriations for American Indian education in five years—from $475,000 in 1880 to $992,000 in 1885—was due in good measure to Alice Fletcher's efforts. Appropriations continued to rise thereafter, but more slowly, as Democratic congressmen urged economy and the Indian Office began to stress reservation schools rather than the more expensive boarding schools.[17]

With philanthropy over for the moment, Fletcher turned to her own concerns. She visited friends in Boston and spent a week with Senator and Mrs. Henry L. Dawes in Pittsfield, Massachusetts. By November she was at the Peabody Museum in Cambridge, arranging in an exhibit case the articles brought from the Sun Dance and talking to Putnam about her future.

The problem was how to make a living for herself while continuing her scientific investigations in the field. She proposed to Putnam that she be paid a fixed salary by the Peabody Museum and sent out on a collecting expedition. "No Museum has or will be likely to have just such an exhibit as I think I can get for you," she offered him.[18] When Putnam expressed interest but indicated that money was a problem, she began on her own to plan a fund-raising campaign for "ethnological investigations" by the Peabody Museum. By Christmas she had put together a scheme. She proposed that a statement on the scientific and practical importance of the work, signed by leading men of science and business, be published in the papers and be coordinated with editorials calling public attention to the appeal.

She would then speak at a large public meeting to which "men of money" had been privately invited. Fletcher also passed on to Putnam the advice of her New York friends—she was spending Christmas with her former pupil Sara Conant Ostrom and her husband Dr. Homer Ostrom in New York—that they ask for an ample amount of money, an endowment, so that the interest from the money alone could carry the work.[19]

Putnam was not a free agent. His museum was firmly in the hands of conservative group of Boston trustees who would have been appalled at the flamboyance inherent in Fletcher's proposals had they been informed of them. But also Putnam was himself somewhat taken aback at Fletcher's eagerness to mix scientific, practical, and even political concerns, and at her assumption that she was qualified to speak for the scientific interests of his museum. Gently but firmly he resisted her program. Perhaps feeling somewhat rebuffed, Fletcher replied immediately that she was not trying to raise money for herself but for "the cause" and the Museum. She quietly backed down, but not away, from the project.[20] At the time, she was visiting Mrs. William Thaw in Pittsburgh, the wife of the industrial and railroad magnate and the aunt of Margaret Copley Wade, a young teacher at the Omaha Presbyterian Mission School. One morning she read her paper on "Indian Home Life" to William Thaw who told her, "I feel as if I had been on the windward side of the Indian."[21] Fletcher reported to Putnam that William Thaw was very impressed with her work and its "practical worth." Thaw insisted that Alice Fletcher accept a gift from him that would allow her to go to Washington to work up her notes on Omaha ceremonies with Francis La Flesche. Although in the short run Fletcher's fund-raising scheme came to nothing, it was to bear a rich harvest for her—through Mrs. Thaw—within a few years.

With William Thaw's gift, Fletcher headed for Washington. "I mean to get the music of the various dances from Frank, and write out all I can that is available," she wrote Putnam.[22] She sent her card around to the leading government anthropologists, including Colonel Garrick Mallery and Professor O. T. Mason, and soon was getting cooperation from the highest circles. At her request Francis La Flesche was given a month's leave of absence from the Indian Bureau to work with her. Red Cloud, the Oglala chief, had brought his case against McGillycuddy to Washington. When he appeared willing to work with Fletcher on the Sun Dance and other ceremonies she had seen the summer before, the secretary of the interior kept him on in the city just for that purpose, and with the help of Francis La Flesche Alice Fletcher wrote out the music that accompanied the Sun Dance. Red Cloud was astonished to learn from Fletcher's questions to him that in Sitting Bull's camp she had been told about the White Buffalo feast. Looking almost frightened, he said it was "the holiest thing" and added, "By it Priests were made."[23]

Not long afterward the White Buffalo feast and Alice Fletcher's work were being discussed at the White House, and Rose Cleveland, the president's sister and official hostess, invited Fletcher to visit. John Wesley Powell at the Bureau of Ethnology in the Smithsonian sent word to Fletcher that he was hoping to publish her work, but she assured Putnam that she wanted it to go to him. Late that spring she sent Putnam her report on five Indian ceremonies, to be published by the Peabody Museum in its annual report in 1884: the "White Buffalo Festival of the Uncpapa Sioux," the "Elk Mystery of the Ogalalla Sioux," the "Ceremony of the Four Winds of the Santee Sioux," the "Ghost Lodge Ceremony of the Ogalalla Sioux," and the "Wa-wan or Pipe Dance of the Omahas." Of this last ceremony Fletcher wrote to Putnam: "Frank has gone over and over it and been very patient. It is all here but two ritual songs. These I could not get for Frank's mother died a week ago and he will not even hum a song."[24]

"Five Indian Ceremonies" was a pioneering exploration of American Indian religious life. Fletcher's descriptions of these religious festivals are straightforward. She described what she had seen or been told. Then in extensive footnotes she commented on the ceremonies and how she had learned about them. The result is a stunning document, a counterplay of event and comment.

She wrote in general terms about the giving away of goods in Indian ceremonies, calling it "a legitimate mode of exchange." To call their religion "nature and animal worship" seemed too "indiscriminate," she thought. Rather, they think of objects in nature as places where "the god has stopped." There are traces of Fletcher's evolutionist orientation, as she suggests that the Indian's feeling for unity with nature "is like the cry of a child rather than the articulate speech of a man. Because he stands abreast of nature, not facing it, he cannot master or coerce it, or view it scientifically and apart from his own mental and emotional life."[25] Nor can Fletcher resist an occasional romantic fillip at the end of an account, with stars coming out, night closing in, and the day (and sometimes also the people) vanishing. But overall, her report is remarkably objective and the footnotes sympathetic.

"Five Indian Ceremonies" was Alice Fletcher's first major work, a demonstration that she could indeed do science, that she was a careful observer and a painstaking recorder. To a keen-eyed reader it showed something else: how crucial Francis La Flesche was becoming to her work. Four of the ceremonies were Sioux. The fifth ceremony was the Omaha "Pipe Dance." Fletcher's account of it was three times as long as her account of any of the Sioux ceremonies and included not just one but eight songs. She showed in it a quantum leap in comprehensiveness for which she was indebted, as she noted, to Frank La Flesche, who had given her "most valuable assistance." Alice Fletcher was learning that an ethnographer needed more than honesty, a good reputation, and a convincing purpose. An ethnographer needed an informant, a knowledgeable insider who was as committed as she was to their joint task of recording for posterity. She was beginning to discover what a treasure she had in Francis La Flesche.

Eight

Allotting Land to the Omahas

I N March 1883 a job suddenly fell into Fletcher's lap. The commissioner of Indian affairs asked her to carrry out the land allotment program among the Omahas.[1] She was to be a special agent of the Office of Indian Affairs and would be paid five dollars a day plus expenses, the same as for men in an equivalent position. Francis La Flesche was detailed to go with her as interpreter.

Fletcher accepted the task with some trepidation. "Everyone wonders at my venturing," she wrote Putnam. "There will be no end of trouble and work but if I succeed as I mean to do, good will come of it to the people."[2] She enjoyed dramatizing and even mythologizing the journey and its potential scientific harvest. "I go to the wild life, and unknown future, where the unknown past may find a voice," she wrote.[3] In fact, she thought of her assignment as a nearly perfect way to combine her philanthropic and scientific work. The government would pay both her expenses and Francis La Flesche's for perhaps six months on the reservation, and in her free time she could continue her ethnological investigations with Francis's help.

Alice Fletcher and Francis La Flesche arrived at the Omaha Reservation in early May. She called a council of the tribe to explain the allotting procedure and spent ten days studying the situation and mastering the technical procedures for surveying and registering land. Many of the land selections from 1871 were in the wooded bluffs and lowlands along the Missouri River where the land was frequently flooded. Fletcher decided that the best agricultural land was in the upland valley of the Logan River, fifteen to twenty miles to the west. That land had the added advantage of being near the railroad. She procured an Indian tent and set up camp on the banks of the Logan with an Omaha matron to do her housekeeping. Joseph La Flesche and his family were the first to take their allotments, and they took them where Fletcher thought they should, west of the right-of-way of the Sioux City and Nebraska Railroad. There they would have white neighbors when land west of the railroad was opened up to white settlement, and they would be near the town already plotted by the railroad on seventy acres of land at the southern edge of the reservation. The Indians called the town Unashtazinga ("little stopping place"). It was to be named by whites for George Bancroft, the historian, and in 1880 had a railroad station, grain elevators, and a post office.[4] Gradually a few other Omahas made their way out to Fletcher's white tent, visible from sixteen miles away on the wide prairie, and took their allotments nearby.

To Caroline Dall in Washington, Fletcher described the inside of her tent. It was "picturesque indeed," she wrote.

> The back part was curtained off with some rich colored patch, behind which was my cot and living comforts. In the center was a camp table

with camp chairs about it. Buffalo robes were thrown down at the sides, and on my Indian matron's side, were the box cupboards which I had knocked up and where my dishes, etc. were duly kept. The Indians knowing of my love of wild flowers kept my table supplied with delicate and lovely blossoms.[5]

Nearly every night thunderstorms shook her tent and left puddles of water an inch or two deep. Once a bolt of lightning hit the ground and burned the grass less than two hundred feet away.

Fletcher worked herself to exhaustion for several weeks "amid torrid heats and torrid storms."[6] On July 3 she was drenched in a sudden storm and, continuing to work in her wet clothing, was soon suffering from a severe chill. Francis La Flesche put her in a wagon and drove her thirty miles to the Omaha mission. For three weeks she lay so ill and in such pain that no attempt was made even to change her bed linen, and she was given narcotics to sleep. "My life dwindled away," she later wrote. "All thought it more than likely I would die."[7] But she rallied. Five weeks after the onset of the illness she was well enough to be moved ten miles on a mattress in a wagon to the agency headquarters at Winnebago. There she lay in bed for the next eight months, recovering from what the agency physician diagnosed as inflammatory rheumatism.[8] Moving her convalescence from the Presbyterian mission to the agency was significant, for it meant going from a skeptical, and even hostile, environment to a supportive one. The Presbyterian missionaries regarded her as a busybody, intent on making trouble both for themselves and for the Omahas. Homer W. Partch, the resident missionary, wrote of her to his chief in Philadelphia that fall, after she had begun to recover, "In order to do much mischief in the world a person must be very talented and rather good."[9]

As she lay in bed, Francis La Flesche brought his relatives and friends to sing to her. "They sang softly because I was weak, and there was no drum, and then it was that the distraction of noise and confusion of theory were dispelled, and the sweetness, the beauty and the meaning of these songs were revealed to me," Fletcher wrote later.[10] The Omahas may have been singing to cure her, for singing was a form of initiation, an opening up to her of a path to supernatural power.

The suddenness and seriousness of Fletcher's illness caused much discussion among the Omahas and lent credibility to the assertions of the conservative group that she was doing a wicked thing for which she, if not the Omahas themselves, would be punished. From the beginning those who hoped for a return of the old times and who knew that Fletcher's program would make that impossible had opposed allotment. One old priest had threatened to work a charm on her, and he claimed success when her white tent suddenly disappeared and she lay ill at the mission. Fletcher wrote later:

> The tribe became troubled, many of the men began to doubt, and for a time the power of charms seemed to take a new lease of life. . . . My prolonged confinement was a triumph and many men who I had located refused to come forward and sign their papers and ratify their choices. "The council fire" [a group opposed to allotment which had supporters in Washington] glowed brightly, the numbers and influence increased, and showed itself in a widespread refusal to send the children to school; and a general outcry that the old religion would revive and the old times return, for was not the woman who had been so strong stuck down and kept there by a spell thrown upon her by the ancient charms? [11]

From her sickbed Fletcher sensed that public opinion was turning against her, and she became determined not to let it happen. She had been perceived before her illness as a strong and powerful person. She would show them that she still was. She had Francis La Flesche set up his clerk's desk by her bed and she moved ahead with the work, making out allotments and taking up some long-festering quarrels among the Omahas in her self-appointed capacity as judicial authority for the tribe. From her bed she held hearings and questioned witnesses. For one such case in which there was much interest, thirty-six Omahas crowded into her room and others listened in at the door and windows. "The Indians would stand at my bed and make their orations at me," she wrote.[12] Repeatedly she insisted that her illness and the stiffness in her right knee were not the result of a charm by which a "worm" was planted in her knee. She had simply caught a cold after having been drenched and chilled in the rain. She refused to have a counter ceremony performed by a friendly priest to remove the worm, despite her ethnological curiosity, "for it would injure many and be a stumbling block to progress," she wrote Putnam.[13]

Gradually the tide turned. Some of the Omahas began to speak not only of the power that had struck her down but also of the even greater power that allowed her to take up their questions and continue her work even though she lay sick and in pain. To her friends in the East she wrote that her illness was "a sort of moral test, and with some, a turning point."[14] It allowed her to prove her determination and to show that charms had no power. It also gave her almost a martyr's status among her Omaha friends. Of Joseph La Flesche and the other members of the "Citizen's Party" Fletcher wrote: "They were sorely stricken by my illness and said, 'If she died our only help is gone.' They brought me gifts of berries, corn, birds—all they had or knew of. . . . I want to get well and serve them."[15] Later she reported: "One man huge in build large featured, with long heavy hair . . . said: 'I see you lying there, your face thin from pain and I feel that it is we who have done this thing.'"[16]

By Thanksgiving of 1883, five months after the beginning of her illness, Fletcher was well enough to sit in a reclining chair for an hour or two each day. By Christmas she was able to stand with the help of crutches, but soon afterward she fell and strained one knee. It became permanently stiffened, bent at the knee in a right angle. She was lame. She had lost thirty pounds during her illness, and most of her hair had fallen out—the beautiful long chestnut-colored hair of which she had been so proud. The new hair, when it began to grow in, was grey. "I look 20 years older, but that can't be helped," Fletcher wrote to Caroline Dall. "The most serious part of the change is that I shall be a cripple. . . . It has been hard to face . . . for it would seem to close my Ethnological career, but it is all in God's hands and I submit."[17]

After seven months on the reservation Fletcher still had about one-third of the allotments to make, and these to the most resistant of the Omahas. They were led by a group of twelve families who had banded together as "the Council Fire" to oppose allotment and to continue the old ways. Fletcher finally decided that force was necessary to make them take their allotments. "By permission of the agent I am now enforcing the attention of the refractory and troublesome element," Fletcher reported to the commissioner of Indian affairs.[18] Presumably by order of Agent Wilkinson the Indian police rounded up the dissenters, forcing them to appear before her and to make their mark in the presence of witnesses indicating that they accepted a designated piece of land. The Omaha agent did not have the power to withhold rations, as was done on many other reservations to enforce compliance with the agent's directives, but he could deny individuals permission to leave the reservation, could remove them from positions of authority, and could harass them in other ways if they refused to do as they were told.

From Alice Fletcher's comments and the number of signatures on various petitions that the Omahas sent to Washington, it can be estimated that one-fourth of the Omahas actively supported the allotment program, one-third actively opposed it, and the rest, although not in favor of the new plan, were persuaded to go along with it.[19] Another estimate of her support is that 326 people, one-fourth of the tribe, took their allotments in the area Fletcher favored, the four townships near the railroad. This number included 69 heads of families, 58 single adults, and 199 children under the age of eighteen, out of 1,179 people in the tribe. She called these "many of the most progressive families in the tribe."[20] Fletcher admitted at Lake Mohonk in 1884 that two-thirds of the Omahas had originally opposed allotment. "It means trouble at first, and Indians are, like the rest of mankind, unwilling to vote for present trouble in order to secure an unknown and uncertain benefit."[21]

In all Alice Fletcher allotted 75,931 acres in 954 separate allotments to 1,194 persons (wives were counted in the census but not given their own allotments; heads of families received 160 acres; single persons over eighteen received 80 acres, and children under eighteen received 40). About 50,000 acres west of the railroad were to be sold to white settlers. The remaining 55,450 acres of the reservation were kept to be given out to the children who would be born during the next twenty-five years.

Fletcher followed correct legal procedures where they existed and tried to create them by precedent where they did not. She gathered and accounted for all the old certificates issued in 1871 that were no longer valid, and in so far as possible she made certain that people got the same land they had before if they wanted it. The choice of allotment was made a weighty and ceremonial procedure. Each person, after choosing a portion of land, was allowed a little time for further thought; then in the presence of witnesses the recipient signed a paper of "Selection," an act that Fletcher declared was binding and not open to reconsideration. The witnesses in turn signed the paper, Fletcher thus attempting to show them how much importance was attached to a signature in legal proceedings and how the process was safeguarded. In contested cases a trial was held, and each party was required to be present with witnesses and an interpreter of her or his choice. After hearing the evidence and having it written down, Fletcher made a decision in accord with the provisions of the law and gave each party a written copy.[22]

Fletcher also made a complete registry or census of the tribe and gave it to the agent. The Omahas were instructed to report to him every birth, marriage, and death, so that the census could be kept up-to-date. Fletcher had great hopes for this registry, which she thought would help settle future questions about inheritance and also might encourage stable family relations. She spent much time trying to explain Nebraska laws of property and inheritance to the Omahas, who could not understand why children should have sole claim to their parents' property or why wives did not have as much right to the land as husbands. In 1893, in response to the complaints of the Omahas, Congress amended the act of August 7, 1882, granting wives eighty acres of land in their own right and raising the amount for children under eighteen from forty to eighty acres.[23]

In the course of her alloting work, Fletcher came to know every man, woman, and child of the Omaha tribe, and she knew them well. In later years, when the commissioner of Indian affairs needed information to settle a particular case, she not only remembered the individual but also could recall the whole situation. Government officials said that hers was "the most thorough and carefully done" of all the allotment programs they had attempted.[24]

She had not done it alone. At the end of her final report to the commissioner of Indian affairs she wrote:

I desire to make especial mention of the faithfulness of Mr. Frank La Flesche, who was detailed to accompany me as my clerk. He worked willingly and uncomplaining from 12 to 14 hours a day and his intelligent knowledge of his native tongue and of English, together with his appreciation of the needs of his people in their onward struggle made his services doubly valuable.[25]

Fletcher left the Omaha Reservation in June 1884 feeling triumphant. Not only had she completed the allotments and eventually won the approbation of many in the tribe, but she had continued her scientific inquiries on a wide range of topics. The letters she wrote to Putnam and to Lucian Carr at the Peabody Museum show that she was an eager student in many areas, trying to learn how to relate what she saw around her to current problems and general issues in anthropology. She wondered if the mounds of earth she saw being built up during certain Indian ceremonies might not be related to the animal effigy mounds Putnam was studying in Wisconsin. "Need I say that I am convinced that the mound builder is another name for Indian," she wrote. "I see too much to doubt it."[26] She knew that Putnam was interested in physical anthropology, and she offered to have Indian skulls and skeletons dug up for him. She also wondered if it would be useful to have photographs made of full-blood Indians, profile and full face, and measurements taken of their height, limbs, chest, and weight in order to study "tribal characteristics."[27] Putnam told her to go ahead, and one result of this was an odd publication in *Science* magazine in 1886: four "composite" photographs of Omaha men and women, an idea she borrowed from Francis Galton, the English eugenicist. Fletcher admitted in the accompanying text, "I don't know exactly what the usefulness of this technic is."[28]

To Lucian Carr, Fletcher reported that the Iroquois custom of referring to a defeated enemy as women was also common among the Omahas. She had observed that when an Omaha warrior recounted his deeds by acting them out, one way of representing the defeat of an enemy was to simulate the sexual act with a grass figure. "It has struck me whether some of the carvings which have been found in America and which have been regarded as obscene were not symbols of victory over enemies," she wrote.[29] She and Francis La Flesche studied earth circles which were the remains of ancient mud lodges and tried to learn from some of the older people in the tribe when the Omahas first began to build earth lodges. "It is difficult to get at

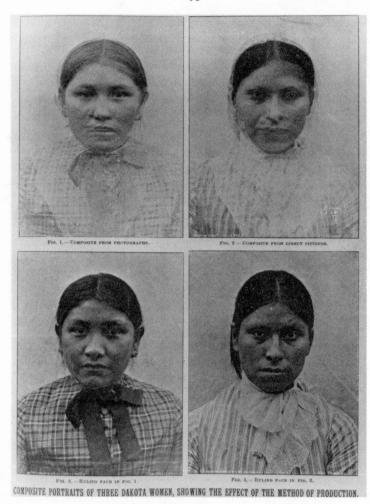

FIG. 1.— COMPOSITE FROM PHOTOGRAPHS. FIG. 2.— COMPOSITE FROM DIRECT SITTINGS.

FIG. 3.— RULING FACE IN FIG. 1. FIG. 4.— RULING FACE IN FIG. 2.

COMPOSITE PORTRAITS OF THREE DAKOTA WOMEN, SHOWING THE EFFECT OF THE METHOD OF PRODUCTION.

Composite and individual photographs of three
Dakota (Sioux) women by Jenness Richardson and
Alice C. Fletcher, 1886. (A. Fletcher, "Composite
Portraits of American Indians," *Science*, May 7, 1886;
photograph by Hillel Burger, Peabody Museum,
Harvard University) "I don't know exactly what the
usefulness of this technic is," she wrote.

tradition on these points, for almost every Indian who cares to listen to these things has an opinion of his own which he loves as dearly as do the scientific folk their theories. Sometimes when I am talking of these matters I am reminded of the proceedings of a certain Anthropological Section, for it won't do to question an Indian's theory any more than that of a member of the A.A.A.S.!" she teased Putnam.[30]

She also studied the Omaha caches, where the winter supply of corn, dried meat, and other provisions was kept along with sacred articles, gala dresses, and ornaments stored in parfleche bags. When new caches were dug, the old ones became garbage pits and were filled with ashes, bones, broken implements, worn-out moccasins, and other refuse, which Fletcher dug up and examined. The Indians were amused at her "queer curiosity," but she thought her observations might help Putnam in his interpretation of the mound builder site he was excavating at Madisonville, Ohio. She made a record of the Indian names still in use in the Omaha tribe, arranged them according to clans, and began to relate these to particular customs, thinking ahead to the comprehensive account she hoped someday to write on Omaha tribal life.[31]

These scattered studies seemed not to add up to much, but as she was finishing the allotments, the Omahas themselves began to help her. Years later Francis La Flesche described one such instance. Fletcher had been trying to gather information about the symbolic haircuts of the children, but she had made little progress because the Omahas were unwilling to talk to her about them. One day at Xo'ga's house an older man suddenly reached over, caught up his little boy and, holding the squirming child firmly between his knees, cut the boy's hair in a particular pattern, the head closely shaved except for locks of hair left uncut here and there. The father swung the little boy up on his back, and announcing "That white woman is my friend and I am going to help her," he carried the child over to where Alice Fletcher was and put him down in front of her. "That's the hair cut of our gens," he told her. "It is a picture of a bison. You can't see it but we can. You may make a sketch of it and write about it as much as you like."

Alice Fletcher was stunned for a minute. She then gave a hearty laugh, clasped his hand, snatched a paper and pencil, and began to make a sketch of the pattern of the shorn head of the little boy before her, to the amusement of all the Omahas present. "Thereafter," Francis La Flesche wrote, "she had no trouble in getting information about the hair cut of the gentes."[32]

The best gift came from Joseph La Flesche. He knew that she was interested in the Sacred Peace Pipe, the famous calumet ceremony of the Plains Indians. One of the five Indian ceremonies she had published was the Omaha version of the pipe ceremony. In a dramatic and knowing gesture which was typical of him, Joseph La Flesche had a special set of pipes made and presented jointly to Alice Fletcher and Francis La Flesche in an all-night ceremony held in a large earth lodge one Saturday in May 1884. As recipients of the pipes, Fletcher and La Flesche were considered the "hosts" for the event and were expected to provide food for the accompanying feast. Several Omaha women helped Fletcher prepare food, stewed meat, fried bread, and coffee, for about fifty people, and at first, like any good hostess, she worried that they did not have enough, as two hundred people pressed into the lodge. But soon she forgot such cares and became caught up in the event itself as the bearers of the pipes made their entrance swaying the pipes in rhythm and she caught the first strains of the Song of Approach, which she recognized. Her excitement was evident and is almost contagious now as we read her description of what happened next. "As they turned into the lodge, the whole company took up the song, and I too joined, able at last to hear and comprehend the music that had through all my difficulties fascinated even while it eluded me." She continued, "[This] occasion . . . was one I can never forget, not only because of the insight it gave me into the music of the people and the meaning of the ceremony I witnessed, but because of its deeper revelation of the heart and inner life of the Indians."[33]

Fletcher was moved by the event, for she knew that it was a sacred ceremony, a pledge of peace, performed between individuals but used to cement relationships between groups. She interpreted it as a sign of friendship to herself and her people, and also as tacit permission to continue her study of Omaha ceremonies and tribal life. This was reinforced soon afterward when several Omaha men gave her formal permission to record this and any other Omaha ceremony she wished.[34] She recognized also the poignancy of the event for the Omahas, for among its other meanings it was inevitably a symbol of capitulation by a proud people, as they attempted to make their peace with a new way of life. She watched one Omaha farmer, wearing white man's clothing but with tears in his eyes, bring his small son forward to touch the Sacred Pipes.[35]

The Omahas had other sacred objects in addition to the peace pipes, which they had kept always with them even when they were out on the hunt. The objects were kept in three sacred skin tents in designated places in the tribal camp circle. The Tent of War contained an ancient Cedar Pole and the Sacred Shell in its leather pouch. Another tent held the White Buffalo Hide, which was connected with success in hunting, and a third tent contained the Sacred Pole, a later version of the Cedar Pole that had come to represent not only tribal unity but also supernatural sanction for their council form of tribal government. The tents and the sacred objects, including the leather packs that went with them, were regarded with awe by the Omahas and treated with reverence, but because of the secrecy their contents were little known except to their hereditary keepers. Alice Fletcher and Francis La Flesche feared that as tribal life declined, the objects would disappear and valuable clues to the nature and meaning of the rituals that were at the heart of Omaha tribal life would be gone forever. They talked to Joseph La Flesche and suggested to him that the objects be sent to the Peabody Museum for safekeeping. La Flesche agreed and began to persuade the keepers of the objects that it would be all right to do this.

The first objects to be transferred were the contents of the sacred Tent of War in June 1884 just as Fletcher and La Flesche were getting ready to leave the reservation. They drove late one afternoon to the lodge of Mon'hin thin ge, the old man who was the keeper of the tent, and found him sitting alone outside, taking a last look at the articles in the fading light. In a low voice he said:

> These sacred things have been in my family for many generations. No one knows how long. My sons have chosen a different path from that of their fathers. I had thought to have these things buried with me but, if you desire to care for them and place them where my children may look upon them when they wish to think of the past and the way their fathers walked you can do so. . . . I know that the

members of my family are willing I should do this thing, and no others have a right to question my action, though there are men in the Tribe who will say hard things to me because of this act.[36]

Then the old man lifted the bundle hastily into the wagon and turned away, and "we too turned and left [broken quote] as the round moon rose over the valley," Fletcher wrote, eager always to dramatize her situation.

Fletcher wrote an excited letter to Putnam describing the transfer and trying to convey to him the significance of what to an outsider's eyes looked like a dingy leather pouch, a leather pack rolled in the shape of a large bird, and an old cedar pole with appendages. Young men made ceremonial preparations for warfare before these objects, she told him, and when the chief led his people into a defensive war he carried the articles into battle with him. The leather pouch was particularly significant for it contained the Omaha Sacred Shell. Although the rites connected with the Sacred Shell had long since been forgotten, it was still regarded with superstitious dread. Men drove thirty and forty miles to warn Fletcher and La Flesche against carelessness in handling the Sacred Shell, for dire consequences—a great heat and the drying up of all the rivers—would occur if the shell were ever allowed to touch the ground.[37]

It was several more years before other keepers could be persuaded to part with their sacred objects. In 1888, on a return visit to the reservation for his vacation, Francis La Flesche persuaded Shu'denaci, the old man who was the keeper of the Sacred Pole, that it ought to be moved from its tent in his backyard to the Peabody Museum, and it was duly sent. La Flesche was arranging to have the White Buffalo Skin transferred to the Peabody Museum when it was stolen from its hereditary keeper, ending up in the hands of a private collector in Chicago.

But no arguments could persuade the tribal leaders to give up the two Sacred Pipes wrapped in their traditional covering. The answer was always, "They must remain."[38] The Omaha keepers were willing to part with symbols that no longer served a purpose: the Sacred Shell, which stood for victory in war; the White Buffalo Skin, which was related to success in the buffalo hunt; and the Sacred Pole, which sanctioned their council form of government. But they were not willing to give up the ancient symbol of peace and prosperity that had seen them through so many changing situations and that might see them through this one too.

Nine

"Made quite a heroine of"

ALICE Fletcher had been on the Omaha Reservation for thirteen months when in June 1884 she packed up her belongings and boarded the train east. She went to Washington, where she took rooms at the Temple Hotel on 9th Street, opposite the Patent Office. This was to be her home for the next seven years.

Her first concern was to try to regain her health and flexibility in her right leg. She consulted various physicians and was soon caught in a maelstrom of contradictory medical opinions and prescriptions causing her almost as much pain and trouble as had the illness itself. The first word was negative. In Washington Mrs. Hawley sent a surgeon to examine her knee, and he pronounced Alice Fletcher a "cripple for life." "It took more courage to face that verdict than to bear all I had gone through," she wrote.[1]

She fled to New York, to seek comfort from her former pupil and substitute family member, Sara Conant Ostrom, whose husband was a physician. There she consulted another surgeon, one whom she "felt like trusting," and he said that her case was not hopeless. "There is no anchylosis of the joint and the muscular adhesions are not so that they cannot be broken up and that probably without surgical operation."[2] The second surgeon said that she indeed had a disease but that it was not primarily rheumatic nor was it an inflammation of the knee joint. He thought that it was an inflammation of the thigh bone which spread to the large muscles, and he prescribed treatment consisting of rubbing and pulling the muscles on her leg for four hours a day. After a week of this regime, Fletcher wrote to

Putnam that she was "nearly dead with fatigue and suffering, but shant die."[3]

Fletcher endured the pulling and rubbing for six weeks, and then she went to Hot Springs, Arkansas, to take the baths for two months. There she was told that her trouble was not any sort of rheumatism but rather the result of a "nervous breakdown."[4] They continued the pulling of her leg, which was "horrible," but the baths she thought were delightful.

Fletcher was content with either diagnosis, rheumatism or nervous illness, for both terms conveyed to her and her contemporaries an actual physical illness, not the physical or mental alternatives they imply to our post-Freudian age. To them, *nervous breakdown* meant a literal breaking down of the nerves. She believed that her nervous breakdown, if such it was, was the result of a deficiency of nervous force, brought on by overwork, worry, or the lack of food or rest. This was in line with the description of neurasthenia, first suggested by George M. Beard in 1869 and popular as a diagnosis up until 1900. Beard liked to compare the human nervous system to the overloaded electric circuit and the overdrawn bank account. He singled out five causes in American life: the periodical press, steam power, the telegraph, the sciences, and the increased mental activity of women, all of which, in encouraging American men and women to experience life more fully, made new demands on their nervous systems.[5] For the rest of her life Fletcher worried when she put in long hours at her desk that she might exhaust her nervous resources and become ill. She frequently did, and this in turn reinforced her fears.

Alice Fletcher sensed, however, that not all of her fellow patients at Hot Springs were there because of overwork or overstimulation. She wrote Caroline Dall that Hot Springs was "a queer place, invalids everywhere. I could not keep from smiling as I made my way into the limping company. It is pitiful and not the most exhilerating [sic] company."[6] The patient who interested her the most was the maiden sister of Washington's influential John Hay, "a rebel and full of queernesses," and pathetically proud of the small gifts her brother sent her.[7] Hot Springs had become a refuge for affluent women who felt useless and unappreciated.

Fletcher was not among their number. Her spirits were soaring, for on the way to Hot Springs she had been received with acclaim both at the annual meeting of the American Association for the Advancement of Science in Philadelphia and at the annual Conference of the Friends of the Indian at Lake Mohonk, New York.

She and Francis La Flesche had given joint papers before the anthropology section of the AAAS on the sacred pipes of the Omahas. *Science* magazine reported that their "thrilling and vivid" account "marked an epoch in the history of the section."[8] In the eleven years that the anthropologists had been meeting together, never before had they had quite such a presentation: a sweet-faced, middle-aged woman and a young, obviously intelligent Indian man singing the strange and discordant music, waving the long, feathered pipestems in rhythm, and then explaining how the pipes were made and the importance of the ceremony as a pledge of intertribal friendship among the Plains Indians.[9]

The emotional tenor of the event for Fletcher's women friends was aptly expressed by one of them a few days later. Dell Hibbard wrote:

> My dear friend Alice, I wanted to hug you bearfashion, after hearing your paper on Tuesday, but my heart was so full that I was afraid to wait to speak with you, lest I should make a foolish exhibition of my feelings. The weird music, the tear in your voice, the loving enthusiasm in your expressive face which seemed to lift you above the suffering leg and yet which meant to me increased pain and exhaustion when the animating thought was spent moved me so deeply that I dared not trust myself even to feebly express to you the pride I felt as a woman and a friend.[10]

Alice Fletcher also gave a paper on "Child-life among the Omahas" at the meeting and was invited to speak to the economics section on her experiences in allotting land to the Omahas.[11]

From "the heat and excitement of Philadelphia,"[12] Fletcher went to Lake Mohonk, New York, ninety miles from New York City, where every fall, beginning in 1883, the Quaker proprietor of a resort hotel, Albert Smiley, convened a group of prominent reformers interested in "the Indian question." In the early years Smiley invited approximately fifty people: members of the Board of Indian Commissioners (an advisory group to the government), leaders of the Indian Rights Association and of the Women's Indian Association, presidents of colleges, and prominent clergymen and journalists. The group was a study group and lobbying organization. Their goal was effective action on behalf of Indian programs that would end the reservation system and that would encourage the rapid assimilation of Indians into American society.

The Lake Mohonk conferences almost immediately had a reputation and political influence far beyond what the number of people involved would seem to warrant. Albert Smiley chose the conferees carefully, and they were well taken care of once they arrived at the picturesque, rambling hotel which looked "as if Mr. Smiley had watered the rocks and the house had grown," in the words of one regular.[13] In 1870 Smiley had purchased an isolated complex: a dance hall, bar, and some bedrooms, built by an enterprising local farmer. Smiley added more rooms and converted it into a liquor-free hotel. On the rugged and rocky terrain he planted six thousand rose bushes, five thousand peonies, four thousand phlox, and eight thousand budding plants, plus a large collection of shrubs and perennials. Having "civilized" the bar, the dance hall, and the landscape, he turned to a bigger task, the American Indians.[14] The conferees held strategy sessions in the mornings and evenings. In the afternoons Smiley provided six carriages, each drawn by four horses and holding ten persons, to take his guests on recreational drives through the surrounding countryside. Many of the conferees, like Lyman Abbott, the editor of *Christian Union*; Herbert Welsh, the secretary of the Indian Rights Association; Amelia Quinton of the Women's Indian Association; John C. Kinney, the editor of the *Hartford Courant*, and his wife, Sara T. Kinney, a leader in the Connecticut Women's Indian Association, returned year after year, happy to combine a pastoral holiday with benevolent activity in defense of a downtrodden and distant people. Theodore Roosevelt called it "an absurd, though useful, Indian conference."[15]

Alice Fletcher attended Lake Mohonk for the first time in 1884 and was "made quite a heroine of," she confessed happily to Caroline Dall.[16] She was one of the few people at the conference who had firsthand experience with Indians living on their reservations, and she was praised for being not only a "scientific student" but also a "practical humanitarian, who had nearly given her life for the benefit of the Omahas."[17] The Lake Mohonk reformers were suspicious of scientists such as John Wesley Powell and others at the Bureau of Ethnology who, they charged, wanted to preserve the Indians in order to study them. Alice Fletcher was "the single brilliant exception"; her "philanthropy swallowed up her anthropology." [18]

Alice Fletcher spoke to the Lake Mohonk assembly, describing her experiences and the continuing needs of the Omahas. Many of the young Indian people were away at school, at Carlisle or Hampton, she told them, and she worried that when they returned to live on the reservation, where the most common dwelling was still the earth lodge, they would be hard pressed to continue the domestic skills they had learned in the East. She proposed that a fund be started for Indian home building. Young couples returning from school could borrow money to build a white-style house and would be an example of civilized living among their own people. This was Fletcher's first public mention of what was to become her celebrated home building project. One man put five hundred dollars in her hand that evening for Indian home building,[19] and the idea was picked up enthusiastically by Sara T. Kinney. Over the next four years the Women's Indian Association helped to build thirty or forty homes for Indians, some at the Hampton Institute and others on the reservation. Inevitably, however, the Indian Home Building Fund foundered, for the young Indian couples tended to regard the loans as gifts, and when pressured could not pay them back. Meanwhile the women in Connecticut, some of whom had made personal sacrifices to contribute to the fund, grew disillusioned and disgruntled when their pleas for repayment went unheeded. Alice Fletcher was caught in the middle, urging patience and an understanding of the reservation situation on the one hand, and prodding the young people to pay their debts on the other.

The Lake Mohonk Conference in 1884 also discussed the Dawes bill, or the Dawes-Coke bill, as passed by the Senate the previous winter. The first general allotment bill for Indians to be debated in Congress had been introduced in May 1880 by Senator Richard Coke of Texas, Henry L. Dawes's predecessor as chairman of the Indian Affairs Committee. The idea for the bill had come from Secretary of the Interior Carl Schurz and Senator Samuel J. Kirkwood.[20] Over the next seven years three different versions of the Coke-Dawes bill were discussed by Congress. The first bill allowed tribes to

choose by a two-thirds vote whether they wanted to receive individual patents to family farms or to continue to hold their land in
common. A revised version of this bill introduced jointly by Senators
Coke and Dawes in 1884 permitted a tribal patent for those Indians
unwilling to accept individual allotments, a provision that grew out
of Henry Dawes's concern that one way or another the Indians
should be guaranteed the right to their land, albeit to a diminished
amount of land.[21] Dawes insisted that the lands secured either by
individual or tribal patent be made inalienable for twenty-five years,
that is, the lands could not be sold or taken away in payment of
debt. During this time it was hoped that the Indians would begin to
adapt themselves to civilized ways. Dawes also insisted on keeping
active the principle of consent, which had been part of Indian treaties, by providing that individual allotments of land could only be
made to everyone in the tribe if two-thirds of the tribe had voted
in favor of them. This was the bill that passed the Senate in March
1884.[22]

At Lake Mohonk in the summer of 1884 Alice Fletcher argued
vigorously against two out of three of Dawes's concerns. She approved of the twenty-five-year period of inalienability, but she insisted that land allotments must be given to individuals. She argued
that the tribal relation had to be broken up, for it was an obstacle to
progress. "Under no circumstances should land be patented to a
tribe. The principle is wrong," she told the conference. She also
thought it was useless to try to get two-thirds of a tribe to vote in
favor of allotting lands. "The work must be done for them whether
they approve or not."[23]

Thus did paternalism, or rather a fierce form of Victorian mater-
nalism, come to hold sway in the United States Indian policy of the
1880s. The American Indians no longer were considered alien
nations to be dealt with by treaty, nor were they feared and hated,
but respected, savages to be defeated on the battlefield, nor were
they wards placed more or less permanently under the government's
care. They were to be treated like children: willful, indolent, ignorant as to their true interests. They were children who needed to be
encouraged to grow up.

The idea that Indians were children was a change in Alice Fletcher's thinking. She had gone west as an ethnographic student, as an investigator into a different mode of life, and she clearly did not think of Sitting Bull, or Wajapa either, for that matter, as a child. In an article published by *Century Magazine* in 1883 she explained that the Indians were not "savages." Although their way of life, their "sociologic status" was different from our own, it was still an effective way of life. But political and personal events carried Fletcher along, and when the Omaha allotment act was applied to every member of the tribe and she found herself having to use force to carry it out, her justification became that the Indians were children and had to be forced to do what was best for them. So Alice Fletcher came to have a dual view of Indians. In their old way of life they were adults—they worked, they worshiped, they governed themselves—but in the new way of life which was unfamiliar to them they were children, not knowing what to do. And she, who had brought them the new way, became in effect their mother. Alice Fletcher's illness among the Omahas became her hour of travail, her suffering for her children. She had brought them forth out of the womb of barbarism into the harsh light of civilization where they stood blinking and confused. They must be helped to stand on their own feet. Alice Fletcher was to pride herself on doing science like a man. But she did her philanthropy with the special claims of a woman, one who had suffered for and who knew what was best for her children. In January 1889 she told the Board of Indian Commissioners that they must "push on the work of severalty," adding, "It is like the birth, a dangerous time, but it is the only chance for life."[24]

One prominent Boston advocate of Indian rights, D. A. Goddard, editor of the *Boston Daily Advertiser* and a friend of Susette and Thomas Henry Tibbles, was skeptical of Alice Fletcher. He warned Herbert Welsh of the Philadelphia Indian Rights Association that Alice Fletcher was "enthusiastic, unconventional and very emotional. She has fallen into a wretched sentimental way of calling the Omahas her children—her babies—and such pet names."[25] A decade later a reporter in Buffalo noted that Fletcher still spoke of the Indians as her "children." It had become part of the public story that she told over and over again: how in 1881 she had found the Omahas destitute, waiting for her to act "with all the confidence of children for their mother," and she had suddenly felt in herself the strength to help them, "the strength of a regiment of men."[26] One aroused mother was as good as a regiment of men.

Alice Fletcher had not invented the metaphor of Indians as children. Horace Greeley wrote in 1859 after he had made a trip through the West:

> The Indians are children. Their arts, wars, treaties, alliances, habitations, crafts, properties, commerce, comforts, all belong to the very lowest and rudest ages of human existence. . . . Any band of schoolboys from ten to fifteen years of age, are quite as capable of ruling their appetites, devising and upholding a public policy, constituting and conducting a state or community as an average Indian tribe. . . . [The Indian is] a slave of appetite and sloth, never emancipated from the tyranny of one passion save by the ravenous demands of another. . . . As I passed over those magnificent bottoms of the Kansas . . . constituting the very best corn land on earth, and saw their men sitting round the doors of their lodges in the height of the planting season, . . . I could not help saying, "These people must die out— there is no help for them. God has given the earth to those who will subdue and cultivate it, and it is vain to struggle against his righteous decree.[27]

The Indians, the "schoolboys, from ten to fifteen years of age," were in other words *adolescents*, a term not yet much used but soon to be popularized by G. Stanley Hall's famous book *Adolescence* (1904). Alice Fletcher, fumbling her way toward the same idea, did not have a word for it. She therefore continued to theorize about Indians in terms of Morgan's scheme of social evolution. But when she learned the psychological term, she seized it, for it fit her ideas. In 1900 at Lake Mohonk she made explicit this change. "It is good to think of the so-called dependent races as children," she told the group, adding that she regretted that the stages in the lives of nations and of peoples should have attached to them the popular names of "savagery, barbarism, and civilization," when they "merely represent these stages, childhood, adolescence, and maturity."[28] Alice Fletcher thus came to reject Lewis Henry Morgan's comprehensive system of evolutionary stages in favor of a superficial biological and psychological analogy. Although *savagery* and *barbarism* had pejorative connotations, they were at least sociological terms meant to designate integrated, coherent, and stable ways of life. For political purposes, if not for her ethnography, Fletcher preferred to equate the Indian way of life with a temporary and immature stage in the life of an individual.

Alice Fletcher went to two crucial meetings at Lake Mohonk, in 1884 and 1885. In between, she continued to work for the government in ways that gave her even greater status as an expert on the Indians. One assignment involved a relatively new medium, photography, and a nineteenth-century passion, world's fairs. New Orleans in 1885 was preparing to host the World's Industrial and Centennial Cotton Exposition. Early that year the commissioner of education asked Fletcher to prepare an exhibit on "Indian Civilization" for the New Orleans Exposition. The Bureau of Indian Affairs was still reeling from the attacks directed at it by Helen Hunt Jackson at the time of the Ponca affair. They were eager to show how much the government was doing for Indians.

Alice Fletcher accepted readily—it meant continuing on the government payroll as "Special Agent" in the Department of Indian Affairs—and she threw herself into the task with her customary energy. She decided to use her experience among the Omahas and to make it a "before and after" story, showing Omaha life before and after they had land allotments and the opportunity for education and self-advancement. At first she planned an exhibit like those in the Peabody Museum, with miniature models of an Omaha earth lodge and of the tribal circle of tents, placed near an actual-size skin tent and Omaha weapons, tools, and clothing. But Putnam was reluctant to loan objects from his museum, and the commissioner of Indian affairs wanted something inexpensive. Fletcher finally decided to do the whole exhibit with photographs. The result was an early demonstration of the power of photography to convey a particular political message, although Fletcher did not see it as that. She believed she was simply telling the Omaha story as she knew it to be.

Fletcher planned the exhibit carefully. She arranged for a photographer from Sioux City, Iowa, a Mr. Hamilton, to go to the Omaha Reservation and take "a series of views," and she specified what she wanted in each photograph. She wrote to the agent, asking his co-

Omaha sod dwelling with a rack for drying corn and
"two women seated in the foreground, one braiding
the corn husks so that the corn can be hung up, and
the other pounding the corn in a large wooden
mortar with a long wooden pestle." Photograph
by Hamilton from Sioux City, Iowa, 1885,
commissioned by Alice Fletcher for Indian Bureau
Exhibit, New Orleans Exposition, 1885. (Peabody
Museum, Harvard University)

operation, and to her friends among the Omahas, asking them to dress in old-time costumes and to be photographed showing their past customs. The exhibit, as finally installed in one of the alcoves in the balcony of the government building at the Exposition site in New Orleans, consisted of sixteen large photographs, two drawings, a map, and a stack of pamphlets.[29]

The first photographs showed the old Omaha way of life. One was of an Omaha earth lodge with a chief in full dress and his wife walking along behind him "according to Indian custom." Another was of a sod dwelling with a rack for drying corn and "two women seated in the foreground, one braiding the corn husks so that the corn can be hung up, and the other pounding the corn in a large wooden mortar with a long wooden pestle." Fletcher was not eager to call attention to polygamy among the Omahas, for she did not want to titilate her audience, but she could not ignore it altogether, for Indians would be seeing the exhibit and she wanted it to ring true to them. She cleverly solved the problem with this photograph. White visitors would see what they were told to see, two stages of corn drying and pounding, but Indian eyes would recognize a household with two wives. Other photographs showed the Omahas transporting and setting up the skin tents that they had used every summer on the annual buffalo hunts.

Next came the heart of the exhibit: two drawings that were summations of the old way of life and the new. On the buffalo hunt the tribe camped in a circle with an opening to the east and with fixed locations within the circle for each of the ten kin groups. Fletcher asked a Washington artist, F. W. Miller, to do a pen-and-ink drawing of a bird's-eye view of this tribal circle. Next to this she put a map of the reservation and then a pen-and-ink copy by Miller of a sketch, done by an Omaha man, of "the village of make-believe white men" where Joseph La Flesche and his friends lived. These two sketches, showing the placing of dwellings in the past and the present, became metaphors for the two ways of life. The Omahas had moved from the constraints of tribal life to the freedom of "civilization," from the tight restrictions of the tribal circle to homes large and small scattered along the main road in the village, each built in accord with a person's own will and by his own effort, and all of them leading, via the road to the steamboat landing on the Missouri River, out to the wider world.

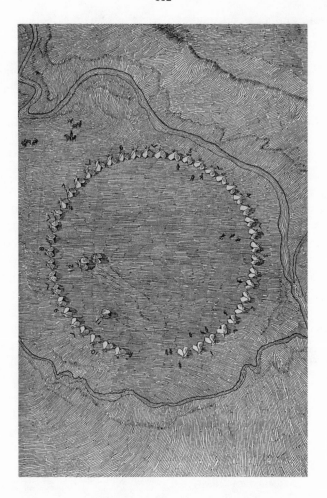

Pen-and-ink drawing of a bird's-eye view of the
traditional Omaha tribal circle. The numbers 1–10
designate the location of each of the ten gentes in
the Omaha tribe. The sacred Tent of War is No. 11.
The tents containing the Sacred Pole and the White
Buffalo Hide are No. 12. Drawing by F. W. Miller for
the New Orleans Exposition, 1885. (Photo by Hillel
Burger, Peabody Museum, Harvard University)

The "village of the make-believe white men" on the
Omaha Reservation. Pen-and-ink copy by F. W.
Miller of a sketch made by an Omaha man for the
New Orleans Exposition, 1885. Joseph La Flesche's
house is No. 7, and his vegetable garden is inside
another fence at No. 25. Wajapa's house is No. 15.
The road going southwest leads to the agency. The
road heading northeast leads to field shops, the
Presbyterian mission, and the steamboat landing on
the Missouri River. (Photo by Hillel Burger, Peabody
Museum, Harvard University)

The final section of the exhibit consisted of photographs showing the Omahas enjoying their new way of life: an Omaha man taking a wagonload of corn to the grist mill; a carpenter at work in his shop; one man's farm complex with his home, machinery, and grain bins, the result of ten years of his labor. There were photographs of the aids to civilization that had been provided by the federal government and by churches: the local agency, the Presbyterian mission school, the government industrial school, the thirty-one Omaha students at Carlisle in 1882, and even a cottage built for a young couple as a result of the Home Building Fund.

Sixteen black-and-white photographs in a second-floor alcove were not much of an exhibit, but in this not particularly promising situation Alice Fletcher launched a major public relations effort. She went to the exhibit every day and spent long hours explaining it to visitors and giving out the pamphlets that retold the story.[30] She also extolled the work of the Carlisle Indian School, which had a display in a nearby alcove. Fletcher herself, in effect, became part of the exhibit and soon a local celebrity. For months New Orleans newspapers had been reporting the activities of Julia Ward Howe, who had charge of the women's exhibit. Mrs. Howe was the leading "personality," the superstar, of the Exposition. In the midst of perfunctory reports on the exhibits from various industries and other nations, the papers gave full coverage to Mrs. Howe's speeches, to her off-again, on-again relations with the ladies on the local committee, to her boarding house bill, and even to the activities and evening gowns of her debutant daughter, Maud.[31] Eventually tiring of Mrs. Howe, the reporters found Alice Fletcher, who offered them an escape from the trivia to which they had been reduced. Fletcher accepted every speaking engagement that came her way, starting with the International Educators Association and local church groups. When she gave one of the official "Noon Talks" at the Exposition, the *Times Democrat* devoted two columns to it, and overflow crowds came to her two talks at the Dakota headquarters. The first of these she modestly titled "Indian Custom," but when she was invited back, she grew bolder and spoke on "Dark and bright sides of Indian social and religious life." Many in the audience were from Dakota and Wyoming territories and thought they knew all about Indians, but they sat entranced, listening to Fletcher's description of the "inward life and ideals" of the Plains tribes. Afterward Fletcher was warmly commended for her "mediatory work" between the races, and as the session adjourned, many of those in the audience pressed forward to urge her to come and present the same story in their home communities. At the end of April, when Fletcher's appointment was up, the director general of the Exposition regretted that she could not stay longer "to put the public and the press more fully in possession of the facts of Indian life."[32]

Fletcher left New Orleans feeling content with the work she had done. General John Eaton was so pleased with her New Orleans exhibit that he gave her another assignment. He asked her to finish a report that he had begun nine years earlier for the United States Centennial in 1876, a report on the progress of Indian education and civilization. She agreed. She worked on the report steadily for the next ten months, the last two without pay, for the appropriation had run out.[33]

In Fletcher's hands the Report on Indian Education and Civilization was expanded and entirely recast, and it became a comprehensive survey of United States government and Indian relations, past and present. In part 1 Fletcher outlined the history and organization of the Indian office, giving a list of all employees, their pay, and their duties. She reported the population and distribution of Indians within the country, the amount of property they controlled, the school population of each reservation, the school accommodations on each, and the cost of these to the government and sponsoring religious societies. Part 1 became in effect a handbook of Indian affairs. Part 2 was a historical sketch of Indian-government relations from the fifteenth century to 1885, and it included a history of every existing reservation, a synopsis of all treaties made with each tribe, and a report on the current situation on each reservation, with emphasis on Indian ideas and forms of social organization and how these would need to be altered to accommodate European ("Aryan") civilization.[34] The report, published in 1888, was 693 pages long.

Fletcher worked on the report all through the hot Washington summer. She spent nearly every day at the Library of Congress, from nine in the morning until it closed at four. "It is hard work digging thro. the statutes and reports," she wrote Putnam.[35] But life was not all hard work, and the work was winning approval in the highest circles. Rose Cleveland invited her to the White House several times. Fletcher was impressed by the President's "clever, sensible, sister." She offered Putnam her wry view of marriage: "If there were a Mrs. Cleveland she would likely be quite the opposite."[36]

In July Fletcher went to Cambridge for a few days to unpack the contents of the Omaha sacred Tent of War at the Peabody Museum. In September she and Francis La Flesche headed for the AAAS meeting at Ann Arbor. Again, as they had the year before, Francis La Flesche gave one paper and Alice Fletcher gave two. La Flesche's was a careful explanation of the Omaha kinship system. *Science* magazine reported, that the "singularly intricate, and to us absurd, system of relationship which has long been in use among the Omahas, was very clearly explained" and noted that the paper was "of special value" because it came from one who spoke of his own people.[37]

But kinship was boring to most people, and it was Fletcher's papers, prepared with an eye to popular appeal, that were the hit of the meeting. "On Friday morning the opening paper was by Miss A. C. Fletcher, on the sacred war-tent, and some of the war customs of the Omahas. Like all of Miss Fletcher's papers, this was a very clear, minute, and valuable account and was received by the section as a most welcome contribution." Later in the meeting she appeared again, presenting what one reporter called "a most delightful account of 'An average day in camp among the Sioux.'" Fletcher began with the taking down of the chief's tent in the early morning as a signal to the rest of the tribe and ended with the setting up of camp again at dusk. "In a most racy and vivid manner the common incidents of such a day were given, and with the zest which comes from actual experience."[38]

In October, Fletcher went again to Lake Mohonk. Senator Dawes was there for the first time, eager to explain the Coke-Dawes bill, which had passed the Senate, and "very anxious to preserve the tribal patent."[39] He had not, however, reckoned with Alice Fletcher, who had become for the fifty-some persons gathered there *the* authority on Indians. She not only had field experience: all summer she had been working on the report on Indian education and civilization for the commissioner of Indian affairs, which included a history of the treaties made with each tribe. She gave three prepared speeches at Lake Mohonk in 1885, and when she was not speaking formally she was constantly deferred to.

At Mohonk, Fletcher was appointed to a committee of nine to lobby in the House for the passage of the Coke-Dawes bill. She persuaded the committee that land ought not to be patented to the tribe, and Dawes rewrote the bill to conform to her ideas. She also prepared a table of unfulfilled treaty obligations promising land in severalty (individually owned) to Indians, which the committee presented to President Cleveland when they met with him that fall.[40]

Grover Cleveland, the newly elected Democratic president, and his secretary of the interior, Lucius Lamar, found the Lake Mohonk "Friends of the Indian" waiting for them when they took office in March 1885. Cleveland and Lamar urged flexibility and caution in Indian affairs. They wanted to move slowly and to be sure they had the consent and cooperation of any Indians who would be affected by a new program before putting it into operation. They even tried delaying the Dawes bill with the familiar tactic of supporting a proposal for a special investigative commission to look into the proposed reforms.

But the Lake Mohonk committee, which included Albert K. Smiley, Sara T. Kinney, Amelia S. Quinton, and Lyman Abbott, as well as Alice Fletcher, would not be put off, and they had converted Henry Dawes, a Republican but a symbol of bipartisan interest in the Indians, to their point of view. They wanted a general bill providing for allotments to individuals and not to tribes, they wanted it soon, and they wanted it to be compulsory. Lyman Abbott, with little knowledge of Indians but very strong opinions, was so outspokenly in favor of breaking Indian treaties in order to secure immediate land allotment that even supporters of the Dawes bill, like Herbert Welsh, privately called his views "crude and radical."[41] But his presence on the committee was balanced by the quiet, authoritative voice of Alice Fletcher.

In 1886, when the House added an amendment to the Dawes bill requiring the consent of the Indians before their lands could be allotted to them, Senator Dawes persuaded the conference committee to drop this clause. The final version of the bill that became law on February 8, 1887, did not contain any provision for a tribal patent or for tribal consent. It simply stated that allotment in severalty to Indians would take place at the discretion of the president of the United States: 160 acres to each head of family, 80 acres to each single person over eighteen and to orphans under eighteen, 40 acres to other single persons under eighteen. The bill kept the twenty-five-year inalienability clause added by Dawes, which Alice Fletcher favored. It also added citizenship for those Indians who accepted their land allotments. At the last minute the Five Civilized Tribes of Indian Territory and the New York Indians were exempted from the provisions of the act, in order to avoid a long debate over whether the size of their preserves ought to be reduced.

Alice Fletcher called the Dawes Act "the Magna Charta of the Indians of our country." She estimated that of the existing 169 Indian reservations, 119 would probably eventually come under the provisions of the act. In a front-page editorial in the *Morning Star*, the newspaper of the Carlisle Indian School, she wrote that the act was a charter of liberties for the Indians for three reasons. First, it guaranteed to each one a homestead, even to those who had been driven off their land or who were living precariously on executive order (as opposed to treaty) reservations. Second, it placed each owner of land under the civil and criminal laws of the state and conferred the rights, privileges, and immunities of citizenship. Third, it freed each Indian "from the tyranny of the tribe as to his property." Land would no longer be held in common. Each individual was free to keep for himself and his family the results of his own labor. Fletcher also mentioned, but did not dwell on, the fourth important provision of the act, that it threw open to white settlement "the surplus lands" on the reservation.[42]

Alice Fletcher was not trying to put something over on the Indians. She truly believed that they were being held back by having too much land, and she argued this freely in *Lend a Hand*, the paper of the Hampton Institute. She wrote that the Indians had much more land than they could ever use and admitted that this "waste," as she called it, "irritates white settlers." She also believed it retarded the Indian "by isolating him from the industries that teem throughout the length and breadth of our land." This isolation "tends to increase his dependence upon the government, to keep him in ignorance of his own short-comings, to leave him without ambition or any stimulus to action, and to make him the victim of conceit and pauperism."[43]

The Dawes Severalty Act of 1887 was the first major statement of federal Indian policy since the Trade and Intercourse Act of the 1790s. It was the culmination of a decade of effort by government officials, private organizations, and a diverse group of missionaries, Indian agents, and reformers. But the form the act finally took was due more to Alice Fletcher than to any other single person. Henry Dawes recognized that when he said of Alice Fletcher's contributions to the Dawes Act, "I stand in reference to that very much as Americus Vespuscious stands to Columbus."[44]

Of all the reformers, Senator Dawes made the most honest public analysis of his change of heart on the Indian question. He readily admitted that the Dawes Act was not his doing. When he had first begun to work for the Poncas in 1879, he told the Lake Mohonk conference in 1886, he had thought the important thing was to get the tribe a secure title to its reservation. But every year he weakened, he explained, as he felt the pressure for Indian land. The Great Sioux Reservation in the heart of Dakota Territory included thirty thousand square miles, or twenty-two million acres, and had a population of twenty-eight thousand Indians, the same as the population of his hometown of Pittsfield, Massachusetts. The Sioux had been put there in 1868 with the idea that the white men would never reach them, but less than twenty years later half a million white people surrounded the Sioux and the tracks of two major railroads had been built up to the boundary of the reservation. For the last six years there had been constant attempts to get bills through Congress that would open up that land. "I became satisfied—no man can go there [the West] and not be satisfied—that those white men will have a large portion of that reservation; that this land cannot be kept by Indians with a population increasing all around them. I made up my mind that I could do more good by accepting the inevitable, and seeing to it that if they part with their land they shall have an equivalent for it."[45]

Dawes was supporting the Sioux bill then in Congress which would allow the Sioux to keep half their land. The other eleven million acres would be sold to settlers for fifty cents an acre, and the resulting five and a half million dollars would be used for the "education and civilization" of the Sioux. Dawes admitted that this would be a violation of the treaty of 1868 made between six Sioux tribes and the United States, which said that not a foot of their reservation could be taken without the written consent of three-fourths of the adults of all six tribes, but he knew they could never get that consent and he saw no other alternative. The principle of consent was being dropped from the Dawes bill. He felt it might as well be dropped from the Sioux bill as well. When Dawes was asked about the tribal patent, he said that he had given that up because of the "strong sentiment" that the tribal relation must be broken up. He was capitulating both to westerners who wanted land and to eastern reformers, whose ideological commitment was to the assimilation of Indians into white society as rapidly as possible. One by one other reformers bowed to what they called the inevitable. Herbert Welsh wrote of Indian reservations as islands around which "a sea of civilization, vast and irresistible, surged."[46]

One Indian rights group, the National Indian Defense Association, did keep faith with the original purpose of the movement. It was an outgrowth of the *Council Fire*, a newspaper founded by Alfred B. Meacham in 1877. Meacham, a rancher and developer in Oregon, had been shot and partially scalped by Modoc Indians in 1873 when he went to deal with them as a member of a peace commission after the Modoc War. Meacham was left for dead on the lava beds which were the site of the supposed peace parley, but he recovered, although his hands and face were permanently maimed. He spent the remaining years of his life traveling around the country giving a lecture, "Tragedy of the Lava Beds," about his experience. Meacham placed the blame not on the Modocs, but on the perfidious officials who had repeatedly betrayed them. He was accompanied on his travels by two friends, a husband-and-wife team of physicians, Drs. Theodore and Cora Bland. After the founding of the newspaper, the three of them decided to settle in Washington in order to try to have more direct influence on Indian policy. Meacham died in 1882, but the Blands continued to publish the *Council Fire*, eventually changing its name to the *Council Fire and Arbitrator*, and in 1885 they founded the National Indian Defense Association. They held meetings in their living room with visiting Indian leaders and tried to keep alive the idea that the Indians had a right to fair dealings and above all a right to choose their own destiny.[47]

Meacham's original purpose in his speaking tour and in founding the monthly newspaper was to promote peace between Indians and whites, and there was a Quaker tone to much of his writing and that of successive editors. The *Council Fire* was not opposed to land in severalty and citizenship for the Indians, or even to the idea of "civilizing" them. But the editors wanted the pace of these transformations to be set by the Indians. They supported allotments of land and citizenship only by choice of the Indians, not by force.[48]

The National Indian Defense Association was a respected organization in Washington with friends in high places. The vice-president of the association, Dr. Sutherland, was President Grover Cleveland's pastor. Henry Dawes called it an organization of "very excellent men," although by 1886 he had come to think the purpose of the group was wrong, for it was "to perpetuate the existing state of things."[49] The association, opposed to the Dawes bill as long as the bill did not require the consent of a majority of the tribe, used delay as its major tactic. But it lost skirmish after skirmish: the proposal for a study commission was rejected, and the last-minute amendment requiring the consent of the tribe was removed by Dawes.[50] Eventually the association members were swamped by the assimilationist policies of the Lake Mohonk reformers, who thought a radically new program would be infinitely better than the fumbling maintenance of the status quo.

Alice Fletcher had guided the deliberations at Lake Mohonk through two crucial sessions in 1884 and 1885. By 1886 the conference had reached a consensus in support of the Dawes bill and the Sioux bill; President Merrill E. Gates of Rutgers thought it was "encouraging how minds are coming together."[51] Alice Fletcher was no longer needed at Lake Mohonk, and she no longer attended. From 1886 through 1891 she was away every fall, in Alaska, Nebraska, and Idaho, working on scattered government assignments, but she sent letters from the field which were read to the assembly. Fewer than five years before, she had been stumbling naively along on the camping trip among the Sioux, struggling to keep her bearings. By 1886, she had turned herself into an expert on contemporary Indian life. She was respected by scientists, revered by reformers, and deferred to by government officials who recognized that her support was invaluable and that she would carry through on a task no matter how difficult. It would be more than ten years before she realized that her attempt to help the Indians had been a disaster.

Ten

The Omaha Aftermath—
A House Divided

BACK on the Omaha Reservation, the Indian situation, presented so glowingly elsewhere, looked rather different. In the fall of 1885 a new agent, Charles H. Potter, reported that the Omahas were "restless over their political condition, past and prospective" and were divided into factions. They were also bitterly opposed to having been made subject to the civil and criminal laws of the state of Nebraska, which they said they had never agreed to.[1] The "Omaha problem" was far from solved.

The Omahas had been left in an anomalous legal position. According to the Omaha Severalty Act of 1882, when they received the patents for their land allotments they became subject to the laws of Nebraska and so were presumably no longer under the jurisdiction of the Bureau of Indian Affairs or the authority of the local Indian agent. But they had not been made citizens. Alice Fletcher did not consider the Omahas ready for self-government. She wanted all vestiges of tribal government and of the "Agency system" to be rooted out first. "The power of the chiefs ought to be broken," she advised the secretary of the interior in 1882. "The Indians as a body can never progress under their leadership. Law faithfully administered must be the substitute."[2]

But the Omahas were so insistent that they run their own affairs that Fletcher finally acquiesced. The sixty-page plan of self-government she worked out at the request of the commissioner of Indian affairs was a compromise. Fletcher was forced to recognize the existence of the Omaha Council, ten elected men who were the governing body of the tribe, but she urged that as much power as possible be transferred to the local three-man Indian Court of Offenses, an innovation introduced in 1882 on many reservations by the Indian Bureau to help the local agents put a stop to such "heathen and barbarous customs" as the sun dance, the scalp dance, war dances, and polygamy.[3] And, even though these judges were not popular with the people, she hoped that some day they could be paid salaries out of tribal funds. Alice Fletcher and the Omahas agreed on one thing: the "Agency system," in which money owed to the Omahas by the federal government was used to pay the physician, carpenter, blacksmith, and miller who were agency employees, should be abolished. Omahas were to set up their own shops and compete with white tradesmen in the nearby towns. Fletcher suggested that the unallotted land being saved for the next generation be fenced in and used as a common pasture. She urged that the Omahas, whose reservation included most of Thurston County, adopt a simple form of county government, with a superintendent of schools, a superintendent of roads, and other county officials on the model of the local governments around them. With these suggestions and with minimal supervision by the local agent (who continued to live at Winnebago, where he had been ever since the two agencies were combined), the Omahas were left to fend for themselves.

The Omahas were soon floundering. When the agency physician resigned in 1885, a group of Omahas wrote to the commissioner of Indian affairs suggesting that instead of replacing him with another physician, Alice Fletcher should be hired to manage their affairs. Neither the commissioner nor Fletcher gave serious consideration to this, but by the following spring Fletcher found herself in the midst of a "hard fight," trying to put down the opponents of her program on the reservation.[4] In the shifting alignments of reservation politics, it was soon apparent that some of the opposition was coming from within Joseph La Flesche's own family.

Fletcher had known from the beginning that Susette and Thomas Tibbles did not agree with all of her ideas. In October 1882, soon after the Omaha allotment bill had passed, rumors began to reach her in Washington that many of the Omahas, including Joseph La Flesche, were dissatisfied with the law and its provision for the sale of "excess" lands, and did not intend to sign the bill. Joseph La Flesche objected not that the land would be sold but that the commissioner of Indian affairs, and not the Omahas themselves, would decide how the sale money was to be spent. Fletcher learned that Susette and Thomas Tibbles were urging the Omahas not to sign. Rosalie, the second La Flesche daughter and Alice Fletcher's closest friend on the reservation, wrote to her: "You know yourself how easily one can influence the Indians even the best of them. When you were here no one had more influence than you had. When you are away they get under other influences."[5] It took a strongly worded letter from Francis to persuade his father to support the bill. The rift in the La Flesche family would last for twenty years, with Susette and Thomas Tibbles pulling them in one direction and Alice Fletcher and Francis La Flesche pulling them in another.

The message that Alice Fletcher preached was that the Omahas could completely change their way of life. They could be born again, as white people, if they put their minds to it and trusted God and Fletcher, who was at work for them in Washington. She urged a version of the Protestant ethic on the Omahas, like the motto of the Carlisle Indian School, "God helps those who help themselves."

Fletcher's program was appealing to reformers and to some Indians on several levels. It was a radical solution, which the situation seemed to require. It was practical, for it was easier to join the stronger civilization than to try to fight it. Finally, her program appealed to the guilt so often latent in a victim who feels or can be made to feel that he or she is responsible for what has happened. Joseph La Flesche had become a convert to the Christian missionary's teachings. He had long been pondering how the Omahas ought to improve themselves. Here was an upright, Christian woman—"a remarkable woman; in thought and expression . . . more like a man than a woman," he had told Francis—reinforcing his own attempts to make the Omahas turn to new ways.

But Joseph La Flesche had another side, one in which his concern was not for the Omahas' duties and obligations and shortcomings but for their rights. When Susette and Thomas Tibbles spoke about the wrongs done the Indians, about their need to be citizens so that they could be under the law and have redress in the courts, and about their right to be treated as adults rather than children, they were expressing his ideas as much as Fletcher was when she talked about how the Omahas should move toward "civilization." The ideological battle was thus waged between the Tibbles and Alice Fletcher. At the same time, a separate, covert, power struggle engaged the two women.

Susette La Flesche Tibbles was her father's eldest surviving child. She was one of a line of outspoken and strong women, from her grandmother Nicomi, who had been more than a match for two husbands, the Army physician Dr. John Gale and then the wealthy trader Peter Sarpy, to her mother Mary Gale La Flesche, who outlived Joseph by many years and remained a central force in the family. Nicomi always used the Omaha language, refusing to speak English or French. When Dr. Gale was recalled and left, she hid with her daughter rather than allow him to take the little girl away. Later, when she married Peter Sarpy, she sent Mary to school in St. Louis, but she herself did not like living in St. Louis in the elegant home Sarpy had built, and she returned to the reservation.

Mary Gale grew up as determined as her mother and as proud of the Indian half of her heritage. She too spoke only the Omaha language, refusing to use the French she had learned at school. She and Joseph La Flesche had four remarkable daughters: Susette, who with Standing Bear and Tibbles sparked the Indian rights movement of the 1880s; Rosalie, the anchor at home for the family and for many in the tribe, and for whom the town of Rosalie on the reservation is named; Susan, who helped to nurse Alice Fletcher when she was ill, decided to become a doctor, and graduated at the top of her medical school class, the first American Indian woman to become a physician; and Marguerite, a teacher and occasional concert singer.[6]

Susette was the first of Joseph La Flesche's children to go east to school. She returned to face alone the severe trial of readjustment to reservation life after an absence of four years. Taught to dress and behave like an eastern lady, she returned in 1875 to an impoverished reservation in which the agent's will was law and which she could not even leave without his permission. The only books available were her college texts and a volume of Shakespeare.[7] She was refused a teaching position at the agency day school, until she reminded them of the ruling that Indians were to be given preference in hiring. She then was taken on as an assistant teacher at twenty dollars a month, half the salary the white teachers received.

In the spring of 1877, Susette La Flesche went with her father to Columbus, Nebraska, to meet the Poncas en route as they were being forcibly moved south to Indian Territory. The despair and misery of the Poncas, one of whom was Joseph La Flesche's brother, Francis, touched them deeply. In 1879 Susette and her father got grudging permission from the local agent to attend Standing Bear's trial in Omaha. There they met Thomas Henry Tibbles, who had taken on the Ponca case. Tibbles helped raise money to send Joseph and Susette La Flesche to Indian Territory to report on conditions among the Poncas. Susette translated the testimony of the Poncas into English, and when she and her father returned she spoke to a large gathering in Omaha, describing to them the Ponca situation. She was intense and eloquent. Joseph La Flesche had begun to look to Tibbles as a man who could help them, and he was soon persuaded that his daughter should go east with Tibbles to interpret for Standing Bear and to speak for herself, and for him. Susette La Flesche and Tibbles went east twice, in the fall of 1879 and again in the winter of 1880–81. Tibbles's wife had been ailing, and she died while they were away. On their return to the reservation in 1881, Tibbles and Susette La Flesche became husband and wife.

Susette La Flesche Tibbles's position was clear. "Allow an Indian to suggest," she wrote in 1881 in an introduction to a book by Tibbles, "that the solution of the vexed 'Indian Question' is *Citizenship*, with all its attending duties and responsibilities, as well as the privileges of protection under the law." The Indians would have been made citizens long ago, she claimed, had it not been for the valuable lands they possessed. Instead they were given the extraordinary status of wards of the government, and under that pretext were deprived of their liberty and were repeatedly plundered. She was proud to be an Indian. What she wanted for Indians was equal rights and equal protection under the law. Under that umbrella they would be free to work out their own way of life. They might eventually adopt much of western civilization, but at their own pace and in combination with some of their old ways. Like Susette, Thomas

Henry Tibbles thought there was much that was admirable and that ought to be preserved in Indian life. Although it might be necessary to plough under the native sod, Tibbles wrote in *Ploughed Under: The Story of an Indian Chief* (1881), what of "the human bodies and souls that go down under the advancing ploughshares of American civilization on the Western plains?" Might there not be some material in the Indian race "worth saving and improving, even for the sake of the white race and its civilization?"[8]

In 1881 Tibbles's plea was unique. Reformers wanted to "civilize" the Indians. Anthropologists wanted to study them before their way of life vanished, as nearly everyone assumed it would. Almost no one else suggested that the Indian way of life contained in itself anything of lasting value. Tibbles and Susette La Flesche were thirty years ahead of their time in arguing the value of cultural pluralism, and they had to fight the assimilationist current that was so strong in late-nineteenth-century America.

For five years Joseph La Flesche walked a wary line between the two outsiders, Alice Fletcher and Thomas Henry Tibbles, seeking help from both of them: land titles from Fletcher and citizenship and legal rights from Tibbles. The La Flesche family took their allotments where Alice Fletcher thought they should, on the western part of the reservation near the railroad. Joseph La Flesche also continued to send his children east to school, despite the growing opposition of Susette and Thomas Tibbles.

Susette Tibbles's objections to the eastern schools were multiple. Along with the other teachers at the agency school and with Reverend William Hamilton, the Presbyterian missionary in charge of the mission school whom Alice Fletcher tried to get removed,[9] she resented the siphoning off of their best students to schools in the East. She also sympathized with parents in the close and affectionate Indian families who could scarcely endure the long separation from their children that such schooling required. Children were usually sent to the eastern schools at the age of ten or twelve, and it was expected that they would remain there for four or five years without any interim visits home. Alice Fletcher wrote movingly of some of the scenes of farewell and of reunion that she witnessed, as she brought children to and from the eastern schools. But she was so convinced the schools were a good thing that she exercised all her persuasive powers on reluctant parents. In 1883 a young Omaha girl, Alice Springer, died suddenly at Carlisle. Her mother dictated a letter to Captain Pratt saying that it was "Miss Fletcher's doing" and begged that her other children be allowed to return home immediately. Captain Pratt agreed to send the other Springer children home, although he discouraged the resulting wave of similar pleas from other parents. But Alice Fletcher was unshaken. "Life and death are in the hands of God," she wrote James and Lena Springer. Before they called their other children home, they should "be mindful of the future."[10]

But an even deeper objection came from Susette La Flesche's memory of her own disorientation upon returning from school to the reservation. The eastern schools attempted to turn Indians into whites, and when they returned, as Sitting Bull had shrewdly commented, they were neither. Tibbles described an experience that was likely Susette's. An Indian girl among her own people is always accompanied wherever she goes and is taught to turn her head away from a man whom she passes on a road and to hold her head down when a man comes into the dwelling, he wrote. In the eastern schools girls, "are taught to hold up their heads when a man addresses them, to look him in the face and to reply to his questions, and they are particularly instructed to practice that which they have been taught when they return to their tribe." But if they do "they become outcasts among their own people," while if they conform to Indian custom it is said that they "have gone back to savagery."[11]

The eastern schools, although controversial, soon became a minor issue compared to other problems on the reservation. The major confrontation came on the question of leasing land. Many of the Omahas had moved away from the cultivated but frequently flooded lands along the river and had taken allotments on the prairie uplands where the sod had never been broken. To break and clear a field required not just small Indian ponies or horses but oxen, "working cattle" as Fletcher called them,[12] and it was hard work. Tibbles tried it—he moved with Susette and two teen-age daughters from his first marriage out to Susette's allotment and tried to become a farmer—but walking all day behind a plow was heavy going for a man who much preferred advocacy journalism and the excitement of eastern speaking tours. He soon sympathized heartily with the

Omahas who did not want to farm their land but wanted to lease it to nearby white men for either farming or grazing. But they found that this was illegal. The allotment act stated that no Omaha could sell or lease his land allotment for twenty-five years. While the intent of this was to protect the Omahas from being cheated, Susette and Tibbles saw it as an infringement on their freedom to do what they liked with their property. Tibbles was also opposed to the common pasture being managed for the Omahas by Ed and Rosalie La Flesche Farley, arguing that the Omahas ought to be able to lease that land also, if they wanted to, and to whomever they wanted (including some of his white supporters in the towns nearby who were not disinterested in the outcome of his efforts).

Susette and Thomas Henry Tibbles began a campaign to win the Omahas the right to lease their land. They held meetings in the Baptist Church in Bancroft and raised money to take their case to Washington. They linked the right to lease the land with the right to become citizens and have the protection of the law. "It is our opinion that these people [the Omahas] are more fitted to become citizens than thousands of foreigners who land in this country," they said.[13]

At first Susette's father, Joseph La Flesche, was solidly behind them. For three decades he had been the leader of the "Citizen's Party" among the Omahas. He was persuaded, with Tibbles, that the white leasees could do more with the land than many of the Omahas could, for they had oxen and reapers and other equipment the Omahas lacked, and he hoped they would make improvements on the land as well as pay rent. Joseph La Flesche was also worried about Ed Farley's pasture, the eighteen thousand unallotted acres the Omahas had leased to his son-in-law to manage as a common pasture. Farley's lease had been approved by the commissioner of Indian affairs, but the United States attorney general had just ruled that Indians could not lease their land for grazing without the consent of Congress. Joseph was concerned that Farley's lease might be ruled illegal. Through Rosalie Farley, Joseph La Flesche wrote to Alice Fletcher in Washington, asking her to straighten out the leasing situation. "Anything you take in your hands to do you accomplish, so dear friend we wish your help in this matter," he dictated to Rosalie.[14] Through Susette he also appealed to the Boston Friends of the Indian, asking them to support the Omahas' right to do what they wanted with their own land.[15]

But then Joseph La Flesche realized that he was confusing two different leasing situations. Alice Fletcher approved of the leasing of the unallotted land to Ed Farley for a pasture—it had in fact been her idea—but she was adamantly opposed to the leasing of individual allotments to white men. She was responsible for the very provision of the law, the twenty-five-year period of trust, that Tibbles was attempting to overturn. And Joseph La Flesche learned that as part of his campaign Tibbles was attacking Alice Fletcher directly, accusing her of keeping the Omahas dependent and of denying them citizenship. "I fear we have made a wrong move," Joseph La Flesche confided to his friend Two Crows. He regretted having encouraged Tibbles to go to Washington to speak for them. "Miss F. is right there and knows what is best for us and in time will see about this matter."[16] Joseph La Flesche liked Tibbles's ideas, but increasingly he did not trust him. Alice Fletcher he did trust, and he did not want to alienate her, for she had powerful friends in Washington. Forced by the growing enmity between Tibbles and Fletcher to choose between them, Joseph La Flesche chose Alice Fletcher.

Through Rosalie, he dictated a long letter to Fletcher, saying that he regretted having had anything to do with Tibbles's plan. He added this heartfelt testimony—and vivid description of Tibbles:

> Before you came to our help we had no one to go to with our troubles. The white people on the reserve turned a deaf ear to our cries for help. You, friend, from the first were willing to listen and it was not long after you heard that you started to fight for us, and as soon as you accomplish one thing you put it behind and take up another, and before you fire off your gun you see that it is loaded right and when you fire you never fail to hit your mark.
>
> This is not so with the man who is talking about you. He doesn't care how his gun is loaded usually it has nothing but powder in it and when it goes off there is a great deal of noise and that is all. All he is saying is utterly false. I can't believe it will do you harm.[17]

Tibbles took his campaign against Fletcher to Boston and Washington. In Boston, where the first wave of the Indian rights movement lingered on, he found support, but in Washington he was virtually ignored. "He could do nothing here. No one would heed him so the danger went by," Fletcher reported to Putnam.[18]

Several delegations of Omahas also went to Washington in April 1886 to make their diverse—and contradictory—wishes known to the commissioner of Indian affairs. Fletcher and Francis La Flesche met with all of them and took down their requests, and together they worked out a county plan of self-government which everyone seemed to accept. The Omaha delegation was received by President Cleveland and his sister at the White House, where Fletcher had "quite a little talk with the President," and she took them around to many other Washington homes.

But the truce was short-lived. Back in Nebraska, the Omaha Council of Ten immediately divided again into two factions. Five of the councilors (Two Crows, Doubasmurri, Sindahaha, White Horse, and Chazaninga) supported the plan of self-government and Ed Farley's common pasture, and five of them (Prairie Chicken, Wahininga, Wasagaha, Little Cow, and Kaiska) opposed self-government, the pasture, and everything else associated with the La Flesches.[19] The latter group sent a letter to the commissioner of Indian affairs saying that they did not want to adopt Fletcher's plan of organization, charging that Fletcher had made misrepresentations to the Indians, to the public, and to the Department of Indian Affairs, that she had shown partiality to a portion of the tribe, that she had aided a white man named Ed Farley in a pasture swindling scheme, and that the leaders in her cause were not honorable men. They were especially critical of Joseph La Flesche, whom they called "a half breed Ponca" who had been "known in the past to have caused much trouble to Indian Agents by dividing the tribe usurping power."[20] There were 150 signatures on this letter, compared with approximately 50 signatures on Fletcher's earlier petition to Washington. Fletcher also learned from Rosalie that Henry Fontenelle, the leader of the other family on the reservation that claimed descent from a French trader, was opposed to her program. The Omaha agent reported in the fall of 1886 that "a large majority of the tribe are opposed to the system which has been formulated for them."[21] Many even favored returning to the system of agency employees and workshops.

The attacks on Fletcher continued and widened to include innuendoes about her relation to Francis La Flesche, who in the fall of 1884 had moved to the Temple Hotel in Washington where she lived. The gossip reached Carlisle and Hampton, where General Samuel C. Armstrong talked to Marguerite La Flesche about it. Marguerite turned, as everyone did, to Rosalie. Everyone is talking about Francis and Miss Fletcher, she wrote Rosalie, and General Armstrong had talked to her about it and wondered if there was any way to break it up. "I wish Frankie could live somewhere else," she moaned.[22]

Rosalie wrote to Francis, who in turn replied:

> I am very sorry that there should be any gossip about Miss F. among those unprincipled people. It is not new to me because I heard it when we were there making the allotments and it isn't something to wonder at. You know how people are even among those sainted missionaries on the reservation [who] make up stories on one another. . . . I wouldn't mind it if they smeared me all over with mud, their nasty stories, but I am *very* sorry that they should talk about Miss F. It isn't from Boston at all but made up by the nasty, dirty man that Susette has given us for a brother-in-law.[23]

Francis had complaints of his own about Tibbles: that Tibbles had held Susette on his lap and had made love to her on their eastern speaking tour while his first wife was still living. Francis continued to Rosalie: "Oh! dear Ro, if you and the other girls were my full sisters I would make it tremendously unpleasant for that selfish couple and an effort to have them driven off the reservation. It could be done as easy as not but you and Marg. and Su. make it hard to do anything."[24]

Three weeks later in Washington, at the annual meeting of the Board of Indian Commissioners, Susette Tibbles testified that "the Omahas could not be worse off than they are now." She spoke bitterly of the common pasture on the Omaha reservation being run by a white man, Ed Farley, "my brother-in-law," and implied that the Omahas were not receiving the rental money due them. Alice Fletcher sat in the audience during Susette's testimony, her face "the picture of despair."[25]

The La Flesche family was a house divided, and so too was the Omaha tribe. Alice Fletcher and Francis La Flesche had visited the

reservation the previous summer—she was on her way to Alaska
and he was on vacation—and the tension they felt was apparent in
a hasty letter she wrote to Mrs. Dawes. "The Omahas are getting
along," Fletcher reported. She immediately had taken charge of
problems, sending one man with property trouble to a lawyer, another who was a victim of assault and battery to a magistrate, and a
third, who wanted to be made guardian of his relative's estate, to a
court. "Until I visited them there was no one bringing the law in, to
show the people what to do," she wrote. "All that is needed is for
someone to set the machinery going and the Indian will soon
learn." [26]

She rejoiced to find the tribe "disintegrating," in her view a necessary step toward progress. "The thrifty ones are going ahead," she
wrote. "Meanwhile the shiftless element becomes more and more
marked and lag behind. They hold feasts and talk over old times,
neglect their work. . . . They are busy dancing, and the days I was
among them (the heathen element) held a scalp dance, no scalps
however, and at that dance passed resolution to remain old time
Indian. I shouted with laughter when I heard it. scalp dance and
resolution, new queer companions." Fletcher was sure some of these
old-timers would come around, but others might never change.
"Many must die. There is no help for them." [27]

The rift, both personal and ideological, between Susette and
Thomas Henry Tibbles on the one hand and Francis La Flesche and
Alice Fletcher on the other was never healed. Within the family and
for a time on the reservation Alice Fletcher seemed to have the upper
hand. She helped all of Joseph La Flesche's younger children go away
to school, at Hampton in Virginia, and after Susan's graduation in
1886 arranged for her to attend the Women's Medical College. [28]
Susette and Thomas Henry Tibbles drifted away from the reservation. There was a speaking tour in the British Isles in 1888 and then
two years spent in Washington, where Tibbles worked for the free-
silver movement. In 1895 they moved to Lincoln, Nebraska, and
Tibbles edited a Populist weekly. Meanwhile the La Flesche family
continued to look to Francis La Flesche and Alice Fletcher for advice. In 1887, when Marguerite was trying to decide whether to seek
a job as a missionary to the Omahas or as a teacher in the government school, Rosalie wrote to Alice Fletcher saying, "Father wants

you and Frank to decide which it would be best for M. to do."[29] In 1888 Ed and Rosalie Farley named their new baby boy Fletcher.

But in the long run, Susette and Thomas Henry Tibbles won out. The Omahas became citizens with the passage in 1887 of the Dawes Act, which granted citizenship to every Indian who received an allotment. Joseph La Flesche proudly gave the Fourth of July address in Bancroft in 1888, two months before his death. Fletcher's plan for self-government faded away as the Omahas continued to look to the Council of Ten as their governing body. The Omahas were technically participants in the county and state governments of Nebraska, but because they paid no taxes county officials were reluctant to spend much money on them. The Omahas were not encouraged to bring cases to court or to make any other requests of the county. With no police force and little law enforcement on the reservation, bigamy and drunkenness increased and there were a few cases of larceny. But the local agent reported in 1888 that, considering they were "without law," it was rather remarkable there was so little crime. He attributed it to a healthy public sentiment that "discountenances wrong in every form."[30]

Leasing of the land remained illegal for several more years, but it was a difficult law to enforce, and there was much surreptitious renting of land. An agent estimated in the late 1880s that 60 percent of the Omahas were too young, too old, or too ill to farm their allotments, or they were away at school. Their land lay unused and yielded no return. He urged that those who were unable to work their land be allowed to lease it under the supervision of the agent, and in 1891 the Dawes Act was so amended.[31] Leasing then became the dominant way of life for the Omahas. The common pasture managed by Ed and Rosalie Farley became less controversial as others were established, and it no longer seemed that the La Flesche faction had an unfair monopoly. But they had to go to court several times in the early 1890s to keep the pasture from being taken over on one pretext or another by scheming whites in the surrounding area.[32]

The intense factionalism that had erupted on the reservation at the time of the allotment program gradually abated, and the Omahas settled into a way of life that was an amalgam of the old and the new. The economic basis of their old way was gone. They lived on rental income from individual and tribal land holdings, with some agriculture and stock raising and small businesses. They also had money coming in from the sale of unallotted land: $116,000 in 1890, $26,700 in 1891.[33] In the 1890s and early 1900s the Omahas were relatively well-off. Economic trouble for the Omahas was to begin later, after 1906 when the Burke Act ended prematurely the "twenty-five year period of trust." Land sharks gathered while many Omahas sold their land or were encouraged to run up big bills in the local stores, forfeiting the land in payment.

Meanwhile the Omahas faced another problem. By the mid-1890s it was apparent that Nebraska was not the agricultural paradise, even for white settlers, that it had seemed to be for several decades. The federal government had created boom times in the trans-Mississippi West by passing the Homestead Act of 1862, which promised 160 acres of land to any head of family who would live on the land or cultivate it for five years, and by giving vast land grants to railroads (approximately 16.6 percent of the total acreage in Nebraska was given to railroads by either the federal or state government). Railroads crisscrossed the state, bringing hundreds of thousands of settlers to Nebraska after advertising for them as far away as Europe. The population of the state quadrupled between 1860 and 1870, trebled between 1870 and 1880, and doubled between 1880 and 1890. Then it abruptly stopped, growing only very slowly ever since.

By 1890 white settlers had discovered that it took more than free land to become a successful farmer in Nebraska. It took capital and experience and a measure of good luck. Of the land claims filed in Nebraska between 1863 and 1895, only slightly over half (52 percent) were carried through to the final patent. This means that almost half of the would-be farmers in Nebraska gave up within five years. Unusually good rainfall in the 1880s seemed to augur well for the future, but crop prices began to fall even before the drought in the early 1890s, which resulted in almost total crop failures in 1893 and 1894. The worldwide depression of 1893 shook the most stalwart farmers. Many Nebraskans like Thomas Henry Tibbles and Congressman William Jennings Bryan turned to Populism and free silver. When Nebraska agriculture recovered after the turn of the century, it was the most aggressive and the best-financed farmers who succeeded, those who were able to buy new labor-saving equipment and who were willing to plant new crops, especially winter

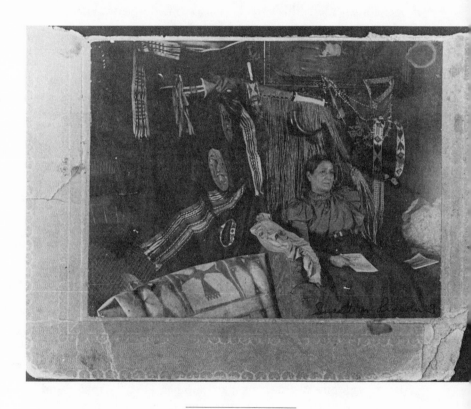

Susette La Flesche Tibbles
in her Lincoln home.
(Nebraska State Historical Society)

wheat and alfalfa.[34] Willa Cather was later to write of these "years of trial" in Nebraska that they "winnowed out" all but the strongest.[35] Among those "winnowed out" of farming were most of the Omaha Indians.

But the Omahas managed to keep their language, their tribal identity, and their political autonomy as a self-governing community. Margaret Mead spent the summer of 1930 with the Omahas and wrote about them, disguised as the "Antlers," in *The Changing Culture of an Indian Tribe*. Mead reported that they had abandoned some of their old customs, including polygamy, the rituals connected with menstruation and early childhood, and the outward marks of kin groups, but they had kept many others, including burial customs, their kin system and marriage regulations.[36] They were shaken but not destroyed, and they were still in Nebraska.

Susette La Flesche Tibbles remained close to her sisters. Marguerite's daughter remembers her as a sophisticated and cultured lady. "It was at her house in Lincoln that I first ate an olive," she laughs.[37] Susette Tibbles surrounded herself with Indian artifacts and clung proudly to her Indian heritage. In 1898 she did delicate sketches of Indian artifacts for a small book on the Omahas which was published for the Omaha Trans-Mississippi Exposition.[38] But her health was poor, and increasingly she was despondent and subject to "wandering spells."[39] Around 1900 she and Tibbles moved back to her allotment on the reservation several miles north of the town of Bancroft, and there in 1903 she died. John Neihardt, the poet and author of *Black Elk Speaks*, was then a young journalist in Bancroft. He recalled years later that Tibbles was not popular in Bancroft, for people thought him abrasive and an agitator, even an anarchist. On the night of Susette's death a neighbor brought Neihardt a message from Tibbles, asking if he could come and keep him company. Neihardt went, expecting that Susette's family would be there too, but they had gone and Tibbles was alone. Neihardt sat through the night with Tibbles as the latter alternately talked of and wept for the woman whose cause had become his own.[40] Tibbles continued to be active in politics. A year later he ran for vice-president of the United States on the Populist ticket.

In the spring of 1887 Alice Fletcher was invited by the president of the Indian Rights Association to write a defense of her work for the Omahas, which the association would publish. She sent him a fourteen-page letter explaining the Omaha situation, but she would not write anything for publication. "I do not care to take the time and thought of people for any self-vindication," she told him. "My work for the Indians (those little ones whom I found in need of a friend, and whom by God's grace I was able to help) has rested between my Maker and myself, and there I am content to let it stand."[41]

Eleven

Francis

I N the summer of 1886 Alice Fletcher abruptly decided to go to Alaska. She was at loose ends after having finished the government report on Indian education and civilization and was worn out from the Omaha controversies. Sheldon Jackson, the well-known Alaska missionary, had been trying for three years to get her to Alaska. Now the time was ripe. She invited Kate Foote, an old friend from her Sorosis days, a geneticist, and the president of the Washington auxiliary of the Women's National Indian Association, to go with her.

Alaska was the new frontier in the 1880s, attracting the attention of journalists, congressmen, educators, and hundreds of well-off tourists who cruised the great fjords of the inland passage and marveled at the scenery and the glaciers. It had not always been so. For fifteen years after Alaska was purchased from Russia in 1867, federal officials were so indifferent and defensive about the new acquisition that they failed even to provide a government for it. When the Russian flag went down at Sitka, the capital of Russian America, and the United States flag went up, the army moved in to keep order. With nothing to take its place, the army stayed on as an occupying force for ten years.

This neglect was not inevitable. It was the result of a deliberate campaign waged by a private fur-trading company, the Alaska Commercial Company, an American version of the old Russian-American Company, which had been granted a monopoly of all of Alaska's resources and the power to govern the area. In 1870 the Alaska Company obtained a monopoly lease on the seal fur trade in the Pribilof Islands north of the Aleutians, and for a modest annual payment to the United States government, the company began to do millions of dollars of fur trade business. Wanting as little public attention drawn to their sphere of operations as possible, the Alaska Commercial Company promoted the view that Alaska was an Arctic outpost, uninhabitable and worth nothing apart from its seal rookeries.[1]

Alaska was a forgotten territory and might have remained so for years, but for the activities of two men: John Muir and Sheldon Jackson. Muir, the romantic naturalist-writer, first went to Alaska in 1879. Traveling with a young Presbyterian missionary, Samuel Hall Young, and some Stikine Indians, he was struck by the majesty of Glacier Bay, with its spectacular mountains and lush evergreen forests that came down to the sea. Muir sent an avalanche of reports back to newspapers in the States, and by the early 1880s dozens of luxury steamers made their way every summer along the Inside Passage through the quiet fjords of the Alaskan panhandle.

Meanwhile government officials began to hear about Alaska from Sheldon Jackson. Jackson made his first trip to Alaska in 1877, to establish a mission school for the Indians. For the next seven years he recruited other missionaries and teachers and, in the words of his biographer, "carried on a one-man campaign in the states on behalf of Alaska and its native population."[2] He appealed to the public and church groups for funds for schools in Alaska, and received subsidies from Congress through his friendship with Senator (later President) Benjamin Harrison, a member of the Committee on Territories. Largely through Jackson's efforts, a civil government was established in Alaska in 1884. But it fell into the hands of his enemies, men in Sitka who were allied with the Alaska Commercial Company and who were vying with Jackson for leadership among the natives.

Jackson could see it coming, and as early as 1883 he had tried to enlist Alice Fletcher's help, for "she is a power in Washington," he told a mutual friend.[3] In March 1883 he asked her to go on a fact-finding mission to Alaska. Fletcher knew something of the Alaskan situation from William Dall, the son of her friend Caroline Dall. Fletcher told Caroline Dall, and the latter wrote in her journal:

> If she does her expenses will be paid that she may defeat the wretches in power there, but it will be kept secret.
>
> Her humility was beautiful. She did not fear anything, cold privation or anything else. The tears came into her eyes as she said, "It seems so presumptuous to think I can do anything! *Do* you think I can?"
>
> Of course I said "Go!"[4]

A letter from Alice Fletcher indicated that she understood clearly what Sheldon Jackson wanted from her. She was to get acquainted with the people, study the possibilities for Indians there, and "hear their cries for help." Then she was to "return to my nest, to make my report heard and bear fruit by legislation." Jackson wanted some sort of territorial or district government for Alaska and a system of government schools under the supervision of the Board of Education. "One thing is needed," Fletcher wrote him, "time enough to master the situation." She thought it would take at least a year in Alaska to learn the facts, and she could not go immediately because she needed to finish the Omaha allotments.[5] She was willing to help but only if she could spend enough time there to speak with authority and confidence.

So the situation in Alaska moved ahead rapidly without her. In 1884, when Alaska was declared by Congress to be a "civil and judicial district," President Chester Arthur appointed men whom Sheldon Jackson considered his enemies to the four top government positions in Alaska: the governor, federal judge, attorney general, and United States marshal. That summer when Jackson arrived in Alaska they had him arrested on a trumped-up charge of knowingly obstructing the road to the cemetery in Sitka. Jackson in turn charged them with incompetence and with failure to enforce the laws. The case was ambiguous. Each side maintained that it was defending the rights of the Indians. The case was also short-lived, for President

Arthur's appointees went out of office with his administration in 1885.

Jackson no longer needed Fletcher to help "defeat the wretches in power," but he was still eager to have her lobbying support for Alaskan appropriations. Since 1883 Fletcher had been too preoccupied with the Omaha allotments, the New Orleans Exhibition, and General Eaton's Report on Indian Education and Civilization to think much about Alaska. But in the summer of 1886 she suddenly decided to go. Her doctor, she wrote Mrs. Dawes, thought the trip would do her good.[6] She and Kate Foote would go not for a year but for a couple of months.

Shortly before she left, Fletcher made a promised visit to Newport, Rhode Island, to speak about American archaeology and her experiences among the Indians. She appeared before a crowd at the casino and met privately with a group of women at the home of Ellen Mason, a well-known classics scholar and a cousin of Henry James. Fletcher talked to the women about F. W. Putnam's work in the mounds of Ohio and the a disgraceful fact that the sites at Fort Ancient and Cahokia were being ruined when they ought to be "bought, restored and preserved." The outcome was that the group of women organized themselves into an association for the preservation and exploration of American antiquities. "They are all rich," Fletcher wrote to Putnam excitedly. "I told them of your work and that you were the person to lead them in this enterprise. . . . I will keep hold of them and help you all I can."[7]

Putnam had learned that the famous Serpent Mound site in Adams County, Ohio, was about to be destroyed. He sent the Newport women a circular of appeal and with their help bought the seventy-acre site. He then arranged to have it turned over to the state of Ohio to be preserved as a state park. The law passed by the Ohio legislature was the first state or federal law in the country concerned with the preservation of American antiquities. It was Putnam's project—he spent most of two summers at the site studying the mounds and helping to plan the layout of the park—but it was Alice Fletcher who had made the preservation possible.[8]

Flushed with success from the Newport venture, Alice Fletcher and Kate Foote set off for the Northwest. They traveled with Francis La Flesche as far as the Omaha Reservation. Then they took a train from St. Paul to Seattle, stopping on the way at Yellowstone Park, which Kate Foote wanted to see. In Yellowstone they met "a gentleman, Mr. Rockyfeller the Pres't of Standard Oil Company," Fletcher reported to Putnam. She promised to pursue him and appeal directly to him for funds for the Peabody Museum.[9]

Kate Foote and Alice Fletcher thought the geysers "wonderfully fine," but Fletcher was really more interested in the mosses that grew in the hot springs, changing colors as the streams grew cooler. She wrote Putnam of this, evidently wanting to impress him with her powers of scientific observation. "It is all grand," she added, "but there should be railroad communication from point to point as the distances are so great and the stage rides very hard."[10] Here as elsewhere in a life of considerable travel, Fletcher was not much taken with the beauties of nature. She did not like wild, untrammeled prairies or mountain ranges any more than she liked wild Indians. She liked wildflowers but in a vase on her desk. She gloried not in nature itself but in the new machines of nineteenth-century civilization that conquered nature and harnessed its powers. Railroads were a symbol of the conquering force of civilization and a model for her of the control she hoped for over the unruly forces within the self and the social order. She did not like nature when it was wild, threatening, intimidating, or overpowering.

But the experience of Yellowstone National Park stimulated her in another direction, coming as it did just after her success in helping Putnam save Serpent Mound in Ohio. The park had been established in 1871, the first national park in the country. Why, Fletcher asked herself, should there not be other national parks set aside to preserve not just natural beauty but archaeological remains, remnants of America's ancient past?

Immediately upon her return from Alaska she moved ahead with this idea. She proposed in an open letter to section H of the American Association for the Advancement of Science that a committee be appointed to request that Congress take such action.[11] Shrewdly she decided to get Matilda Stevenson involved in it, for Stevenson had done fieldwork in the Southwest under the aegis of the Bureau of Ethnology and was president of the newly formed Woman's Anthropological Society, a Washington-based group. Fletcher did not want to step into Tilly Stevenson's territory without her leave. She also thought that she and Stevenson together might be able to get the bill she wanted through Congress. The two women were duly appointed a Committee on the Preservation of Archaeological Remains on Public Lands by the AAAS in 1887. They prepared a report for the AAAS meeting in 1888 and wrote a bill urging that the pueblo area along the Rio Grande west of Santa Fe be set aside under the control of the secretary of the interior, with other sites to be proposed by the director of the geological survey.[12]

Fletcher worked hard on the bill. "Think of a plan of argument to have these reserves under the control of scientific institutions, etc. I wish we could add a western one," she wrote Putnam.[13] The bill floundered on scientific rivalries and on assertions by congressmen that they had already set aside too much land in the West, but the idea did not die. Alice Fletcher's bill was a prototype for the Lacey Act of 1906, the Act for the Preservation of American Antiquities, in which she again had a hand. In the meantime Mary Hemenway helped to get through Congress in 1890 a bill to preserve a single site, Casa Grande in Arizona. These two conservationist women, Alice Fletcher and Mary Hemenway, were fifteen years ahead of the conservationist president Theodore Roosevelt, who would eventually take up their cause.

Beyond Yellowstone, the Alaska trip itself was a disaster from start to finish. They sailed late, after all the scheduled boats had gone. Sheldon Jackson could not leave for Alaska until the appropriation for the next school year had been approved by Congress, which finally took place in August. He then chartered a schooner, the *Leo*, to take newly appointed teachers and supplies to their destinations in Alaska, and he made arrangements for Alice Fletcher and Kate Foote to join them. They finally set sail from Port Townsend, Washington, on September 4, 1886.

The *Leo* was to be their home for the next three months as they toured the Aleutian Islands, the Alaska peninsula, and the Shumagin Islands. They headed west for Atka, far out on the Aleutian chain, but winds drove them instead to Kodiak Island. From there they moved slowly westward along the Aleutian Islands.

For the first month the women enjoyed shipboard life and visits to native villages, salmon canneries, and mission outposts. Even Fletcher was struck by the magnificence of nature. "The beauty of this situation passes description," she wrote from Kodiak Island.[14] But then, increasingly, in the "Alaska Notebook" Fletcher kept, the weather became a main concern. After one stormy and rough night Fletcher wrote, "wind came up . . . everybody sick and a sort of musing of loneliness came over me." They not only were late in the season, but also were sailing with few navigational aids, and the fog was often so thick that visibility was near zero. "The Captain feels his way along. Charts are poor. says Dall's work is all we have," she wrote.[15]

On October 9 they were moving at fullforce off the coast of the Sannelek Islands when the fog lifted suddenly to reveal the rocky sides of Uganik Island looming up in front of them. All hands dropped sail and in less than two minutes the captain had managed to turn the ship aside, but it was an unnervingly close call. "Gales, snow, sleet, hail, high seas and danger on every hand," Fletcher wrote the next day. That night there was "a terrible gale and sea," and she "lay awake in dread and suspense thinking of life and death."[16]

Two days later they were at Unalaska, the headquarters of the Alaska Commercial Company. It was a company town, laid out on a narrow neck of land between the harbor and a river running parallel to it. Company officials came to call on them, and so too did the captains of the whalers that were in port.

Dr. Sheldon Jackson and the ship's captain were soon at odds, which added to the general strain. Jackson was a stubborn, uncompromising man who always needed to be right and who insisted on being in charge even when the decisions to be made, such as whether or not it was safe to land, were outside his competence. "I am tired and disgusted with the endless quarreling. The Captain is wonderfully forbearing," Fletcher wrote after weeks of trouble.[17]

Turning east, the *Leo* reached Sitka on November 6, three weeks behind schedule. Sitka, the oldest settlement in Alaska and the seat of federal authority, was a frontier settlement of 160 white residents and 1,000 Indians. The one main street began at the dock and ran through the town, which was dominated by the spires of the Russian Orthodox church. The Presbyterian mission boarding school was the destination of the six teachers (three married couples) who were traveling with them. They all disembarked, and Alice Fletcher and

Kate Foote moved into the mission for a few days. They visited the mission school, and at every opportunity Sheldon Jackson and Alice Fletcher made ringing speeches on the importance of education.

From Sitka a two-day sail took them to Juneau. The newly appointed governor, Alfred Swineford, made this part of the journey with them, and he and Alice Fletcher had "a long talk" on Alaskan affairs.[18] Juneau was a depressing place, Fletcher thought. It was "shut in from all the world, darkened by vice." She recorded in her journal the stories she heard there of the "licentiousness" of the white men. The Indian women refused to become wives, she was told, as that would make them slaves. Instead "they make the white men wait on them, and this quite enrages the white women who must work hard." As always in her ethnographic inquiries, Fletcher was initially most interested in the relations between men and women and the nature of family life. She justified this, when she needed to, as having a bearing on "the woman question" in her own society, but the intensity of her interest surely also hints at questions that grew out of her own experience.

They went on to Wrangell through the Wrangell Narrows, and there the *Leo* struck a rock and then, caught between two rocks, was left high and dry when the tide went out. Jackson slipped away in a dory with the three other men in the party, leaving the two women alone to face whatever peril there might be as the tide rose on a possibly damaged and listing vessel. A day later he returned alone, having in turn left the three Presbyterian clergymen stranded for the night on a rocky point along the shore. Alice Fletcher and Kate Foote were dumbfounded at his callousness. When the three abandoned men finally made their return to the ship, Jackson was in general disfavor and for some days "meeker in demeanor" than before.

On November 25, 1886, Fletcher recorded "a desolate Thanksgiving." She wrote in her journal, "We had a dinner of clam soup, ducks, and vegetables, but it was a gloomy affair. No one was happy and we all felt the ugly influence of quarrels." They were by then heading south, along the inland route through the Bella Bella straits. At Alert Bay on December 10 they went ashore to visit the Kwakiutl Indians. Alice Fletcher and Kate Foote were taken to several Indian homes, and the missionary and his wife talked about potlatching. In potlatching, Fletcher wrote in her journal, "a man strains every nerve to accumulate blankets to give a feast and outdo all his neighbors." His wife, pressured to help him, finally can do nothing but "go to Victoria, become a prostitute, gather the blankets, and return with the spoils to her husband." Fletcher added that women were so scarce that they were bargained for and were forced to change husbands often; as a result they seldom lived beyond the age of twenty-five or thirty.

These notations reveal Fletcher's frazzled state of mind as they neared the end of their journey. Her fact-finding trip to Alaska had degenerated into a hasty recording of missionary stories. She had had little chance to see things for herself. Alice Fletcher knew better than to try to do ethnography—or politics—in this fashion. She had at first insisted that she did not want to make her Alaskan investigations "under missionary obligations or control"[19] and that she needed at least a year in Alaska to come to an understanding of the situation. Why had she settled for less? Why had she embarked on this dangerous journey which was foreordained to failure?

The answer lies less in what she went to see than in what she was fleeing. For six months she had been under public attack for her work for and among the Omahas. But far more troubling and difficult to deal with was the gossip about her relation to Francis La Flesche. In mid-December on shipboard, Fletcher wrote: "The day was quiet, full of work, thought, care, and a loneliness that makes me heavy hearted. Life is so weary. I long to get away. The journey has become wearisome for the pleasure is gone out of it. and I would I were home. Where I am at rest and happy. Fact is I am homesick."[20] There is a rhythm in the phrases at the end of this entry that any diary writer will recognize as a series of added thoughts, each with a new bit of honesty and insight. After writing that the journey "has become wearisome for the pleasure is gone out of it," Fletcher thinks of the future: "and I would I were home." She remembers what that is like, "Where I am at rest and happy," and analyzes her feelings: "Fact is I am homesick."

Two days later they were in Seattle, where she "sent off a note to Francis." From there she and Kate Foote went to Portland where she "wrote telegram to Francis." They then boarded the train for St. Paul. Fletcher's Alaska journey had been like the weeks of camping with the Sioux: physical hardships through unknown and distant places, unfamiliar companions, and more to experience than she could absorb. But there was one significant emotional difference. In 1881 when she was in despair, she wrote that she felt lost and "alone in the world." On the Alaskan journey in 1886 she felt not lost but lonesome, not alone in the world but homesick.

But where was "home?" Fletcher thought about that often in the mid-1880s. One answer she liked to give was the Peabody Museum. In 1884, when the secretary at the Peabody Museum asked Fletcher what she wanted to list as her occupation and address in the museum records, Fletcher responded blithely: "Write what you will. . . . I dig, delve and dive among the Indians, and I am where my work is, but always faithfully attached to the Museum."[21] In the summer of 1886 she wrote Putnam that "the dear old Museum" was "the only place that binds me."[22] She made a quick trip to Cambridge after her return from Alaska to discuss her projects and writing with Putnam. When she returned to Washington she wrote back to him:

> After I left you I felt sort of wicked. I felt as though I had been like a child that gathers up all its broken playthings and pours them at her father's feet for care and mending. I had burdened you with my mss. Dont think that by my simile I am so silly as to think I am very young and you very old, as you would have to be, to be my father. I am only as a child to you in ability. I hope it has not worried you, for if it was naughty to do it, it was also nice. The world is a cold place, and the Museum my only home.[23]

Fletcher expressed her familiar sense of self: homeless and fatherless, an orphan alone in the world, wanting Putnam to be her father, as she readily admitted, although he was a year younger than she. But there is a hint—in the fact that she could so readily admit it—that this was no longer true. F. W. Putnam and the Peabody Museum had for a time been her anchor, but they were no longer.

Alice Fletcher had a new emotional center in her life: Francis La Flesche. She had first come to know Francis well in the spring of 1882 when she went to Washington to lobby for the Omahas. A year later she got money from William Thaw to go to Washington "and work up my notes with Frank."[24] Francis began to keep a diary in 1883 (it was given him, suitably inscribed, by Alice Fletcher), and he kept one, with only occasional lapses, until after her death forty

Francis La Flesche,
formal studio portrait, ca. 1885.
(National Anthropological Archives, Smithsonian Institution)

years later. Alice Fletcher is immediately a near-constant presence in the diary, referred to alternately as "Miss F" or "my friend." The diary reveals that they were together nearly every day, as he went to her hotel to help her write out the Indian ceremonies or to give her lessons in the Omaha language or to accompany her in visits to people in connection with Indian politics.

Francis's mother died on April 24, 1883, "the saddest day I have spent yet," he wrote in his diary. "For the first time I feel that I am motherless. It is hard, hard but as God wills it so it must be."[25] Alice Fletcher too wrote about this event, in a letter to Putnam describing her work on the Omaha peace pipe ceremony. "It is all here but two ritual songs," she wrote. "These I could not get for Frank's mother died a week ago and he will not even hum a song."[26]

Then, with the Omaha allotments, Francis La Flesche worked tirelessly as her interpreter and clerk, and when she fell ill he showed tender concern for her. As she lay ill, perhaps dying, alone at the Winnebago Agency with all social barriers gone, she reached out to grasp what Francis offered—his concern, his interest and attention, his affection. The emotional bonds that were forged between them then were to last for the rest of her life. During her illness Alice Fletcher came to trust Francis La Flesche as she trusted no one else. Francis seemed like a child to her. He was the son of her friend, Joseph La Flesche, was nearly half her age (twenty-six to her forty-five), and was much her inferior in education and "general culture," qualities she valued very highly in herself. In a moment of frustration in the summer of 1884, Fletcher complained to Putnam of Francis's "lack of objective knowledge and general culture."[27] Francis was admiring, almost worshipful, and yet he gave her in full measure what she yearned for: companionship, attention, and affection. He was intelligent, hardworking, devoted, but not subservient. There was a directness about Francis that she liked and a sense of humor that matched her own.

Alice Fletcher also knew that Francis was invaluable for the work she wanted to do. His interest in "the old things" of the Omahas was even greater than her own. Best of all, he was willing to help her. The lifeline that he threw her in her illness by the simple fact of his presence was both emotional and intellectual. Standing there at her bedside, bringing his relatives to sing for her, helping her to carry on the allotment, he became her reason to go on living.

As Alice's feelings for Francis were shaped by her childhood and adolescent experiences (the comfortableness of a mother role, her yearning for male companionship but distrust of sex), so too were Francis La Flesche's feelings for Alice Fletcher shaped by his past. In an autobiographical memoir published in 1900, Francis La Flesche described a childhood in which he and his friends were born in tepees and earth lodges. Their bones were ripened in cradleboards. His earliest memories were of lessons in Indian etiquette: showing respect for elders, using the proper term of relationship when speaking to another, never addressing anyone by his or her personal name. Indian children were forbidden to pass in front of persons sitting in the tent without asking permission and were taught never to stare at visitors, especially strangers. They were trained in grammatical usage. No slip passed uncorrected, and there was no baby talk. Like their elders, the children were fond of companionship and chattered incessantly. From that comfortable, happy childhood Francis went at the age of eight to the Presbyterian Mission Boarding School, which he attended for three years until it closed in 1869. There children were given vocational training and religious instruction, and were taught arithmetic, geography, history, and English. They were treated kindly enough but were forbidden to speak their own language and were instructed to remain silent until they could make their way in English.[28] This abrupt change in Francis's life was only part of the general reorientation then taking place in Joseph La Flesche's family.

Joseph La Flesche as a young man had chosen to follow his French father's profession but to live in the way of his Indian mother. His first wife, Mary Gale, was half white like himself. He then took another wife, Tainne, also called Elizabeth Esau or Lizzie, who was a full-blood Omaha. Later a third wife joined the household. On December 25, 1857, Tainne, the second wife, had her first child, a son.[29] They named him Francis, in honor of Joseph's Ponca brother. Eight years later Tainne had a daughter, Lucy. Around that time Joseph La Flesche quarreled with the local agent, Furnas, and took his wives and children and left the reservation. When they returned the next year Joseph and Mary La Flesche became converts to Christianity. The missionaries talked to Joseph about his three wives, and after a year or two he sent home the youngest one, who had no children. But he was very reluctant to part with Tainne. Not until after she had given birth to a third child, Carey, in 1872, was Tainne quietly removed from the family circle, although still provided for.

As a result, Francis La Flesche grew up feeling doubly marginal. The La Flesche family, in becoming Christian and in sending their children to school, had moved to the fringes of reservation life. Within the family he, his Indian mother, and his younger sister and brother were vulnerable. Their status was increasingly in jeopardy as Joseph turned toward the white world. The family reached its crisis point, the removing of Tainne from the family circle, when Francis was in his late teens and emotionally sensitive to the humiliation of his mother. The removal had a powerful effect on his life. Joseph La Flesche wanted his son, Francis, to learn the new ways of white civilization, and Francis did. But emotionally and defensively he was drawn to the old ways that his mother represented. Out of this complex situation was born not only his life's work, but also his relation to Alice Fletcher. Here was a woman whom his father greatly admired and who was in many ways the epitome of the white, Victorian civilization toward which his father urged him. Yet what she sought to do, to study and record the Omaha way of life, was for Francis a vindication of his Omaha mother.

When Francis La Flesche returned to Washington after the Omaha allotments, he moved into the Temple Hotel, two Washington row houses that had been turned into a residential hotel, where Alice lived. His address was 604 9th Avenue, NW, and hers was 606 9th Avenue, NW.[30] He no longer wrote in his diary of going to visit "Miss F." Instead he spent many evenings enjoying the lobby of the hotel, and his diary became a record of places where "we" went—to a reception at the Dalls', to a breakfast meeting with Miss Quinton and Mr. Painter, to a "very pleasant evening" at Colonel and Mrs. Stevenson's. He "escorted Miss F" to a reception at Mrs. Dawes's and to one at Mrs. Hawley's. Alice Fletcher he referred to alternately as "Miss F" and as "M," the latter standing for "Mother," a term he gradually used exclusively.

Francis's obvious joy in their new relationship and his enjoyment of life in the hotel and their busy social calendar all suggest that he was the one who initiated his change of residence and defined the terms of their relation to one another. He may have tested it in jest, half-joking that since he was motherless, she should be his mother, and when the idea proved acceptable, pursued it more earnestly. This was to be a pattern in their lives. Francis would express his wishes or discontent in jokes or small comments, sometimes so subtly that Alice hardly understood what was going on, but she would be moved to make the changes he desired, and their relationship would move ever nearer to what he wanted it to be.

Francis La Flesche early on seems to have decided that Alice Fletcher was the woman he wanted to spend his life with. Marriage was out of the question, he knew. She was considerably older than he, which mattered in her social circles although not in his, and she was much too proud of her high social standing to marry a young reservation Indian with only a grammar-school education. Nor would she accept him as an equal partner in their scientific work. She was too jealous of her own prerogatives as a scientist and at the same time too insecure in that status to be willing to share it with him. But the relation of mother and son seemed natural to both of them. Adoption of adults was a widespread custom among American Indian groups, usually to replace a deceased kinsperson or to fill a particular role.[31] In suggesting this, Francis had hit on the one close relationship she would accept. She would be the superior as she needed to be, but the relationship would be sufficiently flexible to permit a wide range of feelings and of commitment.

Alice was at first cautious and tentative. Her primary commitment was to her career. She needed Francis but she also needed to keep him somewhat in the background. In the summer of 1884 she had worried about what she herself could present at the AAAS meeting that fall if Francis spoke on the Sacred Pipes. At that time she wrote to Putnam: "Frank wants to write on these pipes, and all things considered it is not best for me to object. Altho. I feel sure he cannot go into the matter as deeply as it ought to be done from lack of objective knowledge and general culture. Still I will help him." Then she added: "Let me tell you my friend, it is a hard thing to work with Indians, to mix with them, to keep patience, pluck and a steady head. If I were to yield to the sentiments of my education I should wish I were dead. I get so weary and lonely, and feel so strange, but that is only when I am weak. I shan't give up."[32]

The strength of this statement is a measure of Fletcher's inner conflict over the course her life was taking. The happiness in her life was an American Indian. She was moving away from the cultural prejudices of her society toward a profound appreciation of Indians and Indian ways of life, but it was not easy. The intensity of her struggle—"I get so weary and lonely, and feel so strange"—reveals how deeply ingrained was her society's contempt for and fear of Indians.

That fall Francis moved into her hotel, and they tested the possibility of life together as mother and son. One of Francis's requests was apparently that she call him Francis, not Frank, and he was Francis to her ever after. Everything went smoothly at first, but within two years Tibbles had spread the campaign of gossip about them. Alice Fletcher fled to Alaska, needing to sort through her feelings and to come to a decision. In the end, after sleepless nights, she made her choice. She headed home to Francis.

PART 3

Professional Career

Twelve

A Year with the Winnebagos

I N January 1887, less than a month after Alice Fletcher's return from Alaska, the commissioner of Indian affairs telephoned her to ask if she would allot land to the Winnebagos under the provisions of the Dawes Act. Fletcher described her reaction to Putnam:

> It seems as though I have been struck I was so surprised. I hesitated.
> I said I have been cruelly attacked by Mr. Tibbles and persons under his influence in Boston and I hardly felt like doing anything to bring on fresh assaults. "I thought," said the Commissioner, "you were above such things. Don't you think the confidence felt in you by the President, the Secretary, and myself ought to count for something?" So I accepted. The pay is excellent, just the same as the men. The work is very hard for the affairs of the tribe are in a terribly mixed condition. It will take all my powers to do the work. "You know more and are better fitted than any one else," said the Commis. . . . I hope I shall succeed for it will silence many tongues if I do.[1]

In her diary Fletcher expressed herself less circumspectly: "A great triumph! . . . given by God."[2]

This show of support from the highest circles gave Fletcher a new surge of energy. She sent Putnam a flurry of letters, describing the collections of pottery and jade and stone implements she had made for him in Alaska and rejoicing in his recent appointment as professor at Harvard. She was full of plans for her future scientific work. She wanted to pressure the government to preserve ancient monuments and to help Putnam raise money for the museum. She even intended to have more social life. "I am determined to make myself seen in society this year," she confided to him.[3]

In February, she visited the Carlisle Indian School and spoke at their Sunday evening service. She gave a sermon against dependence. "Drop all thought that you are different from any one else in the world," she told the assembled young Indians. She urged them to "work, work, . . . work" and to "fight, fight, fight." She went on,

"You must work, you must fight, you must learn to stand,—stand in the midst of contradiction when you know that you are standing rightfully . . . and the right thing is generally the hard thing to do."[4] It was her own credo.

Alice Fletcher left for the Winnebago Reservation, just north of that of the Omahas, late that summer feeling vindicated and confident that she could again triumph over any difficulties. "I may be gone a year. If I live I'll do good Ethnological work both Omaha and Winnebago. *Don't take me off the Museum.* I'll work hard for you," she wrote Putnam.[5] So she settled in for another round of allotments and attempts at scientific work. This time she was alone, without Francis, who stayed at his desk in Washington.

She began her work confident that the battle was already half won. The Winnebagos knew her from her long stay at their agency during her illness. She had attended an all-night ceremony at their Great Mystery Lodge and had helped six Winnebago children go away to school.[6] After her illness, when she had recovered enough to go out again on the prairie with her white tent, several Winnebago men had driven fifteen miles to spend a day at her camp and "have a good time with" her.[7] The Winnebagos liked her pluck and good humor, and she in turn liked their lightheartedness. She thought the Winnebagos were generally eager for allotments and that the major problem would be straightening out legal complications. She was soon to learn that bringing order to the allotment rolls would be the least of her difficulties. The frontier situation was changing so fast that new problems—and new enemies—could appear almost overnight.

The Winnebagos were very different from the Omahas. Fletcher called them "a lighter, gayer people," fond of mechanical work and fairly good day laborers when they hired themselves out to the railroads or nearby farmers. The local agent said they were "wandering and nomadic" and "as different from the Omahas as a Gypsy from a German." A later agent concurred: they were "roving and restless." But, he asked, how could they not be when they had been moved five times within fifty years?[8]

The Winnebagos had made their first treaty with the United States government in 1816, when the tribe was in Wisconsin. Several other treaties followed, and in 1838 they were ordered out of

Wisconsin. The tribe split at that time, some of them, "The Disaffected," simply refusing to go. The more tractable Winnebagos, the "Treaty Abiding Faction," were moved first to Iowa and then to two different locations in Minnesota. They did well on farms there until 1862 when, in the aftermath of the Santee Sioux uprising, they were driven out of Minnesota with most of the other Indians. They were sent to the Crow Creek Reservation in present South Dakota, a barren and alkaline tract of land. There in the harsh winter of 1862 about a third of their number died. The survivors fled down Crow Creek and the Missouri River, and twelve hundred of them sought refuge with the Omahas.[9]

The Omahas shared what they had with the Winnebagos, and their compassion encouraged the agent, Robert Furnas, to think that a solution to the Winnebago problem would be to sell them a portion of the Omaha Reservation. The sale was made by treaties in 1865 and 1874, the Winnebagos purchasing, with money owed to them for the land at Crow Creek, the northern portion of the Omaha Reservation, a strip twenty-four miles long and six to eight miles wide along the western bank of the Missouri River.

The 1865 treaty promised to both the Winnebagos and the Omahas individual holdings of land if they wanted them and by 1872, 420 patents of land had been issued to Winnebago Indians. The work was so casually done, however, that few of the allottees any longer knew (if they had ever known) the location of their allotments or the English names in which they had been issued. Two-thirds of these early patents were found to be fictitious—issued to names no one recognized.

In addition, the pressure for general allotment in 1887 came not from even a minority faction of the Winnebago tribe, as it had with the Omahas, but from outside forces. Congress had adjourned that year without acting on a bill calling for the sale of a portion of the Winnebago Reservation. The executive department therefore decided to allot the land under the provisions of the recently passed Dawes Act, which would have the same effect. The commissioner of Indian affairs, J.D.C. Atkins, was entirely candid about this arrangement,[10] and he lost no time in carrying out the executive order on which it was based, which did not require the consent of the tribe. He selected for the task one of his most thorough and highly regarded special agents, Alice Fletcher, promising her pay of eight dollars per day plus expenses, up from the five dollars per day for her Omaha work.[11] She was in the field and ready to go when the final instructions came through in August.

Fletcher moved in at the Winnebago Agency and began work. A tribal council was called, and more than two hundred of the old land patents were turned in. Fletcher found that many of the markers from the old survey had burned in prairie fires or had been trampled by cattle. She hired Moses Warner, the son of the local agent, to make a new survey of the reservation, and she took a census. The "agency census is useless," she told the commissioner of Indian affairs, "because it was an old custom to lend children and old people to relatives and friends in order to get larger annuities."[12]

There was opposition at first, led by a white man, a Mr. Perry, who was married to a Winnebago woman and represented the Council Fire point of view that the Indians wanted to remain Indian, but it soon subsided. The more recalcitrant Winnebagos were still in Wisconsin. Those in Nebraska had long since learned to live with shifting government policy and to let it affect them as little as possible. They had settled into life as "timber Indians" in camps along the Missouri where they farmed small gardens, hunted game in the woods, and picked up day labor as they could.[13] Allotment for the Winnebagos was not the intense ideological struggle it had been among the Omahas. Alice Fletcher came to them not as a triumphant crusader allied with one faction of the tribe but as a government bureaucrat. She wanted all the same things for the Winnebagos she had wanted for the Omahas—education, law, county government, and stable Christian families—but her emotional commitment was less and sometimes pragmatism won out.

The Winnebagos had had little contact with missionaries. "I am inclined to think that I have quite a rich field here. The Winnebagos are ever so much more pagan than the Omahas," she wrote Putnam shortly after she had started work.[14] But though that might be good for ethnography, it made allotment more difficult. Their family life, Fletcher complained, was a "kaleidoscopic shifting" of husbands, wives, and children. Another problem was the Winnebago kinship system, which seemed to differ somewhat from the patrilineal Omahas. "Women have some queer privileges here I don't yet get at,"

Fletcher admitted early on in the work. Eventually she learned that in former times a Winnebago child belonged to the clan of its mother, not to that of its father, and that the mother's brother, the child's uncle, was the head of the family, not the father. The anthropologist Paul Radin was later to describe the Winnebagos as having patrilineal clans, but he acknowledged that the avuncular emphasis was strong, writing that "internal evidence, myth, tradition, custom, all point to a period in Winnebago history where descent was reckoned in the female line."[15] Alice Fletcher thought that this lack of paternal responsibility contributed to weak family ties. Although she hoped for an eventual "better order," she bowed to expediency and justice and the Winnebagos' wishes, and the allotment act was adjusted so that every Winnebago man, woman, and child received the same amount of land, 80 acres, rather than the male head of the house getting 160 acres of land and his wife none.

On the Great Plains the hot days of August turned abruptly into the coolness of autumn. In October Fletcher wrote to Caroline Dall, "It is full of delights to ride over the prairie these peerless days, not a cloud, the sky clear to the edge of the horizon, the sun golden, the grass and vegetation turning a rich russet, and here and there a bird rising to sing its goodbye, as it turns southward." As she rode back to the agency at night, some of the Winnebagos rode with her and told stories. "It has taken me some time to win the confidence of a few, I think however when one day as we were all riding along and I broke out into an Indian song, I carried away the barriers." She added: "I would like to give you a day of this free life. I like it. I like to feel the wind blow, and to be with these simple folk, who believe what is said, and are not full of all sorts of notions, at least of notions that are a trouble to such as we are."[16]

She was fascinated by the women's native dress and their love of silver ornaments. They wore earrings, bracelets, and rings, sometimes covering every finger. "The silver work of the Winnebagos is quite creditable. They are a deft fingered people quite unlike the slower and bigger Omahas. The latter like farming better than any other employment but the farm they work on must be their own. The Winnebagos would rather work for wages. They like the money return to come quickly and they would rather have no responsibility except to spend it which they easily do."[17]

Fletcher worked steadily on the Winnebago allotments from August 1887 until March 1888 when suddenly she was ordered home to Washington because the appropriation had run out. She had completed about four hundred allotments, many of them out in the western part of the reservation where the best land was. From her Omaha experience she knew that leasing the lands would be a temptation, and she tried from Washington to forestall this by urging that homes be built on the allotments and some acres broken for farming while the Winnebagos were still under the agent's authority.

But time and human nature and the frontier situation were against her. She returned in August 1888, under a new appropriation, to find that cattlemen had overrun the reservation. "My whole being is outraged," she wrote Isabel Barrows in Boston, describing the sharp bargain that the local cattlemen had made with some of the Winnebagos. "How little you blessed people in the orderly East know of the strife where lines are not well drawn. You have your lower class ignorant and vicious but you have them corralled. They are at large out here, and generally great politicians."[18]

The cattlemen, with their low-paying and illegal leases made without the consent of the agent, were to plague the Winnebagos for years. Fletcher believed that if she had not been called home in March it would not have happened. That fall, when members of the cattle combination bought Winnebago votes at the county election with money and whisky, Fletcher scolded the Winnebagos and condemned the vote buying. Then she was accused by local politicians of meddling in politics and electioneering for the Republicans. A congressman from Nebraska wrote the commissioner of Indian affairs: "This woman must be taken away, or her mouth must be closed. She has been carrying on in this way for several years, and it is high time she should be made to keep quiet or be removed to some other place."[19]

Meanwhile the day-to-day work on the reservation was pleasant. Two little buckskin ponies pulled Alice Fletcher's wagon across the prairie, through creeks and sloughs, up and down gullies, forty or fifty miles a day. Prairie chickens flew up as the wagon passed, meadowlarks sang, and occasionally she heard a rattlesnake—these were the only signs of life on the timeless, sun-baked prairie. Out here, she wrote Isabel Barrows, it seems "only man is vile."[20]

But Fletcher knew that trouble lay ahead. She wrote to her Lake Mohonk friends, begging them not to abandon the Indians now that the Dawes Act had been passed. They needed education, law, and help of all kinds. The Severalty Act "is a radical bill far more so than any one dreamed of at the time," she wrote Mrs. Dawes.[21] At the same time a new tougher note began to sound in her reports from the field to reformers. The continuing barrage of hostility from some of the Omahas and the lackadaisical attitude of the Winnebagos increasingly irritated her, as she struggled to help a people who seemingly would not help themselves.

Although Fletcher was acting primarily as a government agent, she managed to write one scientific paper, during her Winnebago work, a report on the transfer of a new religion from the Chippewas in Minnesota to the Sauks and Foxes, and from them to the Winnebagos. She also noted the transfer from the Sauks and Foxes to the Winnebagos of a phonetic alphabet of nineteen symbols. The alphabet was used in nearly all the letters that went back and forth between the Winnebagos in Wisconsin and those in Nebraska.[22]

The paper reveals Alice Fletcher to be as keen-eyed an observer at anthropology meetings as she was in the field. She wanted to work on the most important problems in anthropology instead of cultivating some fringe area. As she learned what the popular topics were (the transfer of culture traits, the rise of new religions, the written languages among the Indians) she kept her eyes open in the field to see what she might contribute.

In August of 1888, when Alice Fletcher returned to the Winnebagos, Francis La Flesche went to the Omaha Reservation as usual for his annual vacation. It was at this time that he persuaded Shudenaci (Yellow Smoke), the keeper of the Omaha Sacred Pole, to give the pole to him and to Fletcher. They would transfer it as an extended loan to the Peabody Museum for safekeeping, as they had done four years before with the Sacred Shell and the Sacred Pack (the contents of the Tent of War). The Sacred Pole, known as the Venerable Man, was made of cottonwood. With an extra piece of wood (the "leg") attached to the bottom and a scalp tied to the top, it was intended to represent a man. It was never placed upright but was kept propped up at a forty-five-degree angle. The Sacred Pole was the symbol of the authority of the tribal chiefs. It also stood for all the

men in the tribe, particularly in the annual ceremony of the anointing of the Sacred Pole, when the men were honored as defenders
and providers. The Omahas always kept the pole with them, for "it
held the tribe together."[23] When they went out on their annual buffalo hunt, the keeper carried the pole on his back. At night it rested
in its own Sacred Tent in a special place in the tribal circle.

But the Omahas no longer went on buffalo hunts, or performed
the sacred ceremony of the anointing of the Sacred Pole, or tended
the Venerable Man with fear and reverence as they once had. Yellow
Smoke was persuaded to give to Francis what had become a weighty
burden and also to reveal to him the accompanying legend of the
pole. He did so, however, with great misgivings. Not until Joseph La
Flesche promised to take upon himself any punishment that might
result from the telling of these sacred things did the old man begin
to speak.

For three days Yellow Smoke sat with Joseph and Francis La
Flesche and Alice Fletcher in a small room in Joseph La Flesche's
house, speaking with eyes cast down, in a low, deliberate voice, and
seemingly to himself alone. As he talked he tapped the wooden floor
with a little stick in a rhythmic drumming, as if invoking unseen
powers. Francis translated what he said, along with Joseph La
Flesche's comments, and Alice wrote as fast as she could, filling three
notebooks. They stored the Venerable Man temporarily at Rosalie
Farley's, and Joseph La Flesche talked of spending the winter with
them in Washington to give them more information. He promised
to have the full ceremony of the anointing of the pole performed the
following summer so that Francis and Alice could photograph it and
transcribe all the songs. But it was not to be. Two days after Francis
left to return to Washington, Joseph La Flesche became ill. He was
dead within two weeks. Alice Fletcher sat up with the family
through the last several days and nights of his illness, but Francis
could not get back to the reservation in time, and his father died
while he was en route.

Alice Fletcher wrote to Putnam of this "great grief and disaster"
in the dramatic tone she used in times of high emotion. "He lies
silent," she wrote, "while the winds rustle thro. his hundred acres
field of ripe corn, and plays about his towering stacks of wheat, all

ready for the thresher. He had over 140 acres under cultivation had builded himself a house and barn, and all this since he left his old farm in the bluffs and came out on the prairie among the white settlers four years ago. He was the last head chief of the tribe, but died the leader of his people still. . . . Civilization and science have lost a friend in Joseph La Flesche." Through her grief a troublesome question surfaced. "How this sore calamity will effect our work I cant tell," Fletcher confided to Putnam. "Poor F. will be heart broken. His Father was his idol, and I fear the boy will hardly have courage to go on, but he is noble, manly and his father's great interest in this work will be a help."[24]

Joseph La Flesche's sudden death gave new credibility among the Omahas to the power of the sacred objects, particularly because this was not the first time he had been so "punished." Thirty years earlier, after he had decided no longer to take part in the ceremony of the anointing of the Sacred Pole, he had stepped on a nail, developed an infection, and had to have his leg amputated. Many in the tribe had said then what they said again after his death: he had been punished for his disregard for the Venerable Man. But Francis was not deterred. Shortly after his father's death he wrote to F. W. Putnam that it would be more difficult to record the full rituals and songs for the Sacred Pole because "the people are yet in the shades of superstition," but he promised that he and Alice would get what they could.[25]

One era of Alice Fletcher's life ended with the death of Joseph La Flesche. Another began a month later when an intrepid New England woman, E. Jane Gay, arrived on the Winnebago Reservation. She came to visit Alice Fletcher and to practice photography. She was to stay at Fletcher's side for the next eighteen years.

E. Jane Gay was fifty-eight years old and Alice Fletcher fifty in the fall of 1888. Born in Nashua, New Hampshire, in 1830, Jane Gay described herself as a Yankee "of Scottish descent." She was the second child in a large family, and she grew up with well-developed mothering skills and pride in her New England virtues of practicality, forthrightness, and shrewd, quick intelligence. She was a boarding student at the Brooklyn Female Academy and later attended Emma Willard's seminary at Troy, New York. Afterward she went south with a friend to teach at the East Tennessee Female Institute in Knoxville, Tennessee, and later in Macon, Georgia. When the Civil War began, she moved to Washington and worked with Dorothea Dix nursing wounded soldiers. Dix required her corps of army nurses to be "plain-looking women," over thirty, dressed in black or brown, and "with no bows, no curls, no jewelry, and no hoop skirts." She managed them like a general on the battlefield and did not herself take a single day off during the entire course of the war.[26] This was a regimen Jane Gay felt at home in. Yet her energy and irrepressible sense of fun soon made her "a lady well-known in the Army and in Washington society."[27]

When the war was over, Jane Gay tried a literary career, publishing in 1868, under the pseudonym Truman Trumbull, a long, humorous narrative poem about the Civil War, *The New Yankee Doodle*. This book-length poem was not based on her personal wartime experiences but was a light verse account of the coming and course of the war (from the northern point of view) of the sort that a political journalist in a playful mood might write. In 1871 she took a job as a clerk in the Dead Letter Office, a Washington institution that had become a tourist attraction, so great was its fame for the lengths to which the government would go to get a letter to the person for whom it was intended. From a balcony, visitors could look down on the clerks below and watch as they checked the letters for cash, swiftly deciphered the spelling of immigrants just learning English, and read into scanty addresses all kinds of additional data. Jane Gay's quick mind and delight in miscellaneous information made her perfect for the job. But after seventeen years in the Dead Letter Office ("seventeen years in the penitentiary," as she later described it), she was ready for something new.[28]

In the mid-1880s Jane Gay and Alice Fletcher chanced to meet at a public lecture in New York City and remembered one another as fellow students at the Brooklyn Female Academy, where Fletcher, "little Alice," had been the youngest child in the school. Jane Gay's sympathies were once again aroused by "little Alice," now a short, plump, modest-appearing woman who walked with a limp but who was a formidable force in the Indian reform movement and was increasingly respected as a scientist. Jane Gay's name begins to appear in Alice Fletcher's diary in the summer of 1888. "Ill in bed but gaining ... Miss Gay like a mother" and "Miss Gay kindness itself," Fletcher wrote on August 4 and 5.[29] By the time Alice Fletcher left to return to the Winnebagos, she and Jane Gay had decided that Jane should accompany Alice on her future field expeditions as housekeeper and photographer.

That Jane Gay should take up photography was probably Alice Fletcher's idea. For several years she had been wishing that she had a photographer with her in the field. She had hired a photographer to take pictures of the Omahas in 1885 and a year later was thinking about buying some photographic apparatus herself.[30] But she had her hands full. If Jane Gay would learn photography, she could make a contribution in her own right to their ethnographic work.

Jane Gay seized the idea. She went immediately to learn photography from her brother, Ziba Gay, a newspaperman in Chelmsford, Massachusetts. A special darkroom was set up for her. Her niece, then six years old, later remembered that the whole household became involved in the photography lessons. Alice Fletcher came to visit, her "voice and shining eyes" enchanting them, as she sat on a low settee and told stories about her life among the Plains Indians.[31] When Jane Gay decided that she had mastered at least the rudiments of her new trade, she followed Alice Fletcher out to Nebraska.

A few of Jane Gay's photos on the Winnebago Reservation are stunning, but most—close-ups of skin tanning, arrow making, and the making of a Winnebago mat house—have only technical interest. While she struggled to figure out what ethnographic photography might be, Alice Fletcher worked "day and night" trying "to get thro. here," as she wrote to Putnam.[32] In December Fletcher returned to Washington with only the bookwork still to do.

Fletcher worked hard on the Winnebago family registry, for it was the point at which the white and Indian systems of kinship and inheritance had to be brought together. In Indian families the father and the mother belong to different clans, and the children to either one or the other but not to both. They take their identity from one side of the family, inherit from that same side, and consider only the members of that clan as their relatives. But allotment and citizenship put the Indians under the laws of inheritance used in county and state courts, in which a child was heir equally to both parents. The Indians did not like to speak directly the names of their relatives, often instead using elaborate circumlocutions, and they did not understand Fletcher's insistence that she be told not only the aunts, uncles, and grandparents on one side of the family but also those on the other. They could hardly think in those terms. Only after much cross-checking did Alice Fletcher have a family registry she was satisfied with, and that she carefully deposited with the agent, to be used in future litigation. Her registry included parents, lineal and collateral descent, and both Indian and English names. The commissioner of Indian affairs was so impressed by her work that he sent several other allotment agents to her for training, but they lost interest when they realized that what she had done was not mandatory.[33] Not until fifteen years later, when the court cases over land inheritance began to pile up, was it realized how exceptional her work had been. In 1902, Merrill E. Gates, the secretary of the watchdog Board of Indian Commissioners, complained of the lack of family records on most reservations, excepting, he said, "the work done by Miss Alice Fletcher, perhaps the best work in allotting Indians ever done."[34] Part of the reason, of course, was that the Winnebagos were so easygoing—and so resigned to government interference—that although uninterested in allotment, they cooperated with her.

Fletcher turned with pride and relief back to her ethnographic studies. She had a crayon portrait made of herself and sent to the Peabody Museum. "Let me explain the coming of my portrait," she wrote to Putnam sheepishly. "I had it taken for the Museum hoping one day to do something that might make it proper that I should be recalled again after I am dead. I did not mean it to go to you until after my death, but it had to go. So if you will store it away in a corner and then if I fail to accomplish anything burn it I shall be obliged."[35]

Locally—in Washington—she was already becoming famous. Her government report on Indian education and civilization was just out and much in demand. She had been invited to become a member of the exclusive Literary Society, the closest thing Washington had to a literary salon. But this pleasant interlude of work and social life in Washington ended suddenly in May 1889 when the commis-

sioner of Indian affairs ordered her to Idaho to make land allotments
to the Nez Perces. Fletcher would soon be describing the Nez Perce
allotments as "the worst struggle of my life."[36]

Thirteen

Among the Nez Perces

ALICE Fletcher's new assignment took her into a situation many
orders of magnitude more difficult than any she had experienced
before. She went from the rolling prairie of eastern Nebraska to
the rugged high plateau country of northern central Idaho between
the Rocky Mountains and the Cascade Range. The reservation assigned to the Nez Perces by treaty in 1863 consisted of 750 thousand
acres of high grasslands, through which the Clearwater River and its
tributaries had cut deep, narrow valleys. In Nebraska Fletcher had
moved back and forth across small creeks and found the muddy
banks a hazard. In Idaho she and the surveying party had to cross
precipitous canyons, sometimes half a mile deep, with sides so steep
they often walked to save the horses. In Nebraska Fletcher had
grown accustomed to hot summers and cold winters. In Idaho she
was to find that the temperature could change as much as sixty
degrees within an hour or two.

No one knew how many Nez Perces (pronounced today by the
people and their neighbors *nezz purses*) there were. In 1886 the new
agent wanted to make a census, but having no appropriation for that
purpose, he worked out a method of his own. He provided a beef
for a feast, counted the eight hundred Nez Perces at the feast, and
estimated that they were probably two-thirds of the people living on
the reservation.[1] His estimate was too low by about 30 percent. The
commissioner of Indian affairs had been told that the land was agricultural and had designated the Nez Perces as one of the twenty-five

tribes considered "generally favorable" to allotment.[2] With this much information Alice Fletcher and Jane Gay left for Idaho in the spring of 1889. Fletcher was to find when she got to the reservation that the government maps gave no notion of the actual nature of the terrain and that, apart from one man, the Nez Perces had never heard of allotment. When they did hear about it, the opposition was "almost unanimous."[3]

Jane Gay was accompanying Alice Fletcher unofficially without pay as Alice's companion and housekeeper. On the side she would do photography. She took with her a glass-plate camera and tripod, and during her years in Idaho she also purchased one of the new Kodak box cameras invented in 1888. Francis La Flesche stayed at his job in Washington. As with the Winnebagos, he could not go with Fletcher as clerk and interpreter because he did not know the language. Fletcher would hire an interpreter, an English-speaking Nez Perce, when she got to Idaho.

The two women took the train from Chicago to Uniontown, Idaho. Uniontown, one dirt street and several saloons, was temporarily the end of the line. From there it was a drive of two hours behind a team of four horses to the "queer little sunburnt town" of Lewiston, Idaho, the jumping-off point for the reservation. Lewiston lay two thousand feet below the plateau, at the junction of the Snake and Clearwater rivers. The landing had become a supply depot for miners in 1861 and almost overnight had grown to a population of five thousand. The landlady at their hotel assured Alice and Jane that Idaho was the garden spot of the earth, with a fair climate and the best soil in the world, but even as they were listening they choked on clouds of alkaline dust that blew everywhere, sifting into their rooms and their clothing. She admitted that sometimes it did not rain for six months.[4]

The best road to the reservation proceeded out of Lewiston in a slow, circuitous ascent. Next followed ten miles of fairly level dirt trail, after which the road plunged down another canyon to the valley of Lapwai Creek. Fletcher found the agency at Lapwai, the administrative center of the reservation, in turmoil. Five people had served as agent in the previous twelve months, and a former agent who was intensely disliked by the Nez Perces was campaigning to regain his position. No one had bothered to tell the Nez Perces that an allotting agent was coming. Nor, apart from a few Indian police-men who hung around the agency, did there even seem to be any Nez Perces around. On Sunday mornings a small congregation gath-ered at the little Lapwai church, but as soon as the benediction was pronounced, they mounted their ponies and disappeared over the hills. For a month Fletcher waited day after day, in mounting frus-tration. When she and Jane Gay made reconnaissances out from the agency they found nothing but dried-up gardens and empty cabins with two sticks propped up against the door to indicate that the owner was away. No one had told them that the Nez Perces usually moved out in the summer to hunt and gather root crops for the winter, returning to their villages in the late fall. Finally an Indian policeman on a pony was sent out to call the Nez Perces to meet in a council, and a small roomful of them came. They sat on wooden benches or on the floor or leaned against the wall and waited in silence to learn what was wanted of them.

Alice Fletcher was introduced by the agent, and she rose to ex-plain the provisions of the Dawes Severalty Act: each male head of the family was to have 160 acres of land; each child over eighteen, 80 acres; each child under eighteen, 40 acres. Allotments rated as grazing land rather than agricultural would be doubled in size. The rest of the land on the reservation would remain exactly as it was, unless of course the Nez Perces wanted to sell it. Jane Gay, at the back of the room, watched her friend stammer and blush as she added this last provision, for it made only too clear the intent of the program. When Alice Fletcher finished speaking, there was a long silence in the room. Finally one old man rose with great dignity and asked through the interpreter: "How is it that we have not been consulted about this matter? Who made this law?" Another said: "Our people are scattered. We must come together and decide whether we will have this law."[5] Fletcher jumped up quickly to ex-plain that there was nothing for them to decide. They had no choice. It was the law, and the law had to be obeyed. The agent hastily adjourned the meeting, and everyone filed out.

This council and many subsequent events on the Nez Perce Res-ervation might well have shaken Fletcher's resolve, but they did not. When the hostility at Lapwai did not abate—the entire corps of Indian officials at Lapwai, including the police, the judges, and the

First council to discuss allotment at
First Presbyterian Church, Kamiah, on
the Nez Perce Reservation, Idaho. Alice
Fletcher at left. Photo by E. Jane Gay,
1889. (Idaho Historical Society)

Allotting land to the Nez Perces. Alice
Fletcher at left, standing with William
Caldwell and Abraham Brooks (with
cane). Edson Briggs holds surveying
rod. E. Jane Gay, ca. 1890. (Idaho
Historical Society)

traditional headmen, did everything they could to stop her work, including threatening her interpreter, forbidding anyone to talk to her, and sending a medicine man "to look me down"[6]—she and Jane Gay set off for Kamiah, sixty-five miles to the east, where the largest group of "progressive" (that is, Christian) Nez Perces had their homes. There, late that summer, the first of the Nez Perces took their allotments.

To Putnam, Fletcher expressed her sorrow at having suddenly to leave her ethnographic work in order to earn a living. "I had to go, or lose any chance to boil my pot," she wrote him. "It was a very, very hard thing to do. It was to give up what I cared most for. I want to honor your friendship and kindness to me, and here I am down in the canons of the Clearwater, and the rocky steeps that shut me in from all the world, seem like the walls of fate about me. Don't give me up. I will get the work done and before long, I trust." She described her situation, "I am as usual between two, the Indians on one hand, and the greed of the whites on the other." But she vowed, "I will save the people, give them a chance, and I trust open the way for some to wider fields of usefulness."[7]

Unknown to Alice Fletcher, Kamiah was the one vulnerable spot in the solid wall of opposition she faced. The Nez Perces at Kamiah had long taken pride in their contacts with white people, a tradition dating back more than eighty years to the visit of Lewis and Clark. Meriwether Lewis reported that they were "placid and gentle" and "the most hospitable, honest, and sincere people that we have met with in our voyage."[8] The Kamiah Nez Perces in turn were impressed with the white men's medicines and instruments. Lewis and Clark's visit came to be an event of almost legendary importance for the Kamiah Nez Perces—Alice Fletcher collected for the Peabody Museum the hat of "an old woman who remembers Lewis and Clark"—and it was the start of a tradition at Kamiah of special rapport with white people.

Most Nez Perces, however, lived in neither Kamiah nor Lapwai, but in a large area extending one hundred miles to the south and west of the Lapwai-Kamiah axis, along the Snake, Salmon, and Wallowa rivers. Scattered in as many as 130 villages, each with its own headman, the Nez Perces had no central government. Several villages on a stream might form themselves into a band, with a council that included representatives from each village, but that was the highest permanent political unit. This loose structure was well suited to their hunter-gatherer way of life: fishing for salmon in the spring and moving out in the summer and fall to gather roots and berries on the plateaus and to hunt game in the rugged Bitterroot Mountains to the east. Occasionally, for war parties or hunting, the Nez Perces formed themselves into larger political units, but these were always only temporary.

The first treaty between the Nez Perces and the United States, signed in 1855, defined the boundaries of the reservation, an area of some five thousand square miles. Then gold was discovered in the area, and ten thousand miners poured into Nez Perce country. The town of Lewiston was plotted illegally inside the borders of the reservation. In 1863 a new treaty was proposed, whereby the Nez Perces were to give up a large portion of their reservation, including much of the land to the south along the Snake, Salmon, and Wallowa rivers. The tribe split into pro- and anti-treaty factions, with the United States claiming that because a few of the Nez Perces had signed the treaty, all were bound by it.

As white settlers continued to move into the Wallowa Valley, conflicts with the Nez Perces became increasingly frequent and bitter. In the spring of 1877, a band of young Nez Perces attacked a white settlement. In the resulting panic, the United States Cavalry was mobilized and began to attack, and the anti-treaty faction fled into the mountains. For four months General Howard pursued Chief Joseph, his brother Ollokut, the war chief Looking Glass, and their band. The Indians were surrounded and stopped just a few miles short of their goal of the Canadian border. Four hundred and thirty-one defeated Nez Perces were sent to Indian Territory. The rest settled on their diminished reservation.

Twelve years after the Nez Perce War, Alice Fletcher arrived in Idaho. Only at Kamiah could she get any hearing at all. Everywhere else on the reservation she was regarded as yet another sign of the federal government's intent to oppress them. A young Nez Perce activist, James Reuben, was starting for Washington to protest the reappointment of the former agent. He was given a second assignment: to find out if what Alice Fletcher said was true. Meanwhile the Nez Perces would wait and do nothing.

Although the Nez Perces obviously did not want what she had to offer, Fletcher was convinced that she was there to save them, as she wrote to Putnam, from "the greed of the whites." This greed made itself felt immediately. Several delegations of local stockmen called on Fletcher at Lapwai and tried to intimidate her, insisting on their rights to free grazing on the reservation.[9] Fletcher knew that from ten to twenty thousand head of cattle belonging to white men were illegally grazing on the reservation, trampling the Indians' gardens and competing with their stock for the none-too-abundant grass. Her tack with the stockmen was to pretend to be naive, to imply that they too wanted what was best for the Indians. She read her government instructions to them and assured them she would carry out her sworn duty, which was to place the Indians on the best land where they could most rapidly become self-supporting and would not be a burden on the surrounding communities. As the non-plussed men in one group mounted their horses to ride off, one of them grumbled: "Why in thunder did the Government send a woman to do this work? We could have got a holt on a man."[10]

Other settlers pressured her to declare the land agricultural. Then the Indians would receive less, and the settlers' claims would be worth more. The entire border of the reservation was surrounded by white people, occupying every forty-acre lot, even land on the tops of mountains, so that they could jump on the reservation when it was opened.[11] Some of the would-be homesteaders had built houses inside disputed boundaries, while squatters moved boldly into the interior. Fletcher explained to Putnam, "as nearly all the men here abouts are more or less embarrassed financially, they are very anxious to get new settlers here to buy them out with solid cash and to "Open up the country."[12] In order not to seem prejudiced in favor of the Indians, Fletcher was careful in grading the land. She herself went to look at nearly every forty-acre piece to decide how much should be rated as agricultural and how much as grazing land. "I find myself followed, by either self-appointed or in some other way commissioned persons, who propose 'to look after the interests of the settlers,'" she reported to the commissioner of Indian affairs.[13]

There was considerable talk about the fact that the allotting agent was a woman, but this aroused more awe than hostility. A local settler visiting her in camp one day observed, "It is as good as a circus to see a woman boss."[14] The Presbyterian missionary, Kate McBeth, was skeptical and kept her distance, but she was soon won over. "It is said she receives a Congressman's salary—she earns it. She meets the old Medicine Men in Councils who have tried to kill her with a look. She knows no fear and so fully understands the Indian character. She cannot be taken by surprise and withal she is very lovable," McBeth wrote a friend.[15] Fletcher was shrewd enough to use people's initial assumption that she was naive or malleable, and she did not discourage their tendency to think that as a woman she was above politics and had greater moral purity and goodness than the men.

In the late summer of 1889, as the land around Kamiah was parceled out, Alice Fletcher and Jane Gay left their cabin there and moved with a tent to the uplands, where they camped for several weeks. They abandoned the wagon, which was useless on the steep canyons, and took everything—all the office materials, their tent, bedding, food, and forage for the horses—on packhorses. The drought and overgrazing were so severe on the reservation that Fletcher had to buy hay and carry with them every pound of food the horses would eat for the next three months.

To one close friend, Isabel Barrows, Alice Fletcher that summer admitted what she would admit to scarcely anyone else: that the scheme in which she was embroiled could not work. Isabel Barrows, an opthalmologist, was, like Alice Fletcher, a scientist and a reformer. The two women had met at the meeting in Omaha in 1887, recognized one another as kindred spirits, and immediately became close friends.[16] They wrote each other the intimate, affectionate letters that were so often exchanged between close women friends in the nineteenth century. "Oh, but I was glad to receive your dear letter. It was like a caress and so very welcome," Alice wrote Isabel on one occasion.[17] But they could also level with one another, and it was to practical and thoughtful Isabel that Alice turned in times of sorest need.

"This is not agricultural land," Alice Fletcher wrote Isabel Barrows from Idaho in September 1889. The only good farm land was at the bottom of canyons, and at high water everything was likely to be swept away. She watched the white ranchers in the area to see how they managed, and she found that they fenced in and grew what they could on their own land and turned their stock loose to graze free on the reservation. On this basis they became moderately prosperous, but it took a lot of free land to live in this fashion. Fletcher thought that eight hundred acres of grazing land for a single family was none too much, for at ten acres a head that was only enough for eighty cattle. She confessed to Isabel Barrows: "This is my first experience in allotting mixed land, grazing and agricultural and I see plainly that the amount given an Indian for grazing is too small for him to make a living off of, 320 acres for himself and wife, about 30 head of stock and perhaps a small garden of a few acres. Without an outlet for pasture, the white man would fare badly on such contracted spaces."[18]

Alice Fletcher shared these secret doubts with the commissioner of Indian affairs, but not with anyone else, not with the advisory Board of Indian Commissioners, not with other Lake Mohonk reformers, and not, particularly not, with Jane Gay there in the field. Confronted with hostility on every side, from the government agent, from the Nez Perces, from the local settlers who thought she was giving the Nez Perces too much land, Fletcher feared that if she wavered in the slightest, or showed any doubt or indecision, the entire program on which they had ventured might collapse, for it hung by the single thread of her will and determination, although ultimately of course all the power of the federal government was behind her. Fletcher knew she could not get the Allotment Act altered to give the Nez Perces more land. That was politically impossible. It would undercut in philosophical and practical terms all the homestead size allotments for Indians already parceled out. To admit defeat or to waver here would be to admit that Tibbles and other critics of her Omaha work had been right. It would be, Fletcher felt, to betray all those Omahas and Winnebagos and now even a few Nez Perces who had put their trust in her. That she would not do. She saw nothing to do but push ahead, to carry out the law. She could insist on grading most of the land as grazing land, rather than agricultural, but that was the best she could do.

The full allotting party included the surveyor, Edson Briggs, a native Vermonter; Briggs's wife; the Nez Perce interpreter, James Stuart; Stuart's wife; and an ever-changing gang of four Nez Perce chainmen who ran out the boundary lines. But often Briggs and Stuart and the chainmen would be working at a distance away from Fletcher's camp, and the two women had to cope alone with wild horses, wild pigs, bears, mud, snow, and dense smoke from forest fires raging all around them. Once, they let their food supplies dwindle to nothing as they waited day after day for a party of Nez Perces who had agreed to meet them, only to learn later that the would-be allottees had decided instead to go on a three-month hunt in the mountains for their winter food supply. At the end of the summer Fletcher calculated that she had ridden forty miles for each allotment. She had managed to do 169 out of a possible 2,000. At that rate it would take ten to twelve years to finish. In the midst of her calculations an urgent request came from Washington wanting to know the exact number of Indians allotted each week. She worked on into mid-November. Then she and Jane Gay raced a snowstorm back to Lapwai, found the sentiment against allotment as strong there as ever, and returned to Washington for the winter.

In January, Alice Fletcher, described as "fresh from the field," appeared before the Board of Indian Commissioners at their annual meeting in Washington. She put the situation in Idaho in the best possible light. "If I believe in anything for the Indians, I believe in allotment," she told them. She spoke of her family registry system and of how she was grouping family members together on the reservation. She had placed James Stuart, her interpreter, near the railroad. "I always help the progressive Indians first," she told the commissioners. "It helps to break the dead monotony of the tribe." Senator Dawes and some of the commissioners were worrying about those Indians, perhaps half, who were not ready for allotment, but Alice Fletcher insisted that most of "hers" were. She speculated: "Among the Omahas, Winnebagos, and the Nez Perces perhaps one third will make successful farmers, another third will make a scramble, half of the last third will not do much, and the other third will be a miserable worthless lot. But I do not believe in keeping all the others back for this fraction. I have always had to coerce a few, and I rather enjoy it." To this General Clinton Fisk, the chairman of the Board of Indian Commissioners, replied, "Most women do."[19]

En route again to Idaho in April 1890, Alice Fletcher and Jane Gay stopped at the Omaha Reservation, where Fletcher was to allot land to the Omaha children born since 1884. There she was brought up short by an unexpected rebuff from the people she still considered her "children." The Omahas had ten thousand dollars due them in interest from the land sales, and Fletcher made plans for spending it. She wanted the Omahas to buy wagons and harnesses and building materials for more small frame houses, and she and Jane Gay had even stopped in Chicago to get price estimates. But the Omahas, when the whole matter was presented to them, objected. It was their money, they said, and they would decide how to spend it. They chose a per capita distribution as the only fair way and proceeded to carry it out. Fletcher subsided, "a disconsolate puzzled hen," in Jane Gay's words,[20] slightly disgruntled at having had her plans so summarily rejected.

One of their visitors in Idaho their second summer there was Chief Joseph, down from the Colville Reservation in Washington, where he had been allowed to move in 1884. Chief Joseph was willing to take an allotment, but he refused to take it on the reservation. He wanted land in the Wallowa Valley, from which he had been driven, or he would have none at all. He came to talk to Alice Fletcher several times, always through an interpreter, for his English was halting and her Nez Perce nonexistent, and they had long discussions. Fletcher thought him "a singular mixture of conversion to new ideas and non-concession." Joseph believed in obedience to law and in orderly conduct and industry, all of which Fletcher heartily approved of, but he insisted that a system of chieftainships was better than democratic equality and that polygamy was better than the white way. He was, Fletcher thought, "a most interesting blending of the old and the new."[21]

Jane Gay was impressed by him. "It was good to see an unsubjugated Indian," she wrote.[22] She took his picture with Alice Fletcher and the interpreter, James Stuart, and they sent a copy to Mrs. Dawes to show around in Washington. Fletcher explained to Mrs. Dawes that James Stuart had dropped to his knees simply to break the visual line, not out of reverence, as Jane Gay later liked to hint.

The relation between these two strong women—Alice Fletcher and Jane Gay—is one of the intriguing undercurrents through the four years of their arduous work in Idaho. Jane Gay was rather in awe of Alice Fletcher, of her work and national reputation as a scientist and humanitarian. She and other friends sometimes referred

Chief Joseph with James Stuart and
Alice Fletcher, Nez Perce Reservation,
Idaho. E. Jane Gay, 1890. (Idaho
Historical Society)

Monday morning in Camp McBeth,
Nez Perce Reservation, Idaho, 1889.
Alice Fletcher, Jane Gay, and James
Stuart. (Idaho Historical Society)

jocularly to Fletcher as "Her Majesty," hinting at her physical resemblance to Queen Victoria (short, plump, and pulled-back hair), her serene imperturbability, and the genuine respect they felt for her. Jane Gay had offered her services to Alice Fletcher sensing that she could be a help to her friend and eager to share in the adventure. Fletcher, knowing the loneliness and hardships of work in the field, was glad to accept.

But Jane Gay herself was something of a formidable figure. She was observant, witty, and sharp-tongued, with an array of practical talents. A niece later described her as the "famous cook and carpenter" who "could do everything better than anybody."[23] One of the things they soon found that she could do better than Alice Fletcher was write popular accounts of their experiences. Fletcher had for several years been sending short articles to the Carlisle Indian School for their newspaper, the *Morning Star*, later the *Red Man*. She wrote about John Eliot, who founded an Indian town at Natick, Massachusetts, in 1652, and about the Dawes Act, and she also sent accounts of her experiences in Alaska and on the Winnebago Reservation. Fletcher wrote one letter from Idaho, but then the pressure of the work overwhelmed her, and Jane Gay began writing to Captain Pratt at Carlisle in her stead.

Alice Fletcher's letters had been earnest and rather preachy. Jane Gay's were wry and funny, as she described her weekly expeditions to get food, the activities of Gooey, their temporary Chinese cook, and their search for Indians on a seemingly deserted reservation. Captain Pratt loved her first letter. He subtitled it "A Rich and Racy View of a Trying Situation,"[24] and he asked for more. Soon, ever-increasing amounts of space in the *Red Man* were given to letters "from the companion of Miss Fletcher." Through 1889 and 1890 Jane Gay kept him well supplied, and praise for the letters reached Idaho. Caroline Morgan, the wife of the newly appointed commissioner of Indian affairs, wrote Jane Gay: "I read every word you write for the Red Man. I wish you would write ten times as much. With such a pen you ought to accomplish a great deal."[25]

Fletcher bore this with good grace, but she could not have enjoyed being upstaged even when she herself was the heroine of the story being told. Writing never came easily to her. She labored over it mightily, but it never betrayed any of the sense of humor that so endeared her to her friends. Admirers often told her there was power in her voice, but no one had ever told her there was power in her pen. Jane Gay would later say ruefully to Putnam about Fletcher, "I wish writing were as easy to her as talking."[26]

Another problem with Jane Gay's letters was the potential critical edge in her humorous accounts of their work. Humor is risky. With only a slight change of tone, the whole enterprise could have been made to seem the greatest folly. As it was, Jane Gay could not help noting how little choice the Nez Perces had in what was being offered them, or help wondering if "civilization" would be an improvement, especially for the Nez Perce women. Jane Gay had little sympathy for the woman's suffrage movement, but she was a strongly independent woman, and she was impressed by the freedom of Indian women. When she and Alice hired an Indian man for any task, his wife was included in the bargain, she wrote, unless the latter chose not to go, in which case wild horses could not drag her. Indian women had their own tents and ponies and other property. They went where they pleased, whereas the wives of white farmers were tied down on their isolated farms and worn down by loneliness, hard work, and discouragement at the hopelessness of their situation. "This country is good enough for cattle and men, but it is death on women and horses," Briggs, the surveyor told Jane Gay. She concluded, "Civilization has been built up largely upon the altruism of the woman, at the cost of her independency; and is still an expensive luxury to her."[27]

When the Nez Perces at Kamiah gathered at the Presbyterian Church to discuss allotment, Jane Gay noted, "They were all men, the women staying at home in an exemplary manner, just like civilized women when any matter particularly affecting their interests is being discussed by the men."[28] Nor could she help noting the irony of their situation: two women had crossed the country to bring to the Nez Perces the benefits of civilization and citizenship, including the right to vote, a right the women themselves did not have. These were sentiments that Fletcher would once have been sympathetic with, before she abandoned "the woman question" in favor of "the Indian question." Now she had no time for them.

So subtly that she herself probably never recognized what she was doing, Alice Fletcher protected herself from her potential critic and rival in two ways: by keeping their roles sharply delineated and by constructing a front of imperturbable professional confidence. Once or twice, in times of greatest discouragement, Fletcher withdrew into herself and sat silently, unresponsive to Jane Gay's attempts to distract her. But she gave no other sign of despair or doubt about what she was doing. In 1890, Jane Gay wrote:

Behold Her Majesty, triumphant over the hardships of life, seated at the board table, like a queen on her throne, pen in hand, writing her decrees. . . . There she sits in aggravating persistency, listening to the stupid, advising the vicious, stiffening up the weak, forgetting to rest, studying how to help those who won't (she says can't) help themselves; unmoved under abuse, steadfast under calumny.

It is enough to drive a looker-on to madness. There is not an Indian with hair so long and blanket so dirty but can claim her attention, be she ever so faint with hunger and the Cook ever so impatient.[29]

In her letters to Captain Pratt, Jane Gay spoke of herself in the third person, alternately as "she," the Cook, and as "he," the Photographer. The Cook was sensible and practical, the Photographer detached and reflective, in keeping with the nature of the two tasks. But the two persona were also a way for Jane Gay to express the two sides of her character and perhaps, too, a way for her to cope with her status within the allotting party. She was willing to play the supportive "female" role as long as she also had a professional "male" role. Photography was a near-perfect choice. It was a prestigious new technical skill, carrying with it the aura both of science and of art. The bulky equipment—a large camera on a tripod, the heavy glass plates, the darkroom supplies—was at least as cumbersome and important-looking to carry around as Alice Fletcher's land plats and notebooks. A darkroom was as necessary as an office. Willing subjects for Jane Gay's camera could be ordered around just as would-be allottees were, for her camera lacked a shutter and was not fast enough to stop any action. Her subjects had to pose for at least two seconds, as she made an exposure by removing and then replacing the lens cap. They sometimes posed even longer while she timed an exposure with a watch. Her choice of what and when to photograph was a way of bestowing or withholding approval.

During the first two years in Idaho, Jane Gay ran the household, took photographs, wrote letters to Captain Pratt, and enjoyed herself immensely. Everything was new and an adventure. She loved camping and the outdoor life—rising with the sun, making coffee and oatmeal over an open fire, and then "the pulls up and down the canons, and the sunburns, the fierce appetites." She hung a ham and bags of sugar and flour in the trees to keep them out of the reach of wolves. They ate on a board with tin cups and plates and sat on an upturned horse bucket or a bag of oats or the camera box. Their sofa was a fur robe laid over a stack of hay. At night they piled up blankets on the camp cots, for it was often bitterly cold. Then there would be a stillness, broken only by distant sounds that they soon learned to identify: a coyote's howl or the quick click of an approaching pony's feet as an Indian messenger made the rounds to relay the news of a death. When they were not camping, they lived in a cabin at Kamiah, the little settlement in the peaceful valley of the Clearwater River far from the agency and its turmoil. There the sounds Jane Gay learned to listen for were the tramping of cattle on the hills, the making of holes in the walls of their cabin by woodpeckers, the almost noiseless coming and going of the moccasined Indians, and through it all the steady rushing of the Clearwater River.

But tensions began to grow. Jane Gay and Alice Fletcher became aware in mid-summer of 1890 that a reservation-wide campaign was underway to punish Robert Williams, the native pastor at Kamiah who with his family had been the first to take allotments. The church building at Kamiah needed repair, and Alice Fletcher had gotten money for this from Mary Thaw in Pittsburgh. The paint, rough wood, shingles, glass, and putty arrived but remained piled up in the churchyard, for no one would help with the work. This, along with rumors of other punishments that Williams was stoically enduring, aroused Jane Gay's ire. Restoring Robert Williams's church building became for her a symbol that they would accomplish on the reservation what they set out to do. She herself began to paint and varnish. She persuaded the surveyor and the interpreter to work on the church before and after official working hours. Some of the chainmen pounded a few nails, and eventually other Nez Perces, including a few Roman Catholics, came over to help scrape, sand, paint, and put new glass in the windows. In the end Jane Gay proudly took photographs of the restored Presbyterian edifice. But the majority of Kamiah Presbyterians had continued to refuse to help. That fall the church membership split, and a new Kamiah Second Presbyterian Church was built across the river.

Jane Gay thought the restoration of the church a great success, but for the cause of allotment it was in fact a serious error. She had helped to split the Kamiah Presbyterians, a split that survives to this day.[30] She had made Alice Fletcher vulnerable to the charge of misusing men on the government payroll. She had turned the rival pastor at Kamiah, Archie Lawyer, who might have become a powerful friend, into a vociferous opponent of allotment. The church-restoring episode was only a hint of what was to come.

Fourteen

"My honor is involved in getting this done"

FLUSHED with her relative success in the second summer (almost five hundred allotments), Alice Fletcher returned to Idaho in the spring of 1891 determined to finish the work that year. She and Jane Gay settled this time at Lapwai, where the agency, two schools, the best land, and a majority of the Nez Perces were. It was hostile territory, but they could no longer avoid it.

Jane Gay walked into trouble almost immediately at Lapwai, on the Fourth of July. Holidays, like flags, are the emblems of a society, and nowhere do they take on greater significance than in a contested zone between two cultures. The Nez Perce Reservation, like nearly every other Indian reservation in the late 1880s, was a contested zone, no longer a military but a psychological battleground, as the legislators of the Dawes Act and the agents of white "civilization" began to exert their full force. The Roman Catholic priests brought in the bishop with his purple vestments for the Corpus Christi Day procession. The Presbyterian missionaries had Thanksgiving dinner with an indigenous turkey and imported fixings: soup, plum pudding, and a pumpkin, sent by well-wishers in the East. The commissioner of Indian affairs, alerted by Alice Fletcher to the important symbolism of holidays, tried to bring these, too, under his control. He sent out special instructions on how the major American holidays—New Year's Day, Franchise Day (February 8), Washington's Birthday, Decoration Day, the Fourth of July, Thanksgiving, Christmas, and Arbor Day—were to be celebrated in the schools on Indian reservations to help pupils understand their significance.[1] The results were sometimes bizarrely inappropriate. On Decoration Day in 1892 on the Nez Perce Reservation, the principal at the government school marched the Nez Perce children in a parade to place wreaths on the graves of the soldiers who had fought Nez Perces in the War of 1877. The children participated with such innocent goodwill that at least two observers were moved to tears.[2] But the biggest holiday of the year in central Idaho, for it happened to fall in the midst of a traditional Nez Perce festival, was the Fourth of July.

Every year in early summer the Nez Perces had gathered for the annual camas bulb harvest on the Weippe prairie. The camas bulb, a root vegetable, was a staple of their winter diet. The people camped for several weeks for dancing, feasting, horse racing, and trading of the famous Nez Perce Appaloosa horses. A version of this lighthearted time was still being practiced at Lapwai on the Fourth of July in 1883, when the day was given heightened significance by the arrival home of some of Chief Joseph's people from exile in Indian Territory. James Reuben, the young Nez Perce leader who was sent to Washington to check on Alice Fletcher's credentials, had set up a school for the Nez Perce children in Indian Territory. He spent several years persuading Congress that the exiles ought to be allowed to return to Idaho, and in 1883 he led the first of them back. With the dramatic flair for which he was famous, Reuben timed the arrival of their caravan to coincide with the Fourth of July celebration. He rode into Lapwai at the head of the small band of returning Nez Perces, mostly women and children on horseback and in wagons, arranged them in a half-circle in front of the agent's office, and then spoke to the crowd of their sorrows in that far-off land, their hardships on the journey, and their joy at being home again. After-ward, for over an hour, hundreds of people slowly filed by to shake each hand and inquire about friends and relatives still missing.[3]

For the Nez Perces this was "an unforgettable Fourth of July";[4] it affected all future celebrations of the holiday, which came to sym-bolize the unity of the Nez Perces, their pride in their past, and their resistance to the white people. From that time on, a war parade was added to the dancing, feasting, and other activities, with the agent's approval. In 1887, fifty Indians, clad in war paint and feathers, rode in a procession from Fort Lapwai to the old agency and back again, a distance of some four miles each way. The next year six hundred Nez Perces, led by Chief Joseph, rode in the procession. The agent reported that they sang Gospel hymns, "in their peculiar and inimi-table manner, so wild and weird,"[5] but a man who had ridden with Joseph and had been banished with him to Indian Territory hinted that these were not Gospel songs. "If the white people only knew how we feel, if they knew what these songs mean to us, there would be no more Tal-lik-lykts (war procession)," he said.[6]

Agency officials and white settlers from nearby towns looked for-ward to the color and excitement of the traditional ceremony, but the Presbyterian missionaries were unalterably opposed to this con-doning of "heathen" ways. They promoted at Kamiah and at Lapwai an alternate celebration of the Fourth of July, a combination camp meeting and Sunday School picnic. Alice Fletcher described the cele-bration at Kamiah in 1890 in a letter to the commissioner of Indian affairs. About five hundred people took part, and she and Jane Gay were the guests of honor. The day began with a sunrise religious service at 6 A.M., held under a large awning tied to tall pine trees. That was followed by a procession in which people clad in "citizen's clothing" marched along singing a song composed especially for the occasion, "We'll Stand Fourth of July." Next was a church service in which native speakers contrasted the happiness of an orderly Chris-tian life with the wild, roving life that the people had formerly led. After a feast of beef and salmon, canned fruit, bread, cake, and wild potatoes, the list of allotments was read. Each case was considered separately and any omissions were pointed out. Adoptions into the tribe of those of questionable Nez Perce identity were then ap-proved. The day ended with fireworks and a prayer service. "And so as happy and peaceful a day as I ever saw came to an end," Fletcher wrote the commissioner. "As I walked about I was greeted with a hand shake, a nod of the head and smile, and 'Fourth of July' much as we say 'Happy New Year.'"[7]

Tucked away at Kamiah in 1890, Jane Gay and Alice Fletcher were unaware of what the Fourth of July meant to most Nez Perces. The next year they were on the scene at Lapwai as the excitement mounted in anticipation of the holiday. When a small group of Presbyterian Nez Perces at Lapwai grumbled to Jane Gay about the forthcoming heathen celebration into which even the schoolchildren would be drawn, she decided to take action. Instead of preaching tolerance, as in a calmer frame of mind she might have done, she decided that the rights of the underdogs (the small band of protesters, in this case) ought to be defended. She helped them write a letter to the commissioner of Indian affairs, asking him to ban the celebration, since the local agent would not. An answering telegram from Washington arrived at Lapwai about a week before the Fourth. It banned the war procession, horse racing, and gambling in the vicinity of the school, and since the school was in the middle of Lapwai it in effect banned the war procession from the main town on the reservation.

The reaction at the agency was "like a bombshell."[8] Councils and protest meetings were held, and messages went swiftly back and forth all across the reservation. The agent sympathized with the disappointed Nez Perces, but his hands were tied. He canceled the war procession completely but allowed horse racing and gambling for a week out on the uplands. Feelings ran so high that Jane Gay slept for a week with a pistol under her pillow and an armed guard in the kitchen of their small cabin. The Nez Perces were split thereafter into two Fourth of July, or summer, encampments, that of the Presbyterians and that of the "traditionals," a split still evident in the 1960s.[9]

Jane Gay thought the whole event "a great step . . . in the right direction." She predicted, "Henceforth there will be two parties in the tribe and a spirited fight will go on."[10] She seems to have had no regrets at having undone the reconciliation between non-treaty, "heathen" Nez Perces and "progressive," Christian Nez Perces that the agent, who urged the two groups to celebrate together in 1887, and the Nez Perces themselves had worked so carefully to bring about.

Why did Jane Gay abandon her earlier observer's stance in favor of a martinet role at Lapwai? Part of the answer may be that she was bored and restless. Keeping house and producing three meals a day in a camp or rude cabin were no longer a challenge. There was nothing new to write to Captain Pratt for his newsletter at the Carlisle School, and her letters dwindled off. She felt helpless and frustrated as the same Indians appeared again and again at their door, wanting to have the boundaries of their land remeasured because they had forgotten them or were quarreling with someone over them. Even photography, which at first had given her so much pleasure, gradually occupied her time less and less.

Jane Gay took some marvelous photographs in Idaho. The best of her landscapes—magnificent vistas of the Clearwater canyons—are the equal of those by W. H. Jackson, Timothy O'Sullivan, and J. K. Hillers, the first generation of famous photographers of the American West. But there was one significant difference between their situations and hers. Jackson, Hillers, and O'Sullivan were all official members of United States government survey parties. Jane Gay was not. She had hoped when she first studied photography that she might be made an official member of Alice Fletcher's team. But the Bureau of Indian Affairs did not have money to spend on such luxuries. Unlike her male peers, Jane Gay had to be content with unofficial status. Her photography was considered an amateur's pastime. Her use of the pronoun *he* when speaking of herself as "the Photographer" may be an ironic reflection of her feeling that only male photographers were taken seriously. With no official encouragement and no market for her work—Alice Fletcher talked of writing a popular article on the Nez Perces for *Century Magazine*, to be illustrated with Jane Gay's photographs, but nothing came of it—Jane Gay eventually lost interest in it herself. In the end she valued her work so little that she left the glass plates in Idaho. Decades later they were uncovered in the attic of the Lapwai mission house. The only known publication of her photographs within her lifetime is an edition she did herself in 1904, an elegant, two-volume set of her letters and photographs from Idaho, illustrated with pen-and-ink designs by her niece, Jane Gay Dodge. The volumes are hand-written and hand-bound and rest in a specially made wooden case. Two sets are known to exist, one in the Schlesinger Library at Radcliffe College and the other in a private collection. Jane Gay did not continue her photography after she and Fletcher returned to Washington. The career that had at first seemed so promising eventually came to nothing, like the others she had tried: teaching, nursing, journalism, poetry.

On the face of it Jane Gay had all the advantages: a large, loving, and supportive family, a good education, great innate talent. But what she did not have was Alice Fletcher's driving will. Alice Fletcher did not give up when she did not get outside support. She simply persisted until she did. Jane Gay was a character, talented and funny, the sort of person who would stand out in a crowd while Alice Fletcher might easily be overlooked. But Alice Fletcher had character in the old-fashioned sense of that word: moral strength, self-discipline, and fortitude. In a world where no professional status of any sort was given to a woman without a fight, it was Alice Fletcher who got what she wanted.

As Jane Gay grew increasingly restless in her roles as "Cook" and "Photographer," she looked around for other possibilities. She spent more time with Kate McBeth, the missionary at Lapwai, and began to absorb her point of view. But Jane Gay could not become a missionary. The only other role model available to her in the small world in which she lived in Idaho was Alice Fletcher.

In the restless summer of 1891, Jane Gay's two new activities were ventures into Alice Fletcher's terrain. Encouraging a minority group of Indians to write to Washington was what Alice Fletcher had done ten years earlier on the Omaha Reservation, the start of Fletcher's career as a reformer and government agent. After the Fourth of July incident, Jane Gay's brief foray into politics, she tried science, deciding to do a little archaeology, in secret so as to surprise "Her Majesty." She found what she thought might be an Indian grave and dug in it, hoping to find a Nez Perce skull that could be sent to the Peabody Museum. But Alice Fletcher greeted her first reports with an utter lack of interest. Jane Gay knew that her friend had "small faith in the value of lay explorations," and the interpreter, when invited to come and help, told her that what she was digging in was a camas root cooking pit. Jane Gay withdrew, feeling chastened and foolish, and made no further attempt at archaeological exploration.[11]

Meanwhile Kate McBeth, the Presbyterian missionary, became interested in Alice Fletcher's ethnographic researches. Jonathan "Billy" Williams, an elderly leader of the Kamiah Christians, came to Lapwai in the summer of 1891 to talk to Alice Fletcher about the old times and to make a map for her showing the locations of some one hundred Nez Perce villages, trails, and other topographical features. That inspired Kate McBeth to begin to look into customs and beliefs she had previously dismissed as "heathen." She helped Alice Fletcher collect some random ethnographic notes on the Nez Perces.[12] Her sister, Sue McBeth, worked with a Nez Perce, Harry Haynes, on a grammar and dictionary of the Nez Perce language. But Jane Gay could not find a way to take part in these activities.

Buffeted about by the storms at Lapwai, without a satisfying professional role of her own, and lacking a commitment such as Alice Fletcher's to the allotment program, Jane Gay, who had always been so sure of everything, felt totally shaken in Idaho. Early in the season in 1891 she wrote:

> But there sits Her Majesty, calmly writing, a placidity about her that
> is aggravating. Has she come so near the heart of the Universe that
> she can rest content in the stillness of the centre of it all, while I, on
> the outer edge, am whirled by the endless revolution into confusion
> of spirit with no power to listen below the noise of the mechanism?[13]

Alice Fletcher did have, in Idaho in 1891, a placidity about her. Its source was twofold. She had in her pocket, ready to be used as soon as she was finished with the Nez Perces, a fellowship at the Peabody Museum at Harvard. It was to support her future scientific work, and she was excited by the possibilities that lay ahead and at the professional recognition that a fellowship from Harvard implied. Fletcher was also buoyed up by a special charge from the commissioner of Indian affairs, T. J. Morgan, delivered in his parting words to her as she left Washington. He had asked her to be his eyes and ears on the Nez Perce Reservation, to give him in confidence trusty information about what was going on at the agency at Lapwai.[14] This was the kind of special assignment that Fletcher loved, one that acknowledged that she was not an ordinary employee but an expert on Indians, part-author of the law she was assigned to carry out, and someone altogether worthy of unique confidence and trust. It was also a sign of her unusually close working relationship with the commissioner, whose policies she had done much to shape.

Thomas Jefferson Morgan knew nothing about Indians when he took office in July 1889. He was to become, after Alice Fletcher, the second most influential person in the late-nineteenth-century campaign to Americanize the Indians, although he held the office for only four years. Morgan's influence was the combined result of timing and of his own energetic and activist nature. The Dawes Act was in place. It was up to the new commissioner of Indian affairs either to implement it aggressively or to let it languish. Morgan chose the former course.

A former Baptist minister and principal of normal schools in New York and Rhode Island, Morgan had hoped that his old Civil War commander Benjamin Harrison would make him commissioner of education, but he settled, willingly enough, for Indian affairs. President Harrison's only charge to him was to administer the Indian Bureau in a way that "will satisfy the Christian philanthropic sentiment of the country."[15] Morgan knew enough to know that this meant he should satisfy the conferees who met annually at Lake Mohonk. He went that fall to their meeting and assured them of his wholehearted support for their program for "civilizing" the Indians and absorbing the Indians into American life. He pushed vigorously for the allotment of reservation lands. When critics charged that the Indians' land base was being rapidly reduced, he admitted that this was so. But, he argued, the Indians were not using the land, did not need it, probably never would, and were being paid reasonably well for it. If looked at from this point of view, the whole thing took on "a different aspect."[16]

Morgan also knew about Alice Fletcher. One of his first acts after he took office in July 1889 was to have his wife, Caroline, write to Alice Fletcher conveying his desire "to really do something to better the Indians" and asking her advice.[17] So, in addition to her official reports, Alice Fletcher sent long, confidential letters addressed to "My dear Mr. Morgan." Soon not only her ideas but also her very words, quoted at length, began to turn up in his annual reports.

Morgan took a special interest in Indian education. Four months after he took office he had in hand a detailed scheme for a comprehensive system of universal and compulsory education for all Indian children. It was an elaborate program bringing the hitherto somewhat haphazard collection of day and boarding schools, on and off the reservations, run by missionary boards or the government, into one grand scheme, with a prescribed course of study, standard textbooks, and English as the only permitted language.

Morgan's system for Indian education, like other parts of his program for Indian affairs, was a logical grid that he then insisted be set down on the unruly reality of Indian reservations. Increasingly, there was an air of fantasy in the reports of local agents, as they tried to tell the commissioner what he wanted to hear, that allotment was working well and that more acres of land were cultivated and more children were in school each year, while the bulk of the reports gave facts that contradicted their optimistic summaries.

There was no air of unreality, however, about the ultimate effects of Morgan's policies on the reservations. The allotment program moved full speed ahead and children were rounded up, taken forcibly to government schools, and punished there for speaking their own language. To these double blows against the Indians Morgan added a third in 1892 with a new set of rules and regulations outlawing Indian dances, polygamy, the activities of medicine men, and other key elements of traditional Indian culture.[18]

Alice Fletcher agreed wholeheartedly with Morgan's program. When F. W. Putnam and other Grover Cleveland Democrats signed a public statement protesting "corruption in the Indian Service" and Morgan's policies of forced Americanization of the Indians, she chided Putnam, telling him that in his new position as head of the Department of Anthropology at the World's Columbian Exposition he should stay out of politics.[19]

Fletcher moved serenely through the hostility at Lapwai in 1891, confident that she had the ear of the top man in Indian affairs, the commissioner himself. She did not take any part in the stopping of the war procession, but two days before the Fourth of July she telegraphed Commissioner Morgan in Washington: "Please instruct agent by telegraph to prevent Indians leaving reservation until they have reported to me and are allotted. They are preparing for their annual hunt. Fletcher Special Agent." In a follow-up letter Fletcher explained that her request for help was a "last resort." The Indians would leave almost immediately after the Fourth, she wrote, and "then it is impossible to do any work." She had already allotted all the settled Indians; "it is the roving class that remains, and it is very difficult to catch them." Morgan did as he was told, in a telegram that arrived in Idaho on the same day.[20]

Alice Fletcher's request may have been a "last resort," but it was also a deliberate display of authority. She could wire to distant Washington and within a few hours get back an order that was coercive not only for the agent but also for a thousand Nez Perces. The agent could be forced to cooperate, and the Indians made prisoners on their reservation and starved into submission, for they depended on the annual hunt in the mountains for their winter food supply. Alice Fletcher and Jane Gay had together managed to antagonize into open rebellion all the hostile forces at Lapwai already allied against them.

The commissioner's telegram was duly read to the Indians, and Fletcher thought she had conquered. She wrote the confidential report Morgan had requested, criticizing everyone at the agency.[21] A month later, in August, she wrote to Putnam, "I am literally building up this people, and putting on a firm basis some good institutions. I have the confidence now of the best men in the tribe, the teachers and good officials are very friendly, and the Government backs me most cordially."[22] But she was puzzled by the lack of cooperation she encountered everywhere. Even Briggs, her faithful surveyor, was balky, and by late October she had complained about him to Washington.

In early November the bomb dropped. A special agent arrived in Lapwai. While Fletcher had been secretly reporting on others, everyone on the reservation except herself and Jane Gay had known all summer that a man was shortly to be sent from Washington to investigate her work. There had even been published reports that she was to be replaced. Fletcher finally realized why she had made so little progress that summer, why there had been so many "intangible difficulties," why the commissioner's order that unallotted Indians not be allowed to go hunting had been generally disregarded, why, although people smiled and nodded at her and seemed to do what she expected, nothing happened. She had become a lame duck. All of a sudden she understood that there were political forces in Washington more powerful than an appointed commissioner of Indian affairs and that local politicians in Idaho could exert pressure behind the scenes in Washington even more effectively than she could.[23]

Fletcher was hurt and felt betrayed by her good friend Commissioner Morgan. She thought of resigning in protest but immediately decided not to. Morgan was only responding, she knew, to pressures on him, pressures that were much more intense that she had realized. Instead she insisted on attending the investigation of her work conducted by Special Agent Parker at Fort Lapwai on November 6 and 7, 1891, and took notes for her own use.

The turn of events only strengthened her resolve. Despite everything, she had managed to make 780 new allotments that summer and to readjust another 457. She had completed 1,440 allotments, but she had 300 more to do. She would not quit until she was finished. Several days after the investigation she wrote Putnam a letter that reveals her state of mind and iron will. She wrote:

> I have been working harder than ever before in my life. . . . My honor is involved in getting this done. I dare not resign until it is completed. I will not bore you with all I have fought thro, but I have had the worst struggle of my life. I never met such greed, such a determination to rob a people, as I have found here in Idaho. One would think these Indians had hardly a right to live, and not a right to possess their land. There has been a running fight upon me, because I am determined to do justice and give these Indians a chance. I have not had any one here to help me, but every one to oppose me. The Indians cling to me like children, and I must and will protect them. I wanted to complete my Century articles, to gather legends, to make measurements, all of which I could have done but for the disturbances a lot of unprincipled men have been able to make. I have been distressed beyond words at all this, and mainly because I felt I was disappointing you, but I had here a plain duty to perform, a trust to fulfill not only to the Government, but to the Indians who had faith that I could and would protect them. Well, Professor, I am getting thro. If the Sun will only shine so that the Surveyor can use his solar instrument for the next month all will be done. A compass is useless

here. The needle hugs the plate and will not point. There is so much metal in the mountains.[24]

The "Century articles" were popular accounts she was writing for *Century Magazine* about life among the Omahas. The "measurements" were physical measurements of the Nez Perces she had promised to get for the physical anthropology exhibits that Putnam's assistant, Franz Boas, was putting together for the World's Columbian Exposition. She worked into December, camping out in ice and snow.

Again the next spring, in 1892, she and Jane Gay returned to Idaho, "the wilderness" Fletcher called it. That summer they camped along the North Fork of the Clearwater, with the thermometer rising to 110 or 120 degrees every day. Fletcher wrote to Putnam in July of "intense heat" and of "all the troubles that assail me here." She added: "I am nearly used up. I have such a hard time here, but I shall soon push thro." At Lapwai the tension with the agent, Warren Robbins, who had replaced the much-disliked Charles Monteith in 1889, was as great as ever. Robbins was pressing the Nez Perces to sign a leasing agreement with white stockmen which would give the stockmen the run of some of the best land on the reservation, and he challenged Fletcher's work by insisting that a road run through one allotment where a Nez Perce man had already planted a crop. Fletcher wrote Putnam: "The Agent here has been investigated and found guilty of almost every crime. He swears vengence on me and attributes all his trouble (being found out) to me. He has done his best to stir up the Indians and the white settlers against me."[25]

Local settlers in Idaho complained to Commissioner Morgan about the delay in the allotting of Nez Perce lands. This work "has been in progress for the last 4 years and to all present appearances it is liable to continue for the next four," one man wrote in August 1892. Meanwhile, he added, the best wheat land in the country lay idle, land that could have "prevented the Russian famine" if it had been in cultivation.[26]

By mid-September Fletcher was finished. As they left the Nez Perce Reservation for the last time, Alice Fletcher and Jane Gay said goodbye to only a handful of Nez Perces, mostly Kate McBeth's

Christian converts. That night, in the little town of Genesee, Idaho, where they were to board the train the next day, Jane Gay was restless and unable to sleep. She hung out of the hotel window looking at the stars and straining to pick out a recognizable landmark on the Nez Perce Reservation which lay on the horizon. But everything was dark. Had it been good or bad for the Nez Perces that Alice Fletcher had been sent to them, she asked herself, and then admitted that the answer lay also in darkness.[27] Alice and Jane left the reservation not in a flurry of triumph, as Fletcher had left the Omahas, but with the sinking feeling of failure. This time there was no complete family registry. A new surveyor had already been hired to work on disputed boundaries. Fletcher thought that the Nez Perces ought immediately to cede their surplus land. "The sooner these Indians are merged with the people of the state, the better it will be for them, looking at their future in the broad sense," she wrote the commissioner.[28]

But there was intense opposition to that point of view. The Nez Perces were soon to be torn by a four-month struggle over whether or not to release for sale the "surplus" lands—the 542,064 acres left after 179,000 acres had been allotted. The sale was opposed by Nez Perces who had large bands of horses and cattle that they pastured on the reservation and by some headmen who wanted to keep to the old ways, but the poorer Nez Perces, who were a majority, were persuaded that it was in their best interests to sign. In the end the have-nots won.[29] Payment was $3 an acre for a total of $1,626,222, to be paid out to the 1,685 Nez Perces over a period of four years. For a thousand dollars each, the Nez Perces lost half a million acres of land. On November 8, 1895, President Grover Cleveland announced that ten days hence the surplus lands on the Nez Perce Reservation would be opened for settlement. The result was a land rush in Idaho like that in Oklahoma five years earlier.[30]

Alice Fletcher arrived back in Washington in late September, "so tired and used up that I have had to go to bed and stay there."[31] She had ridden in from Chicago with Theodore Roosevelt, the newly appointed civil service commissioner who had been on an inspection tour of Indian reservations in the West, and she had talked with him about "Nez Perce affairs."[32] They met again several weeks later at Lake Mohonk, where Roosevelt spoke encouragingly of what he had seen on the Omaha Reservation. He agreed heartily with Miss Fletcher, he said, that the Indians needed to get out from under the agency system and stand on their own feet.[33] Commissioner Morgan was also at Lake Mohonk that year, his last in office. He had begun to worry that perhaps they were pushing allotments too fast—some eighty thousand allotments were complete or nearly so. Most of the conferees looked at him uncomprehendingly. Why should so eminently desirable a program not be put into effect as rapidly as possible? Only Alice Fletcher agreed with him. Farming was very difficult on some reservations, she said. She wondered whether the Indians could be expected to do what white men could not.[34]

During her ten years work as a special agent of the Bureau of Indian Affairs, Alice Fletcher made allotments to 4,400 Indians, or about 1.5 percent of the 300,000 Indians in the country. The gamut of her experiences was representative for the country as a whole. She had started with a tribe in which allotment, earnestly sought by a minority, was a practical and ideological struggle, and she had sided with one faction of the tribe. Next she went to a reservation where the people were resigned to government arbitrariness, and her work was largely administrative. She ended on a reservation where allotment was an all-out battle, a program forced on the people in the face of almost unanimous opposition. When she had started, the release of surplus land was a secondary consideration (for the Omahas, at least, the first concern had been to remain in Nebraska), and when she ended, this was the main goal. The figures tell the story. The Omahas received 75,931 acres in allotments. Another 55,450 acres were kept for children who would be born during the twenty-five-year period of trust, and 50,000 acres were ceded to the government to be sold. The Winnebagos were allotted 83,120 acres, with 28,240 ceded to the government. But the Nez Perces ceded more than a half-million acres (542,275) after being allotted 179,000 acres, with another 34,000 acres reserved for their children.[35] The Omahas lost 30 percent of their reservation, the Winnebagos 25 percent, and the Nez Perces 75 percent.

Although each of Fletcher's three allotting situations was different, the effects everywhere were much the same. Leasing income and the distribution from land sales resulted at first in general prosperity on the reservations, but there was little assimilation into the nearby white communities such as Fletcher had hoped for. The barriers of white prejudice and the Indians' desire to keep their own ways were too strong. As Commissioner Morgan's radical Americanizing program was felt on the reservations, much of traditional Indian culture went underground. Peyotism spread rapidly, becoming, with the Native American Church, the dominant religion on many reservations.

The allotted Indians were quite well off at the turn of the century, but few of them became farmers as intended. Leasing was nearly universal, leading to the loss of much of the allotted land. In 1902 the Dawes Act was changed to allow inherited allotted lands to be sold. Although seen as a way out of the tangled complications of inheritance, the revision contributed directly to the loss of the land to whites. Ten percent of the Winnebago allotments were sold immediately. In 1906 the Burke Act allowed the secretary of the interior to terminate the trust period for any allotment if he was satisfied the allottee was competent to manage his or her own affairs. Local merchants thereupon allowed the Indians to run up large bills, and much of the land was lost in payment.

Meanwhile the Indian population did not continue to decrease, as was generally expected, but began to climb, in some cases dramatically. The effects of this can be seen from statistics for the Omahas, who are not atypical. The Omaha population more than doubled between 1884 and 1984, from 1,194 to approximately 2,700. In 1884 the Omahas held 131,381 acres of allotted and reserved land. In 1984 they held less than one-fifth of that amount, approximately 25,000 acres—13,000 from individual allotments and 12,000 from tribal lands never allotted (including 2,200 acres now on the Iowa side of the Missouri River, being farmed by the tribe). As a result of this loss of land and increasing population the Omahas today own fewer than 10 acres a person, instead of the 80 acres that the allotment program intended.[36]

The tragedy of Alice Fletcher's life is that she was a benevolent, well-intentioned person who ended up harming the people she tried to help. She was a conservative Victorian woman who feared that the white people in her own society were going to take the Indians' land and resettle the Indians, as they had been doing for a hundred years, until the Indians had nothing left. She had little faith in radical politics, in insisting on the rights of the Indians to the land. The only safety she could envision for the Indians was in individual owner-ship of the land on the same terms as everyone else. She wanted to keep the Indians from being victimized by white people and could not understand why they would resist, except that they were like children who did not know what was best for them. Therefore she had to force them to do what was in their best interest. They should give up large chunks of their reservation if necessary, she thought, because otherwise the white people would take everything. She wanted the Indians to be safe on their own land. That was her goal.

Alice Fletcher did not underestimate the power of the unscrupu-lous in her own society or their ability to undo the best-laid plans and continue to cheat the Indians. For this reason she urged the Indians to adopt white civilization, to get an education, to move into trades and the professions. She wanted them to be able to compete on equal terms with the whites moving in around them. She under-stood the competitive, individualistic nature of American society and, tough-minded as she could be, saw no course ahead for the Indians other than that they prepare to jump into the fray and com-pete, along with everyone else. Yet Alice Fletcher did not understand Indian culture well enough to know what this abrupt and forced about-face in ways of thinking and behaving would do to the Indi-ans. She did not know that to destroy the culture of a people is to break the spirit of that people. She did not, at this time, understand enough about the beauty and value in the Indian ways of life to become a fighter for their preservation.

The question a contemporary critic must ask is whether the Oma-has, the Winnebagos, the Nez Perces, and perhaps all the Indians affected by the Dawes Act would have been better off without her. My answer is no. The Omahas and Winnebagos were among the last Indian tribes left in Nebraska. They would soon have been moved to Indian Territory. The Nez Perces were being cheated when she arrived, their reservation overrun by white stockmen and squatters who would have found one way or another to make permanent their gains. In the Dawes Act, Alice Fletcher in effect insisted that any federal act that takes land from the Indians must at the same time guarantee them homesteads of land where they live. It was not a perfect solution, but it was better than the alternative of removal.

Fifteen

A Fellowship for a Woman at Harvard

MIDWAY through the Nez Perce work Alice Fletcher was released permanently from a need to earn her own living. The Peabody Museum announced in October 1890 a new gift, "the largest and most important"[1] it had received since its founding gift of $150,000 from George Peabody some twenty-five years before. The gift of $30,000 came from Mrs. Mary Copley Thaw of Pittsburgh. It was a fellowship named for her but given in honor of her late husband, William Thaw, the steel magnate and philanthropist. It was to go to Alice Fletcher during her lifetime, to support her "scientific and philanthropic researches" in which Mr. Thaw had been so interested.

The Thaw Fellowship changed Alice Fletcher's life. She was no longer a scientific student, sometime government agent, and part-time journalist and public lecturer. She had become a scientist. The Thaw Fellowship was not a student's stipend. It was a full-scale professional salary, not munificent, by any means, but adequate. At approximately $1,050 per year it was twice as large as the fellowship established the next year by Mary Hemenway for a graduate student in Central American archaeology. But what did it mean that a lifetime fellowship for a woman had been given, at the donor's initiative, to an affiliate of Harvard University, whose president, Charles Eliot, was notoriously skeptical about higher education for women? No one was sure. Mrs. Thaw's gift soon took on ramifications far beyond that of support for a single scientist.

William Thaw was one of the new breed of post–Civil War entre-
prenuers who had pulled together a fortune in canals, railroads,
steamship lines, and coke fields. Both the tough industrialist and
his pious second wife were impressed with Alice Fletcher's "power,"
as were many of Alice's admirers, one of whom compared her to
the 2,500-horsepower Corliss engine that had been the marvel of
the 1876 Centennial in Philadelphia.[2] In 1882, when Alice Fletcher
took her fight for the Omahas to Washington, Mary Thaw encouraged her. "You need hardly be told how much power there is in
your voice. There is no such gift as a voice which satisfies and
charms and you have that gift to an unusual degree," she wrote.[3]
William Thaw was a shrewd judge of character, and he liked Alice
Fletcher. Before his death in 1889, the Thaws frequently supplied
Fletcher with research funds, and she made their home in Pittsburgh a regular stop on her wandering itinerary. The Thaw mansion,
Lyndhurst, was on Beechwood Boulevard in the East End of Pittsburgh, where Henry Clay Frick, Andrew Mellon, and Andrew Carnegie also had homes.

Alice Fletcher's visit to Lyndhurst in March 1890 was particularly
propitious. Mary Thaw was still grieving over her husband's death
the year before and casting around for a suitable memorial. Alice
went to Pittsburgh to comfort her friend in her bereavement, but
when pressed she poured out something of the story of her own
difficulties in Idaho the previous summer. Mrs. Thaw decided to
come to the aid of her struggling scientist friend. "Mrs. Thaw proposed that I resign from government work, she to pay me an annuity
of $1200 to begin July lst. A serious question for me to meet and
decide," Alice wrote in her diary that night.[4]

By October it was settled. But the arrangements were not easy.
Mary Thaw looked at Harvard with a suspicious Presbyterian eye,
regarding it as a hotbed of irreligion. She had enrolled her unruly
eldest son Harry at the College of Wooster, a Presbyterian school in
Ohio, although even there he had not lasted long. Nor was it certain
how Harvard would respond. There were no women students or
faculty members at Harvard, and President Eliot, backed by most of
the alumni, was entirely satisfied with the status quo. Harvard by
1890 had been astir for twenty years, but remained adamant, on the
question of admitting women. The *Boston Daily Advertiser* called it

"the Chinese wall behind which Harvard College had entrenched itself."[5] Through quiet persistence, the self-effacing Mrs. Agassiz had managed to open a "Harvard Annex" for women in 1879 where women could take classes taught by Harvard professors. But the two institutions were administratively and physically separate. When the Annex became Radcliffe College in 1894, it gave its own degrees. Mary Copley Thaw and Harvard University were an uneasy match, requiring mollification on both sides.

Putnam, however, accepted the fellowship enthusiastically. "I had a very pleasant letter from Mrs. Thaw," Alice wrote to Putnam late that fall from Idaho. "I am glad she has modified her feeling toward Harvard, and I can't tell you how grateful I am to you as well as to Mrs. Thaw."[6] But though Putnam was responsive, the trustees of the Peabody Museum were cautious. Francis C. Lowell, the treasurer, emphasized repeatedly that accepting the gift of the fellowship did not mean they had chosen Alice Fletcher for it. "The appointment was made by Mrs. Thaw," he wrote. "No doubt we have the right to remove Miss Fletcher at pleasure, but until we do so she holds the fellowship, as it seems to me, by Mrs. Thaw's appointment, and not by ours."[7] Lowell noted somewhat wryly what was on everyone's mind. "As to the woman question generally, the College will have to settle it. Thank mercy the responsibility of so important a decision does not fall upon us as trustees."[8] So they settled the question by not settling it.

Alice Fletcher's closest friends shared her pleasure at what at first seemed merely a sudden bit of personal good fortune. Jane Gay was "delighted at the turn of affairs,"[9] and Francis La Flesche was relieved when finally the uncertainty was over and the plan was settled. But as word spread, the event began to grow in importance. A woman was to be recognized as an established scholar, a fellow, a title that came directly from the most famous English universities. And that event was to take place at Harvard University, one of the most prestigious universities in the country but one that was notorious for keeping its doors resolutely closed to women. This was the kind of triumph that a generation of feminists had been working for.

The event also gave sudden status to the struggling new science of anthropology. In 1890 "anthropology," a designation Putnam was urging to replace the older and more awkward "archaeology and ethnology," was barely visible. Putnam had his museum in Cambridge and directed summer digs in the mounds in the Ohio River Valley. In Washington, John Wesley Powell moved a handful of miscellaneous workers—linguists, geologists, former missionaries, army officers—back and forth between the Bureau of Ethnology, the National Museum, and the Geological Survey, finding support for them where he could. But that anthropology as a science was worthy of support by patrons like the Thaws was a new and astonishing idea. It did not escape attention in Washington that the most powerful man of science there, the astrophysicist Samuel P. Langley, named secretary of the Smithsonian just three years before, was a Thaw protégé, for Langley often declared his deep indebtedness to William Thaw's friendship and support. In one stroke Mrs. Thaw elevated an anthropologist (and a woman, at that) to this lofty company.

The ripples of criticism that Alice Fletcher's appointment caused in Cambridge were nothing compared to the waves of enthusiasm the appointment aroused in Washington. Fletcher returned from Idaho in November 1890 to find that she was the talk of the town. She worried that she would be an embarrassment to Putnam. "I hope no body blames you because I am a woman," she wrote him not long after her return.[10] At the same time she was pleased to be waving the banner for women in higher education.

In February all the women's organizations in the capital joined to give a reception for Alice Fletcher. Again she worried. "I don't want anything done here which will annoy at Cambridge."[11] But she agreed to let it happen, and she enjoyed herself enormously. Eight hundred people came to the reception held at Wimodaughse, a newly organized umbrella woman's club, on G Street N.W. The War Department lent twenty large flags for the occasion, and the wife of President Harrison sent one of the dozens of baskets of flowers. From 4 to 9 P.M., Alice Fletcher stood in a receiving line with a Senator's wife on either side of her as "one continual stream" of people passed by, a "remarkable" cross-section of Washington, with representatives from the highest official, scientific, philanthropic, artistic, and literary circles down to, in Fletcher's words, "the plain quiet people who do so much and are heard of so little."[12] The reception was intended to honor the appointment of a woman and to help forward woman's work, and Fletcher noted with satisfaction,

"There was no foolishness anywhere." The mood was one of high optimism, as expressed by William T. Harris, the commissioner of education, who prophesized exuberantly, "Fifteen women fellows within the coming year." Susan Anthony and Clara Barton were present, and the scientific men were out in full force, including George Brown Goode from the Smithsonian and Otis Mason from the National Museum. President Daniel C. Gilman of Johns Hopkins sent a telegram explaining his absence.

So Alice Fletcher was launched as a "Fellow" at Harvard University. The death of Maria Mitchell in 1889 left her the preeminent woman scientist in the country.[13] Still ahead, however, were two tasks. She had to finish the Nez Perce allotments. She also had to figure out what the Thaw Fellowship really meant.

Fletcher's first decision was where to live, but that was hardly a decision. Washington was the scientific as well as the political capital of the nation in the 1890s. It was far better to be in the midst of that lively scene as a representative of the distant Peabody Museum than to live in the much quieter Cambridge. But Alice also had a personal consideration which in itself would have been definitive. Francis La Flesche was in Washington. She needed and wanted to be where he was. Early in 1891 she and Francis and Jane Gay moved into a corner brick row house at 214 First Street S.E., which Mrs. Thaw helped her buy. Two months later she signed a formal paper declaring that she had taken Francis La Flesche to be her son and that she would make due and suitable provision for him in her will.[14]

Alice and Francis had intended to go through formal adoption procedures, but at the last minute they realized that Francis would have to give up the name La Flesche, which he was unwilling to do, so they settled on an informal arrangement. Thus did this three-person household, which was to last for fifteen years, come into existence. 214 First Street, familiarly "214," became one of the celebrated addresses in Washington, as Alice, Jane, and Francis invited there a wide swath of Washington society and friends, anthropologists, and Indians from all over the country.

The public recognition could not have come at a better time, for Fletcher was blossoming as a scholar. Ten years of hard work, of isolation, loneliness, and sometimes almost unimaginable difficulties, were beginning to pay off. She was finishing a study of the music of the Omaha Indians, her first full-scale scholarly work. She was writing for the general public. Four articles on the Omahas appeared in *Century Magazine* with her by-line during the next four years. Underlying all the other writing was her long-term plan to publish a full account of traditional Omaha tribal life.

But writing was not enough to keep Fletcher occupied. In 1890 she had been elected president of the Woman's Anthropological Society of America, a Washington group founded five years earlier by Matilda Coxe Stevenson, who was so irked at being left out of the exclusively male Anthropological Society of Washington that she decided to organize her own. The women met on alternate Saturday afternoons, and the seriousness of their purpose was declared in their decision not to serve refreshments. Fletcher sought advice from Putnam, in a letter in 1890 that conveys both the eagerness and the uncertainties of the new group. She wrote:

> The Woman's Anthropolog. Soc. proposes to take up the study of the Negro—archaeologically, ethnologically and socially. There is plenty to do about it and while there is much floating material that we hoped to collect and render useful, there is a sense in my brain that I am at the head of that which I dont know how to manage. I am to prepare a statement of work for the Society and while I would not trouble you yet if you could suggest a little what would be well to attack, what is the best way to begin, I should be deeply grateful. There are opportunities for the ladies to collect a good deal from their servants. Others are Southern born and can gather about their old homes, etc.[15]

This project looks hopelessly naive, and very little in fact came of it. Yet the women were on the right track in their sense of subject if not of method. Franz Boas, the young German anthropologist who had come to the United States in the 1880s, was to labor mightily in the 1910s and 1920s to try to move American anthropology away from its nearly exclusive concentration on Indians and to get it to focus more widely on other groups and other "problems."

Meanwhile Alice Fletcher continued to speak publicly on the problem she knew best, the "Indian problem." In December 1890, at a meeting of the American Folklore Society, she reported on the "Messiah Craze," or Ghost Dance, spreading among the Indians in the West. Fletcher's explanation of the dance was perceptive. The spread of the Ghost Dance, she said, was the result of a crisis in the life of the Indians. They had been crowded onto barren tracts of sand, the buffalo and other game were gone, and their children were being educated in a new language with new ideas. Many Indians could find hope only in supernatural expectations, and they pinned their hopes on a belief that the Indian Messiah would come to their aid. One month after her talk, 140 Sioux Indians at Wounded Knee, South Dakota, were massacred by soldiers who responded to the Ghost Dance with panic. Alice Fletcher was one of the few people, even among anthropologists and folklorists, who understood what was happening on the frontier. In the discussion period after her report Franz Boas, although he was later to change his mind, suggested that crazes like this were probably nervous diseases and should not be attributed to any great extent to politics.[16]

Alice Fletcher saw herself as a scientist, as a reformer, and to some extent as a public spokesperson for anthropology. As the recipient of the Thaw Fellowship, she also considered herself Putnam's assistant. In a flurry of letters to him over the next fourteen months she tried to figure out what that was to mean. What should she do? What were his plans for her? When Putnam and his wife talked of having a reception for her in Cambridge, she discouraged it. "Don't get up a reception for me. Let it all go quietly," she wrote. "You would lack of this reception if I were a man and so let it pass, dear Prof. and Mrs. Putnam. It is lovely in you but too much work just now."[17] She wanted to work the way a man would work but was unsure how to do so. Then she learned that Putnam was to be the head of the Department of Anthropology at the World's Columbian Exposition in Chicago in 1893, and suddenly she saw many possibilities.

Putnam had decided that the Anthropology Department should show American Indian life as it was before Columbus arrived. When Alice Fletcher learned this, she began to flood him with a stream of suggestions. Sheldon Jackson could get a southern Alaska or Northwest Coast exhibit with wooden houses, totem poles, and carvings.

She could have the Nez Perces make a mat house that would "cover in a general view the Indians north of California and west of Rockys." For the Plains Indians he would need a skin tepee and perhaps a bark house from the Winnebagos. "I think I could get one of these made for you, and furnished. Do you want models or life size?" she asked. There should be an earth lodge from the Pawnees and Omahas, and a longhouse could represent the Iroquois. "Now dear Prof. Putnam if I have suggested too much pardon it. Tell me what you want me to do and I will do all I can," she wrote.[18]

Through all her difficulties on the Nez Perce Reservation in the summer of 1891, Alice pondered the Chicago exhibit. Part of her intense frustration that summer was that she wanted to be working with Putnam. Instead she was helpless, stuck away in Idaho, where although she seemed to have the upper hand, nothing much was happening. But gradually the Chicago situation turned out to be as puzzling as the scene on the Nez Perce Reservation.

In May 1891, while in Idaho, Alice learned that she had been elected an honorary and corresponding member of the Woman's Branch of the World Congress Auxiliary of the Columbian Exposition. What did this mean? She wanted to work on exhibits for the Anthropology Building, not for the Woman's Building. She wrote to Putnam: "I have accepted, but I don't see anything for me to do. I don't believe in trying to disentangle work according to sex but many do."[19]

Next Franz Boas sent some special devices for measuring head and body size and asked her to measure some Nez Perces for the physical anthropology exhibit he was doing under Putnam's general direction. Alice Fletcher cooperated as best she could. "Dr. Boas's work interests me much," she wrote to Putnam. James Stuart, her interpreter and driver, was willing to be measured, and Jane Gay did the honors, but the two women could not persuade any other Nez Perces to submit themselves to what must have seemed yet another bizarre and arbitrary demand. They finally gave the tools to the school superintendent, who, as Jane Gay said, could "compel" cooperation, and several dozen Nez Perce children were duly measured and the figures sent to Boas.[20]

In February 1892, as she was preparing to start a fourth season in

Idaho, Alice made one last try with Putnam. She outlined a collecting trip she and Jane Gay could make on their way west, to the Pueblos, the Navajos, perhaps into Indian Territory, to the Northwest Coast, and down through California to look for "just what you want in the way of habitations and native families."[21]

Putnam, harassed and frantic with his whirl of activity—he was still permanent secretary of the American Association for the Advancement of Science, as well as professor of anthropology at Harvard, curator of the Peabody Museum, and curator of new exhibits for an entire building at Chicago—put her off with expressions of concern for her health and with gentle admonitions to get on with her writing.[22] He finally found time in April 1892 to meet with Fletcher at her home in Washington to discuss her future. There Alice learned, to her disappointment, that it was Franz Boas, not she, who was to be Putnam's first assistant at Chicago. The long collecting trip that she and Jane Gay had offered to make would not be necessary, although Putnam did want her to help gather a Nez Perce exhibit and perhaps arrange for something from the Omahas. Fletcher's future work, as Putnam saw it, was the same as it had been in the past. She was to study and write up all her notes, to settle down quietly in Washington and work with Francis.

One other unexpected arrangement was made at the meeting. Alice Fletcher had invited a music expert from Milwaukee, John Fillmore, to meet Putnam and to help plan the work she hoped to do on Indian music for Chicago. In the meeting with Putnam she found herself agreeing to help Fillmore travel among the Indians to study their music for the Chicago Exposition, traveling she herself had wanted to do.[23]

Alice Fletcher bore this deflating of her hopes, and the whisking away of her collaborator, with good grace. She went dutifully to Idaho in the summer of 1892 to finish the allotments, but she worked less with a sense of urgency than a desire to be done. By early September she was finished. Alice Fletcher and Jane Gay's return to the East took them through Chicago, but Fletcher did not stop off long enough even to look at the buildings going up at Jackson Park. She turned her back on Chicago and hurried home.

Back in Washington she wrote to Putnam, "I look forward with delight to the quiet of study this winter and I trust some good may come of it."[24] But in fact she did not. She was accustomed to a life filled with activity, to study leavened with speaking engagements, political lobbying, and money-raising activities, all interspersed with months of travel in the most distant outreaches of North America and with government work for which she had been paid a man's wages to do the job expected of a man. She was accustomed to being a power both in Washington and on Indian reservations where she had a staff of six or eight people at her command and could force the most recalcitrant stockmen, agents, and Indians to do her bidding. Suddenly the battles and the victories and the travel were over. She was a "Fellow," a scholar, but she had not been invited to be part of the whirl of scholarly activity in Chicago centered around the Exposition. She felt she had been put on the shelf, relegated to the sidelines. Paid a stipend that she considered barely adequate, she was to spend her days doing the one thing that was most difficult for her—writing. It was what in her most harassed moments she had said she wanted, but in her innermost being she knew it was not what she wanted at all. The Thaw Fellowship did not make her a Harvard faculty member. It did not make her Putnam's first assistant. It carried with it none of a faculty member's obligations and pleasures: students, classes, local and national committees, the power to make educational and research policy and to steer a course toward the future. It released Fletcher from the need to earn her own living, and it made her scholarly work professional. But that was all the fellowship did. It was not, as she and so many others had hoped, the first light of a bright new day of opportunity and equality for women in higher education.

Putnam was probably certain that he had Fletcher's best interests in mind. Her greatest asset was the close working relationship she had with her Indian informants, particularly Francis. That was the key to the magnificent contribution she would make to American anthropology—the work that she and Francis would do together. Putnam may have done the right thing in sending her back to work with Francis, but it was not a choice that she appreciated. She did not want to concentrate on digging deeply in one narrow scholarly furrow, to become simply an expert on the Omahas. She wanted to master the whole of anthropology, to be recognized by the public and by her fellow professionals as one of the leaders in the field. For the first time, she realized that she could no longer count on Putnam to guide her career, for his view of her future and her view of it did not coincide.

But for the moment Alice Fletcher was defeated, and she knew it. She went back to Washington to work with Francis, but even he was acting strangely. In the spring of 1891, at about the time the Thaw Fellowship was announced, he started taking evening classes in law at National University, a coeducational university in Washington that catered to government employees and others preparing for government service. Francis La Flesche received an LL.B. from National University in 1892 and an LL.M. the following year, and he spoke of being admitted to the bar and starting a career as a lawyer.[25]

Alice was secretly distressed at the prospect of losing her research assistant. She seems not at all to have sensed the turmoil going on inside Francis, who was feeling completely overlooked. He was reacting quietly, in the only way he could, to the Thaw Fellowship that had singled her out as a scientist and ignored him. He was also reacting to her enthusiastic sponsorship two years before of the young Nez Perce, James Reuben, as a candidate for law school. Alice Fletcher had pulled all sorts of strings to get Reuben into the Columbian (later George Washington) University Law School with part-time employment at the Bureau of Ethnology, hoping that this would help him become even more effective as a leader of his people. James Reuben did not attend law school in Washington after all,[26] but Francis must have wondered why Reuben, and not he, was singled out for higher things. Francis was too gentle and too genuinely fond of Alice Fletcher to make a direct protest. But he did protest, by announcing that he was starting on a law career of his own, one that would leave little time for their joint endeavors.

Alice Fletcher finished the office work for the Nez Perce allotments. Then, early in 1893, she collapsed into a serious illness, the first of the mysterious and punishing illnesses that would plague her over the next dozen years. The exact nature of her illness is unclear. Fletcher described it as a combination of "pneumonia and congestion of the brain."[27] It involved her head, perhaps in severe headaches, and was aggravated by stress or excitement. Jane Gay was away taking care of her sisters who were ill, so other friends took over in her stead. This letter from one sickroom guardian to Jane Gay, written after the worst was over, describes the scene:

Dear Miss Gay,

The dreaded ordeal is passed, and safely. I think I told you that Mrs. Tulloch said, on Sunday, that Mrs. Lander was still "frantic," and that, as soon as Miss Fletcher could safely see her, if only to let her look at her, and see that she was not being killed it would be well. Otherwise there was positive danger of a *raid* on the premises. "I never," Mrs. Tulloch said, "knew of so much fuss about anyone's sickness in my life!"—so the doctor was consulted on the matter, and said, if Mrs. Lander was allowed to stay only a few minutes, and would be quiet, she might come. This morning she was sent for, and came in very hilariously, but soon quieted down. I kept out of the way, of course; but was very anxious, until an hour after her visit saw the little woman's head still quiet. Then I began to feel as if I could breathe again. After that, my lady combed her hair—for the first time in three weeks and a day; resting a while at intervals during the performance—she says I am a better barber than she is. Then, after a rest, she assumed shoes and stockings, and wrapper, buttoning her boots for the first time, also doing it "all by her lone," and came in here, in time to eat her usual lunch of raw oysters. Nothing else seems to taste quite so good as those raw oysters do, day after day.

Dr. Hinds came in this morning, in the kindest way, to ask if she and the other ladies could do anything to expedite the sea voyage which I had written her Miss Fletcher hoped to take. And this afternoon in the same connection, Miss Painter came, and brought a map of routes of winter trips; and advised her *not* to take the one she herself had just taken; but suggested other and more desirable ones. She brought a pretty little individual coffee pot, which she had brought from Mozambique.

. . . Now for the last item of the day. I sent to Dr. Harris, today, for Fiske's "Discovery of America," and this evening I began it. I suggested stopping several times, but we went on, *for an hour and a half;* and this long listening with considerable accompanying suggested thought did not upset the head. Do you realize what an immense stride that means? She had walked a great deal today, about the rooms, and she says "tell her I'm pretty well, and it won't be long before I am able to write to her." It's a sort of Hallelujah feeling in my heart tonight; and I think it will communicate itself to yours: to see that so much can be done without suffering. Good night.

Your dear lassie is really getting well, and I know you are happier, than any words can say under all the distress about you, to know it.

Love to you always from the little "house beautiful" on the hill.

Helen [28]

Mrs. Lander was a former actress and a grande dame of Washington society and Jane Gay's whist partner. Mrs. Tulloch was Alice Fletcher's good friend and next-door neighbor. Jane Gay sent this happy report about her "lassie" on to Putnam and told him that now it would be safe for him to write to Alice. Slowly Alice began to recover.

One month after the onset of her illness, Alice Fletcher wrote in her diary: "Doctors ordered me to go out. Felt languid but went and much better for it." [29] The languid feelings and her resistence to getting out suggest psychological as well as physical components to her illness. Nor was she alone. Historian Lee Virginia Chambers-Schiller has noted in a recent study of single, career-oriented women born between 1780 and 1840 that "almost invariably, [these] women's response to vocational crisis involved physical or psychic collapse," particularly when they found themselves conflicting with established male authority and "taking on the university, church, or law." [30]

The Thaw Fellowship, so eagerly heralded as marking the entry of women into higher education and professorial careers, collapsed into what Mrs. Thaw had intended all along: lifetime support for one worthy woman. Mrs. Thaw's inclinations were not feminist. She later gave a Thaw Fellowship to Princeton, the alma mater of another son, and it was designated not for a woman but for an astronomer, in line with William Thaw's principal interest. [31] Harvard would not have a woman professor until almost thirty years later, when Alice Hamilton was named assistant professor of industrial medicine at the Harvard Medical School.

Exhausted by four years of turmoil on the Nez Perce Reservation, feeling both rebuffed by Putnam and at the same time guilty for not having adequately repaid his kindnesses to her, and fearful that she was losing Francis's help with her work, Alice took to her bed. For a month she lay there. Any mental stimulation—any thought—was almost more than she could bear. Only oysters, and the luxurious, pampering care of which they were a symbol, finally revived her.

Sixteen

"The music comes from beyond this life"

F ROM her sickbed in April 1893, Alice Fletcher made the final corrections on the study of Indian music on which she and Francis La Flesche had been working for ten years. A new problem had just come up. "I find that Francis has a great deal of feeling concerning the recognition of his share in the work involved in this monograph," she wrote Putnam. "He wants his name to appear on the title page . . . 'aided by Francis La Flesche.' He has spent several hundred dollars and given much time and labor, moreover he first had the idea of writing out this music. He had several songs taken down by Zimmelgave (or some such name), a professional musician, but the work was a failure. After that I took it up with him, having made a few attempts alone and failed. I shall be glad to have his name added . . . and hope you will be willing."[1]

Putnam, whose Peabody Museum was to publish the study, was willing. Thus it was that *A Study of Omaha Indian Music* appeared with Francis La Flesche's name, as well as Alice Fletcher's, on the title page. The monograph was, with one exception, the first serious study ever made of American Indian music, and it was a remarkable work, the joint product of a woman scholar who had long been searching for a "truly American music," as she had told Sidney Lanier, and a young Indian singer and scholar who had tried independently to transcribe the songs of his people.

When Alice Fletcher first dropped herself down into the middle of Indian life, of all the strange sights, sounds, smells, and other sensations that engulfed her, it was the music, the beat of the drums and the wailing voices, that first truly engaged her emotions. The minutes that Alice spent engrossed in the dancing at Spotted Tail's camp on the Rosebud Agency were a turning point in her life. She had had a detached, intellectual curiosity about the Indian way of life, but the music aroused her to a deep, passionate, lifelong commitment to Indians. The experience of singing, drumming, and dancing in a community in which every nuance was understood was unforgettable. Through the rhythmic beat of feet on the earth she felt the people's oneness with nature and with their land. At the same time she sensed that what she was experiencing was another organized human society, a culture, as complex and unique as her own. "I want to study this thing," she had insisted, when Tibbles had tried to pull her away.[2]

The question was *how* to study it. Not until some six months later when she went to Washington to plead for the Omahas did she find the answer. In Washington she had met young Frank La Flesche, whose previous attempts to write down Indian songs had been a failure, as had hers. When they began to work together, however, they found they could do it. Francis was a good singer. The combination of his knowledge and patience, her understanding of western musical forms, and their joint determination made their work possible.

The single precursor of Fletcher and La Flesche's study of Indian music was a Leipzig doctoral dissertation done in 1882 by a young American, Theodore Baker. Baker had gone to Europe to study music. Stimulated there by the growing European interest in folk music, he returned to the United States in the summer of 1880 to look into American Indian music. He wrote to the recognized authorities on Indians: Major John Wesley Powell at the Bureau of Ethnology; Richard Pratt of the Carlisle Indian School; the Dakota missionaries, Alfred and Thomas Riggs; and a missionary-turned-scholar, J. Owen Dorsey. He went to the Seneca Reservation in New York state, where he transcribed ten songs out of the fifty or sixty that he heard, and to Carlisle, where he transcribed twenty-two more songs from various tribes. Baker's visit to Carlisle coincided with the first anniversary of the school, and he was able to get songs not only from students but also from some tribal chiefs who had been invited to the celebration.

Theodore Baker was aware that his was pioneering work, for his contacts and his search in the available literature produced only ten additional songs: two Dakota songs sent by the Reverend T. L. Riggs; two Walla Walla songs published in the reports of the Wilkes Expedition of 1838–42; five Chippewa, Cherokee, and Muskogee songs collected by a professor in Wisconsin; and one song from Henry R. Schoolcraft's massive *Indian Tribes of the United States, 1851–55*. Travelers' accounts frequently mentioned Indian dances and songs. A French explorer, Claude Dablon, described a mock combat among American Indians, which he witnessed in 1670, as "done so well—with slow and measured steps, and to the rhythmic sound of the voices and drums—that it might pass for a very fine entry of a Ballet in France."[3] But very few attempts had been made to transcribe the songs.

The nucleus of Baker's study is the thirty-two songs he collected, given with melodies and texts, but Baker also attempted some generalizations about the music. The Indians sing in unison, he wrote, usually accompanied by a regular, rhythmic beat, either of rattles, sticks, drums, or the feet, and the general impression given by these performances "is rather a pleasing one." He thought the Indians recognized a dominant note in their songs and the intervals of a diatonic scale. Charting his thirty-two songs on a "Table of Intervals," he found that all of the songs contained a tonic note and the fifth; twenty-five of the songs contained the third degree of the scale, usually the major third; twenty-two of the songs contained the fourth; fifteen of the songs contained the major sixth; and eight of the songs the seventh, either major or minor or both. He noted that the two most common tone series used by the Indians were the oldest of the Greek modes of music: the Lydian—major 2, major 3, perfect 4, perfect 5, major 6, major 7; and the Phrygian—major 2, minor third, perfect 4, perfect 5, major 6, minor 7.[4]

In arguing for the diatonic scale as the foundation of Indian music, Baker was challenging the widespread notion that Indian music was so irregular, so prone to semitones or even smaller intervals and accidentals, that it could not be transcribed in the usual note system. Baker showed that it could be transcribed. He believed the transcriber should restrict himself to the single melodic line that was sung by the Indians and not try to add a subjective and highly arbitrary harmonic accompaniment.

Baker's modest work was sound, but it had little effect on subsequent studies, for Baker himself lost interest in the topic. For thirty-four years he worked as literary editor and translator for the music publishing house of G. Schirmir. He translated several German music books into English but never his own pioneering study. He may have pondered the market for Indian music and decided that there was not one. Baker wrote two standard reference works, *A Dictionary of Musical Terms* and *Biographical Dictionary of Musicians*, but neither book gives any hint of his early interest in Indian music. There can hardly be a clearer indication that serious study of American Indian music was not likely to come from mainstream, classically trained musicians in the late nineteenth century. The subject was too peripheral to their main concerns. Yet Baker's work was not totally in vain, for from him the idea of transcribing Indian music passed via J. Owen Dorsey to Francis La Flesche.

James Owen Dorsey, a former Episcopal missionary to the Poncas and a skilled linguist, had been sent to the Omaha Reservation in Nebraska in 1878 by John Wesley Powell. Dorsey spent two years with the Omahas. Joseph La Flesche was one of his chief informants, with Francis often acting as interpreter. Dorsey was impressed with Francis, at this time in his early twenties, who was "devoted to reading" and "the only Omaha who can write his native dialect."[5]

Dorsey collected several Omaha song texts. When he asked Francis La Flesche about the songs of the ceremony of the Sacred Pole, Francis told him it would be difficult to get them, for it was considered sacrilegious to sing them apart from the ceremony and only those in charge of the ceremony knew them. But, Francis confided, "I myself would like to know it all."[6] Not long after this, Francis apparently tried (with the help of a Professor Szemelenyi, whose name Alice Fletcher understood as "Zimmelgave") to write down the songs of his people.

La Flesche knew what most white people thought of Indian music. One day while he was a student at the mission boarding school, the agent brought three government inspectors to visit the school. The children were quizzed on American history and had a spelling bee, and then one of the visitors said he would like to hear an Indian song. "There was some hesitancy," La Flesche later wrote, for the rule against using their native language at school was strictly enforced, "but suddenly a loud clear voice close to me broke into a Victory song; before a bar was sung another voice took up the song from the beginning, as is the custom among the Indians, then the whole school fell in, and we made the room ring. We understood the song, and knew the emotion of which it was the expression. We felt, as we sang, the patriotic thrill of a victorious people who had vanquished their enemies; but the men shook their heads, and one of them said, 'That's savage, that's savage! They must be taught music.'" After that, every afternoon for an hour the children had singing lessons. They were taught to sing in harmony. The teacher had no trouble dividing the group into sopranos, contraltos, and tenors, but no one would take the bass, so Francis, who was less timid about singing than some of the others, was assigned to struggle with it alone.[7]

Francis La Flesche was not only a good singer with an interest in the traditional songs of the Omahas. He also had an intense interest in the old ceremonies, in part because his own life had several times been touched by supernatural sanctions connected with them. In June 1877, four years before he met Alice Fletcher, the twenty-year-old Francis had married a young Omaha woman, Alice Mitchell, in a ceremony performed by the Reverend Hamilton at the Omaha mission. A year later a group of Otos visited the reservation, and in their honor the Omahas wanted to bring out their sacred pipes. But no one remembered the ritual formulas to be said as the pipes were removed from their coverings. Alice Mitchell's father, the hereditary keeper of the pipes, was reluctant to open them without the prescribed prayers but finally yielded. Within a short time, he, his son, and his daughter, Alice, were all dead.[8]

Francis had other vivid memories of sanctions connected with the

Sacred Pole. His horse had once run over the bearer of the Sacred Pole as the latter trudged along on the annual buffalo hunt bearing the pole on his back, and a special offering had been required to set matters right. The pole had also been implicated in the infection that led to the amputation of his father's leg, and even in his father's death. Francis La Flesche never admitted that he believed in these supernatural phenomena, and he probably did not, but he was intensely interested in them. His lifelong concern for completeness and accuracy in recording ethnographic materials was not simply a dislike for sloppy work. He knew that for his people a sacred ceremony wrongly performed made the path to the supernatural powers crooked, not straight. Music was the preeminent link to the unseen powers. As a Sioux priest had told Alice Fletcher, "The music comes from beyond this life."⁹

As she continued to work with Francis, Alice was forced to give up her own society's stereotypes about Indian music: that it was savage, monotonous, haphazard, and really only noise. She learned that it was intimately bound up with the most important political and sacred aspects of life, with distinct songs for each occasion. Yet the experience of Indian music still eluded her. She heard little, she wrote, "beyond a screaming downward movement that was gashed and torn by the vehemently beating drum."¹⁰ But then came the parceling out of land allotments to the Omahas and Alice's illness, the long months of inflammatory rheumatism when she lay in bed at the agency. Francis brought his family and friends to sing to her, and "the sweetness, the beauty and the meaning of these songs were revealed to me."¹¹ When the Sacred Pipe ceremony was performed for her, she was a participant, no longer simply a scientific observer.

Through all the years that Fletcher worked on her government report and struggled with the Winnebago and Nez Perce allotments, she and Francis continued to collect Omaha songs. They did much of the transcribing in Washington during the winters, persuading Omahas who happened to be in the city to come and sing for them. George Miller, a young Omaha student at Hampton, was a typical informant. He visited them in May 1888, and Alice reported to Putnam: "In four days I have taken down 18 songs. I have now 55 and more coming."¹²

By the fall of that year, when she spoke on "Indian Music" to a meeting of the Round Table Club at Danvers, Massachusetts, she and Francis had a collection of more than one hundred Omaha songs, and she told the group that "if she had time to spend, she could in a few months get five hundred songs, and this would not even exhaust the number of songs known and sung in one tribe alone." Fletcher explained why she thought the study of Indian music was important. "Our continent has been peopled for ten thousand years or more, and processes are lived here that are most worthy of study," she said. "I wish that Americans cared for their own country. They care very little. We are all immigrants. I felt it very much when I stood among the Indians for the first time, and really breathed freely and truly a consciousness that there was an American, that there was something worth turning our powers upon. I am afraid that we shall be rather a shallow people in our culture until we possess what lies here in our own country and hold it, and not feel that all that is worthy of mental struggle lies on the other side of the globe." What we need, she said, is "an honest, earnest American culture," which "while rooted here does not in the least neglect that which lies on the other side."[13]

There were echoes of Ralph Waldo Emerson here, as well as anticipations of D. H. Lawrence, who in 1920 wrote an essay for the *New Republic* titled "America, Listen to Your Own." Lawrence argued, on the strength of Mabel Dodge Luhan's enthusiasm and even before he had come to see for himself, that American artists and writers should take inspiration from Indian culture. Alice Fletcher, in her search of American roots for an American culture and in her choice of Santa Fe in northern New Mexico as a center for art and historical studies of the American Indians, was a generation ahead of Lawrence and his famous contemporaries. Like Mabel Luhan, she came to have a driving sense of mission for bringing Indian culture to the attention of artists, particularly, in Fletcher's case, musicians, whom she looked to for a "truly American" music.

As Alice Fletcher began to realize the value of what she and Francis had in hand, she decided to enlist the help of a professional musician. The songs presented baffling problems of rhythm and scale. She thought she needed professional help, and she wanted to interest musicians in the work. She asked around among her friends, and John C. Fillmore, a pianist and organist, was recommended to her. She sent an Omaha song to Fillmore in 1888 and subsequently relied increasingly on him for technical analysis of the songs.

John Fillmore was in his mid-forties when he met Alice Fletcher. A graduate of Oberlin College, he had spent a year at Leipzig and then had returned to teach briefly at Oberlin, at Ripon College in Wisconsin, and at the Milwaukee College for Women. In 1884 he had founded the Milwaukee College of Music. Fletcher acquired this expert just in time, for she soon learned to her dismay that she and Francis were not the only team studying Indian music. The newly founded and well-funded Hemenway Southwestern Archaeological Expedition had begun to throw its formidable resources into the scientific study of Indian music. Fletcher even had reason to think that Mary Hemenway, the founder of the Hemenway Expedition, had taken the idea of studying Indian music from her.

Mary Hemenway had financed the campaign to save the Old South Meeting House in Boston and to set it up as an institute to promote popular interest in American history, and she continued to be keenly interested in what went on there. Frank Hamilton Cushing lectured there when he came east with a party of Zuni Indians in 1883. Alice Fletcher spoke there on "Indian Music" in the spring of 1886. "Mrs. Hemenway has offered to make all my slides for the series of illustrated lectures next Fall at the Old South," Alice wrote Putnam at the time.[14]

But Fletcher went to Alaska instead of giving the lectures at Old South that fall, and Mrs. Hemenway began to focus her patronage instead on Frank Hamilton Cushing. In the summer of 1886 Mrs. Hemenway invited Cushing, with his wife and some Zunis, to visit her at Manchester-by-the-sea, her estate north of Boston. There Cushing, who could be spellbinding, persuaded her to finance the first major archaeological expedition in the American Southwest, one that would look for the historic roots of contemporary pueblo societies. She supported it with the then-munificent annual sum of $25,000, nearly the equivalent each year of the entire endowment for Fletcher's Thaw Fellowship. Under Cushing's leadership the expedition did mostly archaeology, but when he became ill and was replaced in 1890, Mrs. Hemenway decided to broaden her investigations. She bought one of Thomas Edison's new inventions, a phonograph, and sent J. W. Fewkes, the new director of the expedition, to test it among the Passamaquoddy Indians in Maine. That fall Fewkes and his associates took it with them to the Zuni pueblo in New Mexico.[15]

Fletcher learned of this in the early spring of 1891. She was in Washington celebrating the Thaw Fellowship. She had hoped that the study of Omaha Indian music would be her spectacular debut as a professional anthropologist, but now she felt threatened. She hastily wrote to Putnam, wondering whether she should write a popular article on Indian music to "forestall other claims" or whether she should push ahead with the monograph. "Please tell me what I had better do," she begged, adding in the margin, "Miss Gay at my shoulder says she thinks it is very essential to put an article on music in the Century as many are talking Indian music."[16]

A month later she learned that Mrs. Hemenway had hired Benjamin Ives Gilman, lecturer at Harvard in the psychology of music, to analyze the Zuni wax cylinders. "Who is Mr. Gilman?" she asked Putnam anxiously.[17] She postponed her return to Idaho for a week and immediately wired Fillmore to come to Washington to work with her and Francis, promising to pay his travel and expenses.

So the race was on. John Fillmore spent a week with them in Washington and became increasingly absorbed in the work, which he told her was "remarkable" and "of much deeper interest to musical science" than he had thought.[18] That summer while Fletcher was in Idaho, Francis La Flesche took Fillmore to the Omaha Reservation to hear the music in context, after which they worked together for a week at Fillmore's home in Milwaukee. John Fillmore was at first somewhat patronizing toward Francis, but Alice would have none of it, and by the end of the summer Fillmore could not say enough in praise of him. "Francis is careful, conscientious and persistent; he lets nothing pass with which he is not satisfied," Fillmore wrote Alice. "I can't imagine how this work could have been done without Francis. George Miller is satisfied with any sort of approximation to his song, and the others don't count."[19] In those weeks of close work with La Flesche, Fillmore made harmonized transcriptions of seventy-nine Omaha songs.

Benjamin Gilman won the race to publication. His "Zuni Melodies" appeared in 1891 in the first volume of the Hemenway Expedition's own journal.[20] Fletcher rushed an article, "Indian Songs: Personal Studies of Indian Life," off to *Century Magazine* along with a companion piece by Fillmore, but the magazine delayed publication so long that their first work to appear was "A Study of Omaha Indian Music," published by the Peabody Museum in June 1893, just in time for the World's Columbian Exposition at Chicago. Then what had been a race became a battle, as the two experts, John C. Fillmore and Benjamin Ives Gilman, argued over the nature of Indian music. In the process the pioneering and sensitive work done by Alice Fletcher and Francis La Flesche was almost lost sight of—almost, but not quite.

"A Study of Omaha Indian Music," fifty pages long, contained the largest collection of nonwestern music that had ever been published in one place, ninety-two songs, all from a single tribe. Fletcher and La Flesche divided these into three categories according to who sang them: class songs, which are religious and are sung only by those who have a right to sing them either through initiation or inheritance; social songs, including dance and game songs and the songs of the wa-wan pipes, which are always sung by a group; and individual songs, including dream songs, love songs, sweat lodge songs, captive songs, songs of thanks, prayer songs, and death songs. For each song there Fletcher and La Flesche provided a sentence or two of explanation. Above all Fletcher tried to convey to her readers a feeling for the richness of the tribal culture in which the music was embedded. Her familiarity with Indian life is evident on nearly every page. She wrote: "Among the Indians, music envelopes like an atmosphere every religious, tribal and social ceremony as well as every personal experience. There is not a phase of life that does not find expression in song."[21]

She discussed the Indian manner of singing, including their use of vibrations of the voice to suggest the galloping of a horse or the trotting of a wolf over the prairie. She wrote of their keen ear for rhythm, every bit as good as the legendary eyesight of the Indians. The Indians generally use few words in singing, and their comment on white music, she wrote, was that "we talk a great deal when we sing." She suggested that seemingly meaningless syllables in an Indian song are chosen to express emotion: flowing *h*-sounds, hae, ha, he, hi, ho, hu, for gentler emotions, and sharp, explosive *y*-sounds, yet, yae, yee, yi, for challenges and warlike emotions. She also showed how words are altered, pronunciation changed, and extra syllables added in the songs to make them a form of poetry, an explanation Franz Boas thought was of great importance and "surely correct."[22] Boas also liked her explanation of the briefness of Indian songs. They are simple, direct, and brief, she wrote, because in the closeness of tribal life everyone knows what the songs mean and an elaborate unfolding of ideas is not necessary. "The thought, the scene, the melody, come without warning or prelude, breathe out their burden and are gone almost before a listener of our own race realizes their presence."[23]

Fletcher tried to be descriptive and to avoid theory as much as possible, but she finally did place the work solidly in the context of theories of social evolution, calling it a contribution to "the archaeology of music." She implied that these were songs of a people who were midway up the ladder of social evolution. The songs were organized and fixed. Some singers knew hundreds of songs, which remain remarkably stable over time. But she found in the songs little evidence of sustained musical thinking. She attributed that to the lack of a leisure class among the Indians. The Omahas had not yet advanced to a stage of class distinctions and division of labor. She admitted it was interesting to speculate on how Omaha music might have evolved if their way of life had remained unchanged, but, she said firmly, this would be speculation only, for the old way of life among the Omahas was over. But it was not these social evolutionist sentiments that made "A Study of Omaha Indian Music" controversial, for they were widely shared and quite peripheral to the study itself. The controversy concerned John C. Fillmore's contribution.

Alice Fletcher had discovered that when she played a melody back to the Omahas on the piano, it did not sound right to them until she harmonized it, adding chords. John Fillmore tested this and found it to be true. He did other experiments, such as carefully recording an off-key version of a song by a singer only to have other Indians laugh upon hearing it and insist that the right way was the harmonic way, either sung or played on the piano. As he worked with Francis and other Omaha singers in transcribing songs Fillmore found that though they might sometimes miss an interval they intended to sing, when he played the possibilities for them on the piano, they were always certain which one was intended. From that,

Fillmore concluded that Indian music is based on a natural or latent feeling for the harmonic relations between notes, in fact, for the same harmonies that are more overtly expressed in western classical music. The Indians may sing out of tune, as do white singers, but they have in their heads the goal toward which they are striving. Fillmore thought the discovery all the more remarkable because it was contrary to what they had expected. "We all entered upon the work of transcribing Indian songs with the expectation of finding a different set of intervals from those embodied in our folk music," he wrote.[24] Instead they found them to be the same. There seemed to him to be a universal grammar of music based on the nature of sound.

Fillmore based his claim not only on his and Fletcher's experiences but also on the authority of Hermann von Helmholtz, the celebrated German physicist and author of *On the Sensations of Tone as a Physiological Basis for the Theory of Music* (1862). Helmholtz had demonstrated that so-called simple tones are acoustically complex, with overtones in frequencies that have a set ratio to the vibration frequency of the base note. Fillmore took Helmholtz's discovery, that tones are always accompanied by mathematically related overtones, then simplified and distorted it. He simplified it by implying that there is one scale, the western diatonic scale, that is more basic than the others, acoustically "the path of least resistance." He distorted it by seeming to suggest that this particular harmonic scale was *the* organizing principle of all music. "I am profoundly convinced that the Indian always intends to sing precisely the same harmonic intervals which are the staple of our own music, and that all aberrations from harmonic pitch are mere accidents, due . . . to imperfect training, or rather to the total lack of it," he wrote in an article ingenuously titled "What do Indians Mean to Do when They Sing, and How Far Do They Succeed?"[25]

Although the Omaha people sing in unison, Fillmore transcribed their songs (eighty-nine out of the ninety-two in "A Study of Omaha Indian Music") into four-part harmonies, like hymns or chorales. He did this for two reasons. He believed that these harmonies were latent in their heads because the harmonies were what the Omahas preferred when they listened to their music played on a piano. He also felt it was important to transcribe Indian music in a way that could be understood and used by others. He was highly critical of Gilman, whose charts of notes were incomprehensible to an average reader.

The intriguing question is why Alice Fletcher allowed her work to be tampered with, why, instead of publishing the songs with single melodic lines and rhythmic markings as she had done in "Five Indian Ceremonies," she used Fillmore's harmonized versions. The answer lies in her professional insecurity at that time and the potential threat posed by the Hemenway Expedition. Alice Fletcher was still an amateur when she hired John Fillmore, an amateur in the sense that hers was a labor of love, an avocation while she and Francis earned their livings in other jobs: she as a special agent in the Indian Bureau and he as a clerk. She was determined not to let her work and Francis's be swept aside by Mary Hemenway's well-funded and prestigious expedition. If the Hemenway Expedition had a musical expert, so too did she. And if Fillmore wanted the songs to be readily available to parlor musicians, already transcribed for performance on the piano, so too did she. Popularizing the music had been one of her goals in doing the work.

Alice Fletcher was careful to keep her work separate from John Fillmore's, and she never fully endorsed his theory. In 1898 she wrote that she had become convinced that the Indians sing in tones and intervals "which approximate our diatonic scale" and that the structures of the songs "seem" to be built on harmonic lines,[26] but that is as far as she would go. Yet she used Fillmore's four-part harmonizations in "A Study of Omaha Indian Music" and made no distinction between them and the songs as they were actually sung in unison by the Omahas.

John Fillmore also contributed an essay added at the end, "A Study of the Structural Peculiarities of the Music." This was a thoughtful piece, marred only by Fillmore's overemphasis on the question of scales, harmony, and tonality. He had keen insights into rhythm, phrasing, motifs, and the quality of tone in Indian singing. Rhythm, he thought, was the most elaborately developed element in Indian music, particularly the ability to combine dissimilar rhythms. He liked the richness and variety of the motifs or short phrases in Indian songs and the way a melody was built up out of modified repetitions of these. He responded to the repeated charge that there was no beauty in Indian music because it was loud, out of tune, and so full of noise. It was true, he admitted, that there was an "uncertainty of intonation" and a "lack of sensuous beauty of tone quality" in Indian music, but he explained that the Indians generally sing out of doors and must compete with the winds, the noises of camp, and the drums. To this Fletcher would add that beautiful tone quality is not of interest to the Indians. They sing for themselves. They are participants, not performers.[27] Fillmore insisted that this lack of beauty was balanced by what the music had to offer: "an elaborate, well-developed rhythm" and above all "fresh, original, clear, characteristic expression of the whole range of emotional experience of a primitive people."[28]

Above all Fillmore stressed the emotion, the feeling, conveyed in Indian music. That was Fletcher's theme in what she called her "psychic" analysis of the music, but it was dominant even in Fillmore's more technical analysis. Nine-tenths of the criticism he received from the Omahas as he tried to play their songs, he wrote, had to do not with the melody line or the rhythm or the text, although the Indians were particular about all of those, but with the expression of emotion. The reason casual listeners to Indian music find nothing in it, he suggested, "is that they have not the faintest idea of the meaning and spirit of it." When an observer understands that a ceremony is profoundly religious and sees that its symbols, such as the painted and feathered pipes of the wa-wan ceremony, are treated by the Omahas with reverence as great as that any priest shows for the crucifix, then the music can be powerfully stirring and beautiful.[29]

In contrast to Fletcher's, La Flesche's, and Fillmore's emphasis on the meaning of the music to the Omaha people, Benjamin Ives Gilman tried to do for a strictly scientific analysis. Benjamin Gilman was a philosopher trained in logic, psychology, and aesthetics. He had done graduate study in Berlin and Paris as well as at Harvard and Johns Hopkins, but he had never before heard any "primitive" music. He listened to the Zuni cylinders and then reproduced each melody line as closely as possible on a harmonium, a keyboard instrument based on wind pipes with an equally tempered scale of twelve intervals to an octave rather than the usual combination of twelve whole and half tones of a chromatic scale as on a piano. His aim was to analyze the exact tones that were being sung, and his conclusion was that the Zunis did not sing on a fixed scale, or have any sense of a key note or tonic chord, or have a feeling for latent harmonies.

Gilman was charmed by the patterned structure of Indian songs, usually an introduction, theme, and coda. He also commented, as had Fillmore, on the use of motifs or expressive phrases, often repeated higher or lower for emphasis. But as for scales, he insisted, "what we have in these melodies is the musical growths out of which scales are elaborated, and not compositions undertaken in conformity to norms of interval order already fixed in the consciousness of the singers. In this archaic stage of the art, scales are not formed, but forming."[30]

The rivalry between Gilman and Fillmore as scientific authorities drove each of them into more extreme positions. Gilman used ever more complex recording devices, including a harmonium measurement just invented by the British acoustician, A. J. Ellis, called a "cent system" because it could measure one hundred units within each half tone interval (1,200 for an octave). He used this to show that the Indians sang many different notes and intervals, that the songs were improvised, and that they seldom sang a song the same way twice. Although Gilman admired the ingeniousness of song development—"these wild flowers of fancy"—as revealed by his meticulous analysis, he continued to insist on the primitive, random, even accidental nature of the singing. He suggested there might even be an anatomical reason for this: the Hemenway Expedition had discovered that in ancient Indian skeletons the hyoid bone at the base of the tongue was unusually "elastic."[31] In later papers Gilman concluded that scales were not forming in Indian music and never would. He said it was not a prehistoric art but an "unhistoric" one, a dead branch on the evolutionary tree. Meanwhile Fillmore insisted that not only was Indian music stable and ordered, but it was orderly on exactly the same lines, or rather chords, as western classical music.

From our perspective they were both wrong. Alice Fletcher's first statement on this question, written when she was working with Francis La Flesche but not yet with John Fillmore, is more nearly in line with contemporary theory. In "Five Indian Ceremonies" (1884), she had written, "The Indian musical scale having different subdivisions from our own, the original songs lose a little of their native tone by being forced into our conventional scale." The controversy demonstrates how wrong both a strict phonetic (physical) and a strict phonemic (psychological) analysis can be. Gilman's attempt to be rigorously objective proved to be of little worth and was also inevitably tinged with his evolutionist thinking. Fillmore's attempt to get inside the mind of the Indian was equally warped by his own preconceptions, especially those stemming from the dominant role of the piano and of harmonic music in the classical tradition in the late nineteenth century.

Two instruments shaped, if they did not create, this controversy, the piano and the newly invented phonograph. Pianos (and organs) were everywhere in the United States in the late nineteenth century, in performance halls and classrooms, in mansions, middle-class parlors, and rude cabins. On the frontier they carried a special message, symbols of culture and "civilization" in the most distant outposts. Alice Fletcher spent her first night west of the Missouri River in a settler's home where her hostess proudly displayed an organ. The trader Peter Sarpy had flaunted his wealth and tried to please his Indian wife, Mary Gale, with a piano brought upriver from New Orleans to St. Louis. Rosalie La Flesche's husband had been an itinerant organ salesman before he married and became a farmer. Susette La Flesche played the piano and taught songs to her Sunday School class when she returned to the reservation after having been at school in the East for several years. It is easy to understand why the Omahas preferred to have their songs played on a piano with four-part chords. A line of melody played with single notes was weak and feeble. It sounded incomplete whether compared with the hymns and harmonized songs that were the staple of piano music or with the Indians' customary lusty outdoor singing, in unison but with a wide range of voices and the powerful accompanying beat of the drum. John Fillmore fell easily into the trap of conceiving of other music in terms of its rendering on a piano, for he was a pianist and organist and the author of *A History of the Piano-forte* before he took up Indian music.

Equally significant was Thomas Edison's invention, the phonograph (called a graphophone when it was manufactured by Columbia, the Edison Company's arch-rival).[32] For the first time music could be accurately reproduced and studied at leisure, far from the distracting sights and sounds and the sometimes embarrassing presence of "primitive" people. Rudolf Virchow, the German physician, public health officer, politician, and leading anthropologist, told the Berlin Anthropological Society in 1886 that the one field that anthropology had neglected completely was music.[33] The reason was obvious. Music was hard, if not impossible, to transport or draw or make a record of. But the phonograph changed that, and anthropologists eager to study the physical aspects of Indian music seized upon the new invention avidly. Gilman's strongest supporters were the German ethnomusicologists Otto Abrahman and Erich M. von Hornbostel, who in the early twentieth century built up Carl Stumpf's Phonoarchiv of Primitive Music in Berlin. Several scientists interested in the physics of music gathered around John Wesley Powell in Washington. They included O. T. Mason and C. K. Wead, an examiner for the U.S. Patent Office who wrote an early work on the history of musical scales. Let them "try the blind alley of physics; but they won't get anywhere," Fillmore predicted to Alice Fletcher.[34] He was right in that physics alone is not enough for satisfactory analysis of other music systems. Although the phonograph was to become invaluable for ethnomusicology, the lesson from these early experiments was that the phonograph needed to be supplemented whenever possible by research and experience in the field.

Alice Fletcher at first had reservations about the use of a phonograph. The early models had only a small horn that could pick up the voice of one singer but got little of the drumbeat. It was useful, she thought, primarily for getting the language sounds, but she could get those more accurately and immediately from Francis. Yet if she needed to use the latest mechanical gadgets to be considered professional, she would. "Mrs. Thaw offers to send me a phonograph and I'm inclined to try it. Shall I?" she wrote Putnam soon after she had read Gilman's work.[35] Putnam replied that she should let Gilman "work the phonograph for all it is worth and you stick to the art,"[36] and for a time she did. But she continued to think about a phonograph. In "A Study of Omaha Indian Music" she commented that learning to listen below the noise of Indian music to the music underneath was like learning to listen to a phonograph, ignoring the sound of the machinery.

"A Study of Omaha Indian Music," Alice Fletcher's first major work as Thaw Fellow, appeared in print just as she headed off from Washington for the World's Columbian Exposition in Chicago. There she was to find herself once again pushed aside, although the field of study she had initiated was all the rage.

Seventeen

Disappointment at the World's Columbian Exposition

ALICE Fletcher arrived in Chicago in June 1893 and stayed into October. She and Jane Gay shared an apartment at 3974 Drexel Boulevard near the fairgrounds. "I go to help Prof. Putnam. There will be some other things for me to do . . . papers to give and I hope some things to learn," Fletcher wrote Isabel Barrows.[1]

Putnam's Department of Anthropology had at the last minute been given an entire building, which occasioned a flurry of activity before it finally opened in mid-June. Downstairs in the main exhibit hall Putnam and nearly one hundred assistants arranged exhibits in archaeology and ethnology designed to illustrate the life of the Indians of North and South America at the time of Columbus's arrival four hundred years before. The entrance to the North American Ethnology exhibit was particularly striking, a large Northwest Coast exhibit designed by Franz Boas with totem poles, woven blankets, and wooden house fronts. Across the aisle were smaller displays, gathered by thirty-five assistants, illustrating the habits and customs of the various tribes of North American Indians. Alice Fletcher's collection of Nez Perce, Omaha, and Winnebago objects was among these. She also arranged two smaller exhibits nearby: a display of her work on Indian music including copies of "A Study of Omaha Indian Music" and an exhibit with Francis La Flesche on the Omaha Sacred Pipes.

Visitors having made the rounds of the main floor exhibits went next to the wide gallery on the second floor running along all four sides of the building, where the department offices, the library, and the laboratories of psychology, neurology, and physical anthropology were located. The laboratories were open to the public, and people were invited to be measured with the latest scientific apparatus from the United States and Europe. Two more special exhibits prepared by Franz Boas were on display here: a chart showing the varying rates of growth of over ninety thousand schoolchildren in North America, and diagrams and maps showing the physical characteristics of the Indians of North America, based on measurements of 1,700 Indians made by Boas and seventy-five assistants including Jane Gay and the Nez Perce school superintendent. Outside, next to the Anthropology Building on the shores of the south lagoon, were large casts of Mayan sculptures and "living exhibits": a village of Penobscot Indians from Old Town, Maine; Tuscarora and Seneca Iroquois from northern New York state in a longhouse and other houses of bark; several Navajos, including a silversmith and a blanket weaver, living in a hogan; and a village of Kwakiutl Indians from British Columbia, with totem poles erected in front of the dwellings and their great canoes floating nearby in the lagoon.

The federal government also had an anthropology exhibit at the fair, arranged in the Government Building by William H. Holmes, O. T. Mason, Frank H. Cushing, and their colleagues at the Bureau of Ethnology and the National Museum. The foreign concessions out on the midway contributed more living exhibits, including a Dahomey village of thirty huts and 69 people, a Javanese village with 120 people, a South Sea village with people from Samoa and the Fiji Islands, and a North African village. There were also camps of Sioux, Winnebagos, Navajos, and Pueblos from Laguna.[2]

Alice Fletcher was officially on the staff of Putnam's Department of Anthropology, paid a fee of one thousand dollars plus three dollars per diem and travel expenses, and she was a member of the Board of Judges as one of the judges for the Ethnological Exhibit. In reality, however, once the exhibit cases were arranged she had little to do. She had hoped to pursue her music studies at Chicago, but her collaborator, John Fillmore, was off working with others. Fillmore spent many hours in Chicago listening to songs of the Dahomeys, South Sea Islanders, Javanese, and other groups camped out on the Midway Plaisance, and he worked with Franz Boas on the music of the Kwakiutl Indians.

The Hemenway Expedition was also at Chicago. Mary Hemenway had commissioned Gilman to go there with a phonograph, and he recorded nearly one hundred cylinders of the performances at the Javanese, Samoan, and Serbian exhibits and six cylinders of the tuning of the individual gamelan instruments.[3] Gilman was invited to a Kwakiutl recording session in Franz Boas's office. It was his first experience of live singing by an Indian, and he was impressed by the native singer's lack of self-consciousness. The man was at first a little sheepish as he sang into the phonograph, Gilman noted, but soon he "crooned away as simply and unhesitatingly as if he had been squatting on damp stones in a circle of his mates by a British Columbia river, instead of being seated in an office amid inquisitive Americans."[4]

Pushed aside by the men and feeling somewhat at loose ends, Alice Fletcher turned to her women friends. Jane Gay was there, and Rosalie La Flesche Farley came from Nebraska at Fletcher's invitation. Alice Fletcher spent several days taking Rosalie Farley around and then several days with Mrs. Thaw. She also spent much time in the company of the archaeologist Zelia Nuttall. Nuttall had loomed on the horizon as a potential rival ever since 1886, when Putnam named her special assistant in Mexican archaeology at the Peabody Museum. He had appointed Alice Fletcher special assistant in ethnology in 1882. "I wish I could do as well as she [Zelia Nuttall] does," Fletcher wrote Putnam from Idaho in 1891 after having read Nuttall's paper in the latest annual report of the Peabody Museum. "Miss Gay consoles me by saying I am building up the people I study."[5] But at Chicago they became friends, a friendship that was later to have important repercussions in Alice Fletcher's career.

Alice Fletcher had been invited to give papers at three of the international congresses held in Chicago that summer, the congresses of music, anthropology, and religion, and these became her main activity. The music congress was first, in early July. The anthropology congress met at the end of August and the religion congress in mid-September. Her three presentations are a barometer of what happened to her that summer in Chicago.

At the music congress Fletcher spoke on "Music as Found in Certain North American Indian Tribes." Her presentation, carefully prepared, was superb. She summarized the high points in "A Study of Omaha Indian Music," but she also carried her ideas in new directions, for the first time explicitly comparing the study of music with that of language. "It was not many years since the notion prevailed that the speech of savages was a mere jargon with an exceedingly limited vocabulary, the words being uttered regardless of rule or order," she said. "But we now know that nowhere on earth does there exist a people, from the lowest savage tribes to the cultured Saxon, whose speech is not organized." So must it be, she argued, with music. "The music of savages is still spoken of as purposeless sound . . . but there can no more be a jargon in music than in speech."[6]

What Alice Fletcher was revealing was the theoretical implications of the treasure she had uncovered. Indian music was a system akin to language, kinship, house design, or any other fundamental aspect of culture and was as revelatory of Indian life. It was ordered, stable, and easily transcribed, based as it was not on a minutely divided scale but on note intervals comparable or equal to those used in western music. This was a discovery almost as significant for anthropology as the discovery one hundred years earlier by linguists that Indian speech was not primitive babble but was as complex and stable as Indo-European languages and was similarly transcribed with a limited set of symbols.[7] Francis La Flesche sang Omaha songs to illustrate what she was saying, and Fletcher wrote in her diary that night that the session had been "Quite a success." Her paper was printed immediately both in the journal *Music* and in the *Music Review*.

John Fillmore's paper for the music congress was a hasty summary of the arguments supporting his theory of the harmonic basis of all music.[8] But then Fillmore settled in at Chicago to work on Kwakiutl music with Franz Boas and to listen to other foreign music on the midway. By the time of the anthropology congress in late August, the roles were reversed, and it was Fillmore who had the impressive paper. Alice Fletcher, perhaps hoping to appeal to a large audience, spoke on "Love Songs among the Omaha Indians." It was a topic of continuing interest to her, for she liked to use these songs as evidence that an Indian woman was not treated as a beast of burden or a slave by her husband and as evidence that the Indians were capable of expressing emotion. But she misjudged her audience. The anthropologists were not much interested in Indian love songs. The paper was printed in the official congress volume, but it attracted little attention.[9]

John Fillmore, by contrast, abandoned polemics and simply gave a detailed account of all the work he had done on Indian music, from his first study of Omaha songs and his work on the Omaha Reservation with Francis La Flesche to his experiments with George Hunt and other Kwakiutl singers at the Exposition, testing their preference for a single line of melody or chords on the piano and testing their recognition of wrong notes, the experiments he had learned from Alice Fletcher. He ended with a survey of other music he had heard at the fair, and what he had learned. Fillmore had become interested in rhythm and motifs in the music as well as in latent harmonies, and he was fascinated by the orchestra he had heard at the Dahomey village on the midway, with its seven drums, five bells, and pair of rattles. Fillmore's emphasis on his experiments, a rare phenomenon in anthropology, led one reporter to comment that his was "the only truly scientific work of the session." Frank Cushing in his diary that night wrote, "I think this the first real work in Primitive music yet produced."[10]

Alice Fletcher was sick at heart. Chicago was to have been her debut as a full-time professional anthropologist and as the leading expert in the country on Indian music. Instead her monograph on Omaha music was considered controversial because of the four-part harmonies Fillmore had added, while Fillmore himself was at the center of attention, in part for doing the very experiments she had done first. She wrote tersely in her diary that night: "Read paper on Indian Omaha Love Songs before Internatl Congress of Anthropology at 11 a.m. Professor Fillmore gave paper on Primitive Scales and Rhythm at 11:30."[11] Thereafter the diary is blank for three weeks, usually for Fletcher a sign of troubled times.

Again she took refuge in illness. Immediately after the anthropology congress both she and Jane Gay became ill. Fletcher wrote Isabel Barrows, "I am hovering on the edges of a breakdown but hope to get well."[12] To Putnam's secretary in Cambridge she reported that

Putnam was fine but overworked. "As for me," she added, "I am not good for much. Ever since my severe illness last winter and spring, my head has not been well enough for hard and continuous work."[13]

Alice Fletcher got up after ten days in bed to attend the opening day of the World's Congress of Religions on September 11 and two weeks later spoke to them on "The Religion of the North American Indians." She bemoaned the fact that no American Indian was on the platform at Chicago to join the Buddhists, Hindus, Moslems, Christians, Jews, and representatives of the other great religions. Only she and the Sacred Pipes were there to speak for "the race that for centuries was the sole possessor of this western continent." She spoke of the Indians' feeling of a mysterious, unknowable power that animates all nature, generating and nourishing all life. Fletcher suggested that this view, that everything is alive and active to help or hinder humanity, explains much of Indian ritual but also hinders the development of individual responsibility. Success or failure are seen to come not through human actions but by occult powers. One corollary is that the Indian has little consciousness of evil in himself. "The Indian seldom thought of himself as being in the wrong, his peculiar belief concerning his position in nature having engendered in him a species of self-righteousness."

She explained the Indians' general acceptance of personal immortality. "There was no place of future punishment; all alike started at death upon the journey to the other world, but the quarrelsome and unjust never reached it, they endlessly wandered." She spoke of Indian religious ceremonies, the elaborate dramatizations of myths, with masks, costumes, rituals of song, rhythmic movements of the body, and the preparation and use of symbols. Although the ceremonies have "grotesque features," she said, they are "impressive and instructive" and show the struggle to find an answer to the question of human origin and destiny.

She described Indian ethics. Truth was literal, and nothing excused a person who broke his word. Justice likewise was literal and inexorable, undiluted by mercy. Hospitality was a marked virtue. The richest person was the one who had given the most away. "This deeply rooted principle of giving is a great obstacle in the way of civilizing the Indian, as civilization depends so largely upon the accumulation of property," she noted. Finally, in every home peace was taught, as symbolized by the Sacred Pipe ceremony. "The initiated were told in the presence of the little child, who typified teachableness, that happiness came to him who lived in peace and walked in the straight path, which was symbolized in the pipes as glowing with sunlight." Here, she felt, were implied the first dawnings of mercy and "kindred graces."[14]

Although the paper is tinged with Fletcher's evolutionist presuppositions, it showed how deeply she had come to understand Indian life. It is striking in its display of her ability to comprehend from within and simultaneously to evaluate from without. The paper was followed by "a long discussion of much interest," Fletcher noted with satisfaction in her diary.[15] The paper was printed in an abstract of the congress of religions, but it was lost to anthropologists. It is not listed in Alice Fletcher's professional bibliography compiled after her death and has never been reprinted or even cited in studies of North American Indian religions.

As she left Chicago in early November Alice Fletcher wrote Putnam an odd but revealing note, telling him that her time in Chicago had been "rich in experiences that leave no sorrow behind them." She had "learned much," she wrote, "and this, like so much else that has made my life worth anything, I owe to you." She added: "I can never forget your kindness, and the pains you have taken to open new fields of study to me. I only wish I could render you some return."[16] Fletcher wanted Putnam to know that she left with no ill feelings. Indeed, she could not bring herself to blame him. Putnam was harassed and overworked, kindly and helpful, the man to whom she owed everything.

Yet she knew that she deserved better than she had gotten in Chicago. Her frustration was intense, for she knew that her work was as good as that of her male colleagues. Her pioneering work in Indian music and Indian religion was as significant for ethnology as Holmes's work in archaeology or Boas's in physical anthropology or Cushing's or Mason's work in material culture. Fletcher knew that her studies and the method she had evolved, of long sustained contact and living with the people one wanted to study, were important. Putnam knew this too. In an editorial note to her music monograph he described what she had struggled to achieve: "She is able to put herself mentally in the Indians' place and regard them and their acts from their own standpoint. It is this which gives importance to all that Miss Fletcher writes. She describes the thoughts and acts of her Indian friends as they would describe them, while her scientific training leads her to analytical work and thence to an understanding of the meaning of what she sees and hears."[17]

This dual vision, being able to look at another society from within and without, sympathetically and analytically, has been the goal of all subsequent generations of anthropologists. It is the lure, the perpetual appeal, the very cornerstone of the profession. A later generation would label the method "participant observation," but before it had a name it was invented by Alice Fletcher among the Omahas, Frank Cushing among the Zunis, and Franz Boas among the Eskimos and Kwakiutls. The Chicago Exposition was not the great opportunity for Fletcher that it was for her male contemporaries. It threw her back on herself, still stranded on the great divide between amateur and professional, because no one quite knew how to make a professional place for a woman, and because American science was changing in a way she could scarcely grasp.

Several complex issues that came together at the Chicago Exposition made Fletcher's situation difficult and led almost inevitably to her sense of personal despair and confusion. To begin with, the organization and stature of American science was changing. Fletcher had been trained by F. W. Putnam in the natural history tradition in which Putnam, in turn, had been schooled by Louis Agassiz. Science was learned in an informal, apprentice-like system. A scientist was anyone who did important original work, and no significant distinction was made between an amateur and a professional. But as science became a more complicated and more significant part of American life, it felt the same pressures for order, regulation, division of labor, and status that were apparent elsewhere in turn-of-the-century society. Women were pushed to the periphery of one scientific field after another between 1880 and 1910, as scientists sought to upgrade their profession by requiring graduate degrees and by instituting professional hierarchies, both formal and informal.[18]

Women were given very confusing signals at the Chicago Exposition. In one sense the Exposition seemed a triumph for feminists. Women were everywhere, as exhibitors, as speakers, as judges, and they had a Woman's Building of their own. "As Columbus discovered America, the Columbian Exposition discovered Woman," Mrs. Potter Palmer, the chairman of the Woman's Committee declared triumphantly.[19] But within their professions women felt much less secure, as Fletcher could have testified. Why, when her work was so innovative and so good, did she feel such despair and confusion? Why did she feel outside of things, isolated, out of touch?

Also involved in Fletcher's situation at Chicago was a struggle between the claims of research and popularization.[20] This too was related to the growing professionalization of science, for it involved the question of where one's ultimate loyalties lay. Putnam and Boas were firmly committed to research as the first purpose of museums and, by extension, international expositions. Putnam did not want to waste his time putting up a temporary exposition, and what he built at Chicago became the foundation for the Field Columbian Museum. To Putnam the library and the laboratories were as important as the exhibit cases downstairs. For Putnam and Boas the search for knowledge was the important thing. It was a lifelong and inspiring commitment for both of them. Their peers and their ultimate court of judgment were their fellow scientists. Alice Fletcher learned to talk this line with Putnam, assuring him that all she wanted to do was make an important contribution to science. But her heart was never totally in it. She always had a popularizing, an ameliorative, side. Like Margaret Mead a generation and a half later, she wanted her work to have a wide audience and to change people's lives. It is possible to dismiss Fletcher's desire to have her science be useful as an old-fashioned concern, one related to Victorian optimism, faith in science and technology, and belief in human progress. But it is better, and truer, to see her not as old-fashioned, but as different, as part of a continuing tradition in science but one that has gone almost underground in many scientific fields in the twentieth century.

Overall, the Exposition was not a happy time for Alice Fletcher. She wrote her friend Isabel Barrows that the high point of the Exposition, "the crowning glory of this wonderful Fair," for her had been the World Congress of Religion.[21]

For the next eight months, Alice Fletcher did little other than give occasional talks on Indian music. She spoke at Vassar College in

December 1893, to the Baltimore branch of the Archaeological Institute of America in February 1894, at the Peabody Museum in
Cambridge in late spring, and to the Anthropological Society of
Washington in April. She was heartened by Franz Boas's favorable
review of "A Study of Omaha Indian Music," but in general through
the winter and spring months of 1894 she was restless, weary, and
merely marking time. The enormous burden of the Nez Perce allotments and the years of work on Omaha music had drained her,
seemingly to little purpose. Even more troubling was her inability to
see what lay ahead. She wondered what she should do next and if
anyone cared what she did.

Rescue came suddenly in July 1894, from the usual source. Mrs.
Thaw offered her five hundred dollars for a trip to Europe. "It came
most opportunely," Fletcher rejoiced to Putnam, "for I have been
under the Doctors care my head giving me trouble, and a sea voyage
and rest was ordered but . . . could not be obeyed. Then came Mrs.
Thaw's letter like a gift out of the open heavens."[22] Mrs. Thaw gave
much more than she knew, for the venture that began as a vacation
provided a chance for reflection and opened up new opportunities.

The trip also became a public display of Alice Fletcher's formal-
ized relation to Francis La Flesche, that of mother and son. Jane Gay,
who had been Alice's traveling companion for nearly ten years, was
hesitant to go so far away from a sister who was ill, so Francis went
instead. He took his summer vacation and ten extra days of leave,
and in August Alice Fletcher, Francis La Flesche, and Mrs. Tulloch
and her son, neighbors in Washington, sailed on the *Britannia* from
New York. After landing at Queenstown in Ireland the foursome
spent three weeks traveling through Ireland and Scotland and down
to London. They went through the English lake country, to Bath,
and over to Salisbury, where they visited Stonehenge and a "Druid
circle" at Keswich. The stone circles reminded Fletcher of the Indian
tribal circle and of communal gatherings for religious rites. Cambridge was shut up tight when they went through, but at Oxford
they were able to see the Anthropological Museum. Fletcher thought
the arrangement "unsatisfactory," for it was by topic, such as "musical instruments" or "weapons," rather than by geographical areas,
as Putnam preferred, and La Flesche found mistakes in some of the

labels. Then the two young men returned to Washington, and Alice Fletcher went to Belgium with Mrs. Tulloch. After a tour of Antwerp, Ostend, Bruges, Ghent, and Brussels, they went to Paris for two weeks. On October 1, Mrs. Tulloch returned to Washington, and Fletcher went on alone to Dresden, Germany, to spend two months with Zelia Nuttall.

Zelia Nuttall, Alice Fletcher discovered, was not the formidably confident rival she had at first thought. Nuttall made spectacular discoveries as she burrowed in dusty archives but did not always know what to do with them, and her paper at Chicago on the Mexican calendar system had been controversial. In Dresden Alice Fletcher began to function as a kind of scientific mother confessor to Zelia Nuttall, who was almost twenty years her junior. She encouraged her, advised her, and then interceded for her with Putnam. "Mrs. Nuttall is now at work on her Calendar. She is going to start afresh and gather together all her new material. She has certainly made gains since she left Chicago, and in the end I hope the monograph will be all that you and she may wish. She is very much in earnest . . . and intent on success," Fletcher wrote Putnam.[23]

While Alice Fletcher advised Zelia Nuttall on how to win Putnam's approval of her work, Zelia Nuttall in turn introduced her to important European scientists. They went to Prague, to Leipzig, to Vienna, and spent almost a week in Berlin, where Fletcher met Rudolf Virchow, Adolf Bastian, Eduard Seler, and Carl Stumpf, the preeminent leaders of German anthropology and ethnomusicology. She met a prominent musician, Rudolph Becker, who was much taken with "A Study of Omaha Indian Music" and arranged to have it translated and published in Germany.

From the safe distance of Europe Alice Fletcher reflected on her relation to Putnam and her future in anthropology. "I am sometimes tempted when I think of the Museum and of what I could possibly do there, to wish that I never did wish, to be a man! I am aware that being a woman I am debarred from helping you as I otherwise could—but the bar is a fact," she wrote him.[24] Chicago had taught her a lesson. Alice Fletcher had thought that good scientific work would put her securely on the appropriate rung of the professional ladder. She learned that quite other qualities, including but not limited to sex, determine the professional ladder. Kept off it, she had floundered for a year, wondering how and why to continue with work that interested her deeply but was not its own reward.

In Dresden with Zelia Nuttall, Alice Fletcher found new ways to carry on. She discovered a world of anthropology beyond the American establishment. She saw ways of working apart from the limited professional positions available in American universities and museums. She began to meet an international community of wealthy patrons and scholars, and she found herself appreciated among them. Scientists at home might be indifferent to her work, but European scholars were eager to hear about it and viewed her as an important contact with their American counterparts.

As she prepared to return home, Alice Fletcher thought about her own country and about what she had seen in Europe. She had gone the length and breadth of Ireland and changed her mind about it, she wrote Isabel Barrows, which can only mean that she liked it more than she had thought she would. Scotland was beautiful, she thought, and of England she marveled like an Indian Maharaja she had heard of that "in such a bit of country and such a climate a world, as it were, had been created."[25] But as she moved into Western and Central Europe, the heaviness of tradition began to weigh on her, and she rejoiced in the ideals of America and in "all that it has accomplished." "Dear Friend," she wrote Isabel Barrows, "Europe is interesting and pathetic, but for alive men and particularly alive women, our blessed land is the desirable spot. I would not give our working ideas, for all the beauty . . . here. My sympathies are much aroused for the people here who are so circumscribed and so weighted by their past, which is ever with them."[26]

In Europe, reflecting on America, Alice Fletcher regained her energy and her optimism. She returned to Washington late in 1894 eager to get back to work. She had made her peace with the professional scene at home, although a year later when she learned that the young assistant professor in Putnam's department had signed on to lead a cruise through the Atlantic, Mediterranean, and Indian oceans and was calling himself a "Professor of Archaeology and Egyptology," she was indignant that the "good Professor" was being so trifled with. She sniffed to Putnam's secretary that if she were not a woman and could be in that place, she would study and "stick to business."[27] But in general Alice Fletcher came home ready to push ahead with her career in any way that opened up to her and to create a new life for herself. Her life would increasingly center on "214," the home she shared with Francis and Jane Gay.

Eighteen

Life in Washington

ALICE Fletcher returned from Europe rejuvenated and eager to get to work. On the surface, her life stayed the same. She continued to define herself as professionally associated with the Peabody Museum in Cambridge but living in Washington in order to work with her Indian informant. In reality, however, the focus of her life had shifted. She recognized the limits of what Putnam could offer her. In Zelia Nuttall she had found the example of a woman who was making a career on her own as an independent scholar working out of her home, wherever that happened to be. For Alice Fletcher in 1895, Washington became home. Home most particularly was 214 First Street, S.E., the small but pleasant house on Capitol Hill which she shared with Jane Gay and Francis La Flesche.

This three-person household had already been in existence for five years. During those years, however, Fletcher viewed it more as an extension of her temporary quarters at the Temple Hotel than as a home with all the connotations of permanency and domestic warmth, even happiness, that that term implies. Alice and Jane Gay had been in Idaho for much of 1891 and 1892. In 1893 they were in Chicago, Jane Gay for nearly a year to care for her ailing sisters and Alice for five months during the Columbian Exposition. In 1894 Alice had spent five months in Europe. Although the Washington house was always there waiting—and Alice surely thought of it as her ultimate destination—she had been in no hurry to settle down. But the time had come. In letters to her friends, Alice revealed both

Alice Fletcher.
(National Anthropological Archives, Smithsonian Institution)

E. Jane Gay
(Schlesinger Library, Radcliffe College)

pride and a new note of self-consciousness about the household as she settled in to make a career for herself and a home for Jane Gay and Francis at 214.

"We have all been ill with Grippe—Miss Gay, Francis, Rebecca, the cat, and myself," Alice wrote Putnam in the spring of 1895.[1] She celebrated Easter morning that spring with a cheery letter to Isabel Barrows. "I am all alone," she wrote. "Miss Gay is at church. Francis too. I was late having some duties, but I've had a sweet time, for I have had refreshment in memory—and then Rebecca and I have been reading the Scripture together in the sunshine. She, poor girl, being in her early days a slave can't read and I like when I can to read for her. She does so much for me. so very much."[2]

Alice Fletcher's house was on a corner lot with a small yard in front surrounded by a decorative iron fence. The backyard had a large garden, with a pear tree, a magnolia tree, and roses, wisteria, and other flowers. To Rosalie Farley, on a day in late June 1896, she described their garden. "We have had many flowers. Our dinner table decorations have been from the garden since the last of March, and we have had flowers in the parlor and in my study for the past month or more. Flowers are like living beings to me, and bring many a happy hour to me, as I work alone."[3] Alice Fletcher was fifty-seven in 1895, Jane Gay was sixty-five, and Francis La Flesche forty years old. The three of them made a complex household. Alice was at the heart of it, both for Jane Gay and for Francis, who had little directly to do with one another.

Jane Gay was frank, funny, sometimes abrasive. In 1896 Alice described her friend and something of their relationship in a letter to Isabel Barrows. "Miss Gay is much better, almost like her old self," she wrote. "She is quite ready to poke fun at me, and take down my vanity. Excellent discipline no doubt, and I shall try to profit by it, but I fear I more mind my own stupidity, than her chaffing."[4] When they were apart, Jane Gay and Alice Fletcher wrote to one another two or three times a week, long, newsy, and affectionate letters full of domestic detail. They addressed each other as "Dear Lassie." Of all of Fletcher's letters to Jane Gay, only a few from the fall of 1898 survive, but those reveal the tone of their relationship. On September 21, 1898, Alice wrote: "Tom is picking the pears. . . . They were falling and making the garden a pig pen. . . . Don't hurry home until

Alice Fletcher's home at 214 First
Street, S.E., Washington, D.C.
(National Anthropological Archives,
Smithsonian Institution)

Alice Fletcher with camera and tripod in the back
garden at 214 First Street, S.E., and Francis La
Flesche in the same garden at apparently the same
time, ca. 1903. (National Anthropological Archives,
Smithsonian Institution) They are dressed up and
appear to be on their way to a social occasion.
Fletcher's direct, indeed open and trusting, look at
the photographer (by all evidence La Flesche) is in
remarkable contrast to nearly every other existing
photograph of her, where she appears looking
resolutely away from the camera.

the autumn weather sets in here. You are a troop and I miss you dear. F. sends love. Ever lovingly, Alice." On September 26, 1898, in a letter to her "Dear Lassie," Alice wrote that she was looking for a cook. The one she had hired had left for higher wages elsewhere. "I was glad for I did not like her. She was too talkative and familiar." Alice wrote that she was house-cleaning and that "F." was working hard. "I hope he will not break down."[5]

Alice liked to think that she was "making a home" for Jane Gay, in part in conscious repayment of the latter's devoted service to her in Idaho. When Jane Gay was ill in 1898, Alice wrote her: "You will surely be better dear and no matter what comes your home is here with me where you are tenderly beloved. . . . You must wait until the fall weather sets in before you return otherwise the heat here will harm you." A week later in the midst of having the kitchen painted she wrote: "I am beginning to look for you—I think by the last of next week you could come and by that time I hope to be settled. Ever with the old affection, Alice C. F."[6]

Jane Gay, however, continued to think of herself as taking care of Alice. She offered advice and opinions on every topic. She read and edited all of Alice's manuscripts. She took photographs when Alice needed them to illustrate something, although she seems otherwise to have given up photography. She spent hours making an exact miniature copy of an authentic Omaha earth lodge for the Peabody Museum and was hurt when her friends, stopping in Cambridge to see it, found that it had been stuck off in the basement.[7] After Fletcher complained to Putnam's secretary, the earth lodge was hastily moved upstairs. She was, in short, a supportive, outspoken, and occasionally tumultuous presence in the household. She was a vegetarian, so the meals had to be planned around what she would eat. Much of the furniture in the house, including a spinet piano, was hers, although she made no secret of her dislike for piano music. She paid some rent and shared household expenses, for Alice was saving every penny she could to pay interest on the mortgage. Jane Gay lived her own life in Washington and had her own friends. She and Alice seldom made calls together. Every now and then she would have dinner and spend the night with a "Miss Bradley," the daughter of a judge. Alice was bothered enough about this to note each such occasion in her diary, and she would write "Miss Gay home again" when her friend reappeared.

Francis La Flesche was a quiet and gentle presence in the household, but there were occasional flashes of feeling that betrayed the depth of his emotions. Francis was the only one of the three who went out every day to work. He was one of seventy clerks in the Bureau of Indian Affairs, part of the Department of the Interior which was located in the Patent Office Building. He lived as a son in the household, and Alice exercised over him a mother's authority. After Isabel Barrows's husband had stayed at 214 briefly while Alice was away, she wrote Isabel apologetically, "I fear the house looked like a camp for I found that Francis had broken his bounds and lived all over the premises—a privilege I accord when I am off for months."[8]

Francis bought a bicycle in the bicycling craze that swept Washington in the 1890s. He shared a billards table with the neighbors. He was Alice Fletcher's most frequent escort. They attended many social functions together and went together, sometimes two or three times a week, to the theater and to concerts. But he was a colleague as well as a son. In the evenings and on weekends he was her informant, translator, and co-worker as they labored over their publications. Not only was 214 Francis's home, but it was also the place where he did the work that meant the most to him. The house was almost as much the focus of his life as it was of hers.

Alice Fletcher was on a tight budget. At the end of 1901 she calculated that her household expenses for that year had been $1,469, toward which Jane Gay and Francis together contributed $625. The remaining $850 of home expenses, plus $500 of personal expenses for clothing, travel, and the costs of bringing her Pawnee informant to Washington, gave a total expenditure for the year of $1,350. Her annual stipend from the Thaw Fellowship was $1,050, less than Francis earned as a clerk in the Indian Bureau. She made up the difference through lecturing, writing, and occasional short-term assignments for the government. In 1898, 1901, and 1904 she worked on Indian Bureau exhibits for the expositions in Omaha, Buffalo, and St. Louis.[9]

The household broke up during the hot Washington summers. Jane Gay usually left for several months, going north to visit her brother at North Chelmsford or her sister at Lake Champlain or to stay with Mary Livermore at the latter's summer place on the ocean at Egypt, Massachusetts, south of Boston. Francis had a month's vacation at the Indian Bureau, and he usually went to visit his family on the Omaha Reservation. Alice's plans varied from year to year, depending on her work. She visited various friends, including always Mrs. Thaw, and traveled when she could.

Fletcher was still very loyal to Putnam. Their letters in 1895 and 1896 are full of mutual appreciation, as if both of them, in the aftermath of the Columbian Exposition, were taking special pains to keep up good feeling between them. Fletcher spent three weeks in the summer of 1895 cataloging and arranging the Omaha and Nez Perce exhibits at the Peabody Museum. On returning home she wrote: "I have not had a chance to tell you and Mrs. Putnam how much I enjoyed my visit. I look back [upon] it with delight. Oh: how refreshing to get away from the seething interest of the 'live Indian' and to contemplate Archaeological and historical problems. The heart ache is gone out of them. . . . One of these days I hope to come again."[10] She was eager to keep her professional address at the Peabody Museum. "My living here [in Washington] I consider as a sort of personal disability—but I always count myself as living in the Museum," she wrote Putnam. "I mean by 'in,' all my work, my thought, my interests centre there."[11]

Putnam had just taken a new extracurricular position as curator of anthropology for the American Museum of Natural History in New York, and he repeatedly told Alice how much he needed her to help him with the exhibits there. She in turn reassured him again and again of her loyalty to him and her willingness to help. And in fact she did help him, by having an Omaha skin tent made for the New York museum.

But a subtle change had taken place in their relationship. Fletcher no longer looked to Putnam to guide her work. Instead she began self-consciously to take charge of her own career. One of the first things Alice did as she settled in was buy a phonograph. She mentioned it casually to Putnam. "I have bought a Graphophone and already have taken important records. Monday night I had here three Otoe Indians. I took down on the cylinders 22 songs words and music and got at some very interesting materials," she told him. "We (Miss Gay, Francis and I) talked a good while about the graphophone before I took the expense, but I think it will prove a good thing."[12]

The graphophone was a signal, if Putnam had cared to read it as such, of her new professional independence and determination to set her own course. She wanted to gather new materials and not just write up what she already had. The graphophone proved to be a brilliant solution. Instead of traveling to reservations around the country, which she felt neither her health nor her pocketbook could stand and which Putnam did not want her to do, she would stay at home and work with Indians who came to Washington either on government business or at her invitation. It was her new method of fieldwork. So successful was she that it might well be said that for five or six years, beginning around 1895, the little row house at 214 First Street, S. E., in Washington was one of the more important research sites for anthropology in North America.

Although Fletcher no longer wanted Putnam to plan her activities, she needed him desperately for something else: to read what she had done after the fact and give it his professional stamp of approval. She was afraid of making a mistake, of crossing inadvertently, through an obvious error or gross generalization, the fine line between professional and amateur, which once breached can lead suddenly to a stone wall. She therefore continued to ask Putnam to read over and approve her writings, and when she was elected vice-president of section H of the AAAS that fall, she consulted Putnam about everything from what the topic of her vice-president's address should be to the smallest details of procedure. Chicago had left her feeling vulnerable, and she did not want to make a mistake.

Another reason she so often went beseechingly to Putnam in those years is that he expected her to. No detail was too small to receive Putnam's attention. Every question received a careful answer. Every submission got a thorough going-over: praise where it was deserved, encouragement when it was needed, and detailed criticism nearly always. Putnam was painstakingly meticulous. This is the secret of his organizational success as well as the reason for his frantic busyness. In writing he insisted on clarity, accuracy, and specificity. His red pencil marked out any suggestion of general theorizing, and Fletcher needed this, for she easily made wild statements. Alice Fletcher did not have professional training in anthropology in the sense that she was never formally enrolled in a degree program. She did have it in the sense that for at least fifteen years almost every word she wrote for scientific or general interest publications—and she wrote a lot—was submitted to Putnam for his criticism. She felt justified in doing this because the reputation of his museum was at stake in her work, and because he so clearly expected that she would.

Alice Fletcher's election as vice-president (presiding officer) of section H in 1895 was the most important scientific honor of her career. To be at the head of the major organization for anthropologists was a triumph in itself. Alice's two immediate predecessors had been Frank Hamilton Cushing and Franz Boas, the two brightest young anthropologists in the country. Adding to the significance of her election was that this was the first time a woman had been vice-president of any section of the American Association for the Advancement of Science. No woman had held an office of any kind in the AAAS until 1885, when another of Putnam's protégés, the ethnologist Erminnie Smith, was elected secretary of section H.

Fletcher's election was all the more surprising because for a decade she had not been present at the annual meetings of the AAAS. She had been elected a fellow in 1883, at Putnam's instigation, and was one of the stellar performers at the annual meetings in the mid-1880s, when she and Francis gave a demonstration of the Sacred Pipes and read a series of other papers. Then for ten years she had missed the meetings, either ignoring them altogether or sending papers reflecting her current preoccupations to be read in her name. In 1887 she had sent the paper "On the Preservation of Archaeologic Monuments," in 1889 one on the Winnebago language, in 1891 one on "The Nez Perce Country" based on a map drawn by a Nez Perce man, Jonathan "Billy" Williams. As she dropped out, so did Francis La Flesche, who had been made a member in 1884 and a fellow in 1885.[13]

Ten years later, in 1895, Alice was back with new credentials. She had become Thaw Fellow at the Peabody Museum and a full-time scholar. She read papers on "The Sacred Pole of the Omaha Tribe" and on "Indian Music," to show what her recent work had been, and the anthropologists welcomed her back by electing her to their highest office. Fletcher was extremely pleased. She spent much of the next year thinking about and carrying out her new responsibilities.

Everyone had ideas on what the topic for her vice-president's address should be. Frank Cushing wanted her to talk on "The Indian Woman." Jane Gay suggested the relation between Indian religious ideas and the political development of the tribe. Francis La Flesche urged the Omaha teachings on war and peace, and she herself thought perhaps she should talk about the relation between primitive song and primitive poetry. She asked Putnam for his opinion. "I am anxious to have my Vice-President's address something that shall be the best I can do," she wrote him.[14]

Alice eventually chose a variation of Jane Gay's suggestion, building on the paper on the Sacred Pole of the Omahas that she had given the year before at the AAAS meeting. When Putnam came to Washington for a meeting of the National Academy of Sciences that spring, he went over it carefully with her, after which she rewrote it completely.[15] The result was worth all the effort. Deceptively titled, "The Emblematic Use of the Tree in the Dakotan Group," it was superb, a careful and even intricate discussion, based on her deep knowledge of Omaha traditions, of the evolution of Omaha political ideas as they were symbolized by a sacred tree.[16] Fletcher related the Sacred Pole of the Omahas to the pole used by the Dakota Sioux as the focus of their Sun Dance. She suggested that the poles had once been a symbol of the search for supernatural help via the thunder gods that dwelt in the tops of trees. As scattered bands of Indians began to come together into larger political units, the Sacred Pole evolved into a symbol of group solidarity and of the authority of the tribe. The paper was a *tour de force* of carefully gathered field data interpreted with ethnohistorical sophistication.

Fletcher's interest in the pole as an old symbol that had taken on new meanings showed her growing understanding of Omaha history. From her study of the Omaha language and of their rituals and traditions, Fletcher had become aware of the great changes that had taken place in Omaha life as the people moved west over the course of several centuries, perhaps from as far east as the mid-Atlantic seacoast. Omaha history, as Fletcher saw it, was one of constant contact with other peoples, of splitting off from larger groups and merging with new groups, of incorporating new ideas and material skills, of moving into and adapting to radically different environments. Everything that Alice learned about Omaha history only reinforced her conviction that the Omahas could once again change their way of life. They had adapted before, and they could again. They had, in her view, no choice, for the buffalo on which they had built their most recent way of life were gone.

Fletcher brought Jane Gay and Mary Livermore with her to the AAAS meeting in Buffalo to share her triumph. In addition to presiding at the meeting and reading her vice-president's address, she read a second paper, "Notes on Certain Beliefs concerning Will Power among the Siouan Tribes." Afterward she and Mary Livermore went on to St. John in New Brunswick, Canada, for the annual meeting of the Association for the Advancement of Women. Fletcher had been away from that group for nearly twenty years. She was welcomed back like a heroine and at the evening meeting read a paper on "Rudimentary Art in Relation to High Art." Julia Ward Howe asked her to sing an Indian song, which was "greatly applauded,"[17] and called on her to lead them in "God Save the Queen." "A fine meeting," Fletcher noted in her diary.[18] A reporter for the *Buffalo Courier* described Alice Fletcher as of medium height, with a carriage of "dignity and grace" and features that "while essentially feminine and interesting, suggest the strength of character, the firmness and tenacity of a man." She has "administrative and executive ability to a marked degree," the reporter went on, and "much personal courage."[19]

In her vice-presidential address Alice Fletcher had demonstrated successfully that she was more than a field researcher or data collector. The next year she returned to the American Association for the Advancement of Science with another important theoretical paper, this time on "The Import of the Totem."[20] Sir James Frazer and other European armchair ethnologists had argued that the North American Indians believed they were actually descended from their totem animals. Alice Fletcher disagreed. She had found that, among the Omahas at least, the totem animal was the mascot of a particular individual and then gradually became recognized as the hereditary symbol for a whole clan. Fletcher knew that Franz Boas had come to a similar interpretation of totemism, based on his work on the Northwest Coast, and had published it in Germany the summer before. She wanted to make sure that she received credit for having come to the same conclusion independently. She and Boas began to be jointly credited with the "American theory" of totemism in the minds of Europeans, just as they were being identified (along with John Fillmore) as the new "American school" of ethnomusicology.[21] What distinguished the Americans from their European counterparts in both cases was their actual experience in the field among native peoples, a fact the Europeans were beginning to note, to their discomfort.

Fletcher's activities in 1896, 1897, and 1898 all point to her growing theoretical sophistication and to her interest in being recognized as a leader among American anthropologists. When she was invited to give a lecture at the Brooklyn Institute in the winter of 1897 she wrote Putnam: "I notice that I follow Prof. Haddon of Cambridge, Eng. and that Dr. Boas comes after me. I therefore stand in good company."[22] Fletcher's growing reputation led to numerous invitations to speak: to three hundred women in New York and to two hundred women in Philadelphia, all on one long weekend in March 1897. The British Association for the Advancement of Science wanted something from her for their joint meeting with the AAAS at Toronto in August 1897. She spoke on "The Significance of the Scalp Lock." The paper was published in the *Journal of the Anthropological Institute of Great Britain and Ireland* and was immediately picked up by the classics scholar Jane Ellen Harrison, who used it in her famous book, *Themis: A Study of the Social Origins of Greek Religion*. At the annual meeting of the American Folklore Society that winter, Fletcher read the same paper and was elected second vice-president of the society. In 1898 she appeared at the AAAS with an ingenious presentation on "The Significance of the Garment," illustrated with photographs that Francis La Flesche had provided for her many years before. She showed how Indians could dramatically convey a wide range of emotional states simply through the way they draped the blanket around them.

By 1898 Alice Fletcher was widely recognized as one of the seven or eight preeminent anthropologists in America. She was still president of the Woman's Anthropological Society in Washington and also president of the Science Club, a group of fifty women who met at Columbian University. They encouraged one another's scientific studies and sponsored annually a free course of lectures by an expert in some branch of science.[23]

As a well-known scientist, Alice Fletcher found Washington a nearly ideal place to live. She had returned there to make her home just as the city was beginning its "Golden Age"—one of the most flourishing and brilliant periods in its history. An essayist writing in the *Atlantic Monthly* in 1900 called Washington "the city of Leisure," where the general air of its inhabitants is one of dignified ease." There were no huge factories, no tenement houses, no stock exchange. "There is no feverishness, no excitement, no turmoil, because the loss of a minute does not mean the loss of a fortune."[24] Washington was a city of pleasure, with wide streets and innumerable parks and circles embellished with statues and flowers, but by no means a cultural backwater, for "eventually everyone comes to Washington" and "lions" are everywhere, not stone statues in front of libraries but attention-commanding human beings. Washington was also "the paradise of woman," the essayist wrote, for woman there had more influence than anywhere else. Wives ranked the same as their husbands, but what a man became often depended on his wife and daughters.[25] Society in Washington was not a mere diversion but part of the general scheme of things.

In Washington women were the social arbiters of society; government scientists, literary figures, and politicians were the center of the social whirl. Alice Fletcher had the best of both worlds. She participated in the ritual leaving of cards and in the weekly "at homes," which were a tradition in social Washington. "The Season" in Washington began in early January and lasted until the beginning of Lent. Ellen Maury Slayden, the wife of a Texas congressman and a leader of Washington society for twenty-two years, described the phenomenon in her journal in 1899. "This is the calling season," she wrote, "and in the afternoon from three to seven flocks of little one-horse coupes, some shabby . . . , others highly polished . . . fairly swarm around the big hotels and fashionable streets." The entertainment, whether in a modest home or a palace, was always the same. "A number of women stand about in semi-evening dress and pass you from one to another with an aerial handshake (at the level of your nose is the latest fashion)."[26] In 1904 Ellen Maury Slayden described one of her own receptions. "There is heavy snow and sleet, but the tea was a great success. Clever people are so easy to entertain; they do it for themselves. Mrs. Hill helped me to get dear Miss Alice Fletcher, Mrs. W. H. Holmes, and Dr. Irving, so with

Dr. Rosalie Slaughter, we made quite a showing of clever titled women. . . . There are no people in Washington more agreeable and cheery than those connected with our scientific departments. In a simple, unpretentious way they entertain a good deal too, which is greatly to their credit for they are wickedly ill paid."[27] Another time she rejoiced at having had as one of her luncheon guests "dear Miss Alice Fletcher, so motherly and warm for all she is a 'leading scientist.'"[28]

Alice Fletcher's own "at home" was on Monday, the traditional day for residents of Capitol Hill, and many well-known people made their way to her door. Simon Newcomb, the astronomer and laissez-faire economist, was a frequent guest in Miss Fletcher's drawing room. Jane Gay's niece and namesake, Jane Gay Dodge, sometimes poured tea on these occasions, and she remembered as "the handsomest and most charming of all" an ex-congressman from Massachusetts, Samuel June Barrows, who was also a Unitarian clergyman, a sociologist and journalist, and the husband of Fletcher's good friend Isabel Chapin Barrows.[29]

Alice Fletcher was herself often a dinner guest in the homes of congressmen and government scientists and a visitor to the White House during four administrations. She was invited to join the elite clubs: the Washington Club, the Historical Society, the Friday Morning Music Club, and the prestigious Literary Society. One irreverent young diplomat's wife spoke of an invitation to join the Literary Society as having been admitted "into the enchanted circle of the Brain Club."[30] The Literary Society was limited to forty men and women, not counting the ex-officio members—the president, chief justice, speaker of the House of Representatives, attorney general, and secretary of the Smithsonian—and a few honorary members, who provided both money and prestige, like William Wilson Corcoran and Mrs. Rutherford B. Hayes. The "Literary," as it was called, met every other Saturday night from December through May to hear one another's papers, and its members enjoyed each other's company so much that they seldom broke up before midnight.[31] Politics and religion were forbidden topics, but anything else was fair game, and the discussions were lively. Members of the "Literary" thought of themselves as an aristocracy of the intellect. They ignored formal titles and military rank, prided themselves on having no dues, and served only simple suppers, but the women wore formal gowns and the men white tie and tails. The Literary Society was first organized in 1874. By Fletcher's time it was slightly past its prime, not quite the exuberant group it had been in the early years, when James Garfield, later President Garfield, gave a paper on the habits of aeronaut spiders and George Kennan appeared in a gray uniform, chains, and fetters for his talk on political prisoners in Siberia. Yet it still thought of itself as the center of the artistic and literary life of the Capitol, rivaled only by the all-male Cosmos Club, and those outside the "Literary" wanted in.

Alice Fletcher was one of the feminine luminaries of the "Literary," along with such other Washington women writers as Frances Hodgson Burnett, the author of *Little Lord Fauntleroy*, and the immensely popular Mrs. E.D.E.N. Southworth. Alice Fletcher sponsored Senator and Mrs. Henry Dawes for membership, at their request. The former actress Jean Lander, a longtime member of the Literary Society, always insisted that the society's first meeting in each new year should be "on the Hill" at her home. After Lander's death in 1903, Alice Fletcher kept up the tradition at her little home at 214. Guests were welcomed at meetings of "the Literary." Fletcher took F. W. Putnam once or twice when he happened to be in town, but her customary escort was Francis La Flesche.

As the city became more glittering and fashionable, new wealth poured in and gave a different tone to Washington social life. "Mrs. Thaw is spending the winter here," Alice reported to Putnam in 1903. "Harry took the house next the Lafayette Theater . . . and here Harry has set up, to dive into "the Swim." He has English flunkies, etc., and he dines and dances, I hope to his heart's content. Alice [his sister] is enjoying it, and Mrs. Thaw too in a degree, although she protests as she goes, still she goes. . . . It is funny to see it all. Washington is wonderfully gay—so I hear."[32] Many old-timers in Washington turned their backs on the partying newcomers and withdrew into hidden caves of exclusiveness. "Cave-dwellers" they began to call one another proudly.[33] A "cave-dweller" was anyone whose family had been in Washington for at least two generations. Jane Gay, who had lived in Washington since the Civil War, was a "cave-dweller" and so, by extension and courtesy, was Alice Fletcher.

Meanwhile the fieldwork flourished, fieldwork that was an ongoing part of life at 214 First Street. The three Otoe Indians Alice had mentioned to Putnam were just the beginning. Francis brought other Indians to the house, and by the end of March 1895 they had nearly one hundred graphophone records and "some very interesting material relative to new religions which have sprung up in certain Indian tribes," Alice wrote Putnam. She already knew about the Ghost Dance religion. What she and Francis were getting were hints of a related "new religion"—a synthesis of Christian and traditional ideas and practices along with the use of peyote, a religion that would eventually become known as the Native American Church. "I want to write it and get it out before any one does so before me. Where would you like me to publish this?" she asked Putnam.[34] There is no evidence that she ever published anything on the use of peyote or on the Native American Church, but it is remarkable that she found out about it as early as 1895, before it had spread even to the Omaha and Winnebago reservations. That summer Francis took the graphophone to the Omaha Reservation. He spent six weeks there and returned with "80 splendid records and considerable new material."[35]

Early in 1896 Alice and Francis brought Francis's Ponca uncle to Washington to spend ten days with them. The old man had been very ill and had postponed the trip several times but finally felt well enough to come. Alice and Francis each paid half of his expenses. They recorded on the graphophone more than eighty Ponca songs. They also took down several ceremonies: a ceremony of the "counting of honors"; the early morning ceremony used by a war party complete with its ritual songs; a ceremony used in tattooing symbols upon women; and the Ponca Sun Dance ceremony which the old man had been through three times.

Fletcher was delighted with this wealth of new material that fit into topics she wanted to write on, including the Sun Dance and tattooing. She wrote Putnam:

Francis has worked night and day, and will have to work night and day for some time to come, with me. It would have been absolutely impossible for anyone to have gained this material without him. His

uncle's regard for him has opened many a secret. Francis said jok-
ingly that he thought he was doing enough for the Museum to win
him a place among its workers. He certainly does labor assiduously
and loyally.[36]

Fletcher was hinting to Putnam that Francis ought to receive more
recognition from the Peabody Museum for his work. She may also
have begun to sense that Francis wanted more recognition from her.
In June of that year Fletcher noted in her diary, "Had a significant
talk with Francis touching the future."[37]

The following winter they hosted an Osage delegation. Again
Francis's labors were heroic. "Francis is working every eve. until
midnight getting their names, and rites as far as we can, that we may
compare these with the Omaha," Alice reported to Putnam. Francis
was not only tireless; he was also ingenious. One day he caught a
glimpse of a tatoo on the chest of one of the Osage men. Eager to
get a better look, he built a blazing fire and kept the Indian near it
until the latter removed first his coat and vest and then finally
opened his shirt. The design was remarkable but extended below
the waist, "so F. must try another scheme to see more," Alice wrote
Putnam.[38] Fletcher was so excited about the Osage material that she
started to write up the rite of adoption for the AAAS meeting that
fall, but Francis demurred, suggesting that she should wait until
they had the songs for the ritual and could make it complete. In the
end she decided he was right, and since she was not feeling well
enough to work anyway she withdrew the paper.[39]

Later that spring they worked with some Caddo and Wichita Indians who had come to Washington. These were not randomly chosen tribes. The Caddo and Wichita Indians were from the same
stock as the Pawnees, who before they were removed to Indian Territory had been the largest Indian tribe in Nebraska. Fletcher had
begun to think that the Omahas had drawn much from Pawnee
culture and was eager to do comparative studies.[40]

In the winter of 1898 in Washington, Alice and Francis worked
with some visiting Sioux Indians and then again with Osage Indians,
and Fletcher began to plan a fieldwork expedition to the Osage Reservation in Oklahoma. "The way has opened for me to go among
the Osages, to observe some of their customs, and to get at some of

their material, and if I can, I think I shall go there in the early summer," she wrote Putnam in the spring of 1898.[41] Fletcher was casting her eyes beyond the Omahas—to the major work she might do either on the Osages or the Pawnees. She seems not to have given any thought to what Francis's role in this work would be, simply assuming that he would continue to help her.

Nineteen

"No people can be helped if they are absolutely unrooted"

I N the summer of 1897 Alice Fletcher had gone back to the Omaha Reservation, for the first time in seven years. She went to do research with Francis La Flesche, but she wanted also to see how the Omahas were progressing, and she was shocked at what she found. She was aware that the Omahas were not farming their land themselves but were leasing it and living on rental income. What she was not prepared for was the general sense of "mental desolation" that had replaced the intense factionalism she remembered.[1] She was taken back to learn that Christianity had virtually died out on the reservation, the result both of waning interest and disgust with the local missionaries. Only three Omahas regularly attended the local church. "In consequence, there has been a revival of the old Indian rites, for man cannot live by bread alone," she commented. But in a greatly altered situation these had little meaning. It was a demoralized people who were left to cope with every temptation that local whites could offer, especially alcohol and credit, and the Indians had little will to resist. The old way was gone; the new way had been tried and found wanting. Among even the best-intentioned white people, the Indians found themselves having to face "misunderstanding and a contemptious [sic] sort of pity."[2]

Alice Fletcher sensed cultural disintegration—she called it a loss of self-respect—among the Omahas, and she did not know what could be done about it. What the Omahas themselves were to do about it was to turn to the peyote religion. By 1916 even Francis La Flesche had become a strong defender of the peyote religion.[3] On the Omaha Reservation in the summer of 1897 Fletcher finally had to confront the self-evident results of her disastrous program for the Indians.

While she was pondering that, Fletcher decided to take on another government assignment. She agreed to prepare the Indian Bureau exhibit for the Trans-Mississippi and International Exposition to be held in the city of Omaha, Nebraska, in the summer of 1898. The citizens of the city of Omaha had decided to cope with the depression and financial panic of 1893 by simply denying that it was happening. Led by a local banker, they planned a Trans-Mississippi Exposition, incorporated it in 1896, and carried it off successfully in 1898, despite the continuing business depression and a foreign war. Railroads, utilities, banks, newspapers, breweries, stockyards, merchants, and insurance companies invested in it, and Congress and several states appropriated money for it. A group of "glittering white buildings," in imitation of Chicago's "White City," were put up on the bluffs along the Missouri River and were visited that summer by President William McKinley and nearly three million other Americans.[4]

At the last minute promoters of the Trans-Mississippi and International Exposition decided that a live exhibit of American Indians would be a drawing card. Indians from Oklahoma and Indian territories were invited to camp on the Exhibition grounds and were encouraged to attack one another in sham battles repeated day after day to the delight of large audiences.[5] Alice Fletcher was distressed at the amount of newspaper publicity given these sham battles of "wild Indians" while her own display of handicrafts, designed to show "the fine things that the Indian mind was capable of," was ignored.[6] So provoked was she that she wrote an article for the *Southern Workman* calling attention to her own exhibit at Omaha. She wrote that the exhibit showed how readily Indian children were taking on white civilization at the government schools. Many former students had come by with their husbands and wives, and "one and all recognized that the past life of the Indian was a closed book." She added, "Listening to these representatives of the Indian race, one felt the importance of keeping the book of the past closed, that the past fraught with deep lessons to the student of mankind, but filled with misunderstandings and tragedies in which two races have had their share, might cease to be an obstacle in the path of the rising generation which must be citizens with us under one flag."[7]

Although her message was nearly obscured in her verbose prose, this was one of Alice Fletcher's strongest statements about the goal of her reform work and the purpose of her ethnography. She saw the past life of Indians as closed. It was of no interest to contemporary Indians and should not even be presented to them, for fear of arousing "misunderstandings" and hostile feelings. The past of the Indians was by implication for scientists only, those "students of mankind" who could understand the "deep lessons" that it revealed.

But then Alice Fletcher had what can almost be described as a conversion experience. She happened to read "A Man without a Country," and she was struck by how similar Philip Nolan's plight was to that of American Indian youths. They too were being set adrift, cut loose from their past. Alice Fletcher suddenly understood what she had never understood before, the need for connection with one's past, the need for roots. She immediately sent another article to the *Southern Workman*, ambiguously titled "Flotsam and Jetsam from Aboriginal America" but containing her reflections on Philip Nolan. The articles were published two months apart, in November 1898 and in January 1899.[8] From these we can date Alice Fletcher's change of heart on the Indian question almost to the month, the ground having been prepared by her visit to the Omaha Reservation in 1897. Finally she had to acknowledge that her radical and comprehensive program for Indian "civilization" was a failure and had been a mistake.

Alice Fletcher never made this admission publicly. The evidence that she acknowledged her mistake lies in her actions and in her subsequent curious relation to the Lake Mohonk reformers. After 1899 Alice Fletcher threw herself into scholarship and generally kept out of Indian politics. Her only continuing connection to the Indian reform movement was the annual invitation that came every summer to attend the Lake Mohonk Conference of the Friends of the Indian and Other Dependent Peoples, as it came to be called, and a curious pattern developed in her response to these invitations. Alice Fletcher would accept the invitation and then several weeks later, just as the conference was about to begin, she would write to say that she was unable to attend, giving only the vaguest of reasons: ill health or the pile of work on her desk. She obviously did not want to go. She did not want to give lip service to a program in which she no longer believed nor did she want to admit that she had been wrong. Yet she did not want to cut her ties with Mohonk completely.

It was a dilemma without a solution. Some years (1901, 1906, 1910, 1912, and 1913) she was traveling and could avoid it entirely, but other years she could not. In 1900 she wrangled an invitation to the Lake Mohonk Conference for Francis; they both went, and Francis had a marvelous time. She returned in 1902, in 1907, and in 1909, but at least five times between 1897 and 1916 she agreed to be there and at the last minute suddenly declined. The closest she came to admitting her change of position was in a letter in 1905 to Albert Smiley, the host at Lake Mohonk. After accepting his invitation, she wrote on the opening morning of the conference that "an unexpected and difficult piece of ethnological work has so used up my strength that I dare not venture to leave home." She went on, somewhat enigmatically: "My own ethnological studies widen the aspect of affairs. The revelation of the Indian's thought, of his ancient attempts to express ideals of life and of duty are not only helpful to an understanding of his condition today but they are also encouraging to those who are trying to assist him to cross over into our community. There is much in his past that should be conserved, for no people can be helped if they are absolutely uprooted. It is just here that the Ethnological student can become a practical helper to the philanthropist."[9] If Albert Smiley read this carefully, he must have realized that she had shifted her stance dramatically. What did not change was her sense of herself as an authority. For almost twenty years she had insisted, on the basis of her almost unique field experience, that the Indians needed to give up their previous way of life. Suddenly she was arguing as an "Ethnological student" that there was much in their old ways that ought to be conserved.

In that same 1905 letter to Albert Smiley, Alice mentioned that the Bureau of American Ethnology had just published her account of the ancient intertribal peace-pipe ceremony as performed by the Pawnees. Her scholarship and growing knowledge of Indian religious ceremonies had finally led her to see in positive terms what her observations on conditions on the Omaha Reservation had revealed in negative terms: that the Indians, like any people, were lost without a comprehensive, sustaining world view such as had been available to them in their own religious traditions.

Alice Fletcher came to understand, too late, that massive cultural change cannot be forced on an unwilling people. To her credit, however, unlike many of her contemporaries she did not turn to racist explanations for the failure of the Indians to become what she wanted them to be. As the optimism of the 1880s gave way to pessimism and disillusionment in Congress and the Indian Office at the turn of the century, many federal policy makers began to hint that Indians and blacks were not the equal of whites and could not be expected to do as well as whites. Indians, like blacks, were to be relegated to permanent second-class citizenship, on the fringes, if not at the lowest levels, of society.[10] Alice Fletcher did not join in that new approach to Indian affairs. She never lost her conviction that the Indians were as capable as whites, that they could compete successfully with whites if they wanted to, and that they should be invited to share the best that white society had to offer.

That she knew her philanthropy had been a mistake helps to explain the intensity with which in the late 1890s Alice Fletcher threw herself into her scientific work. A decade earlier she had been acclaimed both as a reformer and as a scientist. By 1898 she knew that only in science might she accomplish something of lasting significance, and only through science could she still try to help the Indians. It was the settlement house women, Jane Addams and Lillian Wald, who would be the reform heroines in America in the early twentieth century,[11] not the women who had tried to solve "the Indian problem."

But as she moved vigorously into new scientific work, Alice Fletcher was brought up short by Francis La Flesche, who was having second thoughts of his own about the course his life was taking. The crisis began in the spring of 1898 as they made plans for the Omaha Exposition. John Fillmore was invited to give a paper on aboriginal music at the congress of musicians, to be held in Omaha in conjunction with the Exposition, but he replied that he would do nothing on Indian music for the event unless Alice Fletcher and Francis La Flesche were included.[12] Fillmore's letter telling Alice of this arrived the same day as did the official invitation to participate, which was addressed to Francis.

Alice Fletcher immediately took over the planning of the event. She decided that Francis should go to the Omaha Reservation in June, gather up a group of singers, and bring them to Omaha, where they would perform to illustrate papers to be given by John Fillmore and herself. The speed with which Fletcher planned all of this is astonishing. She wrote to Fillmore with this proposal the same day that Francis received the invitation to participate in the congress. Within forty-eight hours she had made a visit to the Indian Office—Francis La Flesche's employers—to request that he be detailed to go to the reservation and be authorized to bring five or six singers to Omaha, their expenses to be paid out of the appropriation just then pending before Congress for the Indian exhibit.[13]

Alice Fletcher's eagerness is easy to understand. Here was a chance to do what had been denied her at the World's Columbian Exposition at Chicago. She could work with John Fillmore in recording music from other Indian tribes, for some five hundred Indians were to be camped at Omaha on the Exposition grounds. She saw in the Omaha Exposition a chance to reclaim the attention she felt she deserved as a pioneer in the study of Indian music. She also saw this as a chance to promote Indian music among the general public, where she felt it had never really found its rightful audience. But in making these excited plans she had not consulted Francis. The invitation turned into a quiet crisis, like those they had had several times before, as they attempted to work out the terms of the professional part of their relationship. They were mother and son, but they were also anthropologist and informant, a relationship that can be as long-term, emotional, dependent on trust, and prone to misunderstandings and conflicting interests as the closest of family ties.

The first crisis had come just after they had finished the allotments in the summer of 1884. Alice Fletcher had realized as the Omahas performed the ceremony of the Sacred Pipes for her and presented a special set of pipes to her and Francis that the wa-wan ceremony "is a far greater thing than I dream of or ever supposed it was." [14] She had decided to give a paper on the pipes at the American Association for the Advancement of Science meeting that fall. But then James Owen Dorsey had come to visit her and Francis in Washington and had suggested that Francis join the AAAS and give a paper on the pipes. Dorsey's seemingly innocent suggestion, which Francis picked up eagerly, threw Fletcher into turmoil. She had established a potentially fruitful relationship with an Indian. Was he now to be elevated to the status of anthropologist and she thrust aside? Fletcher knew that Dorsey was right, that it was only fair that Francis receive credit for his share in the work, but at the same time she felt her own career was on the line. The result was a compromise. She and Francis had each given papers on the pipes and sung the pipe songs together for the AAAS, but she had presented two additional papers, on "Child Life Among the Omahas," and "Experiences in Allotting Land Among the Omahas," to establish the seriousness of her professional intentions and the breadth of her knowledge.

The issue lay dormant for several years, as both Alice Fletcher and Francis La Flesche worked for the government and did what little ethnography they still had the time for. By 1890 when she was appointed Thaw Fellow, Alice Fletcher had forgotten that it ever was an issue. She seems to have been oblivious to the discontent behind Francis's sudden decision to go to law school. Two years later, in 1893, she was genuinely surprised at Francis's sudden expression of feeling about being listed on the title page of "A Study of Omaha Indian Music." She had been immediately accommodating, changing the title page to read, "By Alice F. Fletcher aided by Francis La Flesche."

But it was not enough, as Francis La Flesche eventually needed to make clear to her. Exactly what Francis did in 1898 is not known. So subtle was he, in fact, that six months later Alice Fletcher still hardly understood what had happened. Yet somehow he made her understand that she could no longer continue to take him for granted. He did not chide her directly for taking over an invitation addressed to him, nor did he complain about being treated as an errand boy while she and Fillmore received all the credit for their joint endeavors. He was much too gentle—and too genuinely fond of Alice Fletcher—for that. Francis's friends spoke often of his instinctive kindliness; nowhere is it better revealed than in this instance. He apparently simply demurred about the music congress and intimated that he was thinking of leaving scientific work altogether, perhaps to return to law.

The evidence for this, and Alice's only surviving comments on the incident, are in a letter to Miss Mead, Putnam's secretary. She wrote (six months later):

> (Please say privately to Prof. Putnam not to hint to anyone or in any way the personal matter I spoke of last spring—it seems to have been but a passing shower. Science has greater charms. I would not have my little confidence betrayed, for it would do harm. You will do this, but say nothing of it to me in a letter. You will understand the delicacy of my position. I spoke hastily, because I was so disappointed on account of the work, but I did wrong and was too anxious, it seems.) [15]

Whatever the intention Francis conveyed to Alice, she was sincerely alarmed, for she knew how much she needed his help to complete the Omaha work. Immediately she began to get him professional recognition. She arranged that he too would give a presentation at Omaha. The final program for "Indian Music Day" at the National Congress of Musicians in 1898 included talks by John C. Fillmore on "The Harmonic Basis of Indian Music," by Alice C. Fletcher on "The Psychic Nature of Indian Music," and by Francis La Flesche on "The Omaha Indian Songs of War and Peace." In the evening there was what Fletcher had been so yearning for, a concert of compositions based on Indian themes, including "Indian Suite" recently composed by Edward Alexander MacDowell and "Hiawatha" Overture by Ernest Richard Kroeger. When a correspondent, Walter McClintock, wrote to Fletcher that summer asking how he might go about recording the music of the Blackfeet Indians in Montana, she sent him an encouraging reply and a copy of Francis's paper. "Prof. Fillmore, Mr. La Flesche, and I . . . wish you every success," she wrote. "We are the three pioneers in Indian music, Mr. La F. leading, opening the door to me some 18 years ago." [16]

That fall, for the first time in fourteen years, Francis returned to the AAAS meeting with a paper on the "Ritual of the Omaha Sacred Pole," which he had recorded that summer on the reservation, and Fletcher sent advance word to Putnam that it was "a very interesting and valuable paper."[17] Two years later he was again at the AAAS with a paper on "The Shell Society Among the Omahas," based on what he had been told as a child and on what he had witnessed the summer before on the Omaha Reservation.[18] Without telling her directly, Francis had nevertheless managed to let her know that he felt he deserved more public credit for their work, and she had responded as he surely knew she would, in the way that he wanted. But if "science had greater charms" than whatever else Francis had hinted he might prefer to do, the exact nature of their continuing collaboration remained unresolved. Both of them apparently puzzled over it. Francis had begun an autobiographical memoir about five young Omaha boys at the mission school and was collecting material for a biography of his father. He may well have decided that instead of continuing to collect ethnographic data, he would like to write up what he knew in his own way.

Whatever its source, the idea of Francis as a "man of letters" eventually surfaced in his and Alice's discussions. It seemed the near-perfect solution to an otherwise intractable if unspoken problem. Alice Fletcher did not want to share her scientific reputation with Francis La Flesche, but he was no longer willing to remain in the background. The decision they made late in 1898 was that they would go their separate ways professionally. "I stand for science, rather than letters . . . letters will, I trust, be your avocation in the future. Your science will be mainly your general help of me, and all I can do for you to win you a name there," she wrote him in the summer of 1899.[19] It was a good time to make the break, for their major joint work, an ethnography of the Omaha tribe, was temporarily derailed anyway because of the theft of the Sacred White Buffalo hide. Without the hide, the collection of Omaha sacred objects at the Peabody Museum was incomplete. Fletcher and La Flesche postponed their work on the monograph, hoping that the hide would turn up. Fletcher also worried that their Omaha volume was forestalled by J. O. Dorsey's work and that it would be a "twice-told tale."[20] They quietly put aside the Osage studies as well, perhaps in recognition of the unspoken rivalry between them over who would do it. Francis concentrated on his autobiographical book, *The Middle Five*, and Alice turned to new projects, and to a new informant.

The Middle Five is an account of Francis La Flesche's schoolboy days in the Presbyterian boarding school on the Omaha Reservation. The "middle five" were Francis and four friends who were halfway between the small boys who went to bed at 8 o'clock and the Big Seven who were allowed to stay up until 10 P.M. His is a matter-of-fact and sometimes poignant account of young children trying to learn the ways of a strange world. In November 1898 Francis and Alice both appeared before a meeting of the Folklore Society of Baltimore. She read a portion of *Indian Story and Song from North America*, a little popular book she was working on giving Indian stories and melodies for easy use by composers. He read a portion of *The Middle Five* and "brought down the house," Fletcher told Putnam proudly.[21] Both books were published by Small and Maynard of Boston in the same year, 1900. It was an unexpectedly happy conclusion to their decision made some eighteen months earlier, to be henceforth separate but equal.

Meanwhile Francis had not left her stranded. He met in Washington, and brought home to 214 First Street, James R. Murie, a Pawnee they had both known when he was a student at Hampton with La Flesche's younger siblings. For fourteen years Alice Fletcher and Francis La Flesche had been searching for a fuller version of the Peace Pipe ceremony they had seen in a very truncated form among the Omahas. They were sure that it must exist among neighboring tribes and in 1884 had even talked of going to visit the Pawnees to look for it, but they had not been able to do so.[22] James Murie told them of an old Pawnee priest of the Chawi subtribe of the Pawnee confederacy who might know the ceremony. On his return to the Pawnee Reservation, Murie inquired of the old priest about it, and the priest, after thinking about it for a week, was able to recall nearly all of the four-day-long ceremony. The priest was very hesitant to reveal the full ceremony to white people and allow it to be transcribed and published, but he finally was persuaded to work with them because he had been Joseph La Flesche's friend. In the fall of

1898 James Murie brought the old priest, Ti-hi-roos-sa-wi-chi, to Washington. This was the beginning of a collaboration between Alice Fletcher and James Murie that was to last for four years. Murie brought other Pawnee men to Washington, and he returned with the old priest in 1900. Fletcher went twice to the Pawnee Reservation in Oklahoma, in the spring of 1900 and the fall of 1901. In between she sent Murie long pages of questions, which he answered after consultation with Ti-hi-roos-sa-wi-chi.

Alice Fletcher worked for more than three years on the Pawnee calumet ceremony, which she called by a Pawnee term, the Hako. She transcribed and translated the entire four-day cycle, including nearly one hundred songs, and gave an approximate indication of the choreography. When finished, she had 890 pages of manuscript. It was the most complete account of an Indian religious ceremony ever recorded and remains one of the fullest and most sensitive documentations of such a ceremony. Although little noticed as such, it was also her finest work in ethnomusicology.[23]

Both *The Hako* (1904) and eventually *The Omaha Tribe* (1911) were published not by the Peabody Museum but by the Bureau of American Ethnology in Washington, a shift in loyalty that ten years earlier Fletcher would have found unimaginable. Ostensibly the reason for the shift was money. John Welsey Powell had offered to pay her Pawnee research expenses and urged her to let the Bureau publish the volume. Fletcher knew that the government-subsidized Bureau publications were lavish. At the Peabody Museum she would have had to raise the printing costs herself. But she was also feeling somewhat disgruntled with Putnam and was ready to move out from under his supervision. In 1899, during a visit to Cambridge, she wrote in her diary: "Long talk with Prof. P. He disapproves of my work on myths."[24] A week later she wrote: "Spoke in P. M. [Peabody Museum] Read the myth of Serv't, and this Omaha for certain."[25] What she meant was that the myth of the servant was definitely an Omaha myth. Her tone and slightly belligerent comment reveal that she knew the probable source of Putnam's criticism to be Franz Boas.

Franz Boas had already begun to influence American anthropology with his method of trait distribution studies, in which he stressed the geographical dispersion of culture traits, whether designs in weaving, themes in a folktale, or elements of the Sun Dance. Boas emphasized borrowing as a means of cultural change. Alice Fletcher was aware of borrowing and often documented it. But once an item had been borrowed, she considered it part of the cultural resources of a people and treated it as such. She felt intimations of Boas's criticism conveyed through Putnam, that some of what she called "Omaha" was not really Omaha but had been borrowed from other tribes, and she was hurt that Putnam would side with him rather than with her.

The Hako was only the beginning of her Pawnee researches. In the first issue of the new journal *American Anthropologist*, Fletcher published "A Pawnee Ritual Used When Changing a Man's Name," which the old priest had given her soon after his arrival in Washington. For the *Journal of American Folk-Lore* she wrote "Giving Thanks: A Pawnee Ceremony" recording a ceremony that she had been allowed to see in Oklahoma as the old priest's guest in 1900. Most exciting of all were two preliminary compilations of Pawnee star lore that she sent to these journals.[26] Star symbolism and deification was an important component of the Pawnee religion, which up to the early nineteenth century had included a ritual of human sacrifice to the Morning Star. This was one of the few known instances of ritual human sacrifice in North America. When Major Powell and W J McGee at the Bureau of American Ethnology learned that Alice Fletcher was getting Pawnee star lore, they insisted that she telegraph her informants at once and have them come to Washington, promising to pay all expenses. "Mr. McGee says I 'have struck a bonanza!'" she wrote to Putnam in great excitement.[27]

But Alice Fletcher's Pawnee researches ended abruptly a few months later when her informant, James Murie, was wooed away from her. George A. Dorsey, curator of anthropology at the Field Columbian Museum of Natural History in Chicago, had been interested in the Pawnees since 1899. Dorsey was one of Putnam's first Ph.D. students and an aggressive and well-financed collector, supported by the Carnegie Institution of Washington among others. Dorsey had suggested to Fletcher that they might collaborate on a major ethnography of the Pawnees, and she had accepted.[28] Then in the spring of 1902 he offered James Murie one hundred dollars a month and research expenses for four years if Murie would leave

Fletcher and work with him instead.[29] Murie hesitated but only briefly, and Alice Fletcher resigned herself to what was a *fait accompli*. She had been paying Murie at a piecemeal rate, $1.50 per day while he was in Washington, and approximately the same amount to the old priest.[30] Murie worked for Dorsey sporadically for seven years. In 1910 he became a part-time ethnologist for the Bureau of American Ethnology, and in 1912 he began to work with Clark Wissler. He produced a massive body of work, some of which was not published until 1981.[31] As for Alice Fletcher, once again she found herself in the position of having opened up a significant topic, in this case Pawnee star lore, as before it had been Indian music, only to have it and her expert whisked away from her.

After his initial success with *The Middle Five*, Francis La Flesche's career "in letters" began to pale. He wrote a great quantity of short stories, Omaha folktales, and autobiographical bits, but he published very few. Whether this was owing to publishers' indifference, to his own indifference, or to his judgment that the pieces needed more work is not known. In 1901 Alice wrote a chatty letter to her old friend Mrs. Dawes describing all their activities. "Miss Gay is better than for years this winter and Mr. La Flesche is well. He is writing whenever he can get a chance, but the office work is so heavy this winter that he feels little spring for literary efforts. . . . As for me I am preparing quite a little volume on 'The Ceremony of the Hako' which the Bureau of Ethnology will publish. It is a very interesting cult that some 300 years ago was honored through out the Mississippi Valley."[32]

On the surface, the years around Alice Fletcher's sixtieth birthday in 1898 were quiet, particularly when compared to more tumultuous periods in her life, some past and some still to come. Yet beneath the surface some subtle but major changes in her orientation had taken place in these years. She had admitted to herself that the allotment and civilization program for Indians on which she had spent almost ten years of her life had been a failure. She had come to terms with Francis's dissatisfaction and had begun to work separately from him. She had moved from reform activities to the highest level of anthropological scholarship. The past was still prelude for her. Again she was looking ahead to see what she might do. Next to come was politics in her chosen field.

PART 4

Abroad
and at Home

Twenty

"Awful scene at my bed"

A MERICAN anthropology was at a turning point at the end of the nineteenth century. The anthropological community was stunned in 1900 by the death of the brilliant young Frank Hamilton Cushing, who choked on a fish bone while eating dinner and died before help could be summoned. At the memorial meeting for Cushing, Alice Fletcher spoke of the field method they had shared and of his "unconscious sympathy" with the Indians.[1] Two years later the Washington scientific community mourned the death of John Wesley Powell, the famous one-armed explorer, geologist, anthropologist, and founder of the Bureau of American Ethnology. For two decades Powell had given intellectual and organizational leadership to Washington anthroplogists. His death, following so soon after that of his protégé, was the end of an era.

F. W. Putnam was still going strong in Cambridge at the Peabody Museum and in New York as part-time director of the anthropology department of the American Museum of Natural History, where he had hired Franz Boas. Stewart Culin had settled in at the University of Pennsylvania, and Frederick Starr and George A. Dorsey were in Chicago at the new University of Chicago and the Field Columbian Museum.

Alice Fletcher had accepted the fact when she returned from Europe in 1894 that she was out of the running for any of the emerging professional positions. At fifty-seven she was too old, she was a woman, and she lacked a Ph.D, which was becoming the professional prerequisite. Gradually she found that being off the professional ladder gave her a different kind of power. She began to enjoy the heady prospect of being not a supplicant for positions in anthropology but a power broker. In Dresden she had watched with interest as Zelia Nuttall and Sara Yorke Stevenson, wealthy patron and curator of Egyptian archaeology at the University of Pennsylvania, pulled strings behind the scenes to get the German archaeologist Max Uhle an appointment at that university. On her return from

Europe, Alice Fletcher was invited to Philadelphia to speak and to have dinner and lunch the following day with Sara Yorke Stevenson, and soon afterward she was made an honorary member of the University Archaeological Association at the University of Pennsylvania.[2]

Fletcher's friendships with these wealthy women gave a new tone to her letters to Putnam as she became less a student and more a colleague. She sent along bits of gossip and began to enjoy magisterial surveys of the field, trying to decide who should go where. "I was glad to see in *Science* that Dr. Boas has a chair in Anthropology at Columbia," she wrote in 1899.[3] She thought Boas "one of our strongest, if not the best ethnologist we have. He has both brains and culture, he does not go off at half-cock."[4] Soon she would hint to Putnam that not all was well between Stewart Culin and Mrs. Stevenson in Philadelphia.

Moving in these circles Alice Fletcher inevitably made the acquaintance of Phoebe Apperson Hearst, a longtime friend of Zelia Nuttall's and of Sara Stevenson's. Phoebe Hearst was a knowledgeable, energetic, and very wealthy philanthropist. Born in Missouri, at the age of twenty she married a man twenty-two years older than she, George Hearst, and went with him to California where he had made a fortune in mining and real estate. George Hearst occasionally overreached himself. For a time the family was reduced to living in a boardinghouse, but the general trend of his investments was sharply upward. Phoebe Hearst educated herself in extensive European travels in the company of her young son, William Randolph Hearst, entertained at sumptuous parties, and gave to good causes in California until 1886 when her husband was appointed to the United States Senate. She then moved her activities to Washington. After her husband's death in 1891 she stayed on for a time, becoming a patron of numerous Washington institutions, including the Phoebe Hearst School, later the National Cathedral School for Girls. In the mid-1890s her personal physician, Dr. George Pepper, drew her interest to the University of Pennsylvania, where he was provost and the greatest builder in the history of that university. Dr. Pepper had been working with Sara Yorke Stevenson to found an anthropology and archaeology museum at the University of Pennsylvania, and they persuaded Phoebe Hearst to help them build up their collections. She financed Max Uhle's expeditions in Peru in 1894, sent

Zelia Nuttall to Russia on a collecting expedition in 1895, and supported Frank Cushing's archaeological researches in the Florida keys in 1896.

Dr. Pepper died in the summer of 1898 while he and his wife were guests at Phoebe Hearst's hacienda at Pleasanton, California, and thereafter Mrs. Hearst lost interest in the University of Pennsylvania.[5] She had amassed an enormous collection of Egyptian, Greek, Roman, and other antiquities, and in 1901 she decided to found an anthropology department and museum to house these at the University of California at Berkeley, where she was already a regent in recognition of her previous gifts.

Phoebe Hearst sought advice for this new enterprise from a friend from her earliest California days, Zelia Nuttall, the granddaughter of John Parrott, one of San Francisco's wealthiest bankers. Nuttall had returned home to California in 1901 after almost fifteen years in Dresden, and she was as commanding a presence as ever. In Dresden her circle of friends had included Romanov princesses, the wife of the German ambassador to the United States, and some of the leading scientists in Europe. When, back in the United States, she wanted help in the educating of some young Puerto Rican girls as a gesture of opposition to the government policy toward Puerto Rico, she went to Phoebe Hearst for money and directly to the presidents of Harvard and Yale for educational advice.[6] When the *Codex Nuttall*, a Zapotecan manuscript she had unearthed in a European library, was published in 1902, she arranged "a special audience" with President Theodore Roosevelt at the White House in order to present him with a copy. On this occasion she gathered up Alice Fletcher and W J McGee, the acting head of the Bureau of American Ethnology, to go with her and reported to her friends that "it was most interesting to hear them discuss the Indian and negro question with the President."[7]

In Washington in the spring of 1901, Zelia Nuttall brought Alice Fletcher and Phoebe Hearst together. In an intricate social ballet, they exchanged formal calls and then invitations to receptions and musicals, and finally Alice Fletcher and Francis La Flesche were invited to an intimate dinner at Phoebe Hearst's, where they "talked Indian music in the evening."[8] Several days later Phoebe Hearst and Zelia Nuttall came to 214 First Street for Easter dinner. By the time

Zelia Nuttall and Phoebe Hearst left Washington that spring, it had been arranged that they would all meet again—and soon—in California.

Meanwhile Zelia Nuttall sounded out Franz Boas on Mrs. Hearst's behalf. She wanted to know what his own plans were and how he thought scientific work in anthropology could best be started and sustained in California. Boas replied with a long and thoughtful letter. He was not available himself, he wrote, for he was committed to long-term projects in New York. He urged that Mrs. Hearst begin by establishing several fellowships for graduate study in anthropology and by hiring a young graduate student of his, Alfred Kroeber, who for an outlay of three thousand dollars a year could begin to do research in California. Zelia Nuttall sent his letter to Mrs. Hearst with her strong endorsement. "I have the highest opinion of Dr. Boas," she wrote. "I most strongly advise that his views and propositions be carefully considered by you and Mr. Wheeler."[9] But Phoebe Hearst wanted more than graduate fellowships. She wanted to start a full-fledged department of anthropology at the University. She quietly arranged to have F. W. Putnam spend the summer in California and take up some of the archaeological work he had begun years before on one of the United States Army surveys.

Alice Fletcher was also bidden to California. Her journey out in early August was harrowing. A trap had been laid by striking railway workers for the Canadian Pacific train she was on, but because her train was six hours late a freight train was dispatched ahead of theirs. It hit the opened switch and was completely wrecked. Fletcher's train was halted for twenty-six hours several miles east of the wreckage while a way was cleared through the piled and broken cars. "Strikes are often the excuse for many strange actions," she wrote a friend.[10]

At Phoebe Hearst's Hacienda del Poza de Verona, a converted old ranch, Alice Fletcher found herself in the midst of conspicuous consumption that was the obverse of the labor struggle she had just witnessed. "Mrs. Hearst is a royal hostess and I am in the lap of luxury," she wrote Putnam.[11] One of the stories she liked to tell about the hacienda was of a sunken tub so large and deep that once in she found she could not get out again and had to call for help. Her droll account of this could leave her listeners convulsed with laughter.[12]

But the luxuriousness of life at the hacienda could not stave off her loneliness. Phoebe Hearst was away for days at a time, attending to business from her suite of rooms in the Hearst Building in San Francisco thirty miles away, and her guests were expected to entertain themselves. Alice Fletcher was modest and unassuming but proud. At Mary Thaw's in Pittsburgh where she often visited, she was usually the only guest and the center of whatever activities were planned. At the hacienda she was one of numerous guests, and the others paid little attention to her. She spent much of her time in her room or in the library, plucking books off the shelves and writing letters to every friend she could think of. "Sick all last night. Homesick," she wrote in her diary after she had been there a week.[13] After three weeks of this, Phoebe Hearst sensed her misery and telegraphed Francis La Flesche to come out.

Francis set out at once on the train journey across the continent. He arrived in early September and immediately changed the situation. His confident presence, his interest in seeing the sights, his obvious enjoyment of everything, aroused some of the same feelings in Alice, and best of all was his constant personal attentiveness to her. She blossomed when Francis was around, and the appearance of a handsome, cultured young Indian man on the scene as Miss Fletcher's adopted son transformed her in the eyes of Mrs. Hearst's entourage—from a quiet little nobody into an intriguing and possibly important woman. Nearly every evening there were concerts of Indian music at which Francis sang, and Alice moved near the center of attention where she liked to be.

Francis's arrival came in the midst of a sudden whirl of activity. Phoebe Hearst had not brought Alice Fletcher to California simply for pleasure. F. W. Putnam arrived at the hacienda in early September, as did Zelia Nuttall. They all made numerous trips to Berkeley and held conferences with university officials. On September 7 Mrs. Hearst announced that she was establishing a department of anthropology at the University of California, to be managed by an honorary advisory committee that included herself, President Benjamin I. Wheeler, Dr. John C. Merriam, assistant professor of palaeontology and historical geology at the University of California, Franz Boas, Zelia Nuttall, Alice Fletcher, and as chairman, F. W. Putnam. Two days later the board of regents accepted the new department. It was arranged that Alfred Kroeber would be hired to take charge under

Putnam's direction. Mrs. Hearst also agreed to provide a two-year fellowship for Zelia Nuttall to pursue her studies in Mexican archaeology, and to fund for five years Putnam's continuing searches in California for signs of ancient people in America.[14]

All through September there were extended discussions about the new department. Fletcher talked several times with young Alfred Kroeber. She met Charles Lummis, journalist and enthusiastic promoter of all things having to do with the Far West, later to be her ally in the Archaeological Institute of America. Putnam gave the inaugural lecture on the study of anthropology. Fletcher gave a lecture on Indian music. She finally left in early October, stopping at the Pawnee Reservation in Oklahoma and at Mary Thaw's in Pittsburgh on her way home.

In retrospect the California venture seemed such a success that Alice Fletcher was pleased to accept an invitation to return the following year. This time she arrived at the hacienda in mid-June, but within two weeks she was again so forlorn and ill—"head ache all night," she wrote in her diary[15]—that Phoebe Hearst decided to send her on a trip to the Hawaiian Islands. She was to be accompanied by one of Phoebe Hearst's oldest and closest friends from their childhood in Missouri, a Mrs. Anthony. Fletcher was ecstatic. The two women set off on July 3 and were gone for nearly a month. When they returned, Fletcher tried to settle in at the hacienda, but again she was restless and miserable. On August 1 she wrote in her diary: "unpacked. Mrs. H. went early to San F. tried and can't get settled."[16] Again Mrs. Hearst telegraphed for Francis to come, and he was there within five days. When he had to leave after ten days to return to work, Alice Fletcher was sent to visit Charles S. Wheeler, one of the regents of the University of California, and his wife at their summer home, "The Bend," on the slopes of Mt. Shasta. Fletcher spent a week with them and had a wonderful time, for they entertained her personally, inviting her on long walks through the woods, and in general were charming and attentive. Then it was back to the hacienda, where at Phoebe Hearst's urging and despite her own desires she stayed for another month.

Phoebe Hearst needed Alice Fletcher, which is why she went to such great lengths to keep Alice around. She was not pleased with the anthropology department she had set up. She did not like Kroeber. She felt that Putnam's long-distance managing of the department was not satisfactory. She admired Max Uhle, still doing work in Peru, and George Reisner, the preeminent authority on Egyptian archaeology, and she wondered why she had allowed the California department to become so concentrated on North America. She needed someone to talk to, someone who was knowledgeable but had no stake in the current arrangement, and Alice Fletcher was the only such person.

So they talked frequently, and in carefully worded letters to Putnam, which she read aloud to Phoebe Hearst before she mailed them, Alice Fletcher conveyed some of Phoebe Hearst's dissatisfaction. "The Department has become so strong and important that a crisis has come and a reorganization is demanded by those who are here and in authority," she wrote.[17] She bemoaned Putnam's inability to come to California that summer and urged him to come as soon as possible. "The Advisory Com. has done little save to put Zelia on her feet. All other matters remain for your visit here," she warned him.[18]

In mid-September Phoebe Hearst invited 150 people to an Egyptian dinner "to meet Dr. and Mrs. Reisner."[19] A special train brought the guests to the hacienda, elaborately decorated with palm trees and waterfalls. President Wheeler presided over a head table that seated 60 people, and afterward George Reisner gave a talk on Egyptian archaeology illustrated with lantern slides. Fletcher wrote Putnam that it was "a wonderful spectacle."[20]

The implications were not lost on Putnam, who feared he might lose both Phoebe Hearst's support and the department to the classical and Egyptian archaeologists. In New York that fall, where they all gathered for the International Congress of Americanists, Zelia Nuttall and Alice Fletcher met Kroeber again, and "Alice gave him some sound advice," Zelia reported to Phoebe Hearst.[21] Putnam hurried to California that winter and, on the scene, was able to persuade Phoebe Hearst that Kroeber should stay and that the department was on the right track. The honorary advisory committee to the department was replaced by a smaller executive committee of Putnam, President Wheeler, Mrs. Hearst, and John C. Merriam. Meanwhile George A. Reisner and Max Uhle were added to the staff of the anthroplogy department as Hearst Lecturers.[22] In 1903 Putnam took a leave of absence from Harvard to accept an appointment as professor of anthropology at the University of California for nine months. Phoebe Hearst remained loyal to him thereafter, but a reversal in her financial affairs led her to pull back after 1904. By 1908 Putnam was begging her for money simply to keep the museum at the University of California in operation.

After 1902 Alice Fletcher was not involved in the California department, and she was never again invited to the hacienda. This hurt and puzzled her. "I shall not see that land again for many a day," she wrote bitterly in 1904.[23] She felt she had been suddenly dropped by Phoebe Hearst, and she did not understand why. She worried that she had not been appreciative enough or expressed often enough her enjoyment of what Phoebe Hearst was providing. She spent the summer of 1903 at Mrs. Anthony's summer home in Fairhaven, Massachusetts, an invitation that was probably prompted by Phoebe Hearst, and Hearst continued for years to send occasional greetings and small presents. To these Alice Fletcher replied always with fulsome and ingratiating expressions of thanks, as she continued to puzzle over what had gone wrong.[24]

One answer is that in retrenchment Phoebe Hearst did not need the advice she had sought from Alice Fletcher when they were making plans to move swiftly ahead. But more fundamentally, Alice Fletcher did not realize how visible her loneliness had been when she was Phoebe Hearst's guest at the hacienda. Phoebe Hearst recognized something Alice Fletcher did not yet know about herself: how much she had come to need the loving and steady attention that Francis provided best. Alice Fletcher depended on her friends, on Jane Gay, and especially on Francis to care for her. She needed to be the focus of their attention and solicitude. Only so could she fend off the dreadful feeling of abandonment, of being alone in the world. Without their love and care she could hardly function. Phoebe Hearst was herself no stranger to loneliness. Her solution was to keep at her side a series of young women, her niece, the daughter of a cousin, and others, whom she took to concerts and parties, introduced to eligible young men, and treated as daughters.[25] She recognized what Alice Fletcher needed, acknowledged that it was a need she could not satisfy, and gave up trying.

Alice Fletcher's two years of service as Phoebe Hearst's advisor had one lasting outcome. On Phoebe Hearst's advice, Alice Fletcher bought shares of stock in the Homestake Mining Company and had Francis La Flesche do so too. The shares soared in value over the years, and Francis in particular was quite well off when he died.

When she arrived home from California in the fall of 1902, Alice Fletcher immediately became immersed in other kinds of anthropological politics. First there was the uproar over the appointment of John Wesley Powell's successor as head of the Bureau of American Ethnology. W J McGee, a geologist and ethnologist at the Bureau, was the heir apparent, but Secretary Samuel Langley of the Smithsonian did not like him and refused to appoint him. Fletcher telegraphed Putnam and also Franz Boas and James McKeen Cattell at Columbia and urged them to support McGee. "I have been moved to do this from a sense of justice as well as in the best interests of anthropology," she explained.[26] All that fall the battle raged, but Langley was adamant, and finally W. H. Holmes, who had been head of anthropology at the National Museum, agreed to take the job.

Fletcher's support for McGee was not crucial in this incident. Most of the anthropological community felt as she did, and their protests were ineffective. What is significant about her participation in the lobbying effort is that for the first time she took a strong and aggressive position in anthropological politics without first consulting Putnam or trying to figure out what he would want. She was beginning to trust her own judgment. It was a foretaste of things to come.

Fletcher felt herself entitled to express an opinion because she had begun to work closely with the Bureau. Her Pawnee work, *The Hako*, was to be published by them, and she was writing entries for the *Handbook of the North American Indians*, the famous Bulletin 30, edited by F. W. Hodge and published by the Bureau of American Ethnology in two volumes in 1907 and 1910. Fletcher agreed to write the entries on "Totemism" and "Music and Musical Instruments," and she did these so promptly and well that Holmes asked her to do more. In all she wrote thirty-five entries, ranging from "Adornment," "Agency System," and "Buffalo" to "Tepi," "Trading Posts," and "War and War Discipline." The pay was ten dollars for every thousand words, the standard rate for encyclopedias, but better than the money was the camaraderie with her scientific peers, which Fletcher, who spent so much of her time working alone, enjoyed enormously. She described the work to Isabel Barrows: "Aside from the research and writing we have triweekly meetings of all present in this city where each article is read and criticized. These meetings are delightful, but they take time so I've not had time to call on a mind, to write a note or do a thing."[27] Of her contributions to these classic volumes, "Music and Musical Instruments" in particular was outstanding and has been reprinted several times.

The *Handbook* work lasted for two and a half years, from 1903 to mid-1905. These were busy and, on the surface, happy years. At the same time Fletcher was serving a term as president of the Anthropological Society of Washington. The Woman's Anthropological Society of Washington had merged with the men's group in 1899, and in 1903 Fletcher was elected president of the combined group. "It was a great surprise. The gentlemen are very kind, and I hope no one will regret the election," she wrote Putnam.[28]

She worked hard at the office, using it to expand her own and her fellow members' horizons. "Since I have been President, I have aimed to bring men from outside the city before the Society—and to broaden the topics which are presented," she wrote Phoebe Hearst in 1903.[29] But Fletcher's presidency, through no fault of her own, coincided with a decline in status of the society. In 1902, a new national professional organization, the American Anthropological Association, had been founded, and it took over the publication of the journal *American Anthropologist* from the Anthropological Society of Washington. The latter collapsed almost immediately from being a quasi-national society, by virtue of its location in the nation's capital and its journal, to being a local society. Alice Fletcher was the only woman among the forty people invited to the founding meeting of the American Anthropological Association. She was immediately elected to the council, but she was never elected president.[30] Not until 1940 was a woman (Elsie Clews Parsons) elected president of the American Anthropological Association. Alice Fletcher's election as vice-president of section H in the American Association for the Advancement of Science in 1895 was her highest honor in anthropology, the only time she stood at the head of a group representing all the anthropologists in the country. In 1905 Alice Fletcher was elected president of the American Folklore Society, an honor but not of comparable scope.

Francis La Flesche announced when he returned from his summer vacation in 1904 that he was going to pay for the changes in the dining room at 214 that they had long been contemplating. For four months they lived in a mess of renovation, of carpenters, painters, and paperhangers. When it was finished Jane Gay was able to expand out of one room into two, and everyone was pleased with the new domestic arrangements.[31]

But the domestic harmony was not to last, and one suspects that the renovation may have been, as is sometimes the case, a first hint of restlessness and discord. In the spring of 1905, Alice Fletcher lapsed again into illness. Her friends were worried about her, not about any specific, tangible disease but about her own reports that she was on the verge of "breaking down." Adela Breton, an English scholar and friend of Zelia Nuttall's, wrote to Putnam: "Someone ought to insist on Miss Fletcher's taking a rest. From a letter she wrote to Mrs. N. she is evidently on the point of breaking down which would be such a pity."[32] Fletcher wrote Phoebe Hearst in April that she had had "an enforced rest incident to a fever, from which I am now recovering"[33] and to Isabel Barrows that she had had "catarrhal fever."[34] In her diary in April, Fletcher called her illness "Catarrhal fever and nervous breakdown."[35] The doctors repeatedly did blood and urine tests and assured her that she had no organic disease. Then it was decided that she had malaria, and she and Jane Gay fled Washington for the healthier climate of Mary Thaw's country home at Cresson, Pennsylvania. From there Fletcher went alone to stay for some weeks with Mary Livermore at her seaside place in Egypt, Massachusetts.

Alice Fletcher had recovered enough by late summer to think of going to California for the annual meeting of the American Association for the Advancement of Science. A flurry of letters from Putnam, Kroeber, and Phoebe Hearst all urging her to come encouraged her, but in the end she decided not to go, giving as her reason the expense of the long journey. That fall she was ill again. In October 1905, Fletcher wrote Mr. Smiley of Lake Mohonk, "I have been more or less of an invalid for the past 6 or 8 months."[36] She was too preoccupied and distraught even to keep up with professional matters. "I cannot recall who is vice-Pres. of Sec. H this year," she wrote Putnam.[37] In December she ground to a halt. "Never before was it not possible for me to do my allotted task," she wrote to Putnam. "Now I cannot. My address as president of the Amer. Folk-Lore Soc'y is unfinished and I cannot finish it. There is no hope of my being able to do so. I cannot go to Ithaca [to the annual meeting of the AAA] nor can I attend any of the meetings or do anything on the Committee where I would gladly serve. . . . I am sorry, grieved, never before have I failed. You will not blame me I know, for you are generous and trust me, but I may be blamed and yet I am not to blame, save that I should have stopped months ago."[38] In January 1906, she wrote Mrs. Hearst that she had been ill and that the cause was "tired nerves" but added, "I am gaining slowly."[39]

The vagueness of these symptoms and diagnoses suggests that Alice Fletcher's problems in 1905 were not physical as much as emotional, that they likely were related to changes she could sense coming in "the family," as she sometimes referred to her happy household at 214 First Street.[40] For it was the only family she had. Her occasional contacts with distant relatives only increased her sense of aloneness. In the spring of 1904, when she had gone to St. Louis to work on the Indian Bureau exhibit for the 1904 Exposition, she looked up the widow and the daughter of her half-brother, Frank H. Fletcher, who lived there. They passed on to her a packet of letters written by Thomas Fletcher to his only son. Alice Fletcher spent some days in bed in St. Louis with what she thought might be pneumonia and, as she was recovering, "began reading my father's letters and getting to know him better."[41] After several days of this she noted in her diary: "Finished Father's letters. a sad story. Feel more than ever alone-in both worlds. Wrote Miss G. and F."[42]

What did Alice Fletcher mean when she wrote that she felt alone "in both worlds?" Her religious convictions included the hope for an eternal world where she would meet again those whom she had loved, but she implied that loved ones were so long gone from her that it would be as if they were strangers. She may have been thinking of her father who had died when she was twenty-two months old, but there is one hint in her surviving papers that she was thinking of someone else, that she may at one time have been romantically involved with a man. In the summer of 1905 Alice Fletcher joined the Barrows family at their camp in Canada for the wedding of their only child, Mabel. Fletcher described the wedding in her diary as "a wonderful ceremony sacred and full of spiritual meaning," but it left her feeling "pretty badly and upset."[43] A day or two later Alice Fletcher wrote Isabel Barrows a long letter thanking them for letting her share in the event. "The gates of eternal joy opened," she wrote, ". . . and from my inmost soul I thanked God that I had been permitted the glimpse within. I cannot tell you how much the experience was to me. How it strengthened memories of the deepest joy of my life, and how it helped and helps me to the power to serve and await, if so God grant it, the day of fulfillment."[44] Was she thinking back to someone she had planned to marry, someone with whom she hoped someday to be reunited in "the day of fulfillment"? Isabel Barrows would have known what she was referring to. We cannot know. All we have is Fletcher's sorrowful final assessment of her situation, that she was alone "in both worlds." She turned as always to Francis and Jane Gay.

But now it appeared that she was about to lose even them. Jane Gay was ostensibly still living at 214, but she stayed away for longer and longer periods of time. She checked in briefly at 214 in early October 1903. Fletcher had hurried home to be there when she arrived, but a series of family emergencies came up and Jane Gay did not finally return to Washington until mid-May 1904. She stayed for a month and then was off again. Francis's decision that fall to renovate the house and enlarge Jane Gay's quarters may have been an effort on his part to keep her happy, so she would stay with them.

Francis was on the surface as loyal as ever. He had given up his aspirations toward "letters" and had begun again to collect material for their joint work on *The Omaha Tribe*. In October 1905 he took a week's leave of absence from his job in order to work with Silas Wood, an Omaha who had come to stay with them and give them information on the Shell Society among the Omahas.[45] But Francis La Flesche had a new interest. Early in January 1906 the name Rosa begins to appear in his diary. On March 15, 1906, at eight o'clock in the evening, Francis was married in the parlor at 214 First Street, S.E., to a part-Chippewa Indian woman, Rosa Bourassa.

Alice Fletcher pulled herself together for Francis's wedding. She and Jane Gay went shopping with the bride for the wedding dress. Fletcher arranged for a clergyman, planned the wedding supper, and sent out handwritten notes inviting their closest friends to the wedding "of my dear boy Francis to Miss Rosa Bourassa." She helped Francis rearrange his bedroom to make room for Rosa, and she went shopping a few days before the wedding and "bought sheets and a napkin ring."[46] Rosa was simply to be filled into the routine of the household: another place at the table, another napkin ring. The weather on the wedding day was stormy, but Fletcher filled the house with flowers and that night wrote in her diary: "A beautiful wedding. 40 guests present. Good supper. Many congratulations."[47] The date had been carefully chosen to make it a special celebration. It was Alice Fletcher's sixty-eighth birthday.

But almost immediately afterward it did not seem like a beautiful wedding at all. Two weeks after his marriage Francis came home from the office one afternoon feeling ill. "F. came home sick," Alice wrote in her diary.[48] There was a flurry of doctor's visits and much nursing. Within three days Francis was well enough to take a walk in the country with Alice. Then it was Jane Gay's turn to be ill.[49] Then four days later Fletcher took to her bed with double pneumonia. She was very ill for a month, so sick that a trained nurse was hired and news, including that of the California earthquake, was kept from her.[50] The denouement came on May 13. "Awful scene at my bed. Miss Gay and F. Nurse heard much," Alice wrote in her diary.[51] Two weeks later Jane Gay packed up and left for New England and Europe, never to return to 214 First Street.

What was said at that bedside we have no way of knowing, but the "awful scene" between Francis La Flesche and Jane Gay was the culmination of sixteen years of latent rivalry for Alice Fletcher's love and attention. Jane Gay had hinted at the rivalry years before in a letter from Idaho as their long co-residence was about to begin. Her letter is so revealing of her expectations that it is worth quoting nearly in full. She wrote to "My dear Francis," from Fort Lapwai on May 27, 1890, that they were very relieved to get his letter.

We had taken it into our busy heads that you were ill, it seemed so long since we had heard from "the boy" we feared that your eyes had given out from overwork. Take care of those eyes—for everything depends upon your keeping them in good health. All our work we are looking forward to—all the digging and the photographing, all the gathering and keeping—depend upon you—we can't do anything without you, you know—

Well! We are still at Lapwai. The growing work holds us here. The last kicker has surrendered and now it is how to take allotments fast enough. Indians rise up out of every cañon and are claiming land on top of each other like geological strata.

. . . We hope soon to go to Kamiah. The surveying is very difficult and takes so much time. This surely must be the hardest piece of allotting work in the country. I wish you were here—we look forward to meeting you with great comfort in the thought, when we are tired. We cannot yet see how it is to be done—but the way will open I hope.

Miss F. is well and more blessed than ever, the dearest little woman on earth, as you know, and you do not mind my knowing it also do you? Do not be lonesome but take care of your health and strength. I am taking a picture now and then. I shall ask you to bring me more plates when you join us. I have them at Miss Bradley's, and we must have plenty. Don't forget that I am as ever,

Sincerely your friend, E. Jane Gay [52]

Jane Gay thought of herself as an integral part of what was going to be a three-person ethnographic team, but that is not the way it worked out in Washington, where there was really nothing for her to do. The team was Alice Fletcher and Francis La Flesche, and Jane Gay felt pushed more and more to the periphery. She may have hoped that Francis's marriage would alter the situation at 214, but it did not, and she and Rosa Bourassa La Flesche found themselves allies as they tried to pry apart a mother and son who would not be separated. When Jane Gay packed up and left, it was Rosa who went with her to the train station. [53]

Two weeks after Jane Gay's departure, Alice Fletcher set off for Mexico to stay for six months with Zelia Nuttall. It was a spur-of-the-moment decision, the result of a visit to Zelia Nuttall in the hospital at Johns Hopkins, where she had been recovering from a serious operation. The threesome that had been a happy family for sixteen years was suddenly rent asunder, as the two women hurtled off in opposite directions and Francis was left at 214 First Street alone with his wife.

Twenty-One

Mexico

ZELIA Nuttall's connections with Mexico went back twenty years. After a brief marriage to the French linguist and ethnologist Alphonse Louis Pinart, she had moved with her small daughter and in the company of her mother and younger brother to Mexico City. She spent several months in 1884 working in the National Museum, learning the Nahuatl language, and making a collection of small terra-cotta heads from San Juan Teotihuacán. From these simple beginnings, Zelia Nuttall built a distinguished career as a Mexican archaeologist, relying on her own boldness, her skill at languages, and a wide-ranging curiosity. A paper on the terra-cotta heads published in the *American Journal of Archaeology* in 1886 brought her to the attention of F. W. Putnam, who made her an honorary special assistant in Mexican archaeology at the Peabody Museum, a position she held until her death.[1]

Nuttall had a particular talent for ferreting out in Europe lost or forgotten manuscripts having to do with Mexico. The *Codex Nuttall* was a Zapotecan manuscript she had traced from a monastery in Florence to the library of an English lord. *The Book of the Life of the Ancient Mexicans* was based on the Codex Magliabecchiao she had found in a Florentine library. Part 1 was published by the University of California in 1903. Part 2, which was to have included her commentary on the text along with a translation, never appeared. Her major book was *The Fundamental Principles of New and Old World Civilizations* (1901). In it she traced the swastika around the world, arguing that it was an astronomical symbol representing the North Pole and the four quarters of the world. The book was speculative and seemed quaintly old-fashioned when it appeared but was quite widely read.[2] A copy she gave to D. H. Lawrence became one of the chief sources for his novel about Mexico, *The Plumed Serpent*, and Zelia Nuttall herself appears as a character in the novel, scarcely disguised as the archaeologist "Mrs. Norris."

In 1902, having been "put on her feet" with a two-year fellowship for research in archaeology from Phoebe Hearst,[3] Zelia Nuttall decided to settle in Mexico. She bought a large Spanish colonial–style house called Casa Alvarado, for Pedro de Alvarado, one of Cortes's deputies, who was said to have lived there in Coyoacán on the outskirts of Mexico City. Massive doors in the ornately decorated street facade led into the central court, where the conquistadors once rode on horseback. From the courtyard, worn stone steps led up to a long first-floor corridor and the living rooms. "The house and all its belongings save the bath rooms and electric lights are all in the 16th century," Fletcher marveled to one friend.[4] Outside was an orchard and a garden, which Zelia Nuttall, whose passion besides archaeology was gardening, turned into one of the showplaces of Mexico City. Casa Alvarado had needed extensive repairs, which Phoebe Hearst had paid for. But the money had been a loan, not a gift, and Nuttall struggled to pay it back.[5] In 1909, she finally sold part of the orchard near the house so that she could settle accounts with Phoebe Hearst.

Alice Fletcher spent six months in Coyoacán. "Mexico is far more beautiful than I fancied and the people are a study, not only the natives but those of Spanish descent," she wrote Putnam. "Mrs. Nuttall's residence fits her admirably. . . . All her beautifully carved furniture which she had in Dresden fits into the rooms here as though it had always belonged here. . . . The garden laid out in the Italian style is a wonder of roses, and other flowers. . . . Very soon she can take up regular work, and she is looking forward to it and counting her store of new strength every day." She added: "As for me I am gaining. . . . I shall look changed when we meet for I fear I am going to lose all of my hair. I have already lost over half of what I had. It is my sense illness the Doctors say. . . . I am living in hope of being able to work when I return in the Fall. I am expecting an old Omaha to be with me for a few weeks and go over with him my notes that are about ready for publication. He is the last one who remembers the old time ceremonies."[6]

What Alice Fletcher had to look forward to when she returned to Washington was the enormous task of pulling together the Omaha ethnography and the no-less-taxing problem of getting accustomed to daily life with Rosa, Francis's wife, instead of Jane Gay. It was a future she was willing to put off as long as possible. But these concerns faded away when one afternoon a middle-aged American archaeologist, Edgar L. Hewett, appeared at the door of Casa Alvarado. Hewett was in Mexico on a fellowship from the American committee of the Archaeological Institute of America. Alice Fletcher was a member of that committee, so he quite naturally stopped to see her. The subsequent weeks they spent together in Mexico were to reorient both their lives and the course of American archaeology.

Alice Fletcher's connection with the venerable Archaeological Institute of America (A.I.A.) went back to the year of its founding, 1879, when at Putnam's suggestion she had become a member. The Archaeological Institute of America was originally a Boston group, the creation of Charles Eliot Norton, professor of the history of art at Harvard University, who believed that the mark of an educated man was his vicarious participation in the great civilizations of Greece and Rome. Norton also thought it was time for Americans to do their share in the explorations into the foundations of classical civilization, and to this end he founded the A.I.A.

F. W. Putnam was invited to the initial meeting, along with the American historian Francis Parkman, but despite Parkman's eloquence, the two of them barely managed to get American archaeology included as one of the potential concerns of the Archaeological Institute of America. In its early years the A.I.A. had one token American project. They sent Adolph Bandelier, a Swiss-American businessman who was an expert on the Spanish chroniclers of the New World, to the Southwest and Mexico to study ancient ruins and contemporary Indian life, and they published his long reports in their annual volumes of *Papers*. But after 1884 the American work was dropped completely and Putnam dropped his membership in the A.I.A.

Alice Fletcher continued hers. When the Archaeological Institute of America was reorganized in 1884 to consist of local affiliated societies, Fletcher became a member of the New York Society. In 1889, when she was about to become Thaw Fellow at the Peabody Museum, she transferred to the Boston Society. In 1891, during the turmoil of her Idaho years, she dropped out, but she reappeared in 1895 as vice-president of the new Washington Society. When that one collapsed in 1899, she moved to the Baltimore Society.

The Archaeological Institute of America established the American School of Classical Studies in Athens in 1882 and a similar school in Rome in 1895. They sponsored excavations in Greece and Italy and began to publish an official magazine, *American Journal of Archaeology*, in 1884. A few people complained about the lack of attention to archaeology here at home, but most of the wealthy patrons of this predominantly lay organization preferred classical ruins to prehistoric America. The Archaeological Institute of America spread slowly westward. Four local societies of the A.I.A. had been launched in the Midwest by 1890, in Chicago, Detroit, Minneapolis, and Madison, but most of the money for its projects continued to come from New England.[7]

What finally shook the Archaeological Institute of America out of its indifference to American archaeology was a drop in membership in the organization in the 1890s. The decrease coincided with the national financial depression, and the leaders of the A.I.A., deciding that they needed to broaden their base of support, hoped that some American explorations might do this. In 1897 John Williams White from Cornell, who had succeeded Charles Eliot Norton and Seth Low from Columbia University as president of the A.I.A., appointed a committee to look into the matter. The committee's report a year later was discouraging, at least from the standpoint of the A.I.A. So much archaeological work was going on in the United States, funded by the federal government, private organizations, and individuals, that there was hardly a place for the A.I.A. with its limited resources. But as a first step they suggested that a council member be elected who would represent the interests of American archaeology.[8]

The person chosen was Charles P. Bowditch, a Boston businessman and major benefactor of the Peabody Museum at Harvard. For ten years, ever since he first encountered Mayan antiquities while on a pleasure trip to Yucatan in 1888, Bowditch had planned and largely financed the annual Peabody Museum expeditions to Central America. Beginning in 1898, Bowditch became the prime force in the A.I.A. behind American projects, urging in particular Central American projects.[9]

In 1899, the Archaeological Institute of America held a grand twentieth anniversary celebration of its founding. Charles Eliot Norton gave the major address at the meeting, and half of the papers were by people connected with the School of Classical Studies at Athens. But Charles Bowditch presided over one session on American archaeology in which Putnam, again a member of the A.I.A. after a lapse of nearly fifteen years, and Alice Fletcher both participated. Alice Fletcher spoke on Indian music. She sensed that her invitation was owing to Sara Yorke Stevenson.[10] In the light of later events, it is interesting to note that Fletcher came to prominence in the A.I.A. not through her male associates at the Peabody Museum, but through the support of her woman friends.

The men did not even include her on a committee for American archaeology that was formed two years later. Franz Boas joined the A.I.A. in 1901, when the annual meeting was held in New York City. He read a paper on "Some Problems in North American Archaeology,"[11] and subsequently he, Bowditch, and Putnam were named to a committee for American archaeology in the A.I.A. In 1901, they recommended young Alfred Tozzer, a student of Putnam's, for the fellowship in American archaeology that Bowditch had just established to match the existing A.I.A. fellowships for Greek, Roman, and Christian archaeology. Tozzer set off for Mexico to study the Maya and Lacandon Indians.

The New England–New York male academic establishment seemed firmly in control of American archaeology in the A.I.A. But this arrangement was shaken to its foundations by an unexpected surge of activity in the Far West, led by two promoters and entrepreneurs par excellence, Charles F. Lummis and Edgar L. Hewett. Lummis was an eccentric California journalist. Hewett was an educator turned archaeologist, solemn and rather pompous, but well-meaning and a hard worker. Together, with Alice Fletcher's help, they managed to get control of the American committee in the A.I.A. and, for the next twenty years, of much of the archaeology in the American West, a theft to eastern eyes.

In the 1880s, when Lummis arrived in California, the Franciscan missions were abandoned and in ruins, remembered if at all as places of penal servitude, disease, and starvation for thousands of so-called Mission Indians. Lummis, probably at that time ignorant of these facts, started an Association for the Preservation of the Missions in 1888, which, aided by the popularity of Helen Hunt Jackson's romantic novel *Ramona*, led to a glorification of the role of Franciscan fathers and Spanish dons in southern California.[12] But Lummis soon began to look on Indians with a much more sympathetic eye. After a physical breakdown in the early 1890s, he went to the pueblo of Isleta in New Mexico to recover, staying there for almost four years. On his return to Los Angeles, he transformed the Association for the Preservation of the Missions into the more broadly conceived Landmarks Club.

In 1901 Lummis used the occasion of a two-week stint in Washington, as one of Theodore Roosevelt's advisors on western affairs, to form the Sequoyah League, an organization officially founded in 1902 whose vague goal was "To Make Better Indians by Treating Them Better." Many of the nation's prominent anthropologists were on its advisory board, including Powell, McGee, Hodge, Putnam, and Fletcher. The league's primary importance was as an ideological way station between the Dawes Act of 1887 and John Collier's Indian Reorganization Act of 1934. Lummis and other spokesmen for the Sequoyah League had begun to give up on allotment and assimilation and had started to think it was both inevitable and preferable that the Indians retain at least some of their traditional culture.[13] Not much came of the league, however, and it soon dwindled away.

In 1903 Lummis expanded his Landmarks Club into the Society of the Southwest in Los Angeles. He had by then two purposes. He wanted to campaign for the preservation of the history of the American Southwest, Indian as well as Spanish. He also wanted to put a stop to the wholesale destruction of archaeological monuments in the Southwest. Travelers and traders were pillaging cliff dwellings, abandoned pueblos, and other ancient sites. Even members of the United States Army, Lummis declared indignantly, had been known "to push an ancient building over a cliff into the canyon below 'just to see how it would sound.'"[14]

Lummis could have accomplished, and indeed did accomplish,

the first of these purposes without any outside help. Under his guidance the Society of the Southwest founded the Southwest Museum in Los Angeles, sent out two archaeological expeditions, collected hundreds of folksongs in Spanish and in twenty-four Indian languages, and gathered up photographs of southern California and books and paintings from the Franciscan missions. But Lummis was not averse to adding the name of a prestigious national organization to his efforts, and he knew that to accomplish his second goal, which would require federal legislation, the Society of the Southwest would need help.

When an emmisary of the A.I.A., Martin D'Ooge from the University of Michigan, appeared at Lummis's door in September 1903, Lummis was eager to cooperate. Within two months the Society of the Southwest had become one of the fifteen branch societies of the A.I.A., and the lusty infant was soon the marvel of the entire organization. It had more than three hundred members out of a total A.I.A. membership of approximately fifteen hundred, the result, Lummis explained happily, of applying modern business methods to the service of scholarship. Lummis was a great believer in printer's ink and postage stamps. But also, Lummis emphasized, "an important reason for the success of the Southwest Society is that it is *doing things.*"[15]

Charles F. Lummis personified not simply the coming together of business principles and scholarship, for that was fully developed in the austere Bostonian Charles P. Bowditch, but a new flamboyance in both. He gave the hitherto staid A.I.A. a sudden injection of western drive, energy, and impulse to action. As he wrote to Charles Eliot Norton, who had been his teacher at Harvard: "Our public is intensely conscious locally and intensely patriotic . . . we are incredibly strained to be not only good citizens of our own generation, but to be our own fathers, grandfathers, and great-grandfathers, none of whom were here to provide us with the things that as thoughtful Americans we desire to have."[16] What "thoughtful Americans" who were new citizens of California, Colorado, New Mexico, and Utah desired to have was a sense of home, a sense of place, a sense of the history of the American West. Lummis spoke for hundreds of newcomers to California who had prospered there and wanted to find roots there, people like Phoebe Hearst, who was a good friend of his.

Lummis editorialized in *Out West*, "It has been relatively easy to get generous funds for classical study in the Mediterranean countries; but our own far less hackneyed and equally rich field has been shamefully neglected by our scholars, and atrociously looted by others."[17] This he proposed to change. The leaders of the Archaeological Institute of America were pleased to cooperate. For the first time, and with scarcely any effort on their part, they were truly a national organization. In 1904, the president of the A.I.A., the classicist Thomas Seymour, appointed a large committee to work to secure legislation for the protection of ruins of ancient America. Alice Fletcher, F. W. Putnam, Charles P. Bowditch, Franz Boas, Charles Lummis, and Edgar L. Hewett (then a member of the Colorado Society of the A.I.A.) were among the many members, and they met with a similar committee from the American Anthropological Association to plan their lobbying strategy.[18] But congressional opposition to a bill that promised to remove more land from the public domain was intense. For twenty years efforts to pass a law providing for the preservation of American antiquities had been stalled, and there was every indication that this was going to happen again.

Lummis and Hewett finally grew impatient with the committee approach and decided to take matters into their own hands. They gathered up William H. Holmes, the chief of the Bureau of American Ethnology, and James Garfield, the secretary of the interior, and went to call on Theodore Roosevelt at the White House. Roosevelt was readily persuaded to back their cause. In 1906 Congress passed a general bill for the preservation of American antiquities, the Lacey Act, and also a special bill for the preservation of the cliff dwellings in the Mesa Verde region of Colorado, a project of Hewett's. Hewett and Lummis nominated the scientific institutions to be given permits for excavation, which became the official list, with approval to be given in each case by the chief of the Bureau of American Ethnology.[19] Among the committee members, Putnam and Boas in particular were disgruntled, not wanting the granting of permission to fall into the hands of a single government official, but after the fact there was nothing they could do about it.[20]

The influx of western members into the A.I.A. led the organization to lobby for a national antiquities act. It also helped to redress the long-standing imbalance in the Institute between classical and

American explorations. Most of the income of the A.I.A. came from membership dues. Suddenly, with so many new western members, there was a surplus in the treasury, and it seemed only fair to spend it on American projects. The committee on American archaeology— Putnam, Bowditch, and Boas—was enlarged in 1905 to include J. Walter Fewkes of the Bureau of American Ethnology, Francis W. Kelsey from the University of Michigan, Alice Fletcher, and Charles Lummis, and they were given extra appropriations to spend. They published Tozzer's final report on his four years as fellow in American Archaeology, gave Putnam five hundred dollars for explorations in California caves, and returned some money directly to the Southwest Society.[21]

In 1905 Edgar Hewett applied for and received the American Fellowship. Robert Lowie had also been a candidate, supported by Boas and Bowditch, but Fewkes and Alice Fletcher were impressed by Hewett's experience in exploration and his knowledge of French, German, and Spanish, and in the end, after Lowie pulled out, the committee had given the fellowship to Hewett.[22] Hewett was not a young Harvard student, like Alfred Tozzer, but was forty-one years old. He had just spent five years as president of a teacher's college, the New Mexico Normal University in Las Vegas, New Mexico. When his contract was not renewed in 1903 he decided to turn his passion for archaeology into a full-time profession. He tried to get the attention of the eastern anthropology establishment by appearing at scientific meetings and dropping in at museums to call on the professional staff. In 1903 he inquired about the possibility of spending a year or two under Putnam's direction, either at Harvard or Berkeley,[23] but eventually he and his wife went off to Europe and he enrolled in a graduate program in archaeology in Geneva, Switzerland. The work Hewett proposed to do in 1906, a broad survey of the Southwest and Mexico suggested to him by Fewkes, was essentially an expansion of the survey of prehistoric ruins in the Southwest that Hewett had done in 1904 for the department of the interior. The committee decided to let him proceed.[24] So in 1906, besides winding up his lobbying activity in Washington for the Lacey Bill, Hewett did surveys in Utah and Colorado, assisted in explorations sponsored by the Southwest Society, and traveled down through Mexico to Mexico City.

Alice Fletcher, marking time in Mexico City with Zelia Nuttall, was happy to see him. Not long after he appeared, she wrote Putnam: "Just a line to tell you that I have seen Mr. Hewett twice and am delighted with the reports of his work. . . . He has traveled thro. the country from the border to this valley—and has kept his eyes open, and has blocked out the various culture areas. . . . He works hard but with intelligence and training. He is careful, earnest and unselfish. I am very much pleased with him."[25]

Alice Fletcher helped Hewett get a graphophone to record an all-night ceremony at the ancient temple of Tepoztlan. Soon he was inviting her to go on field expeditions with him, sometimes accompanied by Zelia Nuttall. They went out to the valley of Mexico and then farther afield, to Puebla and Cholula and down to Oaxaca, Monte Alban, and Mitla. Alice Fletcher was impressed with his field methods, and they had long discussions about the nature and needs of American archaeology and about the eagerness of the western societies of the Archaeological Institute of America to support such work, literally in their own backyards.

Alice Fletcher began a program of self-education in Mexican archaeology through reading. Before Hewett's arrival she had been taking Spanish lessons. After talking to him she turned to archaeological reports, including the one on Honduras recently published by the Peabody Museum. Two months after Hewett had arrived in Mexico, Alice Fletcher wrote Putnam a long letter. "I . . . am feeling something of my old vim," she told him. "I want very much to see you and Mr. Bowditch about the work of the American field. . . . There is a fine opening for great usefulness if it is taken and used as it should be." She described her travels with Hewett and what she had learned about the eagerness of the western societies of the A.I.A. Then she added dramatically, "I have held on from the foundation of this Organization thro. all the years waiting for the dawn of the day that now seems to be coming."[26] Putnam passed her letter on to Bowditch with a pencilled note at the top, "Dear Mr. Bowditch, Please return after reading. FWP." The stage was set for a struggle.

What Alice Fletcher rightly sensed was that they were, as she said, "at an important juncture of affairs" in American archaeology.[27] Eight years earlier it had seemed that there was so much archaeological activity in the United States that there was hardly room for the Archaeological Institute of America. That situation had been changed by the death in 1902 of John Wesley Powell. John Wesley Powell had created a government agency, the Bureau of Ethnology (after 1894 the Bureau of American Ethnology), in 1879, the same year in which Charles Eliot Norton had founded the private and classically oriented A.I.A. For the next twenty years Powell thought of himself as the coordinating hub and theoretical synthesizer of work in archaeology and anthropology within the United States. But under Powell's quiet and more modest successor, W. H. Holmes, the Bureau had declined in activity, appropriations, and aspirations. At the same time the museums and university departments of anthropology that had been built up with private philanthropy by Putnam in Cambridge, Chicago, New York, and Berkeley, and by William Pepper in Philadelphia began to look farther afield than the Americas. Phoebe Hearst's collections in California included materials from Greece, Rome, Egypt, and Peru. The Jesup Expedition under Franz Boas and F. W. Putnam at the American Museum of Natural History had gone into Siberia, and Boas was trying to extend work to China. Even had they been willing to limit their work to the confines of the United States, no single university department or museum could take the Bureau's place as a coordinating agency because of rivalry and because none had the inherent power of a government agency.

The decline of the Bureau of American Ethnology left a void, and it was Alice Fletcher, from her ringside seat in Washington, who sensed this and set about to fill it. She also knew that the western societies of the Archaeological Institute of America needed to be convinced that the national organization could continue to be of value to them. She decided to solve both problems by bringing them together. The A.I.A. could become the new coordinating agency for work in North American archaeology. It would need to have a center in the Southwest, near the western societies and in the heart of the most important archaeological area in the country.

Alice Fletcher presented her plan to the Committee on American Archaeology in December, shortly after her return home. She proposed that the A.I.A. undertake "the preparation of a map of the culture-areas of the American continent, as a contribution to the world-study of the human race," that a director of American archaeology be appointed to coordinate the work of the local societies in accord with the basic plan, and that a school of American archaeology be established to give instruction in field research.[28] The committee accepted her plan as a general, long-range program, hoping it would inspire the western societies to full cooperation. As a first step the committee appointed Edgar L. Hewett Director of American Archaeology in the A.I.A. Edgar Hewett, at forty-one, was started on a new career. Alice Fletcher, at sixty-eight, had found a new cause and perhaps a new son.

Not the least remarkable aspect of this new direction Alice Fletcher had suddenly taken was that she had never been in the American Southwest apart from her two visits to Phoebe Hearst's hacienda in northern California and had never before been to Mexico. She apparently did not even consult her hostess, a well-recognized Mexican archaeologist, about her forthcoming plans for archaeology on the entire North American continent. And Zelia Nuttall was not altogether pleased with Fletcher's sudden interest in Mexican archaeology. On one occasion, when Fletcher arrived back at Casa Alvarado at five in the evening after an expedition with Hewett to Guadalupe, she found Zelia Nuttall angry because she had not been told when to expect her. "Mrs. N. . . . very unkind. would not take dinner with me or speak," Fletcher wrote in her diary that night.[29] But Alice Fletcher stayed on in Mexico City for another six weeks, and she and Zelia Nuttall remained friends. On her return to Washington, Fletcher tried to get money from the Bureau of American Ethnology to support Zelia Nuttall's researches.[30]

Twenty-Two

"My life is over"

FRANCIS La Flesche's marriage to Rosa Bourassa was doomed from the start. An oral tradition survives among senior anthropologists that when Francis La Flesche got married and moved his wife into 214 First Street, Alice Fletcher told him, "There is to be no co-habitation in this house." Twice in the days just before

Francis's wedding Alice Fletcher noted in her diary, "had long talk with Rosa." Many years later Rosa Bourassa La Flesche bemoaned to Richard Pratt her tendency to let white people push her around.[1]

It was soon evident that the marriage had been a mistake. On July 13, Francis wrote in his diary, "R. left breakfast table without a word." Then the diary is blank for three months. The next entry, on October 3, reads: "R. went to the Scholts to sleep. Entirely unnecessary." In mid-November Francis took a four-week leave from the office. He traveled with Rosa to Michigan, where he left her with her family, and went on alone to the Omaha Reservation. He stayed there until December 17, when a letter arrived from Alice Fletcher, just back from Mexico, urging him to come home. La Flesche headed back immediately. He arrived at 214 on December 22, and that night he and Alice Fletcher talked until three o'clock.[2] He did not want Rosa to return to 214. His marriage was over.

In retrospect it seems to have been an impetuous middle-aged fling. Francis La Flesche had been married twice in his youth, in June 1877 to Alice Mitchell, who died the next year, and in August 1879 to another young Omaha woman, Alice, the daughter of Little Prairie Chicken (Horace Cline). Separated from his second wife before he went to Washington to work as a clerk in 1881, he divorced her on the grounds of infidelity in 1884, around the time the allotments were being completed. She later married Sioux Solomon, brother of Two Crows.[3] Thereafter Francis had lived for twenty years as a pampered bachelor son in a house with two older women. When the marriage to Rosa took place, Francis was fifty years old, Alice Fletcher was sixty-seven, and Jane Gay was seventy-five.

Rosa Bourassa was an attractive woman, with a background similar to his own, and Francis succumbed, perhaps thinking of her as a long-term companion after Alice Fletcher was gone. But he could not make the break with Alice Fletcher—to move out of her house—that might have allowed his marriage to succeed. And Francis soon realized that he had sacrificed the present for an illusory future, for Rosa Bourassa's presence in the household drastically diluted not only Alice Fletcher's loving care and attention but also her congenial companionship. One cannot read Fletcher's and La Flesche's diaries and letters to one another without sensing again and again how much they enjoyed one another, whether working together, attending the theater, concerts, scientific and literary meetings together, or simply spending evenings at home playing bridge with their neighbors. On the surface they were so different, the well-educated, earnest, socially well-placed, and very determined New England lady and the retiring Nebraska Indian. But their personalities were very similar. Both of them were sentimental, but they were also clear-eyed and blunt about human foibles. They loved jokes and wry comments. With Alice Fletcher, the quiet-seeming Francis La Flesche spoke his own mind at length. He was as set on his course as she was on hers. He loved and admired her and basked in her attention, having learned how to keep it. Alice Fletcher, for her part, had come to feel that she had not really experienced an event until she had shared it with him. In marrying Rosa Bourassa, Francis La Flesche had gained a wife but had lost his companion of choice, the person who for twenty-five years had been at the center of his life.

But for Francis La Flesche to return home alone to the person he most truly loved meant making public something easily misinterpreted, and a storm of gossip broke about their heads. It was fed by Rosa Bourassa La Flesche, who was determined not to let Francis so easily cast her aside. Alice Fletcher's concern at first was simply for Francis. "My boy is here," she wrote Isabel Barrows in February, "a saddened boy but manly and true. The clouds are still thick about him—when and where and how the storm may come I know not."[4]

Anticipating that Rosa might accuse her of having undue influence on Francis, Fletcher made tentative plans to go away for a time, to Europe with Isabel and Samuel Barrows. But then the gossip that swirled about them began to touch her personally, as reproaches came from her closest friends. The essence of the gossip, which resurfaced periodically over the next several years, was that she had broken up Francis La Flesche's marriage in order to marry him herself. Matilda Stevenson spread that word in Santa Fe in 1908, according to Edgar Hewett.[5] In Washington Mrs. Tulloch, Alice Fletcher's neighbor and long-time friend, would scarcely speak to her,[6] and Captain Richard Pratt, who had known Rosa as a student and later an employee at the Carlisle Indian School, took her part in the controversy.

Jane Gay, meanwhile, was staying away from 214, far away. She and her niece and namesake, Emma Jane Gay, had gone to England in the summer of 1906. There they looked up Caroline Sturge, a Quaker physician and friend of Jane Gay's physician in Washington, Anne Wilson. Dr. Sturge was a practicing midwife in London and examiner in operative midwifery at the Royal Free Hospital Medical School. She was living alone at 14 Nottingham Place and was lonely. Dr. Sturge was thirty years younger than Jane Gay, but the latter at seventy-six was "still young in heart and mind," according to her niece.[7] The two women liked each other immediately, and Jane Gay decided to stay on in England with Dr. Sturge. In the troubled spring of 1907, Jane Gay sent a form letter from Europe and, Alice Fletcher noted, "no word of interest or care about the trouble with Rosa."[8]

With Jane Gay gone, the immediate problem was to find someone to share the house at 214. Alice Fletcher needed the money, but more pressing in the midst of the gossip and a possible legal suit was the need not to be alone in the house with Francis. Alice Fletcher's half sister-in-law and her niece from St. Louis came in mid-December and stayed for three months, but then they had to return home.[9]

There were other troubles. The newspapers were full of the trial of Mary Thaw's son Harry for the murder of Stanford White, and Alice Fletcher suffered for her friend and patron. From Nebraska came word of continuing controversy on the Omaha Reservation. "Bad news of Omahas. It is hard to see one's work a failure," Fletcher wrote in her diary.[10]

Not all her friends deserted her. She and Francis were invited to Theodore Roosevelt's White House for an evening of Indian music by the American composer Arthur Finley Nevin in late April. "Invitation thro. kindness of Mr. Leupp [Commissioner of Indian Affairs Francis E. Leupp]," Alice noted. But a few such acts of kindness could not dampen the controversy that Rosa kept inflamed with newspaper interviews and scenes at Francis's office.[11] Two days after one such confrontation, Rosa wrote Francis a letter which he kept in his personal papers until his death. It read:

> My dear Francis, It is necessary for me to ask you for $25.00 to cover the expense of my trip from Chicago. Also . . . that you give me more than $30.00 per month allowance; that does not cover expenses here . . . regarding my re-instatement in the Indian Service . . . [they] re-

quired I take Civil Service examination again, since I have been out over a year . . . this, too, is an added expense. Since you would give me no intimation of your wishes where I should stop . . . told me to do as I liked . . . I went to my friend, who take me in until you make other arrangements for me. In view of your desire that I not come to Miss Fletcher's . . . I assume you . . . prefer I do not send there. . . . I ask you to send [to] the above address, my summer hat and the contents of the box in which it was left and my tan voile dress. An early response to the above requests will greatly oblidge,

Your wife Rosa.[12]

Rosa's possessions were duly packed up and sent to her by taxi. As this letter makes abundantly clear, Rosa La Flesche's stance was that of an abandoned wife. By early June, Rosa's lawyers were threatening to involve Alice Fletcher, if necessary, in order to get Francis to pay more money, and Francis hired a lawyer.[13]

Alice Fletcher responded to the growing crisis in a way that had become a pattern for her—flight. In 1885, during the first round of gossip about herself and Francis, she had fled to Alaska. In 1906, after the confrontation at her bedside between Jane Gay and Francis, she had gone to Mexico. This time she decided to take off again, preparing as if she might not be back, so tired and ill did she feel. She rewrote her will, and she spent a week destroying her papers, "getting all things ready to leave and have no trouble behind," she wrote in her diary on April 4. A week later she wrote: "Working on destruction of letters. Read over all my past life. a very busy one and with some results." The next day she was less sanguine: "Worked all day over letters, and all evening. a sad day."[14] She wanted her professional career to be remembered, so she kept her professional papers. But she ruthlessly destroyed everything else, everything having to do with the first forty years of her life and anything personal from the years after that. She was determined to leave nothing for gossip to feed on.

Deciding where to go was her next problem. For a time she changed her mind daily, like a frantic and distracted bird, alternating between Europe and a return visit to Mexico. In mid-June she fled to Europe with the Barrows. She had no plans other than "to drift with my friends," she wrote Putnam's secretary. "I hope to come back a better and wiser woman."[15] They were to be gone for four months.

In London she met Jane Gay, who was full of the latest news from home. "Rosa has been simply wicked, I did not know how wicked, until I learned from Miss Gay in London what she had been saying and doing. She has tormented Francis and rushed into the newspapers and the court, a species of blackmail. She says it is dollars and cents she is after and she lies past belief about F. . . . I only tell you this that you may know the truth," Fletcher wrote Putnam.[16]

But Alice Fletcher had little time to worry about the trouble at home, so fast did they move—from London to Oxford, then to Copenhagen, Stockholm, Finland, and on to Russia. Everywhere they "breathed penological air,"[17] for Samuel Barrows had been appointed to the commission that was to decide how to replace Sing Sing, and their European tour was actually an inspection tour of European prisons. They looked at prisons from Spain and Portugal to Moscow. In Russia they also spent three days on a Volga steamer and took the trans-Siberian railroad east nearly to Siberia.

Alice Fletcher was overwhelmed by a men's choir they heard in a Russian Orthodox church in St. Petersburg. Her long study of American Indian music had prepared her for new kinds of music, and she was enthralled by what she heard. The priests chanted the ritual, their voices rising in a chromatic scale to a great crescendo, which then at its highest point was picked up by a choir of fifty to seventy-five male voices and was carried on in complex harmony. "I shall never hear its like again," she wrote a friend.[18]

The culmination of their travels in Russia was a visit with Leo Tolstoy at Yasnaya Polyana, his country home 130 miles south of Moscow. Tolstoy was seventy-nine years old and would be dead within three years. He had long since repudiated his great novels *War and Peace* and *Anna Karenina* and was trying to live a life of peace and simplicity. Alice Fletcher and the Barrows arrived at the Tolstoy estate at midday, in time for dinner. Afterward the countess took them upstairs to see Tolstoy's study, and then the great man himself escorted them on a walk on his estate. Tolstoy was utterly uninterested in Samuel Barrows's mission. "What's the use of prisons, anyway?" he wanted to know.[19] But he was fascinated by what Alice Fletcher could tell him about the religious ideas of the American Indians,[20] and he talked quietly with Isabel Barrows about his belief in immortality. Both women felt the visit was a success, although afterward Alice Fletcher decided there was something regressively "primitive" about Tolstoy's apparent need to live his beliefs so dramatically. The countess seemed less sympathetic toward the Russian peasants than was her husband and was perplexed and angered by their increasing belligerence. Fletcher left feeling that she understood Tolstoy much better after having seen him in his Russian environment. Tolstoy gave her a copy of his essay on "Shakespeare and the Drama," in which he charged that Shakespeare's works were "trivial and immoral" because they were without religious foundation. Fletcher read the essay the following winter to the Literary Society and dutifully reported the members' comments to Tolstoy, as she had promised to do.[21]

Then it was on to prisons in Warsaw and to a meeting of the International Prison Commission in Lausanne. Twenty-five letters, a month's worth, were waiting in Lausanne for Fletcher, and they brought back all the troubles at home. "Could not sleep because of distress of mind. Spoke to Mrs. Barrows of the trouble. Good friend," Alice Fletcher wrote in her diary that night.[22]

From Switzerland they traveled through France, went for a "delightful swim" in the Mediterranean at Barcelona, spent nearly a month in Spain and Portugal—prisons again—and finally sailed for home from Gibraltar on September 25, 1907. In all, Samuel Barrows had visited and taken voluminous notes on thirty-six prisons in fourteen countries, and the two women had been with him most of the time. It had been an odd trip but an absorbing one. Barrows's empiricism-with-a-purpose, so representative of American social science at the turn of the century, before the latter became a strictly academic enterprise, was the kind of thing that Alice Fletcher appreciated. "I have had a wonderful summer," she wrote Putnam. She returned with many memories, but little else, for in Granada a pickpocket snatched her purse and got her money, her passport, and the journal she had kept along the way.[23]

Two incidents on the steamer home reveal her state of mind. Fletcher found that she had been put with someone's servant, but she "made a fuss" and ended up sharing her stateroom with a pleasant girl, a Miss Harris.[24] Alice Fletcher would never allow herself to be trifled with. But in the mid-Atlantic when a violent storm came up, she decided solemnly that if the boat floundered and they headed for lifeboats, she would not try to escape "but let those who have dear ones have my place. My life is over."[25]

Alice Fletcher returned home with her head held high and began to reestablish her household, but the situation was as complicated and dreadful as ever. The "trouble with Rosa" was by no means over. Alice Parsons, the daughter of a close friend and neighbor, spent the night at 214 the day Alice arrived home, so that she and Francis would not be there alone together. The next day Sara Ostrom came from New York for an extended visit. The long-term solution was Emily Cushing, Frank Hamilton Cushing's young widow, who arrived in mid-November. She was to share their home (with long interludes at her sister's in California) for the next twelve years.[26]

Emily Cushing was never the close friend that Jane Gay had been. Charming and attractive, she could be somewhat imperious. Frank Cushing liked to imply in the years of their marriage that "my little lady" was a handful and that she gave her loyalty and friendship to only a few carefully chosen people.[27] After Cushing's death his good friend, Stewart Culin, was her frequent escort and a daily guest at 214 when he was in town. Alice Fletcher did not care much for Culin, who had left the University of Pennsylvania after a quarrel with her friend, Sara Y. Stevenson, and this led inevitably to some strain. Correspondingly, Emily Cushing did not care much for Edgar L. Hewett, who was a frequent visitor to 214, and she often contrived to be absent when he was around.[28]

Alice and Francis braced themselves for the lawsuit, which came in November. Francis was served a summons to appear in court, and Alice was subpoenaed by Rosa Bourassa to appear as a witness. "Rosa's lies were fearful," Fletcher wrote in her diary the day of the hearing. "It was all an insult to me. Great nervous strain."[29] The case dragged on for months. Rosa wanted not only alimony but also court costs, and Fletcher began to worry that she might lose her house. The judge's decision, delivered finally on April 24, 1908, that Francis was to pay Rosa forty dollars a month and court costs but no back alimony and no counsel fees came as "a great relief."[30] The amount set was about a fourth of his salary, and he wrote the checks dutifully, month after month and year after year. He was still paying

it faithfully in 1927, more than twenty years after a childless marriage that had lasted for less than eight months.[31]

Rosa Bourassa La Flesche was reinstated in the Indian Service
after the divorce. She worked as an assistant clerk at Chilocco, Oklahoma, and later for the Crow agency in Montana. In 1911 she returned to Washington to work without pay for the newly formed Society of American Indians, a pan-Indian group founded by Arthur C.
Parker, among others, that was assimilationist in orientation but
also had a strong concern for Indian rights. Rosa Bourassa La Flesche
was elected to their fifteen-member advisory board, served as corresponding secretary in their central office, and was pictured and
commended warmly for her dedication in one of the first issues of
their *Quarterly Journal*.[32] Rosa La Flesche lived at this time at 310
First Street, S.E., in Washington, one block away from 214, where
her former husband lived.[33] They both attended the Second Annual
Conference of the Society of American Indians, held in Columbus,
Ohio, in October 1912,[34] but thereafter that organization carefully
ignored both Francis La Flesche and Alice Fletcher. In 1914 the
Quarterly Journal printed a "list of Indians in government employ"
that did not include Francis La Flesche and a list of "noble women
who have befriended the Indian" that included Helen Hunt Jackson
and Amelia S. Quinton but not Alice Fletcher.[35] This may reflect
Rosa Bourassa La Flesche's influence, or it may have been the decision of Thomas L. Sloan, an Indian lawyer (one-sixteenth Omaha)
who was one of the founders of the society and who would be
elected its president in 1919.

Thomas Sloan was Francis La Flesche's alter ego in the sense that
he became a lawyer and an activist for Indian rights, a career that
Francis the scholar occasionally looked at yearningly. Their paths
diverged early. In 1880, while Francis La Flesche was serving as an
interpreter for the ethnologist James O. Dorsey, Thomas Sloan was
employed as a herder by cattlemen running stock on the Omaha
Reservation. Francis La Flesche so impressed government officials
that he was invited to become a clerk in Washington. Thomas Sloan,
meanwhile, ended up in jail on the reservation for making public
the fact that the Omahas were being cheated by the stockmen. When
he complained to the commissioner of Indian affairs and the secretary of the interior, Sloan and Hiram Chase, the son and grandson

Rosa Bourassa La Flesche, formal
portrait by Harris and Ewing,
Washington, D.C., in the *American
Indian* 2 (1914), 179. (Hillel Burger,
Peabody Museum, Harvard University)

of Omaha chiefs, were thrown into jail for thirty days on a trumped-up charge. Sloan later went to Hampton Institute, graduating in 1889 as class valedictorian and one of the most outstanding students in the history of the school. He read law with Hiram Chase, a graduate of the Cincinnati Law School, and the two men practiced law together in the little town of Pender, on the border of the reservation. In the aftermath of the Winnebago allotments, when the reservation was overrun with white stockmen grazing their cattle under illegal leases, Sloan did legal work for four years for the special agent sent out by President Grover Cleveland to remove trespassers from Indian lands. He continued to be a legal fighter for Indian rights and to represent the tribe in cases of concern to them. One of his most famous cases was his own, Sloan v. the United States, in which he challenged Alice Fletcher's 1884 ruling that his grandmother, Margaret Sloan, was not entitled to an allotment, even though she was half-Indian, because she was married to a white man and was not living on the Omaha Reservation on August 7, 1882. Fletcher's ruling was upheld, but tribal sentiment was overwhelmingly with Margaret Sloan and her grandson. Even the secretary of the interior and the commissioner of Indian affairs felt that Alice Fletcher was sometimes too rigid in her application of the eligibility requirements for allotment and had urged her to refer questionable cases to them. In 1905, Thomas Sloan finally received the allotment due him.[36]

Inevitably there was some rivalry, and ill feeling, between Thomas Sloan and Francis La Flesche, although they were often on the same side in controversies affecting the tribe. Both of them were opposed to peyote initially, and then both became strongly supportive of the peyote religion. Whether because of Rosa or Thomas Sloan, Francis La Flesche seems to have been deliberately made to feel unwelcome in the Society of the American Indians. He took the hint and dropped out.

Francis was stoical about his brief marriage, regarding it as his mistake. In 1919 he wrote to Alice Fletcher: "I am glad Pratt is coming around to recognize you because I think he has been unjust to you in holding you responsible for my extricating myself from a situation that started out to be the torment of my life. It was none of his affair but he seems to have taken sides in the matter and tried to be disagreeable."[37] Rosa Bourassa La Flesche never let up on her claim on Francis. She collected alimony until his death in 1932 and then successfully challenged his will, in which she had not been included.

Francis's divorce was not the only court case Alice Fletcher was involved in during the winter of 1907–1908. In January, in response to Mrs. Thaw's pleading, she agreed to testify at Harry Thaw's second trial for the murder of Stanford White, after the trial held the previous year had ended in a hung jury. Fletcher met with one of the lawyers the day before and "told him what I was willing to say."[38] William Travers Jerome, the prosecuting district attorney, tried to befuddle her on the witness stand, but "soft-voiced, dignified, and singularly clear in her answers to question and expressions of opinions, she made a witness that Mr. Jerome realized was eminently fair and honest," a *New York Times* reporter wrote.[39] "Horrid experience," was Alice Fletcher's own summation of the morning's events.[40] Two weeks later Harry Thaw was acquitted on an insanity plea.

There were bright spots in that fall and winter. She went to Lake Mohonk in October and was immensely cheered by the warm welcome she received. In January, in the midst of the Thaw trial and of Francis's trial, the American Anthropological Association elected her to a four-year term as vice-president, the Literary Society greeted her paper on Tolstoy with an ovation, and 150 people came to her first "Monday at-home" of the season. Her health was better, perhaps because for the first time in many years there was an obvious external enemy—Rosa—on whom any troubles could be blamed. "Oh it is so good to be well!" she wrote Cora Folsom at the Hampton Institute. "I am well after so many years of feeble health. My last summers vacation set me on my feet. I went abroad with Mr. and Mrs. Barrows, and to Russia, back through Spain and Portugal."[41]

She also had plenty of work to do, two tasks in particular. The Bureau of American Ethnology wanted her Omaha book, and they wanted it immediately. She and Francis plunged into the final composition of what they regarded as the culmination of their work together, twenty-five years of study and research. The terms of authorship this time were clear. It was to be "by Alice C. Fletcher and Francis La Flesche." Alice reported to Putnam that Francis was going to write a considerable part of the book. "He will have to write it for I want it to have the true Omaha flavor and not be diluted thro.

me."[42] They worked steadily on the monograph for a year. On January 15, 1909, Alice Fletcher wrote the last paragraph. Emily Cushing, who delighted in creating parties, produced ice cream, and they had a celebration. Alice Fletcher read proof for the book off and on for another two years. *The Omaha Tribe* was finally published in 1911 by the Bureau of American Ethnology.

The second job awaiting Fletcher that fall and winter was the exciting task of planning work in American archaeology for the A.I.A. After years of watching anthropological politics from the sidelines, Alice Fletcher was at last in the driver's seat. In the fall of 1907 Charles P. Bowditch had resigned as chairman of the American Committee of the Archaeological Institute of America. Bowditch was weary of trying to rein in Edgar L. Hewett, Charles Lummis, and others more interested in the American West than in the ancient Maya. He suggested that Miss Fletcher take his place. To Bowditch she seemed the ideal candidate. She was sympathetic to Hewett and Lummis, but she was Putnam's protégé and would surely let herself be guided by Putnam. But Bowditch had her wrong. He did not know how confident Alice Fletcher had become in her own judgement and powers and how eager she was to exercise them.

Fletcher had kept in touch with Edgar Hewett, and Hewett in 1907 had had a busy summer. In response to a notice tacked up by Tozzer at Harvard, three young students, A. V. Kidder, Sylvanus Morley, and J. G. Fletcher had gone to Colorado in 1907 to learn field archaeology under Hewett. Jesse Nusbaum began his work as a photographer at Mesa Verde that summer, and the Utah Society of the A.I.A. sponsored an expedition led by Byron Cummings that included Neil Judd among the student workers. It was a golden summer, for these men were to be the leaders in Southwest archaeology for the next several decades. Their eagerness suggested the need for a regular School of American Archaeology, to be located somewhere in the Southwest. Hewett had been talking about such a school, and five cities had made informal overtures to him. "The Western people are alive and willing—more so than the East at present realizes," Alice wrote to Putnam.[43] Although Putnam, Boas, and Bowditch were not convinced, the national officers of the Archaeological Institute of America were, for they viewed the restlessness of the western societies as the chief problem confronting the A.I.A.[44] It was a problem they looked to Alice Fletcher to solve. In December she pushed the proposed school through the annual meeting of the Archaeological Institute of America, and it became an established fact.

Putnam cautioned Fletcher to go slowly, but more serious opposition began to come from Franz Boas, who had a plan of his own for an International Archaeological School in Mexico City.[45] The confrontation came in November 1908, when the committee on American archaeology met in Cambridge. Alice Fletcher had called the meeting so that they could vote on Santa Fe as the site for the new school, but Bowditch unexpectedly took the floor and for three hours argued against turning the American committee into an American school. His point of view carried, for Putnam and Boas voted with him, with Fletcher and Hewett opposing. But the controversy was only beginning, for Fletcher and Hewett undid the results of the meeting by sending mail ballots to the four absent committee members (Francis W. Kelsey and Mitchell Carroll, ex officio members as president and secretary of the A.I.A., Mrs. John Hays Hammond, and Charles Lummis), all of whom voted with them.[46]

That was too much for Charles Bowditch, who was by then wrathful. He sent a strongly worded protest to Alice Fletcher, and he sent Alfred Tozzer as his and Putnam's emissary to the annual meeting of the council of the Archaeological Institute of America to protest recent actions of the American committee. Then it was Alice Fletcher's turn to express her "sorrow, regret, and astonishment" that Putnam had joined Bowditch in calling her actions into question. "Dr. Tozzer tells me that you and Mr. Bowditch do not wish to have the American School take its place beside the other schools of the Institute," she wrote. But, she protested, the American school already existed. It had been established a year earlier. There had to be a school, for they needed an endowment for research, and no one would endow a committee. "I have always deferred to you in every way for I hold you in deep respect and affection, but . . . I must dissent," she wrote Putnam.[47] Two days earlier she had written, "You must remember I did not seek this position of Chairman but being in it I shall endeavor to do my duty however difficult it may be."[48]

Fletcher and Hewett had their way. The Committee on American Archaeology vanished, and in its place appeared a School of American Archaeology. Francis Kelsey, the president of the Archaeological

Institute of America, stood firmly behind Fletcher, calling her "one of the most clear-headed and capable administrators that I have met."[49] Bowditch's actions, on the other hand, particularly his vilifications of Hewett and his attempts to override Fletcher's authority, made Kelsey wonder about his sanity.

The feelings of hurt were intense on both sides. Alice Fletcher set off in mid-March 1909 on a month-long, A.I.A.-sponsored traveling lectureship that took her to the West Coast and north into Canada. She spoke at Boulder, Denver, Colorado Springs, Pueblo, Salt Lake City, San Francisco, Spokane, Seattle, Winnepeg, and Detroit, trying everywhere to arouse support for American archaeology. The lecture tour caused Fletcher to miss F. W. Putnam's seventieth birthday dinner, and this gave rise to subtle recriminations. Had she not been invited because they did not want her or because it was an all-male dinner or because they knew she could not come? Putnam did his best to soothe her feelings.[50]

Alfred Kroeber tried to set himself up as peacemaker in April 1909, deploring "the whole nasty business," which was "exceedingly unfortunate and harmful to the cause of anthropology and archaeology." Kroeber could foresee the results of a split between the eastern establishment and the westerners, and he wanted to avoid it at all costs. He sent Alice Fletcher a single-spaced, five-page letter urging her to try to reconcile the two sides. "You are in a position to do more than anyone else to preserve harmony in the Institute . . . to spread a little of the oil of peace, which you both as chairman of the Managing Committee and as being a woman, and a tactful one, are particularly qualified to do." Hewett, Kroeber thought, was a person of integrity and administrative ability, although his administrative ability and his scientific capacity were as yet unproven and "he labors under one serious disadvantage, which is his complete ignorance of ethnology." Kroeber thought it was possible for Hewett to continue as director of American archaeology in the Archaeological Institute of America but urged that Hewett be kept subordinate to a governing body in which the minority point of view—and the interests of ethnology—would be represented. Otherwise, he hinted, Boas, Bowditch, and Putnam might all pull out, which would be "extremely disastrous to all the prospects of the School and to the Institute's American work." He went on:

So far as I can see, you are the one person in the entire matter who is entirely disinterested, who has no scheme up his sleeve, and no ax to grind, and to whom interested or purely personal motives have not been attributed. . . . I must confess that I was a little disappointed when I learned a year or more ago of your having been selected as Chairman of the Committee, because it seemed to me that Professor Putnam's age, record, and general position in the anthropological world made him so obviously the man for the place after Mr. Bowditch's resignation, that it was by implication almost a slight upon him to select anyone else. . . . As things have developed, however, I have come to feel entirely the other way. In the present crisis you can do far more than Professor Putnam, who as the head of an institution, or rather two institutions [the Peabody Museum and the anthropology department of the University of California], has and must have schemes of his own, who has innumerable entanglements of many sorts, and who in his long official career has made both friendships and enmities that it would be impossible for him to disregard entirely. You enjoy the happy distinction of being the only one among us who is entirely independent and unentangled, and who has every opportunity to be as disinterested and unselfish in this matter as it is possible for a human being to be.[51]

But it was too late for what Kroeber had in mind. Alice Fletcher brushed off his suggestion that because of her sex she had special peace-keeping qualities. She was simply doing what was right, she told him.[52] There was nothing she could do but push ahead.

And push ahead she did. In August Alice Fletcher returned to Santa Fe to discuss with Hewett plans for renovating the Old Palace. She spent ten days at his field camp, looking over the ruins at Puye, watching the excavations, and participating in the evening campfire sessions. One night around the campfire she told of Omaha rituals. She read *The Delight Makers*, a novel by Adolph Bandelier set in the ruins on the Pajarito Plateau of the Jemez Mountains, but wrote in her diary, "Do not like it."[53] In Santa Fe she met with the local leaders who were Hewett's supporters—Frank Springer and Judge John R. McFie—and found inexpensive lodging at St. Vincent's Sanitarium.

All through 1909, Putnam, Boas, and Bowditch deliberated as to what form their opposition to the new American school under Hewett's direction should take. Putnam continued to try to smooth things over. Finally, however, when it was apparent that Fletcher and Hewett intended to go ahead with the school, and when the newly established Bowditch-Bixby Fund for Central American research was put in the general treasury, making Bowditch feel almost deliberately insulted, F. W. Putnam, Franz Boas, and Charles P. Bowditch sent their resignations from the American committee and withdrew from the Archaeological Institute of America. Bowditch composed two memoranda: "My Reasons for Distrusting Dr. Edgar L. Hewett" and "My Reasons for No Longer Trusting Miss Alice C. Fletcher." With these in hand he appeared before the council meeting of the Archaeological Institute of America in late December 1909 to explain his actions.[54] Fletcher in her diary that night called his statements "venemous" and a letter from Franz Boas about Hewett "abusive." Fletcher took to her bed two days later with nervous exhaustion, but she was not deterred, not even when some of the A.I.A. council members echoed Bowditch's criticisms of the voting methods used in her committee. She left the Baltimore meeting feeling "very tired in mind and body and rather discouraged. Yet determined to forward and work for the school," she wrote in her diary.[55]

What is striking throughout this bitter episode is the esteem in which Fletcher continued to be held, and her own composure. She was said to have been "made use of," "deceived," and "hoodwinked," and she was charged with assuming powers that were not rightfully hers, but no one ever doubted her goodwill or accused her of self-interest.[56] Nor did she become vindictive. The wonder is that she stood firm, for she had the most powerful forces in American anthropology arrayed against her, including two of the people whom out of all her colleagues she respected the most: F. W. Putnam and Franz Boas. But Alice Fletcher had a history of standing firm. And she had caught the vision of a nation that was a continent wide, a nation in which the leaders in science and scholarship need not and ought not always come from the East. She understood enough of Phoebe Hearst's and F. W. Putnam's dreams for the University of California to appreciate the need for great universities and intellectual centers in the Far West. She understood that amateurs could sometimes make contributions as great as those of professionals.

And she understood, from her long years in Nebraska and Idaho, that if anthropology were to concern itself with Indians, it ought to be carried on where there were Indians, where the past and the present merged, where the land and the sky that shaped the Indian view of the world could still be felt, and where local and regional pride could grow in tandem with scholarship. Edgar Hewett may have been the wrong person to guide the new school, but there was not much choice in American archaeology in 1908, and ultimately that did not matter. What Alice Fletcher was building was an institution for the future, one that would outlast him. And it did.

Twenty-Three

"Be my own dear Francis always"

IN the summer of 1910 an unexpected invitation came from England. Would Alice Fletcher travel there to help Jane Gay celebrate her eightieth birthday? She would indeed, especially when Jane Gay offered to pay her passage. Francis urged Alice to go, much preferring that she go to England rather than back to Hewett's summer field school in Santa Fe, and she gladly acquiesced. "It is a great pleasure to go as I do, and to see my life-long friend again, and know that she wants to see me," Fletcher wrote Putnam's secretary.[1]

Alice Fletcher had been preoccupied with A.I.A. affairs for much of 1909. She had made the demanding lecture tour for the Institute in the spring of 1909 and had returned to the Southwest for several weeks in August for the summer field school at Frijoles Canyon and for a stay in Santa Fe. In October Edgar Hewett came to Washington and stayed for several months, tending to A.I.A. business with Alice Fletcher and Mitchell Carroll, the Secretary of the Archaeological Institute of America. Hewett and Alice Fletcher had frequent conferences in his office, and he often came for dinner or spent the evening at 214. Neither Emily Cushing nor Francis La Flesche liked him much, and Francis's response to Hewett's frequent presence was to absent himself more and more from the house. He cultivated friendships with several young women, daughters of Alice Fletcher's friends, and he went away for Thanksgiving, spending several days with friends in Pittsburgh. He was home at Christmas but Hewett was there too, with a few other close friends invited for a late supper on Christmas day. Hewett was back a week later for New Year's Day dinner and on January 2 as well. "Dr. Hewett in Eve. stayed very late," Fletcher noted in her diary.[2] Hewett was a widower—his wife had died in 1905 after a long illness—and Fletcher's beleaguered protégé. She was offering him only kindness, friendship, and professional support, but Francis began to wonder if something more was afoot between his dear M., as he addressed his letters to her, and the hard-driving, intensely serious archaeologist who was ten years Francis's junior.

Francis La Flesche's own professional life was changing. On September 10, 1910, he was to be transferred from his clerkship in the Indian Bureau to the Bureau of American Ethnology, where his new title would be Ethnologist. After almost thirty years of working informally with Alice Fletcher, he was finally to be employed as a professional anthropologist in his own right. La Flesche was assigned to study the Osage people, a tribe related to the Omahas. The new position pleased him and Fletcher, but it meant that he would be away from 214 First Street for months at a time, working in Oklahoma. From aboard the S.S. *Devonian*, which took her to England in July 1910, Alice Fletcher wrote Francis: "All the way across the ocean, for we shall D. V. see land tonight, you have been in my thoughts. . . . It was more of a parting than we have ever had before, for it seems as tho. we had come to a parting of the ways, you to enter a field where I shall not be with you constantly and I to return to a home where the one for whom I have so long made a home is gone." Francis had apparently given her a ring as a parting gift, for she wrote, "My opal ring is a great comfort. I enjoy it and all it stands for and try not to be homesick."[3]

Alice was heading for England with some trepidation, not sure how she would actually be received by Jane Gay when she got there. But she need not have worried. As they neared port the captain passed two letters on to her, one from Jane Gay, who was making every arrangement for her comfort, and the other from Professor J. L. Myers of Oxford, welcoming her to England on behalf of the English anthropologists. These set the tone for her entire visit.

Jane Gay and Dr. Sturge had moved from London, where the winters were hard on Jane Gay's health, to the little village of Congresbury, in Somerset. They lived in a large stone cottage called Fair Orchard, which looked out on a wide lawn and down over the village. "Miss Gay is the centre of Dr. Sturge's care and . . . is very happy, for which I am very glad. She is far better off than when with me," Fletcher wrote Francis not long after her arrival.[4] Three weeks later she expanded her observations: "Dr. Sturge is very fond of Miss Gay, makes her the center of everything, everything is shaped to her wishes and likes and Miss Gay speaks her mind as she used to do, but Dr. S. does not seem to mind it. So no hurt is felt. I think Miss Gay is far happier than ever before and I am very glad to know and to see it. The change was well every way. Miss Gay is I think gentler than she was."[5]

The birthday celebration on July 27 with two of Jane Gay's nieces and several other guests as well as Alice Fletcher was a great success. Then for several weeks Fletcher enjoyed life in rural England, seeing the sights and accommodating herself to what she thought were strange food habits. Breakfast was at eight, followed by a dinner (called lunch) at one o'clock, the inevitable tea at four, "when ladies of culture come together," for "the people do not make calls as with us," she explained to Francis, and another dinner (called supper) at seven.[6] In August she spent several days in Suffolk with Dr. William Sturge, the brother of Jane Gay's friend, who was a physician and avid amateur archaeologist. He had a large collection of stone tools and weapons, most of them gathered locally. She also visited Bath, the cathedrals at Wells and Ely, and an old Saxon church at Glastonbury. "I wished for you as I always do when I enjoy anything," she wrote Francis.[7]

In early September Fletcher went to Sheffield for the annual meeting of the British Association for the Advancement of Science. She had been invited to present a paper, and she shrewdly prepared two. She wanted to tell about "anthropological activity in America" and did so in a comprehensive and well-received summary, but she also wanted to talk about her own work. Her second paper, "A Side-Light on Exogamy," was based on material in *The Omaha Tribe*, and it "excited considerable discussion and was on the whole very well received."[8] Fletcher was made a vice-president of section H (anthropology) and was asked to preside at one session, although she declined. Anthropologists in the British Association for the Advancement of Science were trying to make amends for a snub she had received at their hands in 1897, when they had met in Canada. She alone of all the American officers had not been made an officer in the corresponding British section because she was a woman. Fletcher learned in Sheffield that the Canadian incident had produced a fight over "the woman question" that went on for years in the BAAS and was not yet resolved.[9] She was, in 1910, the first woman ever to have been named vice-president of a section of the British Association for the Advancement of Science. Unknowingly, Fletcher had stepped into a major feminist battle in England.

What disturbed Alice Fletcher most in England was what she observed of the relation between the sexes there. "Women are not respected by men over here," she wrote Francis. "Truly the laws here are horrid and here there are two standards of morals, one for women and one for men. . . . I shudder as I meet them [men] in the road."[10] The issue touched her personally because she wanted to travel on to Italy and Greece to see the archaeological investigations going on there, but she could not find a woman friend to go with her. She thought of going alone, but the more she thought about it, the more fearful she became.

Fletcher's fears were natural for a seventy-two-year-old woman contemplating the discomforts of traveling alone. But she also was genuinely shocked by the position of women in England and by the contrast between their position there and in America. It was almost enough to call her back to the feminist cause she had put aside thirty years before. Even Jane Gay, who had never been sympathetic to the cause of woman suffrage in America, had become "stirred up" by the situation in England. In one of the great London demonstrations Jane Gay rode in the procession, seated on a horse-drawn coach that was wrapped in a long scarf in the colors of the militant party and said "Votes for Women" in large letters at each end. "I am glad she is interested," Fletcher sniffed. "It has done her good. She has become broader." Fletcher went on to Francis: "She has spoken with much interest and feeling concerning you and your troubles. Time has made her see things differently, for which I am glad for her sake. I've not gone much into matters but I can discover that there was a great deal of false statement that was poured into her ears. How I do hope you will be able to get some evidence that will enable you to get free from the great trouble."[11]

From England Alice Fletcher sent a stream of letters to "My dear F.," commenting on his new work and giving him advice, for this was the first time he had been on his own and she wanted him to be a success. "I am very desirous that you should do good work and win a name for yourself," she explained.[12] She also admitted her loneliness. In mid-September she wrote: "Some way I feel so homesick today that I have to send you a line if only to remind you to write me often that I may keep in touch with your work, and all that you are doing. When I feel so homesick I remind myself that no one is at home. You are far away and even if I could go back tomorrow I would find the place empty."[13] In early October she ended one long letter: "How I wish I was going to see you. Sometimes I think I must go to see you. Ever affly, M."[14]

Alice Fletcher attended a suffrage meeting at Queens Hall in London on October 31, and two days later took tea with Dr. Beatrice Webb. "A very interesting woman," she wrote in her diary. She stayed on in England until mid-November and then sailed for home. Fletcher arrived back in Washington on December 6 and found two letters from Francis, announcing that he would be home in just a few days, earlier than expected. "The news was joyful. Welcome! welcome home! dear Francis," she wrote him.[15] Edgar Hewett was invited to dinner the day of Francis's arrival, and they settled back into their routine through Christmas, which was also Francis's birthday. Then Alice Fletcher left to attend the annual meeting of the Archaeological Institute of America in Providence.

On the last day of 1910 Fletcher contentedly summarized the year just past in her diary. "A year of many and varied experiences," she wrote. "I have been happy to have the clouds lift between me and old friends. Much enjoyment with friends. The work on the Omaha records completed. F. transferred to congenial tasks in the Bureau of Eth. The School of Am. Arch. has weathered the storm and may God grant that needed Endowment may come so that we can surely help our worthy young men."[16]

But this contentment was not to last. When Alice Fletcher returned to 214 from Providence, Francis was gone. Alice at first thought nothing of his abrupt departure for Oklahoma, but as the days wore on without any word from him, she began to be uneasy, for he usually wrote nearly every day. Finally a letter came that "astonished and pained" her.[17] Francis felt that she was no longer interested in him now that *The Omaha Tribe* was finished and he was not needed for her work. He accused her of hurrying home from England to see Hewett and of rushing off to Providence after Christmas in order to be with Hewett. He wondered if she were thinking of marrying Hewett.

Alice Fletcher was genuinely shocked at his fears. "You are beset by a phantom," she wrote him. Hewett was planning to marry someone else and meant nothing to her. "I am deeply interested in your work. . . . You are the one dear thing in life to me," she assured him.[18] But Francis was not easily appeased, and over the next days and weeks Alice poured out, in letter after letter, her deep affection and love for him, while chiding him for his "very unkind" letter and his subsequent silence.[19] On January 5 she wrote: "I want to see you more than I can tell. . . . I carried away with me the joy of your parting caress and I think of that now to give me comfort. I am utterly alone when you are gone. . . . I have a bad headache and I am very sad. I was so happy before. Do not you be sad. There is nothing to trouble you. Our work and our close friendship is all there is in life and all there has been for these many years."[20]

Four days later she wrote: "No letter from you since your very unkind letter of a week ago Sunday. Don't do so, my dear. There is no reason why you and I should make each other uncomfortable. There is not a particle of ground for your thought as expressed. I have respect for that person's ability and character. That is all there ever was or ever could be. There is no connection with my own personal life. You know that."[21] And two days later, "I am very sorry that you can find it in your heart to refrain from writing me."[22]

She filled her letters with comments about his work. "I shall do everything I can to help you," she wrote on January 12, "just as long as God spares my life. If you will be kind and loving it will help me to live. I've been almost sick since your naughty letter of New Years Day. Be my own dear Francis always."[23]

Francis did begin to write again occasionally but without his customary warmth, and as the weeks wore on Alice grew increasingly despondent and weary. "Very tired" appears over and over in her diary. On February 7, 1911, she wrote: "not well—very weary and heart sick. . . . Wrote F. but did not send the letter. destroyed it. . . . Had a bad night."[24]

A few days later she decided to resign as chairman of the managing committee of the School of American Archaeology. "I shall do so, without fail," she wrote Francis. "I think it is best every way and by so doing I shall be able to conserve my strength, for I want to live to help you with your book on the Osages."[25] She expressed concern about his health and about his rheumatism and urged him to be careful around people with tuberculosis. "I feel very anxious about you," she wrote. "You have never been so long away from and under circumstances where I cannot look after you and protect you."[26] In March she talked of going to Oklahoma to visit him. "I miss you more and more, every day I miss you, my dear Francis."[27]

When he discouraged that, she made plans so that they might spend his summer vacation together. The years of gossip had made her wary of their traveling together, but now she threw caution to the winds. "I think we could go to Miss Wolcott's place [in the Adirondacks] and be together and no one have anything to say about it. . . . Or would you rather that I come west and you and I go to the Yellowstone Park, or would you like me to meet you somewhere and you and I go to the Grand Canyon?. . . I am willing to go anywhere with you."[28]

Fletcher arranged with her lawyer to transfer her shares of Homestake stock to Francis so that he would be provided for if she died suddenly.[29] She went through his letters from Oklahoma, copied bits of Osage ethnography he had included, and began to organize them. She cleaned his room and his closet. She packed his good suit and sent it to Oklahoma when he asked for it. And increasingly she made explicit in letters to Francis what she before had scarcely been willing to acknowledge even to herself: that he was the emotional center of her life, the person who mattered more to her than anyone else in all the world.

Gradually Francis was appeased. It helped that his work in Oklahoma was going well, for behind his charge of having been abandoned lay some understandable nervousness at finally having his work judged in its own right. He wrote in detail about what he was doing. He was working with an Osage Indian, Saucy Calf, who had asked him about the horizon, whether it was the edge of the sky and the earth.

> So I had to give him a lecture in astronomy—using the globe of the gas fixture to represent the sun and my hat as the earth. I moved my hat in a whirling fashion around the globe and told him we started around the sun in that fashion and made the trip in 365 days. He saw at once the naturalness of the thing and exclaimed, "How ignorant we are!" But I explained to him that it was many hundreds of years of hard study for the white people to find that out and from force of habit they still speak of the sun going down when it reality it did not go down. He was as much interested in my talk as I was in his where he talked of the earth and its relation to the sky.[30]

Francis wrote that he was having trouble with the music arranger, Charles Cadman, who was in Oklahoma working with him and was full of self-importance. But, Francis wrote, Cadman finally realized "that his work would be absolutely worthless without my help and now he is perfectly docile and is behaving himself like a rational white man." Francis added, "You do the things quicker than he does, very much quicker, and the work is more accurate."[31]

He grew bolder in telling Alice how much she meant to him. Planning his summer leave he wrote: "I want to see as much of you as I can. In doing this work I have given up a great deal that is of personal interest to me. Your companionship is worth much to me and I have given up a great deal of it."[32]

Francis La Flesche stayed away from 214 for six months, while Alice Fletcher, sad and lonely, repeatedly sought to assure him that matters between them were as they had always been, that she wanted to continue to share his life, and that she wanted to help him with his work. Francis kept these letters—almost alone of all the letters she had written him over the years—and with good reason, for they are a witness to the terms on which they lived out their final twelve years together. Their long-unspoken love for one another had finally been acknowledged. Fletcher, who had kept the upper hand in their relationship for thirty years, at last tossed it aside to admit how much she needed him and how much she wanted his love and care. As he had for so many years assisted her in her work, henceforth she would assist him. His work would be what mattered. Francis's love would preserve Alice's life, and she in turn would devote what remained of her life totally to him. Those were the terms established in their long-distance correspondence. Alice was seventy-three years old; Francis was fifty-six. Francis, who knew his own mind as always, had once again managed to work their relationship around to what he wanted. When Francis finally arrived back in Washington on June 30, 1911, Alice was waiting for him at the train station.[33] Their new life, in which she was to be his research assistant, was about to begin.

But new beginnings are seldom without second thoughts and some foot dragging. Alice Fletcher did not actually resign as chairman of the managing committee of the School of American Archaeology until 1912. The Homestake stocks were not transferred officially to Francis La Flesche until 1920. But the commitment had been made, the intent expressed. Francis was satisfied.

Twenty-Four

"There is no story in my life"

FROM 1911 on, for the last twelve years of their life together, the emphasis in the little house at 214 First Street, S.E., in Washington was on Francis La Flesche's career. Alice Fletcher immediately began to work on the Osage song transcriptions, redoing those "very poorly done by Cadman," she wrote Putnam's secretary.[1] By mid-July she had transcribed eighty-one Osage songs.

Francis, with their relationship clarified, no longer felt the need to keep her away from Hewett. In August they both went to New Mexico for Hewett's summer field school, stopping at the Grand Canyon on the way. "Francis is with me on his vacation and greatly enjoying every moment," she wrote to Putnam.[2] From Santa Fe they traveled to the summer field camp at Rito de los Frijoles. A wagon took them to the canyon rim, and they climbed down the precipitous trail to the camp beside the small stream, where she was greeted with "Cheers for Miss Fletcher." Alice Fletcher cheerfully limped around the ruins, eager to see everything, and at the evening campfire discussions she and Francis gave presentations. A few days later she had to climb back out of the canyon. "Dr. H. pulled, F. pushed," she wrote in her diary.[3]

The School of American Archaeology in Santa Fe had begun well enough. Hewett had excellent people working with him, including Adolph Bandelier for documentary history, Byron Cummings for excavations in Utah and Arizona, Sylvanus G. Morley for the archaeology of Central America, John P. Harrington for ethnology, Jesse L. Nusbaum for architectural reconstruction and photography, and Kenneth M. Chapman as secretary and illustrator.[4] Hewett was particularly proud of J. P. Harrington, whom he recognized as a genius in linguistic work. Others associated with the school in the early years included Earl Morris, Ralph Linton, Barbara Freire-Marreco, A. V. Kidder, and Neil M. Judd. Kidder excavated at Pecos, in a site owned by the Museum of New Mexico. Earl Morris worked at Aztec, New Mexico, under the auspices of the St. Louis Society of the Archaeological Institute of America, and later, along with Morley and Judd, in Guatemala.

But almost immediately Hewett's tendencies to spread himself too thin, to act dictatorially, and to make exaggerated claims for his projects began to cause trouble. In 1910 he and Morley began four years of excavations at Quirigua in Guatemala, sponsored by the St. Louis Society of the Archaeological Institute of America. But a lack of results, especially artifacts wanted for the St. Louis Museum, irritated the sponsors, and his haphazard accounting procedures alarmed Alice Fletcher. Hewett was director of the Museum of New Mexico as well as of the School of American Archaeology, and he freely intermingled the affairs of the two institutions. In 1911, he announced his intention to add to his other positions that of director of anthropology exhibits for the Panama-California Exposition to be held in San Diego in 1915. The Exposition was intended to celebrate the completion of the Panama Canal and, not incidentally, "to bring the climate of California to the attention of the world."[5] San Francisco's men of wealth and influence were planning a rival Panama-Pacific Exposition, which was to be a full-fledged world's fair. San Diego fair-makers settled for a slightly smaller and regionally oriented Exposition and chose anthropology, "the science of man," as its main theme. They sought out Edgar L. Hewett, from their perspective "the highest scientific authority" on the subject, to be the director of exhibits.[6]

Hewett wanted the power and the money the new position would bring, $3,500 a year in salary to add to the $1,500 he received from the Archaeological Institute of America as director of American archaeology. He argued that his new position would solve the financial problems of the School of American Archaeology, for the San Diego Exposition would pay the costs of all the excavations they wanted to do, just as the World's Columbian Exposition in Chicago had enabled Putnam to hire a hundred people to work for him. But Alice Fletcher and Francis W. Kelsey, the president of the Archaeological Institute of America, were appalled. Alice Fletcher wrote Hewett a very firm letter, warning him that the affairs of the school were in such a serious state as to imperil its future. She feared "a disaster that may prove to be irretrievable. . . . Do not think I use too strong words; unfortunately I do not."[7] She was not sanguine about the plans for the San Diego Exposition. She begged him not to consider the new post, and as best she could from across the continent, she tried to help him clear up his bookkeeping.[8]

Hewett brushed aside her concerns. He insisted on going ahead with the San Diego Exposition. "I don't see any way to get out of directing that," and as for the excavations at Quirigua, "Miss Fletcher, there has never been a more businesslike expedition conducted than this, nor could there be."[9] He made a trip to Washington to explain his plans for San Diego to her and others on the managing committee of the American school, and they reluctantly agreed to let him accept the position.[10]

The smoke had hardly cleared from this, and from an "Open Letter" critical of Hewett's administrative methods, which Franz Boas was sending around, when Hewett enraged many of the leading archaeologists in the country by giving an interview to the *New York Times* in which he claimed that his and Morley's work in Guatemala

would solve the problem of the Mayan hieroglyphs. Bowditch protested these "extravagant and sensationalist statements,"[11] and one
long-term Institute supporter wrote Kelsey, "That anything so utterly
crude should be connected with the Institute that Norton founded
is one of the ironies of fate!"[12]

Alice Fletcher passed these complaints along to Hewett, but when
Putnam wrote her to complain about the article, she rose to a spirited defense of Hewett. "We who live here in Washington learn not
to pay attention to the newspaper statements. . . . Everyone here is
a prey to newspaper men. I am bothered continually. They call me
up over the telephone, force their way in the house, until sometimes
I feel like running away," she wrote him.[13] This was to be her stance
ever after in relation to the school. In private she would offer Hewett
frank advice and counsel but publicly she stood firmly behind him.
On December 30, 1911, Hewett married Mrs. Donizetta Jones Wood
of Santa Fe, and three days later he brought his bride to 214 First
Street for dinner.

In 1912, in keeping with her promise to Francis, Alice Fletcher
resigned as chairman of the managing committee. The committee
accepted her resignation reluctantly and named her Chairman
Emeritus, her name "to be so carried on the roster of the Managing Committee in perpetuity."[14] She was succeeded as chairman by
William Henry Holmes, an artist, geologist, archaeologist, and head
of the department of anthropology at the National Museum in Washington, who decided to overlook Hewett's obvious faults, recognize
his virtues, and let him carry on as he would. For a decade Holmes
gave only token supervision to Hewett's activities. In retirement
Alice Fletcher's interest in the school remained as strong as ever. She
made several trips to Santa Fe and continued to be one of Hewett's
closest advisors. Hewett in turn regarded himself as her protégé for
the rest of his life.

The Omaha Tribe, by Alice C. Fletcher and Francis La Flesche,
finally appeared in November 1911, sumptuously published by the
Bureau of American Ethnology. Alice Fletcher wrote the foreword,
explaining that she had striven as far as possible to make the Omaha
his own interpreter. Plate 1 in the book is a formal photograph of
Francis La Flesche. There is no corresponding photograph of Alice

Francis La Flesche, formal portrait by
Towles, Washington, D.C., ca. 1908.
Plate No. 1 in *The Omaha Tribe*, 1911.
(National Anthropological Archives,
Smithsonian Institution)

Fletcher. Francis's was the knowledge behind the book; she was the instrument that brought it into being. "It is an honest piece of work, that I can say for it," Fletcher wrote to Putnam.[15]

The Omaha Tribe was an ethnohistorical work. It was an account of how the Omahas had lived in the early part of the nineteenth century before the appearance of white people and the disappearance of the buffalo, based on what was still practiced or remembered by the Omahas in the late nineteenth century. The book included the Omahas' knowledge of their environment; their tribal organization and government; hunting and agricultural practices; social life including child care, courtship, etiquette, clothing, and amusements and pastimes; their music; warfare; disease and burial customs; secret societies; and religion and ethics. An appendix summarized the recent history of the tribe, beginning with contact with white people. It was "one of the most sought after studies ever published by the BAE [Bureau of American Ethnology]"[16] and is today widely recognized as one of the classics in ethnography.

Alice Fletcher expected to rest on her laurels with the publication of *The Omaha Tribe*. She had not counted on the changing currents in American anthropology. She found herself facing an unsympathetic generation of younger anthropologists, many of them connected with Columbia University, who were eager to assert themselves and to disavow the mistakes of their elders. Controversy over *The Omaha Tribe* began even before it was officially published. A graduate student at Columbia, Paul Radin, criticized certain of Fletcher's statements in his Ph.D. dissertation on the Winnebago Medicine Dance, which was published in the *Journal of American Folk-Lore* in the summer of 1911.[17] Alice Fletcher was furious that Radin had been allowed to see the proofs of the manuscript without her permission and "greatly incensed" that their work was being publicly misconstrued and torn apart before it was available to other scholars. Her complaints reverberated through the halls of the Bureau of American Ethnology and were relayed to Radin. Forty years later, in response to an interviewer's question, Paul Radin, still smarting from her justifiable rebuke, dismissed Alice Fletcher as a "dreadfully opinionated woman."[18]

Next came the review in *Science*, which was written by Robert Lowie. Alice Fletcher and Francis La Flesche thought that J. Owen

Dorsey's work on the Omahas was marred by many errors, the result of his imperfect knowledge of the language, and had decided that they would ignore it rather than fill their book with criticisms of Dorsey. In *The Omaha Tribe* they presented "only original material gathered directly from the native people."[19] But the developing canons of professional scholarship called for review and incorporation of earlier studies. Lowie chided Fletcher and La Flesche for the "well-nigh complete neglect of the work of their predecessors," including the "classic" work of "so sane, conscientious, and competent an ethnographer as the late Rev. J. O. Dorsey." He criticized them for classifying the material in accord with "aboriginal" rather than "scientific" logic and for attaching historical value to the origin accounts of a primitive tribe, a "tendency, now definitely abandoned by ethnologists." He complained that they slighted topics like material culture and decorative designs, such as Clark Wissler and Alfred Kroeber had been studying, adding archly, "Every professional ethnologist may reasonably be expected to pay some attention to points that have come to be of theoretical interest to his fellow-students."[20] It was the review of a young scholar who, having imbibed the research program of one scholarly camp, looks contemptuously at everything done outside it.

Both Alice and Francis were indignant at Lowie's hostile and one-sided review. "Mr. Lowie reviews in *Science* 'The Omaha Tribe' criticizing and condemning and extolling Dorsey's work," Alice wrote in her diary on June 13, 1913. The next day she thought it "unfair, unjust and faultfinding," and a day later she wrote, "At church laying down life taking it up on higher plane. very suggestive and must apply it to Lowie's article whether I will reply."[21] In the end it was Francis La Flesche who wrote a response to the "animadversions and innuendos of the would-be reviewer." La Flesche wrote simply that they had not wanted to criticize and point out the errors of a well-intended man who was no longer around to rectify them. (J. Owen Dorsey died in 1895 at the age of forty-seven of typhoid fever.) La Flesche rested their case on the "unusual advantages" they had enjoyed in that one of the authors was an Omaha and well versed in both his native language and English.[22] In his view there could be no comparison between the two works, *Omaha Sociology* (1884) by J. O. Dorsey and *The Omaha Tribe* (1911) by Fletcher and La

Flesche; nor was there, on disputed points, any question about who was right. Another critical review appeared, anonymously, in the *American Historical Review*, again comparing *The Omaha Tribe* with Dorsey's book and charging that it contained too little history.[23] To this Fletcher and La Flesche sent a joint response.[24]

Alice Fletcher felt once again, as she had after the publication of "A Study of Omaha Indian Music," that their work was not getting the appreciation it merited. She was twenty years older now, seventy-five instead of fifty-five, but she cared as much as ever. In March 1913, she went to New York for a conference at the American Museum of Natural History and that night wrote in her diary, "See that the future is closed to me—all over."[25]

Happily, the European reviews were better. Alfred Haddon reviewed *The Omaha Tribe* in the British journal *Nature*, praising it highly.[26] The two foremost leaders of French sociology, Emile Durkheim and Marcel Mauss, each wrote a review in their journal *L'Année sociologique*. Mauss reviewed the book first, calling it a contribution of great importance not only to descriptive sociology of the American Indians but to sociology in general. Mauss had a few reservations. He was critical of Fletcher, whom he assumed was the main author of the book, for ignoring Dorsey's work, and he commented on her "exclusively empirical knowledge of the language," her "taste for doubtful entymologies," and her tendency to be overly philosophical and abstruse. On the other hand, he wrote, there was a certain "mystique," a power of expression in Fletcher's writing, as she chose deliberately to avoid laborious scholarly discussions and sought instead to describe the depth of the Omaha soul.[27]

Mauss's reservations apparently provoked Emile Durkheim into re-reviewing the book for his journal, for he gave it unstinting praise. Alice Fletcher and Francis La Flesche had sought to grasp the internal principles of Omaha life and to reveal both its unity and its complexity, he wrote. He considered their work much better than Dorsey's "fragmentary" and "superficial" attempts at analysis.[28] Durkheim, from his towering position in French sociology, could look out across the international scholarly landscape and recognize *The Omaha Tribe* for the unique work that it was, and he wanted others not to miss it.

With Francis away for months at a time working with the Osages in Oklahoma, there was nothing to keep Alice Fletcher in Washington. She went again to England in the summer of 1912, to spend five months with Jane Gay and Dr. Sturge at Fair Orchard in Congresbury. Since she was to be in England anyway, she was named an official delegate to the International Congress of Americanists meeting that summer in London. The congress had been founded in France in 1875 and had become a prestigious biennial gathering of the leading Americanist scholars from Europe, North America, and South America. Alice Fletcher tried to interest Americans in it. One of her last publications was a "brief history" of the congress for the *American Anthropologist.*[29]

The next winter, back in Washington, she transcribed the Osage songs Francis had recorded. "I have just completed my 49th song," she wrote Putnam in March of 1913. "Some of them are quite difficult as to rhythm. Not infrequently one song will occupy four hours of hard, close work. Rarely a song takes less than an hour and a half. . . . So you see, Professor, I am not idle but working for the Science to which I have devoted my life."[30] By summer she had finished 217 Osage songs.[31]

In 1913, Alice decided to go to England again. She sailed in late July and found "Miss Gay looks well but the years count."[32] She stayed at Fair Orchard for two and a half months, with occasional trips to London and Stratford, and sailed for home in mid-October. Thereafter she did not see her old friend again. In 1915 Jane Gay and Caroline Sturge decided to move from Congresbury to the nearby Quaker village of Winscombe. Dr. Sturge hired a well-known architect in Bristol to design a "cottage," in reality a large and very solidly built country home with four bedrooms on the second floor and three maids' rooms in the attic, for "Miss Sturge and Miss Gay." The house was set at the top of a large, sloping field overlooking the village and the playing field of the famous Quaker school nearby. The design included two large ornamental letters, *S* and *G*, carved in the plaster on gables on opposite sides of the house. They named the house "Kamiah" for the peaceful place in Idaho that Jane Gay had loved. Both the name, out of Jane Gay's past, and the large initials placed so prominently on the exterior walls reveal that Jane Gay had at last found the totally dedicated companionship Alice Fletcher had never been able to give her. Jane Gay died at Kamiah in 1919 at the age of eighty-nine. Caroline Sturge died three years later of a brain tumor at the age of sixty-one.[33]

Alice Fletcher learned on her arrival home in 1913 that Isabel Barrows had died. "I am a good deal broken up about it. It is a great loss to me," she wrote Francis from Boston, for she had gone directly from the steamer to the funeral. "I can say little but I am thinking a good deal." She told Francis when she would be arriving in Washington. "Then you will meet me, and o! I shall be so glad to see you again, dear Francis. . . . It is a hard experience that I have met, but death is a part of life. I know it is such. Still it is human to feel the change when it comes. Good night. God bless you and keep you safely and grant we may meet again. Love to Mrs. Parsons. Greetings to Dora. Ever affly, M."[34] Two years later Fletcher traveled to Cambridge for the funeral of her longtime friend and mentor, F. W. Putnam.

Francis La Flesche had an operation on his right eye for glaucoma in May 1914 and then went to the Omaha Reservation for three months rest.[35] Fletcher went to San Diego to see preparations for the Exposition, which was to open on January 1, 1915, and to Santa Fe for the annual meeting of the managing committee of the American School. J. P. Harrington was recovering from typhoid fever, so she filled in for him at the summer field school, giving six lectures on ethnology.

In 1917, she returned to Santa Fe for the opening of the Art Museum, which Hewett had added to the Old Palace. Edgar Hewett had returned from San Diego eager to expand the scope of the School of American Archaeology. In San Diego he had met Robert Henri and invited him to Santa Fe. Robert Henri arrived in 1916 and was followed shortly by George Bellows, John Marin, and John Sloan.[36] Hewett gave the artists studio space in the Museum of New Mexico, arranged for exhibitions in the Old Palace, and made plans for an Art Museum addition to the Old Palace building. In 1917, the school was renamed the School of American Research and established as an independent corporation, retaining only a loose affiliation with the Archaeological Institute of America. The new name, Hewett wrote, embraces "anthropology, ethnology, psychology, sociology, art, history, and religion." He explained: "No reason is recognized for limiting research to scientific subjects. The artists who are painting here

are just as truly researchers as are the scientists. . . . In truth, anthropologists, with a few conspicuous exceptions, have done scant justice to the Indian culture. . . . It is through the artists and poets and
scientists combined that this remarkable race is at last being truly
represented."[37]

Whatever the truth of Hewett's statements, most leading anthropologists thought that he was again wasting resources and superb
opportunities by spreading himself too thin. Clark Wissler of the
American Museum of Natural History spoke for many when he
urged that though the School of American Research was making
Santa Fe the "art center of the Southwest," it also ought to make
Santa Fe a center of scientific anthropology, for, he wrote, you "have
in your canyons and Indian villages one of the finest natural anthropological laboratories in the world."[38] But Hewett was past the point
of taking advice.

Alice Fletcher would return to Santa Fe in 1922, the year before
her death, noticeably feeble but still remarkably alert. It was a poignant visit. The friends who gathered around her realized that it was
likely to be her last visit and that no one else could take her place as
a backer of the school. She was the last link between the school and
the East Coast establishment, for in 1922 Holmes was replaced as
chairman of the managing committee by Frank Springer, a Las Vegas
attorney who was the school's most generous benefactor and the
donor of the new Art Museum. Hewett held on until his death in
1946. Then, almost immediately, the School of American Research
and the Museum of New Mexico were merged with a rival Santa
Fe institution, the Laboratory of Anthropology, which had been
founded in 1927 partly as a way of maneuvering around Hewett.
The School of American Research was reestablished as a private institution in 1958.

Through these final years there was always Francis, as constant a
presence in her diaries as he was in her life. The long absences from
Washington that Francis's work required were a trial to both of them
and the only drawback in his new assignment. In 1912 the superintendent of the Indian agency at Pawhuska, Oklahoma, tried to
persuade Francis to take the position there of chief clerk. "The position has a big salary and I could do the work," Francis wrote Alice,
"but I cannot take it. I can't leave Washington, you know why."[39] He

started bringing informants to Washington, as Fletcher had done, and soon was making only occasional brief visits to Oklahoma.

When he was away, either in Oklahoma or on his annual visits to the Omaha Reservation, they wrote to one another several times a week and sometimes every day. Francis was frank about his family, colleagues, and informants and sometimes very funny but also increasingly tender. On January 15, 1917, he wrote her from Oklahoma, "When I am home we will go out [riding] often so that your health may not be weakened by staying indoors all the time." He noted on the sixteenth: "Yesterday I received 3 letters from you, 2 dated the 10th and one the 11th. I was very glad to hear from you as I always am." And he wrote again on January 31, "Preserve your strength for I am going to need your wise counsel in this work."[40] When he was home he offered drives, walks, and games in the evenings, and he conspired with the cook to have special treats like strawberry shortcake and surprise dinners. Alice Fletcher in turn thought about him constantly, kept house for him, and translated songs and organized research material for him. Emily Cushing left in 1915 to make her home permanently with family members in California. They worried only about the loss in income that this meant and how they would keep the house going. Fletcher thought after Jane Gay's death in 1919 that her niece, Emma Gay, might return to Washington and live with them at 214, but it did not happen. Francis wrote Alice, "It may be for the best. I was hoping she could be with us in order to help you in keeping up the home, but we can get along."[41]

Alice Fletcher had become an anachronism by the end of her life, from her Victorian ideas of social class and social propriety to the voluminous black dresses she habitually wore while women all around her were becoming flappers in skinny sheaths with dropped waists and short skirts. Mabel Barrows, the daughter of Fletcher's beloved friend Isabel Barrows, accused her of being snobbish in her choice of friends, which drew from Fletcher an indignant and spirited response. But others had a similar impression. Emlyn Hodge, the daughter of Smithsonian ethnologist Frederick Webb Hodge, remembers Alice Fletcher as an occasional guest at her parents' open house at Garret Park, Maryland, on Sunday evenings in the years between 1912 and 1919. Alice Fletcher was very serious and dignified and always wore black and great bustling skirts. When she arrived, she would pause in the door, waiting for everyone to rise and escort her to the most comfortable chair in the room. Emlyn Hodge and her sister called her "Lady Alice" behind her back and were mortified when their aunt, Emily Cushing, passed this information on to Alice Fletcher. But the latter took it as a joke and urged the two young girls to come with their mother in response to Alice Fletcher's calling card, which read "At Home—Mondays in January." Francis La Flesche appeared to the young girls to be a stereotypical silent Indian. The Hodge daughters thought that both Emily Cushing and Alice Fletcher were elitist, rejecting what they considered distasteful and deigning to associate only with people they considered worthy.[42]

This snobbishness of Alice Fletcher's, if such it was, was a key element of her ethnography. In Fletcher's view, one of the tragedies of American history was how little the native race and the incoming race knew of "the better elements of the other."[43] The races came in contact with one another in the worst possible circumstances, on the frontier or border between their two societies, where Indians acting outside tribal control and custom interacted with white men who had placed themselves beyond the legal and moral restraints of society. "All white people lie," she had heard on her first visit among the Indians, and she insisted that this was not true. She knew equally well the stereotypes and prejudices that white people clung to about Indians, that at worst they were vicious savages and at best they were stolid, sullen, morose, and untrustworthy. Alice Fletcher worked all her life not just for some vague understanding between the two societies but for appreciation by each of the highest and best that the other was capable of.

Inevitably this colored her ethnography, and it led to at least one sharp exchange with Franz Boas and Alfred Kroeber around 1902. As Boas described it:

> I had asked him [Kroeber] to collect Arapaho traditions without regard to the "true" forms of ancient tales and customs, the discovery of which dominated, at that time, the ideas of many ethnologists. The result was a collection of stories some of which were extremely gross. This excited the wrath of Alice C. Fletcher who wanted to know only the ideal Indian, and hated what she called the "stable boy" manners

of an inferior social group. Since she tried to discredit Dr. Kroeber's work on this basis I wrote a little article . . . in which I tried to show . . . the necessity of knowing the habits of thought of the common people as expressed in story telling.[44]

Another observant visitor to 214 in these years was Carobeth Laird, then the wife of the anthropologist and linguist John P. Harrington. The Harringtons were invited to dinner by Alice Fletcher soon after they first arrived in Washington in 1918, for Fletcher admired Harrington and wanted Francis to get to know him. They made their way to 214 First Street, S.E., not far from where they themselves had taken a cheap apartment, and found a very old, Washington red-brick row house in a rundown area. Capitol Hill had deteriorated by then, and most of the scientific community lived either in the Northwest section of the city or out in the suburbs. The house, Laird later wrote, was "perhaps a little overfurnished in the Victorian way, but it had a lovely atmosphere, a comfortable *atmosphere*. Miss Fletcher was elderly, full-figured, pale, mentally alert. She was diabetic, and Mr. La Flesche watched over her diet with an eagle eye. We ate, I remember, a delicious roast, but I believe there was no dessert. Mr. La Flesche explained that Miss Fletcher could not eat sweets." Carobeth Laird described Francis La Flesche as "a full-blooded Omaha, middle aged, and heavy from years of city living, but still a fine figure of a man. A certain female clerk at the Bureau, trembling on the verge of confirmed spinsterhood, was said to have cast sheep's eyes at him, but I never heard of his responding."[45]

Later J. P. Harrington, without his wife, attended a testimonial dinner in honor of Alice Fletcher, having been informed ahead of time that "Miss Fletcher would be the only woman present." When Carobeth Laird, waiting at home and eager to hear all the details, asked him how she was dressed, he replied, "Same as the men, black with something white in front." Neil M. Judd, in his history of the Bureau of American Ethnology, also mentions her clothing. She had come to be known as "the gracious lady of the B.A.E.," he wrote. "It was her warm, sympathetic interest in everyone and everything rather than her snow-white hair and widely flowing dresses that endeared her to all."[46]

In the summer of 1922 Francis La Flesche escorted her to Santa

Fe and to the Omaha Reservation for the last time. "At both places she was highly honored," Francis wrote his niece, Marguerite Conn. "She enjoyed the trip and was very happy. She had much to tell about the visit when she came home about the honors paid her."[47]

Alice Fletcher fell ill with grippe on February 6, 1923, and then suffered a paralytic stroke, from which she never recovered.[48] Once again her woman friends rallied around. Mary Thaw sent money to help with the expenses of nursing care, and Emma Gay, Jane Gay's niece, came to help.[49] On April 6, 1923, Francis wrote in his diary: "Clear, warm. M. passed away just at 8:10 this evening, quietly and no suffering."[50] Services were held two days later at 214 First Street, the home out of which she had worked for thirty years. Dozens of her friends gathered there for the last time for services conducted by Dr. Ulysses Grant Baker Pierce of All Souls' (Unitarian) Church. The honorary pall bearers were the leaders of Washington anthropology: William H. Holmes, director of the National Gallery of Art and formerly chief of the Bureau of American Ethnology; J. W. Fewkes, chief of the Bureau of American Ethnology, and staff members Truman Michelson, J. R. Swanton, W. E. Myers, and J. N. B. Hewitt; Ales Hrdlicka, Walter Hough, and Neil M. Judd of the National Museum; and one longtime friend and neighbor, F. H. Parsons. A week later J. P. Harrington moved into 214 to share the house with Francis La Flesche.

"I miss the dear lady at every turn," Francis wrote Emma Gay, "but it is well, and I am content, that the end came for if she had partially recovered she would never have been happy. . . . She has been to me like a real mother, and it was fortunate for me that I became associated with her in her work. I have indeed lost a true friend."[51]

Alice Fletcher's estate was valued at $35,000, not including the 125 shares of Homestake stock (worth $8,656) she had formally transferred to Francis La Flesche in 1920. In her final will, dated September 18, 1919, Fletcher had set up a trust with the bulk of her estate, the income to go to Francis La Flesche during his lifetime and then to the School of American Research in Santa Fe, New Mexico, to establish a fellowship in the name of Alice Fletcher. The will and the gift of Homestake stock were contested by Genevieve F. Crayton of Lebanon, Illinois, and Wendell C. Fletcher of Montreal, Canada,

Alice Fletcher, Hartley Burr Alexander,
Robert Douglas Scott, Henry Purmont
Eames, and Francis La Flesche in
Lincoln, Nebraska, ca. 1915. (Nebraska
State Historical Society)

children of Fletcher's half-brother, who claimed "mental weakness at the time of her making the will" and "undue influence."[52] In probate hearings held in November 1924, Francis La Flesche was able to produce Fletcher's statement signed on April 3, 1891, and enclosed in the will, which read: "I Alice C. Fletcher have taken Francis La Flesche to be my son. And I make due and suitable provision for him in my Last Will and Testament. Alice C. Fletcher, signed in the presence of J. C. Heald." In the probate hearings Charles J. Kappler, attorney at law, testified that in 1920 Fletcher had come to his office to hand over formally to Francis La Flesche her 125 shares of stock in Homestake Mining Company. The case was decided in Francis La Flesche's favor.

One of Alice Fletcher's and Francis La Flesche's good friends in her last years was Hartley Burr Alexander, a poet and philosopher at the University of Nebraska and later one of the founders of Claremont Colleges. For three years, from 1915 to 1917, he wrote annual pageants in honor of the semicentennial of the state of Nebraska, using Indian themes and the Fletcher–La Flesche collection of Omaha music. A 1916 photograph of Alice Fletcher and Francis La Flesche with Hartley Alexander and Dr. Henry P. Eames, librettist and composer for "Sacred Tree of the Omaha," is the last known photograph of Alice Fletcher.[53]

Fletcher was mourned in places scattered widely across the country. The Hampton Institute paper in Virginia called her their "constant and consistent friend."[54] The *Omaha Bee* announced proudly that her two finest works, *The Omaha Tribe* and *The Hako: A Pawnee Ceremony*, were "Nebraska's own." The reporter added: "Her personality was a rare combination of gentleness and force—the grit and moral determination of the old-fashioned New Englander, coupled with shining sweetness of character which was irresistible. She was in Nebraska only last fall, an interested spectator at Ak-Sar-Ben pageant, and many will remember the dear old lady with the cane, whose bright eyes and eager voice still bespoke the youthful enthusiasm of her spirit."[55]

Nowhere were the tributes to Alice Fletcher more heartfelt than in Santa Fe, where a memorial meeting was held in the Old Palace.[56] She who had been on the fringes of the academic world all her life had founded there a scholarly institution that survived her and is well-known today as the School of American Research. Charles Lummis wrote of a "plain, gentle, modest little woman" who had the power that comes from knowledge, from knowing to the roots whatsoever she attempted to write or speak about. "Some of her opponents never were quite aware what quiet, deep river had just drifted along and left them stranded far from their selfish hopes," he said. "She didn't fight—any more than the snowflake and the sunbeam fight. Like them, she Just Kept On." In the earliest years of the School of American Archaeology, when the executive committee had many problems, "the tallest spirit in all that stout company was the unruffled, gentle-eyed, far-seeing little woman who limped from tent to council-fire at the Rito, or from room to adobe room of the Old Palacio, and never worried, never hurried, nor ever failed in wisdom or in cheer."[57]

Francis La Flesche stayed on at 214 First St. and at the Bureau of American Ethnology for six more years, working on *The Osage Tribe*. In the end the study was four volumes long, the work of nineteen years—a monument of American Indian scholarship. The Osage Indians, who speak a language cognate to that of the Omahas, had been moved from Kansas to Oklahoma in 1870, after an earlier removal from Missouri to Kansas. They were a large tribe of four thousand people, unexpectedly prosperous, for the land they were given in Oklahoma was found to have oil beneath it. When La Flesche began his work, they were reputed to be the wealthiest community in the country. They lived in three villages: Grayhorse, Hominy, and Pawhuska.[58] The sudden wealth and change in living conditions had led to a rapid dying out of the ceremonial life of the people, and La Flesche decided to give this his first attention.

Alice Fletcher had expected, and probably the Bureau of American Ethnology did too, that La Flesche's Osage work would lead to another comprehensive, single-volume ethnography like *The Omaha Tribe*. To Putnam in 1911, Fletcher had described La Flesche's project. "Francis has been transferred from the Indian Bureau to the Bureau of Ethnology and has been working among the Osage since last September. He has secured some very rare and valuable material for the Nat. Museum and also the rituals attendant upon ceremonies. If all goes well, we will have in time another complete account of tribe in the same linguistic group. Comparative study can be made, and the influences of different environments, both physical and social, observed. I am much interested that this should be done."[59] But it was not to be, for Francis had quite other intentions.

Francis La Flesche could write summaries of broad interest when he wanted to. In 1916 he contributed a paper on "Right and Left in Osage Ceremonies" to a volume in honor of William Henry Holmes. The paper is a masterpiece of sensitive ethnological writing, beginning with careful analysis and opening up to wider issues. It was reprinted in 1973 in a structuralist volume, *Right and Left*, edited by Rodney Needham.[60] In 1920, La Flesche wrote "The Symbolic Man of the Osage Tribe" for the popular journal *Art and Archaeology*, a highly readable account of the gradual development of the Osage tribal form of government, including symbolic linkages between natural and social phenomena.[61] La Flesche's writing is as sophisticated and his understanding of the social origin and nature of religious conceptions as keen as that of Emile Durkheim, whose *Elementary Forms of the Religious Life* in 1915 was a milestone in the sociology of religion.

But La Flesche's general attitude was that this kind of thing was almost too easy. Far more difficult was getting the material in the first place, the slow, painstaking work he did as he sought to record not just one version of a particular ceremony but every surviving version, coaxing it from not just one but several informants. La Flesche was driven by the knowledge that this material was vanishing, even as he was recording it. Three of the old Osage men whom he depended on to sing for him died during his first year in Oklahoma.[62] The work was made even more difficult by the intense tribal sanctions against telling outsiders of the sacred ceremonies. La Flesche was surprised when one old Osage man, Playful Calf, took the initiative during a trip to Washington on tribal business, and actually invited La Flesche to come to Oklahoma and "write down on paper" some of the rituals of his clan. La Flesche complied immediately, and in the winter of 1911 Playful Calf returned with him to Washington, thinking to get away from those on the reservation who objected to the telling of the sacred things. They made numerous cylinder recordings, and Playful Calf returned home, but shortly after his arrival in Oklahoma he died suddenly under mysterious circumstances, and his house burned.[63] The death of Playful Calf made La Flesche's work harder, but he persevered, following up every lead, getting every scrap of ceremony he could.

What made *The Osage Tribe* so different from *The Omaha Tribe* was Francis La Flesche's different ethnographic goal. Alice Fletcher intended her work for anthropologists and the public, to help them better understand Indians. She eventually appreciated Francis La Flesche's desire to preserve the material for future generations of Omahas, and she stressed this in her foreword to *The Omaha Tribe*, but it had never been her primary motivation. She wrote comprehensive summaries designed to explain the Omahas to outsiders. This was true of *The Omaha Tribe* and it was true of "A Study of Omaha Indian Music," where her approach was to identify a broad range of musical genres and to record representative examples of each.[64] The result was two landmark studies: one of the most comprehensive ethnographies that exists for any North American Indian group and a pioneering study of the various forms of musical expression in one Indian tribe.

Francis La Flesche had little interest in general ethnographies or summaries of tribal culture. What he cared about were the sacred ceremonies at the heart of Indian life, and he went at their study with a passion for accuracy and thoroughness that came from his respect for the power of the sacred things. At the same time this passion for thoroughness made completion of the project impossible. The Osage tribe was divided into twenty-one clans, each with its own duties and its own version of certain ceremonies. Potentially, then, there were twenty-one versions of some of the ceremonies. To get all twenty-one was manifestly impossible, for many of the clans had disintegrated and knowledge of the ceremonies had vanished, but La Flesche tried to get different versions when he could.

What Francis La Flesche published under the general title *The Osage Tribe* is four separate volumes totaling 2,242 pages and appearing over nine years. The whole is so demanding to read that it deters, as it was surely meant to do, all but the most dedicated inquirer. The first volume, published in 1921, contains the "Rite of the Chiefs," in which is preserved the story of the gradual development of the ceremonial life and tribal institutions of the Osage people, and "Sayings of the Ancient Men," the thoughts in the minds of the Seers as they were formulating the preceding rite. Later volumes contain two versions of "The Rite of Vigil," "Two Versions of the Child-Naming Rite," and "Rite of the Wa-xo'-be and Shrine Degree." With this last, La Flesche moved beyond the ceremonies common to the Osages as a whole to those that belonged to a single clan. "The Rite of the Wa-xo'-be" was the first of seven tribal war rituals as practiced by one clan of the Osage tribe. With this ritual he started—and finally had to abandon—a recording task that was virtually endless and that could at best be piecemeal, as he tried to record what was still remembered of the once-voluminous Osage ceremonial practices. It was in both conception and in execution a staggering project. *The Osage Tribe*, for all its incompleteness, has rightly been called "the most complete single record of the ceremonies of a North American Indian people."[65] Francis La Flesche did it, not for anthropologists, but for future generations of American Indians.

Francis La Flesche rounded out his Osage work with *A Dictionary of the Osage Language* in 1932 and a paper on "War Ceremony and Peace Ceremony of the Osage Indians," published in 1939 after his death. La Flesche continued to live quietly at 214 First Street in Washington. A distant cousin of Alice Fletcher's remembers his graciousness as he showed them around the house he kept like a museum. There were rumors among anthropologists that he drank heavily.

In 1926 the University of Nebraska conferred an honorary degree on Francis La Flesche. He was an engaging guest, noting in a brief speech that as a boy he had planned to be a great buffalo hunter, but the white people came and ate up the buffalo, so he had turned to writing instead. He regretted that Alice Fletcher had not lived long enough to witness the honor. To a friend he wrote: "The dear Lady would have been joyed at the honor conferred on her pupil. The homecoming was a bit sad as I thought of her and how happy she would have been over my recognition by a great University."[66]

Later that year Francis suffered a paralytic stroke. He was hospitalized for several months and remained a semi-invalid, looked after by a nurse-caretaker, Grace Woodburn, who traveled with him when he went to the reservation for several months in the summer of 1927. Although he could have taken a disability retirement, La Flesche continued to work for the Bureau of American Ethnology through 1929, the end of twenty years of service. Then, without the caretaker, he returned to live on the reservation with his brother Carey. In the bitter depression winter of 1931 he often gave ten dollars to needy families for supplies.

Francis La Flesche died on the Omaha Reservation the next fall, on September 5, 1932. His funeral was as eclectic as his life had been. He had been a member of the Presbyterian Church since his youth, and in Washington he had joined the Masonic Order. At his burial three separate rites were held. The Mormons led a religious service at the home of his brother, Masonic rites were conducted at the cemetery by the lodge at Walthill, and after the casket was lowered into the grounds, Indian rites were led by Henry Turner, White Bear, and Henry Morris. The local newspaper reported that these last were "very serious and impressive."[67]

Equally eclectic was the dispersal of Francis La Flesche's estate, a situation complicated by the fact that he left two wills. La Flesche had drawn up a will in Washington in 1928. In it he reaffirmed his earlier arrangement to leave 125 shares of stock in the Homestake Mining Company to the School of American Research for a Fletcher and La Flesche Memorial Foundation. He made small gifts to his sister, Marguerite, to Rosalie's surviving six children, and to his nurse-caretaker, and left everything else to his brother, Carey.

Then La Flesche went back to the reservation to make his home with Carey, and there in 1932, without any mention of the first will, he wrote a second will leaving everything to his brother. The second will was challenged by Rosa Bourassa La Flesche, by Edgar L. Hewett for the School of American Research, and by the nurse-caretaker. A probate court in the District of Columbia ruled that they had rightful claims. La Flesche had purchased stocks in consultation with Alice Fletcher, whose business acumen he respected, and these, particularly his 235 shares of Homestake stock, had increased greatly in value. After an out-of-court settlement had been reached with Hewett and the nurse, Carey and Rosa were left heirs to an estate of $60,000.[68]

Carey was fifteen years younger than Francis La Flesche, as handsome as his older brother but less serious. After six years at Hampton Institute he had returned to the reservation, where he worked at various jobs, including assistant clerk at the agency, assistant teacher at the government school, and as a policeman. For a time he was a professional baseball player. His sister, Lucy, worried about him, not approving of all his comings and goings and the crowd he hung out with, and in the early 1890s she and Rosalie urged Francis to get Carey a job in Washington. But Francis, whose position in Washington was not as lofty as it looked from the reservation, could be judgmental and probably did not want to cope with Carey's presence at 214 First Street. He replied that the latter could look after himself.[69] Carey was indignant at first, but he could not hold a grudge for long, and he and his wife, Phoebe, eventually named one of their sons Frank.

In the midst of the Great Depression, on an impoverished reservation, Carey La Flesche found himself a wealthy man. He spent the money in the traditional Omaha fashion, in generous gifts and feasts for those around him and in exuberant display. He and his wife bought the first automobile on the reservation and, since they could not drive, hired a chauffeur, who took them on long journeys to visit distant relatives and friends.[70] The money was soon gone. Carey La Flesche's time of good living is still a topic of conversation on and around the Omaha Reservation some fifty years after the event, and opinions about it are as varied as they ever were, from disgust at this "squandering" of resources to an amused admiration for the flamboyant display of oldtime Omaha values. Carey La Flesche died in the Indian Hospital at Winnebago in 1952 and was buried in the cemetery at Macy, not far from Tainne's other children, Francis and Lucy.

Alice Fletcher's remains were cremated, as she had requested, and placed behind a bronze plaque in the patio of the Art Museum at Santa Fe. For the plaque, William Henry Holmes edited the preface she had written to her last book, a small collection of *Indian Games and Dances* (1915) dedicated to "the youth of America." The plaque reads:

Living with my Indian friends I found I was a stranger in my native land. As time went on, the outward aspect of nature remained the same, but a change was wrought in me. I learned to hear the echoes of a time when every living thing even the sky had a voice. That voice devoutly heard by the ancient people of America I desired to make audible to others.[71]

That is the story of Alice Fletcher's life that she wanted known to the world. It is accurate but incomplete, for here as always she had left out the early struggles that had shaped her. "There is no story in my life," she had protested to an interviewer when she was in her late seventies. "It has always been just one step at a time—one thing which I have tried to do as well as I could and which has led on to something else. It has all been in the day's work."[72] To posterity she gave the same answer, implicitly, by destroying all her personal papers. What she kept was a record of work done that led on to other work, forty years of it. Across her emotional life—her affections, her motives, her yearnings—she pulled a nearly impenetrable curtain.

Behind the curtain lay the wretched experience of finding herself alone in the world; her struggle against male power for a position for herself; her long search for a home, a family, and a cause, and her finding all of these among the American Indians. She found love there too, and secure in that love, her own thinking underwent the transformation she was willing to make public. She had moved from the European-oriented world of Brooklyn and Manhattan to the prairies of Nebraska and the deserts and mountains of New Mexico, where land and sky assert themselves. "I found I was a stranger in my native land," she had written, but gradually she learned to hear "echoes of a time when every living thing even the sky had a voice." What she discovered was the sacred geography of America as it was experienced by Indian peoples. She never pretended to share the Native American view of the world, but she came to understand and appreciate it. That understanding she sought to convey to others.

Notes

PREFACE

1. Gertrude Stein, *The Making of Americans* (1925; reprint, New York: Something Else Press, 1966), 141.

2. Gertrude Stein, "The Gradual Making of *The Making of Americans*," in *Writings and Lectures, 1909–1945*, ed. Patricia Meyerowitz (1967; reprint, London: Penguin Books, 1971), 86.

3. Alice Fletcher, "Indian Music," MS, speech at Round Table Club, Danvers, Mass., June 18, 1888, Alice C. Fletcher and Francis La Flesche Papers, National Anthropological Archives, Smithsonian Institution, Washington, D.C. (hereafter cited as Fletcher Papers); Fletcher, *Indian Games and Dances with Native Songs* (Boston: C. C. Birchard, 1915), v–vi.

4. Harry Stack Sullivan, *The Fusion of Psychiatry and Social Science* (New York: W. W. Norton, 1964), 220–21, and Helen Swick Perry, *Psychiatrist of America: The Life of Harry Stack Sullivan* (Cambridge: Harvard University Press, 1982), 226.

5. Stein, *Making of Americans*, 217.

CHAPTER ONE

1. Edward H. Fletcher, *The Descendants of Robert Fletcher of Concord, Mass.* (New York: Rand, Avery, and Co.,1881), 50.

2. Ibid., 42.

3. Gertrude A. Barber, comp., *Marriages from New York Evening Post, 1837–39*, vol. 8. (New York Public Library, 1935).

4. Memo No. 3 left with Alice Fletcher's will, copy in La Flesche Family Papers, Nebraska State Historical Society, Lincoln, Nebraska.

5. A. C. Fletcher, autobiographical sketch, ca. 1890, MS, Fletcher Collection, Peabody Museum of Archaeology and Ethnology, Cambridge, Massachusetts.

6. William B. Browne, comp., *Genealogy of the Jenks Family of America* (Concord, N.H.: Rumford Press, 1952), xi, xiii, 45, 77.

7. A. C. Fletcher will, Fletcher Papers.

8. *Articles of Association and By-Laws of the Brooklyn Female Academy*, Brooklyn, New York, 1847, p. 7; *Circular of the Brooklyn Female Academy*, Joralemon Street, Brooklyn Heights, New York, 1847, p. 6; Marjorie L. Nickerson, *A Long Way Forward: The First Hundred Years of the Packer Collegiate Institute* (Brooklyn, N.Y.: Packer Collegiate Institute, 1945), 30.

9. Stephen M. Ostrander, *A History of Brooklyn and King's County*, 2 vols. (Brooklyn, N.Y.: privately printed, 1894), 2:100.

10. *Circular of the Brooklyn Female Academy*, 1847, p. 2.

11. Ibid., 10.

12. Deborah Warner, "Science Education for Women in Antebellum America," *Isis* 69 (1978): 58–67, 60.

13. Alice C. Fletcher, "Biographical statement," 1890, MS, Fletcher Papers.

14. Alice C. Fletcher at Carlisle graduation, February 24, 1892, quoted in *Red Man* 11 (May 1892): 6.

15. Fletcher, "Dickens," 1915, MS, Fletcher Papers.

16. Fletcher to Isabel Barrows, Feb. 2, 1896, Samuel J. and Isabel Barrows Papers, Houghton Library, Harvard University, Cambridge, Massachusetts.

17. Fletcher, "Dickens."

18. Caroline H. Dall Journal, Jan. 11, 1885, Caroline H. Dall Papers, Massachusetts Historical Society, Boston, Massachusetts. Reference from Gary Goodman, biographer of Caroline Dall. I am immensely grateful to Gary Goodman for her interest, generosity, and quick perception that what she had read about Alice Fletcher in Caroline Dall's diaries was of extraordinary interest.

19. Charles Storrs, *The Storrs Family, Genealogical and Other Memoranda* (New York: privately printed,1886), 130, 134, 267.

20. A superb book on this subject is Altina L. Waller, *Reverend Beecher and Mrs. Tilton: Sex and Class in Victorian America* (Amherst: University of Massachusetts Press, 1982).

21. Oliver C. Gardiner to Horace Mann, Dec. 12, 1843, and E. M. Shurston to Horace Mann, May 4, 1848, Horace Mann Papers, Massachusetts Historical Society.

22. Oliver Cromwell Gardiner, *The Great Issue; or, The Three Presidential Candidates, being a brief historical sketch of the Free Soil question in the United States from the Congress of 1774 and '87 to the present time* (New York: Wm. C. Bryant; Boston: B.B. Mussey and Co., 1848).

23. Frederick Odell Conant, *A History and Genealogy of the Conant Family in England and America* (Portland, Maine: privately printed, 1887), 483.

24. Judith Lewis Herman's pioneering book *Father-Daughter Incest* (Cambridge: Harvard University Press, 1981) has shaped my understanding of the family dynamics that may result in abuse situations and of the possible long-term effects on the daughter-victim.

25. "Memoir of T. G. Fletcher, Aug. 8, 1878," Fletcher and La Flesche Papers.

CHAPTER TWO

1. Sidney Lanier, *Letters, 1869–1873*, vol. 8, ed. Charles R. Anderson and Aubrey H. Starke (Baltimore: Johns Hopkins University Press, 1945), 417–18.

2. Fletcher to Sidney Lanier, Nov. 14, 1873, Fletcher Papers; also printed in *Letters of Sidney Lanier: Selections from His Correspondence, 1866–1881* (New York: Charles Scribner's Sons, 1899), 79–80.

3. Appendix to *Papers Read at the 4th Congress of Women*, Philadelphia, Oct. 4–6, 1876 (1877), 121; also Jane C. Croly, *Sorosis: Its Origin and History* (New York: J. J. Little, 1886). Minutes of the early Sorosis meetings are in the Sorosis Papers, Sophia Smith Collection, Smith College Library, Northampton, Massachusetts.

4. "Sorosis," *Woman's Journal* 3 (March 30, 1872): 104; Maria Mitchell, Lecture Notes and Notes on Women Subjects, Maria Mitchell Memorabilia, Maria Mitchell Library, Nantucket, Massachusetts.

5. Celia Burleigh, "Our New York Letter," *Woman's Journal* 1 (June 11, 1870).

6. "What Is Sorosis?" *Woman's Journal* 4 (Dec. 28, 1872): 409.

7. *Association for the Advancement of Women, Historical Account, 1873–1893.* (Dedham, Mass.: n.p., 1893), 3; *Woman's Journal* 3 (Nov. 15, 1883): 364.

8. Henry B. Blackwell, *Woman's Journal* 4 (Nov. 22, 1873): 373.

9. Laura E. Richards and Maud Howe Elliott, *Julia Ward Howe, 1819–1910*, 2 vols. (Boston: Houghton Mifflin, 1916), l: 251.

10. Extracts from the *Chicago Tribune* in *Woman's Journal* 5 (Nov. 28, 1874): 380.

11. Ibid., 360. On Julia Ward Howe see also her own *Reminiscences, 1819–1910* (Boston: Houghton Mifflin, 1900); Deborah Clifford, *Mine Eyes Have Seen the Glory: A Biography of Julia Ward Howe* (Boston: Little, Brown; Atlantic Monthly, 1979); Mary Grant Hetherington, "Private Woman, Public Person: An Account of the Life of Julia Ward Howe from 1819 to 1868," Ph.D. diss., George Washington University, 1982.

12. Mary A. Livermore, "What Shall We Do With Our Daughters?" printed in *The Story of My Life; or, The Sunshine and Shadow of Seventy Years* (Hartford, Conn., A. D. Worthington, 1897), 615–29.

13. Ibid., 619.

14. Ibid., 518.

15. Maria Mitchell, "Lectures on Women's Rights," Item 17, Mitchell Memorabilia; Dorothy J. Keller, "Maria Mitchell, An Early Woman Academician," Ed.D. diss., University of Rochester, 1974, p. 136. On Maria Mitchell see also Helen Wright, *Sweeper in the Sky: The Life of Maria Mitchell* (1949; reprint, Nantucket, Mass.: Nantucket Maria Mitchell Association, 1959); Henry Mitchell, "Biographical notice of Maria Mitchell," *Proceedings of the American Academy of Arts and Sciences* 25 (1890): 331–43; Maria Mitchell, *Life, Letters, and Journals*, comp. Phebe Mitchell Kendall (Boston: Lee and Shepard, 1896); Sally Gregory Kohlstedt, "Maria Mitchell and the Advancement of Women in Science," *New England Quarterly* 51 (1978): 39–63; and a perceptive book of poetry based on her life, by Carolyn Oles, *Night Watches: Inventions on the Life of Maria Mitchell* (Cambridge, Mass.: alice james books, 1985).

16. Maria Mitchell, "Address of the President," *Papers Read at the Third Congress of Women*, Syracuse, Oct. 1875. On the six committees see Keller, "Maria Mitchell," 102, and *Woman's Journal*, Oct. 23, 1875.

17. Maria Mitchell, "Commonplace Book, 1874–1880," June 20, 1875, Mitchell Memorabilia.

18. Maria Mitchell, "The Need of Women in Science," *Papers Read at the 4th Congress of Women*, Philadelphia, Oct. 4–6, 1876, (1877), 11.

19. Mitchell, "Commonplace Book, 1874–1880," Nov. 15, 1876, Mitchell Memorabilia; "Fourth Woman's Congress," in *Woman's Journal* 7 (Oct. 14, 1876).

20. Mitchell, "Commonplace Book, 1874–1880," Nov. 15, 1876, Mitchell Memorabilia.

21. Ibid., June 20, 1875.

22. Lita Barney Sayles, "History and Results of Past Congresses," in *Papers Read Before the AAW at Its 10th Annual Meeting*, Portland, Maine, Oct. 1882, pp. 13–44. It is an odd historical coincidence that Alice Fletcher took charge of the program for the annual meetings of the AAW the same year that her future mentor in science, Frederic Ward Putnam, did so for the AAAS in his capacity as permanent secretary of the AAAS. But then again it is not so odd, for it shows that they had in common enormous energy, organizational ability, and the respect of their peers.

23. Items 45 and 46, Mitchell Memorabilia. Not long after Maria Mitchell used statistics to try to advance the cause of women in science, the Association of Collegiate Alumnae sent questionnaires to its members in an attempt to learn whether college attendance threatened their health and physical being, as Dr. Clarke alleged it would. See Rosalind Rosenberg, *Beyond Separate Spheres: Intellectual Roots of Modern Feminism* (New Haven: Yale University Press, 1982), 20.

24. *Report of the Ninth Congress*, Buffalo, New York, Oct. 19–21, 1881, p. 7.

25. Lita Barney Sayles, "History and Results of Past Congresses," 13–44, 30.

26. J. W. Howe to M. Mitchell, May 22, 1879, Mitchell Memorabilia.

27. Fletcher to E. E. Miles, treasurer of the AAW, June 18, 1874, MS files of the New York Historical Society Library, New York, New York.

28. Julia Ward Howe, "The Second Woman's Congress," *Woman's Journal* 5 (Oct. 31, 1874): 350.

29. Phebe A. Hanaford, *Daughters of America; or, Women of the Century* (Boston: B. B. Russell, 1883), 154.

30. Frances E. Willard and Mary A. Livermore, eds. *A Woman of the Century: 1470 Biographical Sketches* (Buffalo: C. W. Moulton, 1893), 293.

31. Alice Fletcher spoke to the Saturday Morning Club on William Blake, Jan. 22, 1881, and on her personal life with the Omahas, Dec. 23, 1882. Both talks were recorded almost verbatim in the club minutes. (The Saturday Morning Club Papers, Vol. 2, Schlesinger Library, Radcliffe College, Cambridge, Massachusetts).

32. Julia Ward Howe, "How Can Women best associate their efforts for the Amelioration of Society?" *Papers and Letters*, First Woman's Congress of the Association for the Advancement of Women, Oct. 1873 (New York: Mrs. Wm. Ballard,1874), 6.

CHAPTER THREE

1. Catherine Johnston to Fletcher, Sept. 6, 1876, Fletcher Papers.

2. Mary S. to Fletcher, Dec. 23, 1877, Fletcher Papers.

3. Conant, *A History and Genealogy of the Conant Family*, 483.

4. These quotations are from the publicity folder for "Lectures on America" by Miss A. C. Fletcher, in Fletcher Papers.

5. As quoted in *Woman's Journal* 7 (Aug. 5, 1876): 253, 321; Walter Muir Whitehill, *Boston: A Topographical History* (Cambridge: Harvard University Press, 1959), 168 n. 230.

6. Publicity folder, Fletcher Papers.

7. These three quotations are in a publicity folder included in a letter from Fletcher to John Wesley Powell, Aug. 10, 1881, Fletcher and La Flesche Papers.

8. "Report of the Woman's Congress," *Woman's Journal* 10 (Oct. 25, 1879): 341.

9. Fletcher to secretary of the Smithsonian (S. F. Baird), Oct. 2, 1979, Fletcher Papers.

10. Baird to Fletcher, n.d., Fletcher Papers.

11. Fletcher to F. W. Putnam, Sept. 9, 1879, Peabody Museum Papers, Harvard University Archives, Cambridge, Massachusetts.

12. Fletcher to J. Smith, Sept. 21, 1879, Peabody Museum Papers.

13. Fletcher to Putnam, Jan. 31, 1880, Peabody Museum Papers.

14. Quoted in the flyer for A. C. Fletcher, "Lectures on Ancient America," Fletcher and La Flesche Papers.

15. Hazel W. Hertzberg, "Nationality, Anthropology, and Pan-Indianism in the Life of Arthur C. Parker (Seneca)," *Proceedings of the American Philosophical Society* 123 (1979): 47–72, 53; Henry Miller Rideout, *William Jones: Indian, Cowboy, American Scholar, and Anthropologist in the Field* (New York: Frederick A. Stokes, 1912).

16. Eben Putnam, "Frederick Ward Putnam," *Putnam Leaflets*, vol. I, 1896, nos. 10–11, 76–79; personal conversation with Ralph W. Dexter.

17. Putnam to L. H. Morgan, Jan. 9,1880, Lewis Henry Morgan Papers, University of Rochester, Rush Rhees Library, Rochester, New York.

18. Clipping, "Popular Science," 1880, Fletcher Papers. The "Professor" title was a courtesy in 1880, as Putnam was not made a professor until 1887.

19. *Boston Daily Advertiser* 135, n.d., Peabody Museum Scrapbook, 1 (1872–1889), Rare Books Collection, Tozzer Library, Harvard University, Cambridge, Massachusetts.

20. Stanley Clark, "Ponca Publicity," *Mississippi Valley Review* 29 (1943): 495–516.

21. Thomas Henry Tibbles, *Buckskin and Blanket Days: Memoirs of a Friend of the Indians* (Garden City, N.Y.: Doubleday and Co., 1957), 236; Fletcher to Putnam, Feb. 24, 1881, and Fletcher to Lucian Carr, Aug. 3, 1881, Peabody Museum Papers.

22. Mary R. Parkman, *Heroines of Science* (New York: Century Company, 1918), 218; I thank Carl Nagin for these identifications.

23. Emily F. Rogers to Fletcher, July 25, 1879, and Sept. 11, 1879, Fletcher and La Flesche Papers.

24. Fletcher to John Wesley Powell, Aug. 10, 1881; James Pilling to Fletcher, Aug. 11, 1881; Fletcher to Garrick Mallery, Aug. 23, 1881, all in Fletcher and La Flesche Papers; Fletcher to Putnam, Aug. 10, 1881, Peabody Museum Papers.

25. Fletcher to L. Carr, Aug. 3, 1881, Peabody Museum Papers.

CHAPTER FOUR

1. L. de Hegermann-Lindencrone, *The Sunny Side of Diplomatic Life, 1875–1912* (New York: Harper and Bros., 1914): 22.

2. Alice Fletcher, "Camping with the Sioux," 1, MS, Fletcher and La Flesche Papers. There are three accounts of Fletcher's six-week journey among the Sioux Indians in the fall of 1881, in addition to a chapter in a book by Thomas Henry Tibbles written in 1905 but not edited and published until 1957. Fletcher kept a journal and filled two sketchbooks with drawings of what she encountered along the way. Six years later she revised the journal, hoping to break into the popular market with a "true story" of herself as a heroine among wild Indians. In this version, fortunately perhaps for her subsequent career never published, she omitted any mention of her traveling companions and wrote as if she were alone, living with the Indians. After her death Francis La Flesche started to pull together yet another account of her journey, based on her journals and sketches and on his recollections of what she and others had told him. His version is very detailed for the early events of the journey and then ends abruptly. All three manuscripts are in the Fletcher and La Flesche Papers.

3. Fletcher, "Camping with the Sioux," 4.

4. Fletcher, "Life among the Omahas," MS, Fletcher and La Flesche Papers; Tibbles, *Buckskin and Blanket Days*, 237–38.

5. Francis La Flesche, "Alice C. Fletcher's Scientific Work," MS, Fletcher Papers.

6. Fletcher, "Camping with the Sioux," 19, and A. C. Fletcher, "Tribal Life Among the Omahas: Personal Studies of Indian Life," *Century Magazine* 51 (January 1896): 450.

7. Fletcher, "Camping with the Sioux," 8.

8. Ibid., 19.

9. Tibbles, *Buckskin and Blanket Days*, 239.

10. Fletcher, "Camping with the Sioux," 22.

11. Ibid., 28.

12. Tibbles, *Buckskin and Blanket Days*, 261.

13. Fletcher to Putnam, Nov. 7, 1881, Peabody Museum Papers.

14. Fletcher, "Camping with the Sioux," 31.

15. Ibid., 38, 25.

16. Tibbles, *Buckskin and Blanket Days*, 252.

17. Fletcher, "Camping with the Sioux," 32.

18. Ibid., 47.

19. Ibid.

20. Tibbles, *Buckskin and Blanket Days*, 256.

CHAPTER FIVE

1. Fletcher, "Camping with the Sioux," 55.

2. Tibbles, *Buckskin and Blanket Days*, 268.

3. J. M. Lee, "Spotted Tail Agency," in *Annual Report of the Commissioner of Indian Affairs*, Washington, D.C., 1877, p. 66; Cicero Newall, "Rosebud Agency," in *Annual Report of the Commissioner of Indian Affairs*, Washington, D.C., 1879, p. 41; E. A. Hayt, *Annual Report of the Commissioner of Indian Affairs*, Washington, D.C., 1878, pp. 28–31; William Seagle, "The Murder of Spotted Tail," *Indian Historian* 3 (1970): 10–22; Fletcher, "Camping with the Sioux," 35.

4. Fletcher, "Camping with the Sioux," 62.

5. Tibbles, *Buckskin and Blanket Days*, 278.

6. Fletcher, "Camping with the Sioux," 63.

7. V. T. McGillycuddy, "Pine Ridge Agency," and James G. Wright, "Rosebud Agency" in *Annual Report of the Commissioner of Indian Affairs*, Washington, D.C., 1884, pp. 41, 46–47.

8. Henry E. Fritz, *The Movement for Indian Assimilation, 1860–1890* (Philadelphia: University of Pennsylvania Press, 1963), 219.

9. Alice C. Fletcher, "Indian Songs: Personal Studies of Indian Life," *Century Magazine* 47 (January 1894): 421–22.

10. Tibbles, *Buckskin and Blanket Days*, 279.

11. Ibid., 280.

12. In 1908 the Belgian ethnologist Arnold van Gennep would show that rites of passage marking stages in human life have a common pattern, including separation from the group, a journey of transition, and then reincorporation into the group with a new status. (Arnold van Gennep, *Les rites de passage*, trans. Monica B. Vizedom and Gabrielle L. Caffee (1908; reprint, Chicago: University of Chicago Press, 1960). What Alice Fletcher experi-

enced in the days immediately after the Sioux dance can be understood as an informal version of this pattern.

13. Fletcher, "Camping with the Sioux," 70.

14. Ibid., 71–72.

15. Ibid., 73.

16. Ibid., 86.

17. Ibid.

18. Ibid., 88.

19. Fletcher to Putnam, Nov. 7, 1881, Peabody Museum Papers.

20. Fletcher, "Camping with the Sioux," 97.

21. As quoted in Frederick E. Hoxie, "Beyond Savagery: The Campaign to Assimilate the American Indian," Ph.D. diss., Brandeis University, 1977, p. 13; the article appeared in the March 1881 issue of the journal.

22. Fletcher, "Camping with the Sioux," 98.

23. *Morning Star* (March 1882), 3, reprinting an article by Alice C. Fletcher, "Among the Omahas," *Woman's Journal* 13 (Feb. 11, 1882): 46–47; also Alice C. Fletcher, "The Indian Woman and Her Problem," *Southern Workman* 28 (1899): 172–76.

24. Fletcher notebook, No. 2, Fletcher Papers.

25. Fletcher to Putnam, Nov. 7, 1881, Peabody Museum Papers.

26. Fletcher, "Camping with the Sioux," 74.

27. *Woman's Journal* 12 (Dec. 10, 1881): 393.

28. Fletcher, "Among the Omahas," 46.

29. Fletcher, "Tribal Life Among the Omahas," 461.

CHAPTER SIX

1. Clipping, "A Boston Girl Joins an Indian Tribe to Learn Their Traditions," *Sioux City Journal*, n.d., Peabody Museum Scrapbook, I (1872–1889).

2. Fletcher to Jane Smith, Nov. 14, 1881, Peabody Museum Papers.

3. Fletcher to Putnam, Feb. 4, 1882, Peabody Museum Papers.

4. Ibid.

5. Fletcher to Jane Smith, Nov. 14, 1881, Peabody Museum Papers.

6. Alice C. Fletcher and Francis La Flesche, *The Omaha Tribe*, Smithsonian Institution, Bureau of American Ethnology, 27th Annual Report, 1905–1906 (Washington, D.C., 1911), 70.

7. G. Hubert Smith, "Notes on Omaha Ethnohistory, 1763–1820," *Plains Anthropologist* 18 (1973): 257–70. The smallpox figures are ambiguous. R. H. Barnes reviews the data in *Two Crows Denies It: A History of Controversy in Omaha Sociology* (Lincoln: University of Nebraska Press, 1984), 7–9.

8. In the 1950s in a suit brought before the Indian Claims Commission, the Omahas recovered the difference between what was paid in 1854 and the

value of the land at that time (Barnes, *Two Crows Denies It*, 7).

One provision of the 1854 treaty, written in ignorance of the shifting nature of the Missouri River, is still, more than 130 years later, a source of legal contention along the Missouri. The treaty set as the eastern border of the reservation "the center of the main channel" of the Missouri River, but that channel (and with it the border of the reservation) has since moved west of where it was in 1854. In the Blackbird Bend area east of Blackbird Creek, in particular, an estimated 4,480 acres of land, which in 1854 were west of the central channel of the Missouri River, now lie on the Iowa side of the river. The Omaha Tribe has brought suit claiming this land. (David Henry Ehrlich, "Problems Arising from Shifts of the Missouri River on the Eastern Border of Nebraska," *Nebraska History* 54 [1973]: 341–63; personal communication, members of the Omaha Tribe, August 1985).

9. Fletcher and La Flesche, *The Omaha Tribe*, 84.

10. Ibid., 633; Fletcher, "Life among the Omahas," MS.

11. La Flesche did not get credit for his innovation. The commissioner of Indian affairs first mentioned a tribal police force in his *Annual Report* for 1869, when he noted that the Iowas had one. By 1873 the Winnebagos, Santee and Oglala Sioux, and Navajos had tribal police, and the commissioner was urging other tribes to do likewise. (Norma Kidd Green, *Iron Eye's Family: The Children of Joseph La Flesche*, [Lincoln: Johnsen Publishing Co., 1969], 24; Loring Benson Priest, *Uncle Sam's Stepchildren: The Reformation of United States Indian Policy, 1865–1887* [New Brunswick, N.J.: Rutgers University Press, 1942], 139).

12. Green, *Iron Eye's Family*, 35; Dorothy Clarke Wilson, *Bright Eyes: The Story of Susette La Flesche, An Omaha Indian* (New York: McGraw-Hill, 1974), 103. Conversation with Dennis Hastings and Paul Brill, Aug. 7, 1984.

13. Report of Omaha Agent George W. Wilkinson, *Annual Report of the Commissioner of Indian Affairs*, Washington, D.C., 1883, p. 105.

14. James Owen Dorsey, *Omaha and Ponka Letters*, Smithsonian Institution, Bureau of Ethnology, Bulletin no. 11 (Washington, D.C., 1891), 29–33, 553–54.

15. James Owen Dorsey, *The Degiha Language: Myths, Stories, and Letters*, Smithsonian Institution, Bureau of Ethnology, Contributions to North American Ethnology, VI (Washington, D.C., 1890), 677, 717.

16. La Flesche quoted in Neil M. Judd, *The Bureau of American Ethnology: A Partial History* (Norman: University of Oklahoma Press, 1967), 52. By the time the letters were published, Dorsey felt it necessary to add a preface saying that several of the writers had told him they had had reason to change their opinion of Mr. Tibbles and no longer trusted him or wished him to speak for them.

17. Fletcher to Jane Smith, Nov. 14, 1881, Peabody Museum Papers.

18. The petition and some of the accompanying "remarks" are reprinted in *The Omaha Tribe*, 637–39.

19. Fletcher to John Morgan, Dec. 31, 1881, Fletcher Papers.

20. Personal communication from Dennis Hastings, August 1984.

21. Fletcher, "Among the Omahas," 46.

22. Fletcher, "Life Among the Omahas," MS.

23. Fletcher to S. J. Kirkwood, Feb. 2, 1882, Records of the Bureau of Indian Affairs, National Archives, Washington, D.C.; Fletcher to Dawes, February 1882, and Fletcher to Kirkwood, Feb. 8, 1882, Fletcher Papers.

24. Anna L. Dawes to Fletcher, May 13, 1882, and Emily Talbot to Fletcher, May 13, 1882, Fletcher Papers.

25. Amelia S. Quinton, "Remarks," *Third Annual Lake Mohonk Conference of the Friends of the Indian*, 1885, p. 46.

26. Herbert Welsh, "'The Indian Problem' and What We Must Do to Solve It," *Wowapi: A Magazine Devoted to the Cause of the Indians* 1 (1883): 3–9.

27. Priest, *Uncle Sam's Stepchildren*, 86; Ruth Odell, *Helen Hunt Jackson* (New York: D. Appleton-Century, 1939); Helen Hunt Jackson, *A Century of Dishonor* (New York: Harper, 1881).

28. *Annual Report of the Commissioner of Indian Affairs*, Washington, D.C., 1879, iv.

29. Ibid. 1880, xvii.

30. Ibid., 1882, xliii.

31. Ibid., 1878, viii–ix.

32. Fletcher and La Flesche, *The Omaha Tribe*, 639.

33. *Twenty-fifth Annual Lake Mohonk Conference of the Friends of the Indian*, 1907, p. 179.

34. Fletcher to Mrs. Dawes, Jan. 25, 1883, Henry L. Dawes Papers, Library of Congress, Washington, D.C.

35. Fletcher, "Personal Studies of Indian Life: Politics and 'Pipe-Dancing,'" *Century Magazine* 45 (1893): 441.

36. Fletcher to Com. Morgan, Feb. 4, 1882, Fletcher Papers.

37. Alice Fletcher was familiar with Lewis Henry Morgan's work, which she considered "suggestive" and speculative (see Fletcher to Putnam, July 15, 1880, Peabody Museum Papers). She probably had met Morgan either in 1880 at the AAAS meeting in Boston or earlier through Erminnie Smith, her colleague in Sorosis and a student (like Morgan) of the Iroquois.

38. Lewis Henry Morgan, "The Hue and Cry Against the Indians," *Nation* 23 (1876): 40–41; Morgan, "Factory Systems on Indian Reservations," *Nation* 23 (1876): 58–59; Morgan, "The Indian Question," *Nation* 27 (1878): 332.

39. A. Fletcher, "Notes on an evening spent with Frank Cushing and a Zuni friend, 5-10-82," MS, Fletcher Papers. Cushing scholar Jesse Green suggests that the Zuni man may have been Naiiutchi.

CHAPTER SEVEN

1. Pratt to Fletcher, July 1882, Fletcher Papers.

2. Report of V. T. McGillycuddy, Pine Ridge Agency, *Annual Report of the Commissioner of Indian Affairs*, Washington, D.C., 1882, p. 39.

3. A. C. Fletcher, "The Sun Dance of the Ogalalla Sioux," *Proceedings of the American Association for the Advancement of Science* 31 (1883): 580–84.

4. Julia McGillycuddy, *McGillycuddy Agent* (Palo Alto: Stanford University Press, 1941), 171–74.

5. Fletcher to Ida Conant, July 4, 1882, Fletcher Papers.

6. McGillycuddy, *McGillycuddy Agent*, 175.

7. Fletcher to Ida Conant, July 4, 1882, Fletcher Papers.

8. Alice C. Fletcher, "The Elk Mystery or Festival, Ogalalla Sioux," *16th Annual Report of the Peabody Museum* 3 (1884): 280n.

9. Ibid.

10. Alice C. Fletcher, "The White Buffalo Festival of the Uncpapas," ibid., 274n, 275.

11. Ibid.

12. Ibid.

13. Fletcher to Putnam, Aug. 4, 1882, Peabody Museum Papers.

14. Caroline H. Dall Journal, Sept. 8, 1882, Dall Papers.

15. Hiram Price to Fletcher, Oct. 27, 1882, Fletcher Papers; Fletcher to H. M. Teller, Oct. 8, 1882, Records of Bureau of Indian Affairs.

16. Caroline H. Dall Journal, March 6, 1883, Dall Papers.

17. Hoxie, "Beyond Savagery," 161, 148, 162.

18. Fletcher to Putnam, [fall 1882], Peabody Museum Papers.

19. Fletcher to Putnam, Oct. 30, 1882, Dec. 26, 1882, Peabody Museum Papers.

20. Fletcher to Putnam, Jan. 21, 1883, Jan. 20, 1883, Peabody Museum Papers.

21. Fletcher to Putnam, Jan. 12, 1883, Peabody Museum Papers.

22. Fletcher to Putnam, Jan. 20, 1883, Peabody Museum Papers.

23. Fletcher to Putnam, Feb. 1, 1883, Peabody Museum Papers.

24. Fletcher to Putnam, May 1, 1883, Peabody Museum Papers.

25. Alice C. Fletcher, "Five Indian Ceremonies," *16th Annual Report of the Peabody Museum* 3, (1884): 260–333, 274n, 276n, 308n.

CHAPTER EIGHT

1. *Annual Report of the Commissioner of Indian Affairs*, Washington, D.C., 1883, lxii.

2. Fletcher to Putnam, May 1, 1883, F. W. Putnam Papers, Harvard University Archives, Cambridge, Massachusetts.

3. Fletcher to Putnam, March 17, 1883, Peabody Museum Papers.

4. Exhibits in John Neihardt Center, Bancroft, Nebraska.

5. Fletcher to Caroline Dall, Sept. 7, 1883, Dall Papers.

6. Fletcher to Dall, Sept. 7, 1883, Dall Papers.

7. Fletcher to Dall, Jan. 20, 1884, Dall Papers.

8. A contemporary diagnosis would probably be rheumatoid arthritis.

9. Partch to Lowrie, Oct. 13, 1883, in files, Presbyterian Board of Foreign Missions, quoted by Barnes, *Two Crows Denies It,* 15–16.

10. A. C. Fletcher, "A Study of Omaha Indian Music," *Archaeological and Ethnological Papers,* Peabody Museum of Archaeology and Ethnology, I, (1893): 237.

11. Fletcher to Mrs. Hawley, Jan. 6, 1884, Dall Papers.

12. Fletcher to Dall, Jan. 20, 1884, Dall Papers.

13. Fletcher to Putnam, Jan. 27, 1884, Peabody Museum Papers.

14. Fletcher to Mrs. Hawley, Jan. 6, 1884, Dall Papers.

15. Fletcher to Dall, Sept. 7, 1883, Dall Papers.

16. Fletcher to Dall, Jan. 20, 1884, Dall Papers.

17. Fletcher to Dall, Jan. 20, 1884; on losing thirty pounds, Fletcher to Major Larrabee, Aug. 28, 1883, Records of Bureau of Indian Affairs.

18. Fletcher to commissioner of Indian affairs, March 11, 1884, Records of Bureau of Indian Affairs.

19. Fifty-three men signed Fletcher's first petition in 1881, and 52 men signed a letter to the commissioner of Indian affairs in 1885 requesting that Fletcher be appointed as their Matron and Business Manager, in place of the Physician and Farmer who had just resigned (Geo. Wilkinson to Com., May 10, 1885, Records of Bureau of Indian Affairs). By contrast, there were 140 signers on a request to Washington in 1886 that an allotment of land be given, contrary to Fletcher's decision, to a part-Omaha woman, Margaret Sloan, and her grandson, Thomas (Records of Bureau of Indian Affairs, 1886, document #13786) and 131 signatures on a letter dated July 22, 1886, opposing Fletcher's plan for reorganization of the tribe (Records of Bureau of Indian Affairs, 1886, document #25585).

20. Alice C. Fletcher, "Lands in Severalty to Indians; Illustrated by Experiences with the Omaha Tribe," *Proceedings of the American Association for the Advancement of Science* 33 (1885): 663.

21. *Second Annual Lake Mohonk Conference,* 1884, p. 26 quoted in D. S. Otis, *The Dawes Act and the Allotment of Indian Lands,* ed. Francis Paul Prucha (Norman: University of Oklahoma Press, 1973), 42.

22. Fletcher to commissioner of Indian affairs, June 1884, Fletcher Papers.

23. Fletcher and La Flesche, *The Omaha Tribe,* 640.

24. Fletcher to Putnam, July 28, 1884, Peabody Museum Papers.

25. Fletcher to commissioner of Indian affairs, June 1884, Fletcher Papers.

26. Fletcher to Putnam, Aug. 25, 1883, and Fletcher to Lucian Carr, Feb. 12, 1884, Peabody Museum Papers.

27. Fletcher to Putnam, March 20, 1884, Peabody Museum Papers.

28. Alice C. Fletcher, "Composite Portraits of American Indians," *Science* 7 (1886): 408–9. Francis Galton described his technique in *Inquiries into Hu-*

man Faculty and Its Development (London: Macmillan, 1883), having previously presented it at anthropological meetings in England in 1877 and 1878.

29. Fletcher to Lucian Carr, Feb. 12, 1884, Peabody Museum Papers.

30. Fletcher to Putnam, Dec. 3, 1883, Peabody Museum Papers.

31. Ibid., and Fletcher to Putnam, Jan. 20, 1883, Peabody Museum Papers.

32. Francis La Flesche, *The Osage Tribe*. Part Three: "Two Versions of the Child-Naming Rite," *Smithsonian Institution*, Bureau of American Ethnology, 43rd Annual Report, 1925–26 (Washington, D.C., 1928): 94–95, see fig. 5, no. 2. The study was incorporated into *The Omaha Tribe*.

33. Fletcher, "Indian Songs," 423; Fletcher, "Life among the Omahas," part II, "The Omahas at Home," MS, Fletcher Papers.

34. Francis La Flesche, "The Scientific Work of Miss Alice C. Fletcher," *Science* 57 (1923), 115–16.

35. Fletcher, "Politics and 'Pipe-Dancing,'" *Century* 45 (1893): 455; Fletcher to Putnam, May 13, 1884, Peabody Museum Papers.

36. Fletcher to Putnam, June 6, 1884, Peabody Museum Papers; a slightly different version appears in Fletcher and La Flesche, *The Omaha Tribe*, 453–54.

37. Fletcher and La Flesche, *The Omaha Tribe*, 455.

38. Ibid., 209.

CHAPTER NINE

1. Fletcher to Dall, July 29, 1884, Dall Papers.

2. Fletcher to Dall, July 20, 1884, Dall Papers.

3. Fletcher to Putnam, July 22, 1884, and July 28, 1884, Peabody Museum Papers.

4. Fletcher to Dall, Oct. 10, 1884, Dall Papers.

5. Barbara Sicherman, "The Uses of Diagnosis: Doctors, Patients, and Neuroasthenia," *Journal of the History of Medicine and Allied Sciences* 32 (1977): 33–54.

6. Fletcher to Dall, Oct. 10, 1884, Dall Papers.

7. Fletcher to Dall, Oct. 1, 1884, Dall Papers.

8. *Science* 4 (1884): 345.

9. Francis La Flesche, "The Sacred Pipes of Friendship," *Proceedings of the American Association for the Advancement of Science* 33 (1885): 613–15, and Alice C. Fletcher, "Observations upon the Usage, Symbolism, and Influence of the Sacred Pipes of Friendship among the Omahas" (Abstract), *Proceedings of the American Association for the Advancement of Science* 33 (1885): 615–17.

10. S. Dell Hibbard to Fletcher, Sept. 12, 1884, Fletcher Papers.

11. Fletcher, "Land in Severalty to Indians"; 654–65.

12. Fletcher to Dall, Oct. 1, 1884, Dall Papers.

13. Fletcher to Dall, quoting Dr. Lyman Abbott, Oct. 1, 1884, Dall Papers.

14. Bernard L. Fontana, "Meanwhile, Back at the Rancheria," *Indian Historian* 8 (Winter 1975): 13.

15. T. R. to Henry Cabot Lodge, Oct. 16, 1892, quoted in William T. Hagan, "Civil Service Commissioner Theodore Roosevelt and the Indian Rights Association," *Pacific Historical Review* 44 (May 1975): 194.

16. Fletcher to Dall, Oct. 1, 1884, Dall Papers.

17. *Hartford Courant*, n.d., quoted in *Second Annual Lake Mohonk Conference in Behalf of the Civilization and Legal Protection of the Indians* (Philadelphia: Indian Rights Association, 1883), 23.

18. Philip Garrett, *18th Annual Report*, 1886 (Washington, D.C.: Board of Indian Commissioners, 1887), 51.

19. Fletcher testimony before the Board of Indian Commissioners, Jan. 22, 1890, *21st Annual Report*, 1889 (Washington, D.C.: Board of Indian Commissioners, 1890), 148.

20. Henry L. Dawes's address, *Third Annual Lake Mohonk Conference of the Friends of the Indian*, 1885, p. 38.

21. Frederick E. Hoxie, *A Final Promise: The Campaign to Assimilate the Indians, 1880–1920* (Lincoln: University of Nebraska Press, 1984), 72.

22. Priest, *Uncle Sam's Stepchildren*, 185–86.

23. Alice Fletcher, *Second Annual Lake Mohonk Conference of the Friends of the Indian*, 1884, p. 25.

24. *20th Annual Report*, 1888 (Washington, D.C.: Board of Indian Commissioners, 1889), 111.

25. D. A. Goddard to Herbert Welsh, Aug. 2, 1886, *Indian Rights Association Papers*, Historical Society of Pennsylvania, quoted in Rebecca Hancock Welch, "Alice Cunningham Fletcher, Anthropologist and Indian Rights Reformer" (Ph.D. diss., George Washington University, 1980), 47.

26. "Life with Poor Lo," *Buffalo Courier*, August 31, 1896, clipping, Fletcher Papers.

27. From James Parton, *Life of Andrew Jackson*, 3 vols. (Boston, 1866), 1:401, quoted by Michael Paul Rogin, *Fathers and Children: Andrew Jackson and the Subjection of the American Indians* (New York: Knopf, 1975), 117.

28. Alice C. Fletcher, "The Registration of Indian Families," *Eighteenth Annual Lake Mohonk Conference of the Friends of the Indian*, 1900, p. 73.

29. Alice C. Fletcher, "The Indian Bureau at the New Orleans Exposition," Report to the Commissioner of Indian Affairs, May 6, 1885 (Carlisle, Penn.: Carlisle Indian School Print, 1885), 12 pp.

30. Alice C. Fletcher, "Historical Sketch of the Omaha Tribe of Indians in Nebraska" (Washington, D.C.: Bureau of Indian Affairs, 1885).

31. *Daily Picayune*, Jan. 29, Feb. 1, Feb. 15, March 4, 1885.

32. Fletcher, "The Indian Bureau at the New Orleans Exposition," 3.

33. Fletcher to Putnam, April 26, 1886, Peabody Museum Papers.

34. Fletcher to Mrs. Dawes, Sept. 21, 1885, Dawes Papers.

35. Fletcher to Putnam, Dec. 11, 1885, Peabody Museum Papers.

36. Fletcher to Putnam, June 20, 1885, Peabody Museum Papers.

37. *Science* 6 (1885): 232.

38. Ibid., 233. The paper was published in the same volume, 285–87, as well as Fletcher, "An Evening in Camp among the Omahas," 88–90.

39. Address by Dawes, *Fourth Annual Lake Mohonk Conference of the Friends of the Indian*, 1886, p. 31.

40. Henry E. Fritz, "The Board of Indian Commissioners and Ethnocentric Reform, 1878–1893," in *Indian–White Relations: A Persistent Paradox*, ed. Jane F. Smith and Robert M. Kvasnicka, (Washington, D.C.: Howard University Press, 1976), 68–72; *17th Annual Report*, 1885 (Washington, D.C.: Board of Indian Commissioners, 1885), 106.

41. Priest, *Uncle Sam's Step-Children*, 246.

42. Alice C. Fletcher, "The Crowning Act," *Morning Star* 7 (March 1887): 1.

43. Alice C. Fletcher, "Between the Lines," *Lend a Hand* 1 (July 1886): 430.

44. *Tenth Annual Lake Mohonk Conference of the Friends of the Indian*, 1892, p. 126.

45. Henry L. Dawes, *Fourth Annual Lake Mohonk Conference of the Friends of the Indian*, 1886, p. 33.

46. Welsh, "'The Indian Problem,'" *Wowapi* 1 (1883): 4.

47. T. A. Bland, *Life of Alfred B. Meacham* (Washington, D.C.: T. A. and M. C. Bland, Publishers, 1883).

48. "The Council Fire Platform," *Council Fire* 6 (September 1883): 122.

49. Address by Dawes, *Fourth Annual Lake Mohonk Conference*, 1886, p. 31.

50. Priest, *Uncle Sam's Step-Children*, 239.

51. Address by Gates, *Fourth Annual Lake Mohonk Conference*, 1886, p. 46.

CHAPTER TEN

1. *Annual Report of the Commissioner of Indian Affairs*, Washington, D.C., 1886, p. 186.

2. Fletcher to Henry J. Teller, Oct. 8, 1882, Records of the Bureau of Indian Affairs.

3. J.D.C. Atkins, *Annual Report of the Commissioner of Indian Affairs*, Washington, D.C., 1885, xxi.

4. Fletcher to Putnam, March 19, 1886, Peabody Museum Papers.

5. Rosalie Farley to Fletcher, October 24, 1882, Fletcher Papers.

6. Wilson, *Bright Eyes*, 8–10; Green, *Iron Eye's Family*.

7. Herbert Kelly, "Books Presented to Historical Society," clipping, La Flesche Family Papers.

8.   Inshta Theamba, "Introduction," in Thomas Henry Tibbles, *Ploughed Under: The Story of an Indian Chief* (New York: Fords, Howard, and Hurlbert, 1881), 4–5; Tibbles quote, p. 7.

9.   Fletcher to Rev. Mr. Harsheo, April 2, 1883, Fletcher Papers.

10. Fletcher to James and Lena Springer, Dec. 6, 1883, Fletcher Papers.

11. T. H. Tibbles, "The Indian Emancipation Act," *Lend a Hand* 1 (1886): 285.

12. Fletcher to commissioner of Indian affairs, April 12, 1888, Records of Bureau of Indian Affairs.

13. *Bancroft Weekly Journal*, Feb. 12, 1886, clipping, Fletcher Papers; Jan. 8, Jan. 15, Feb. 12, 1886, clippings of accounts of meetings and speeches, Fletcher Papers.

14. Joseph La Flesche to Fletcher, May 14, 1885, Fletcher Papers.

15. Martha LaB. Goddard to Fletcher, May 23, 1885, Fletcher Papers.

16. Joseph La Flesche to Fletcher, March 13, 1886, Fletcher Papers.

17. Joseph La Flesche to Fletcher, March 13, 1886, Fletcher Papers; Joseph La Flesche's friends among the Omaha delegation that went to Washington in 1886 also told J. O. Dorsey that they had changed their opinion of Mr. Tibbles. Dorsey, *Omaha and Ponka Letters*, 29.

18. Fletcher to Putnam, April 29, 1886, Peabody Museum Papers.

19. Sindahaha to Fletcher, May 25, 1886, Fletcher Papers.

20. Wahininga to C.I.A., July 22, 1886, Records of the Bureau of Indian Affairs.

21. *Annual Report*, Bureau of Indian Affairs, 1886, p. 187.

22. Marguerite La Flesche to Rosalie La Flesche Farley, late 1886, La Flesche Family Papers.

23. Francis La Flesche to Rosalie Farley, Dec. 16, 1886, La Flesche Family Papers.

24. Ibid.

25. *18th Annual Report*, 1886 (Washington, D.C.: Board of Indian Commissioners, 1887), 119–23, 135.

26. Fletcher to Mrs. Dawes, Aug. 13, 1886, Dawes Papers.

27. Ibid.

28. Fletcher to Rosalie Farley, May 21, 1886, La Flesche Family Papers.

29. Rosalie Farley to Fletcher, May 11, 1887, Fletcher Papers.

30. *Annual Report,* Bureau of Indian Affairs, 1888, p. 170.

31. *Annual Report of the Commissioner of Indian Affairs*, Washington, D.C., 1890, p. 137.

32. Green, *Iron Eye's Family*, 93–95.

33. *Annual Report*, Bureau of Indian Affairs, 1891, p. 289.

34. James C. Olson, *History of Nebraska* (Lincoln: University of Nebraska Press, 1955), 159–63, 230, 251.

35. Willa Cather, "Nebraska: The End of the First Cycle," in *Roundup: A Nebraska Reader*, ed. Virginia Faulkner (Lincoln: University of Nebraska Press, 1957), quoted in Olson, *History of Nebraska,* 249.

36. Margaret Mead, *The Changing Culture of an Indian Tribe* (New York: Columbia University Press, 1932), 28–29.

37. Conversation with Marguerite Diddock Langenburg, August 1984.

38. Fannie Reed Giffen, *Oo-Ma-Ha Ta-Wa-tha* (Lincoln: privately printed, 1898).

39. Rosalie Farley to Francis La Flesche, early 1897, La Flesche Family Papers.

40. John G. Neihardt, *Patterns and Coincidences: A Sequel to All Is But A Beginning* (Columbia: University of Missouri Press, 1978), 43–45.

41. Fletcher to J. E. Rhoads, April 7, 1887, Fletcher Papers.

CHAPTER ELEVEN

1. Jeannette Paddock Nichols, *Alaska: A History of Its Administration, Exploitation, and Industrial Development During Its First Half Century Under the Rule of the United States* (Cleveland: Arthur H. Clark, 1924), 19; Ernest Gruening, *The Story of Alaska* (New York: Random House, 1954); "The Alaska Society of Sitka," *Science* 10 (Dec. 9, 1887): 280–81.

2. J. Arthur Lazell, *Alaskan Apostle: The Life of Sheldon Jackson* (New York: Harper, 1960), 14.

3. R. S. Fellows to Fletcher, Nov. 17, 1883, Fletcher Papers.

4. Caroline H. Dall Journal, March 9, 1883, Dall Papers.

5. Fletcher to Sheldon Jackson, March 17, 1883, Sheldon Jackson Papers, Presbyterian Historical Society, Philadelphia, Pennsylvania.

6. Fletcher to Mrs. Dawes, July 28, 1886, Dawes Papers.

7. Fletcher to Putnam, July 27, 1886, Peabody Museum Papers.

8. F. W. Putnam, "The Serpent Mound of Ohio," *Century Magazine* 39 (April 1890), 871–88.

9. Fletcher to Putnam, Sept. 3, 1886, Peabody Museum Papers.

10. Fletcher to Putnam, Aug. 13, 1886, Peabody Museum Papers.

11. Alice C. Fletcher, "On the Preservation of Archaeologic Monuments," *Proceedings of the American Association for the Advancement of Science* 36 (1888): 317.

12. Fletcher, "Report of the Committee on the Preservation of Archaeologic Remains on the Public Lands," *Proceedings of the American Association for the Advancement of Science* 37 (1889): 35–37.

13. Fletcher to Putnam, Aug. 5, 1887, F. W. Putnam Papers; also Fletcher to Putnam, July 23, 1888, Jan. 14, 1887, Peabody Museum Papers.

14. Fletcher to Dall, Sept. 24, 1886, Kodiak, Alaska, Dall Papers.

15. Alice Fletcher, Alaska Notebook I, Sept. 29, Nov. 12, 1886, Fletcher Papers.

16. Ibid., Oct. 10, 1886.

17. Ibid., Oct. 12, 1886.

18. Ibid., Nov. 16, 1886.

19. William Thaw to Jackson, March 17, 1883, Fletcher Papers, quoted in Welch, "Alice Cunningham Fletcher," 102.

20. Fletcher, Alaska Journal, Dec. 13, 1886.

21. Fletcher to Jane Smith, June 17, 1884, Peabody Museum Papers.

22. Fletcher to Putnam, July 4, 1886, F. W. Putnam Papers.

23. Fletcher to Putnam, March 11, 1887, Peabody Museum Papers.

24. Fletcher to Putnam, Jan. 20, 1883, Peabody Museum Papers.

25. Francis La Flesche Diary, April 24, 1883, Fletcher and La Flesche Papers.

26. Fletcher to Putnam, May 1, 1883, Peabody Museum Papers.

27. Fletcher to Putnam, July 2, 1884, Peabody Museum Papers.

28. Francis La Flesche, *The Middle Five: Indian Boys at School* (1900; reprint, Madison: University of Wisconsin Press, 1963), xvi; Michael C. Coleman, "The Mission Education of Francis La Flesche," *American Studies in Scandinavia* 18 (1986): 67–82.

29. Handwritten note, Fletcher and La Flesche Papers, Box 14.

30. City Directories, District of Columbia, 1885, 1887.

31. I thank Nancy O. Lurie for alerting me to this.

32. Fletcher to Putnam, July 28, 1884, Peabody Museum Papers.

CHAPTER TWELVE

1. Fletcher to Putnam, Jan. 14, 1887, Peabody Museum Papers.

2. Fletcher Diary, July 12, 1887 (the day the appointment came through), Fletcher Papers.

3. Fletcher to Putnam, Jan. 25, 1887, Peabody Museum Papers.

4. "Brave Words of Miss Fletcher to our Students at Their Sunday Evening Service, Feb. 20th." *Morning Star* 7, (February 1887): 5.

5. Fletcher to Putnam, Aug. 5, 1887, F. W. Putnam Papers.

6. Fletcher to commissioner of Indian affairs, Oct. 15, 1883, Records of Bureau of Indian Affairs.

7. Fletcher to Putnam, May 14, 1884, Peabody Museum Papers.

8. Fletcher to commissioner of Indian affairs, Oct. 16, 1883, Records of Bureau of Indian Affairs; *Annual Report of the Commissioner of Indian Affairs*, Washington, D.C., 1883, p. 118; Robert Ashley, Agent, *Annual Report of the Commissioner of Indian Affairs*, Washington, D.C., 1890, p. 136.

9. Nancy Oestreich Lurie, "Winnebago," *Handbook of North American Indians*, 15 (Washington, D.C.: Smithsonian Institution Press, 1978), 690–707.

10. J.D.C. Atkins, *Annual Report of the Commissioner of Indian Affairs*, Washington, D.C., 1887, lxviii.

11. Upshaw to Fletcher, July 23, 1887, Fletcher Papers; Fletcher to Putnam, Jan. 14, 1887, Peabody Museum Papers.

12. Fletcher to commissioner of Indian affairs, Jan. 4, 1888, Fletcher Papers.

13. *Annual Report of the Commissioner of Indian Affairs*, Washington, D.C., 1891, p. 287.

14. Fletcher to Putnam, Sept. 25, 1887, F. W. Putnam Papers.

15. As quoted in Lurie, "Winnebago," 695.

16. Fletcher to Dall, Oct. 5, 1887, Dall Papers.

17. Fletcher to Dall, Dec. l, 1887, Dall Papers.

18. Fletcher to Isabel Barrows, Aug. 14, 1888, Barrows Papers.

19. John A. McShore to Com. J. H. Oberly, Oct. 13, 1888, and Fletcher to Com., Oct. 27, 1888, Records of Bureau of Indian Affairs.

20. Fletcher to Isabel Barrows, Aug. 14, 1888, Barrows Papers.

21. "Letter from A. C. Fletcher from Winnebago Agency, Nebraska, Sept. 23, 1887," *Fifth Annual Lake Mohonk Conference of the Friends of the Indian*, 1887, pp. 14–17; Fletcher to Mrs. Dawes, Sept. 18, 1887, Dawes Papers.

22. Alice C. Fletcher, "The Phonetic Alphabet of the Winnebago Indians," *Proceedings of the American Association for the Advancement of Science* 38 (1889): 354–56.

23. Fletcher and La Flesche, *The Omaha Tribe*, 229.

24. Fletcher to Putnam, Sept. 26, 1888, Peabody Museum Papers.

25. Francis La Flesche to Putnam, Dec. 3, 1888, Peabody Museum Papers.

26. Ann Douglas Wood, "The War Within a War: Women Nurses in the Union Army," *Civil War History* 18 (September 1972): 197, quoting from Agatha Young, *The Women and the Crisis: Women of the North in the Civil War*, (1959).

27. *Morning Star* 9 (November 1889).

28. Jane Gay Dodge, "Brief Biography of E. Jane Gay," MS, Jane Gay Dodge Papers, Schlesinger Library; E. B. Borden, "Visit with Miss Jane Gay Dodge, '04," Sept. 19, 1951, MS, ibid.; Jane Gay Dodge to E. B. Borden, May 25, 1952, ibid.; Joseph West Moore, *Picturesque Washington* (Providence: J. A. and R. A. Reid, Publishers, 1884, 209–10; Mrs. John A. Logan, ed., *Thirty Years in Washington; or, Life and Scenes in Our National Capital* (Washington, D.C.: A. D. Worthington, 1902, ix, 330.

29. Fletcher Diary, Aug. 4, Aug. 5, 1888, Fletcher Papers.

30. Fletcher to Putnam, April 29, 1886, Peabody Museum Papers.

31. Dodge, "Brief Biography of E. Jane Gay"; see also the Jane Gay sources given in note 28, above.

32. Fletcher to Putnam, Nov. 18, 1888, F. W. Putnam Papers.

33. Fletcher to Putnam, Feb. 4, 1889, Peabody Museum Papers; Fletcher, "Registration of Indian Families," 73–76.

34. *Twentieth Annual Lake Mohonk Conference of the Friends of the Indian*, 1902, p. 121.

35. Fletcher to Putnam, Feb. 4, 1889, Peabody Museum Papers.

36. Fletcher to Putnam, Nov. 11, 1891, Peabody Museum Papers.

CHAPTER THIRTEEN

1. Agent George W. Norris, *Annual Report of the Commissioner of Indian Affairs*, Washington, D.C., 1887, p. 70.

2. Ibid., 4.

3. Fletcher to commissioner of Indian affairs, Oct. 10, 1889, Records of Bureau of Indian Affairs.

4. E. Jane Gay, *With the Nez Perces: Alice Fletcher in the Field, 1889–1892*, ed. Frederick E. Hoxie and Joan T. Mark (Lincoln: University of Nebraska Press, 1981), 8.

5. Ibid., 24.

6. Fletcher to commissioner of Indian affairs, Nov. 30, 1889, and Oct. 10, 1889, Records of Bureau of Indian Affairs.

7. Fletcher to Putnam, Aug. 2, 1889, Peabody Museum Papers.

8. *The Journals of Lewis and Clark* (New York: New American Library, 1964), 311.

9. Fletcher to commissioner of Indian affairs, Sept. 16, 1889, Records of the Bureau of Indian Affairs; Gay, *With the Nez Perces*, 9–10, 15; "Letter from Miss Alice C. Fletcher," *Seventh Annual Lake Mohonk Conference of the Friends of the Indian*, 1889, pp. 13–15.

10. Gay, *With the Nez Perces*, 11.

11. Fletcher to Captain Pratt, June 25, 1889, Fletcher Papers.

12. Fletcher to Putnam, Sept. 20, 1889, Peabody Museum Papers.

13. Fletcher to commissioner of Indian affairs, Sept. 16, Aug. 26, 1889, Records of Bureau of Indian Affairs.

14. Fletcher to commissioner of Indian affairs, Oct. 5, 1889, Records of Bureau of Indian Affairs.

15. As quoted in Allen C. Morrill and Eleanor D. Morrill, *Out of the Blanket: The Story of Sue and Kate McBeth, Missionaries to the Nez Perces* (Moscow: University Press of Idaho, 1978), 325.

16. Remarks by Mrs. Barrows, *Fifth Annual Lake Mohonk Conference of the Friends of the Indian*, 1887, p. 51.

17. Fletcher to Isabel Barrows, Nov. 10, 1894, Barrows Papers. Two essays by Carroll Smith-Rosenberg are particularly helpful for understanding women's friendships in the nineteenth century: her well-known "The Female World of Love and Ritual: Relations Between Women in Nineteenth-Century America" and the recent and stimulating "The New Woman as Androgyne: Social Disorder and Gender Crisis, 1870–1936," both in Carroll Smith-

Rosenberg, *Disorderly Conduct: Visions of Gender in Victorian America* (New York: A. Knopf, 1985).

18. Fletcher to Isabel Barrows, Sept. 10, 1889, Barrows Papers.

19. *21st Annual Report*, 1889 (Washington, D.C.: Board of Indian Commissioners, 1890), 150–52.

20. Gay, *With the Nez Perces*, 83.

21. Fletcher to Mrs. Dawes, Oct. 2, 1890, Dawes Papers.

22. Gay, *With the Nez Perces*, 90.

23. Jane Gay Dodge, "Sketch of My First Meeting with Alice C. Fletcher in 1888," MS, 1939, Schlesinger Library.

24. *Red Man* 9 (November 1889): 5–6.

25. Caroline S. Morgan to Jane Gay, Oct. 12, 1891, Fletcher Papers; Isabel Barrows to Fletcher, Sept. 17, 1891, Fletcher Papers.

26. Jane Gay to Putnam, March 18, 1891, F. W. Putnam Papers.

27. Gay, *With the Nez Perces*, 34, 35.

28. Ibid., 48.

29. Ibid., 86.

30. Deward E. Walker, Jr., *Conflict and Schism in Nez Perce Acculturation: A Study of Religion and Politics* (Pullman: Washington State University, 1968), 67–68.

CHAPTER FOURTEEN

1. *Annual Report of the Commissioner of Indian Affairs*, Washington, D.C., 1890, xviii–xix.

2. Gay, *With the Nez Perces*, 90; Fletcher to Mr. and Mrs. Dawes, May 23, 1892, Dawes Papers.

3. Kate McBeth, *The Nez Perces Since Lewis and Clark* (New York: Fleming H. Revell, 1908), 100.

4. Allen P. Slickpoo, Sr., *Noon-Nee-Me-Poo (We, The Nez Perces)* (Privately published, 1973), 210.

5. George Norris, *Annual Report of the Commissioner of Indian Affairs*, Washington, D.C., 1888, p. 86.

6. Gay, *With the Nez Perces*, 132.

7. Fletcher to commissioner of Indian affairs, July 12, 1890, Records of Bureau of Indian Affairs.

8. Gay, *With the Nez Perces*, 133.

9. Slickpoo, *Noon-Nee-Me-Poo*, 216; Alvin M. Josephy, Jr., *The Nez Perce Indians and the Opening of the Northwest* (New Haven: Yale University Press, 1965), xx.

10. Gay, *With the Nez Perces*, 134.

11. Ibid., 140–41.

12.   Fletcher's ethnographic notes on the Nez Perces are in her papers in the National Anthropological Archives.

13.   Gay, *With the Nez Perces*, 129.

14.   Fletcher to commissioner of Indian affairs, July 11, 1891, Fletcher Papers.

15.   Francis Paul Prucha, "Thomas Jefferson Morgan (1889–93)," in *The Commissioners of Indian Affairs, 1824–1977*, ed. Robert M. Kvasnicka and Herman J. Viola (Lincoln: University of Nebraska Press, 1979), 194.

16.   Ibid., 195.

17.   Fletcher to Morgan, Aug. 27, 1889, Fletcher Papers.

18.   *Annual Report of the Commissioner of Indian Affairs*, Washington, D.C., 1892.

19.   Fletcher to Putnam, Oct. 18, 1892, F. W. Putnam Papers.

20.   Fletcher to Morgan, July 2, 1891, Records of Bureau of Indian Affairs. The evidence for Morgan's telegram is a note written on Fletcher's telegram: "tel. to Robbins, Agt. July 2, 1891."

21.   Fletcher to Morgan, July 11, 1891, Fletcher Papers.

22.   Fletcher to Putnam, Aug. 6, 1891, Peabody Museum Papers.

23.   The impetus for the investigation came from Congressman Willis Sweet, based on two contested cases on which Fletcher had worked, that of Mrs. Cox and Mrs. Fairfield. Fletcher to Morgan, Nov. 2, 1891, Fletcher Papers.

24.   Fletcher to Putnam, Nov. 11, 1891, Peabody Museum Papers.

25.   Fletcher to Putnam, July 31, 1892, and July 13, 1892, Peabody Museum Papers.

26.   John O. Beede to T. J. Morgan, Aug. 20, 1892, Records of Bureau of Indian Affairs.

27.   Gay, *With the Nez Perces*, 169.

28.   Fletcher to Morgan, Aug. 20, 1892, Records of Bureau of Indian Affairs.

29.   James Reuben to commissioner of Indian affairs, April 21, 1893, Records of Bureau of Indian Affairs; *Annual Report of the Commissioner of Indian Affairs*, Washington, D.C., 1896, p. 141.

30.   Slickpoo, *Noon-Ne-Mee-Poo*, 222.

31.   Fletcher to Putnam, Oct. 3, 1892, F. W. Putnam Papers.

32.   Fletcher Diary, Sept. 19, 1892, Fletcher Papers.

33.   *Tenth Annual Lake Mohonk Conference of the Friends of the Indian*, 1892, pp. 80, 81, 86; Hagan, "Civil Service Commissioner Theodore Roosevelt," 187–200; Robert E. Jensen, ed., "Commissioner Theodore Roosevelt Visits Indian Reservations, 1892," *Nebraska History* 61 (Spring 1981): 85–106.

34.   *Red Man* 9 (1892): 6.

35.   *Annual Report of the Commissioner of Indian Affairs*, Washington, D.C., 1890, p. 136; Slickpoo, *Noon-Ne-Mee-Poo*, 224; *Annual Report of the Commissioner of Indian Affairs*, Washington, D.C., 1896, 140–41.

36.   Personal communication, Edward Cline and Dennis Hastings, Aug. 6, 1984.

CHAPTER FIFTEEN

1. *24th Annual Report of the Peabody Museum* (1890): 103–4; Lowell to Putnam, Oct. 2, 1891, Dec. 9, 1891, and Sept. 14, 1892, Peabody Museum Papers.

2. Charles F. Lummis, "In Memoriam. Alice C. Fletcher," *Art and Archaeology* 16 (1923): 75–76.

3. Mary C. Thaw to Fletcher, April 20, 1882, Fletcher Papers.

4. Fletcher Diary, March 28, 1890, Fletcher Papers.

5. *Boston Daily Advertiser*, May 14, 1873, quoted in Paul Buck, "Harvard Attitudes Toward Radcliffe in the Early Years," *Proceedings of the Massachusetts Historical Society* 74 (May 1962), 36; Barbara Miller Solomon, *In the Company of Educated Women: A History of Women in Higher Education in America* (New Haven: Yale University Press, 1985); Samuel Eliot Morison, *Three Centuries of Harvard, 1636–1936* (Cambridge: Harvard University Press, 1946), 391.

6. Fletcher to Putnam, Oct. 27, 1890, Peabody Museum Papers.

7. Francis C. Lowell to Putnam, Oct. 7, 1892, Peabody Museum Archives.

8. Lowell to Putnam, Oct. 3, 1892, Peabody Museum Archives.

9. Fletcher to Putnam, Aug. 20, 1890, Peabody Museum Papers.

10. Fletcher to Putnam, [November 1890], Peabody Museum Papers.

11. Fletcher to Putnam, Jan. 8, 1891, Peabody Museum Papers.

12. Fletcher to Putnam, Feb. 8, 1891, F. W. Putnam Papers; Caroline H. Dall Journal, Feb. 5, 1891, Dall Papers.

13. For example, G. Stanley Hall—in *Adolescence: Its Psychology and Its Relation to Physiology, Anthropology, Sociology, Sex, Crime, Religion, and Education,* 2 vols. (New York: D. Appleton & Co., 1904), 2: 634–35—in pleading for more women scientists can name only one example, "Miss Fletcher."

14. Paper enclosed with Alice Fletcher's will, Sept. 18, 1919, dated April 3, 1891, Fletcher Papers.

15. Fletcher to Putnam, Dec. 21, 1890, Peabody Museum Papers.

16. A. C. Fletcher, "The Indian Messiah," *Journal of American Folk-Lore* 4 (1891): 57–60. Boas's comments are in the same volume, pp. 5–6. Fletcher's remarks were borne out by James Mooney in his *The Ghost Dance Religion and the Sioux Outbreak of 1890,* Smithsonian Institution, Bureau of American Ethnology, 14th Annual Report (Washington, D.C., 1896).

17. Fletcher to Putnam, March 23, 1891, Peabody Museum Papers.

18. Fletcher to Putnam, April 4, 1891, Peabody Museum Papers.

19. Fletcher to Putnam, May 22, 1891, Peabody Museum Papers.

20. Ibid.; Gay, *With the Nez Perces,* 138.

21. Fletcher to Putnam, Feb. 14, 1892, Peabody Museum Papers, and Feb. 29, 1892, F. W. Putnam Papers.

22. Putnam to Fletcher, July 25, 1891, Fletcher Papers.

23.   Fletcher to Putnam, April 30, 1892, F. W. Putnam Papers.

24.   Fletcher to Putnam, Oct. 3, 1892, Peabody Museum Papers.

25.   Fletcher to Putnam, Oct. 3, 1892, F. W. Putnam Papers. Diplomas in Fletcher Papers.

26.   Fletcher to J. W. Powell, Sept. 7, 1889, Fletcher Papers; Columbian University records make no mention of a James Reuben in attendance at the Columbian Law School. Information from Lori Neiswander, Office of the Registrar, George Washington University, Oct. 18, 1984.

27.   Fillmore to Fletcher, March 29, 1893, Fletcher Papers.

28.   Helen [H. P. Kane?] to Jane Gay, Feb. 14, 1893, Peabody Museum Papers.

29.   Fletcher Diary, Feb. 25, 1893, Fletcher Papers.

30.   Lee Virginia Chambers-Schiller, *Liberty, A Better Husband. Single Women in America: The Generation of 1780–1840* (New Haven: Yale University Press, 1984), 163, 165.

31.   Information from Earle E. Coleman, archivist at Princeton University, Oct. 3, 1984.

CHAPTER SIXTEEN

1.   Fletcher to Putnam, April 12, 1893, Peabody Museum Papers.

2.   Tibbles, *Buckskin and Blanket Days*, 280.

3.   Robert Stevenson, "Written Sources for Indian Music until 1882," *Ethnomusicology* 17 (1973): 20.

4 .   Theodore Baker, *The Music of the North American Indians*, trans. Ann Buckley (1882; reprint, Buren: Fritz Knuf, 1976), 73; "Vita," Theodore Baker, *Ueber die Musik der nord Amerikanischen Wilden*, Leipzig, 1882.

5.   Dorsey, *The Degiha Language*.

6.   J. Owen Dorsey, *Omaha Sociology*, Smithsonian Institution, Bureau of American Ethnology, (Washington, D.C., 1884), 211–368, 291. Dorsey's song texts are in J. O. Dorsey, "Omaha Songs: Songs of the Inkugci Society as given by Fred Merrick," *Journal of American Folk-Lore* 1 (1888): 209–13; Dorsey, "Ponca and Omaha Songs," *Journal of American Folk-Lore* 2 (1889): 271–76; Dorsey, "Songs of the Hecula Society," *Journal of American Folk-Lore* 1 (1888): 65–68. This last contains two songs "written down by Professor Szemelenyi," to whom Frank La Flesche sang the songs (p. 68).

7.   La Flesche, *The Middle Five*, 96, 100–101.

8.   Dorsey, *Omaha Sociology*, 24. Alice Mitchell's death one and a half years after her marriage is confirmed in F. La Flesche's obituary in *Walthill Times*, Walthill, Neb., Sept. 15, 1932.

9.   Fletcher, "Five Indian Ceremonies," 263n.

10.   Fletcher, "A Study of Omaha Indian Music," 237.

11.   Ibid., 237.

12.   Fletcher to Putnam, May 18, 1888, F. W. Putnam Papers.

13. Fletcher, "Indian Music," MS, speech at Round Table Club, Danvers, Mass., June 18, 1888, Fletcher Papers.

14. Fletcher to Putnam, April 29, 1886, Peabody Museum Papers.

15. Fewkes's Passamaquoddy records are the oldest recordings known of American Indian music. They are part of the Federal Cylinder Project at the Folklife Center at the Library of Congress.

16. Fletcher to Putnam, Feb. 25, 1891, Peabody Museum Papers.

17. Fletcher to Putnam, March 23, 1891, Peabody Museum Papers.

18. Fletcher to Putnam, March 31, 1891, Peabody Museum Papers.

19. Fillmore to Fletcher, Aug. 2, 1891, Fletcher Papers.

20. Benjamin Ives Gilman, "Zuni Melodies," *Journal of American Archaeology and Ethnology* 1 (1891): 63–91. For biographical data on Fillmore and Gilman see the entries by Sue Carole de Vale in Stanley Sadie, ed., *New Grove Dictionary of Music and Musicians* (New York: Macmillan, 1980), 6: 547; 7: 382–83.

21. Fletcher, "A Study of Omaha Indian Music," 10.

22. Franz Boas, Review of "A Study of Omaha Indian Music," *Journal of American Folk-Lore* 7 (1894): 169–71.

23. Fletcher, "A Study of Omaha Indian Music," 17.

24. John C. Fillmore, "What do Indians Mean to Do when They Sing," *Journal of American Folk-Lore* 8 (1895): 141.

25. Ibid.; see also John C. Fillmore, "The Harmonic Structure of Indian Music," *American Anthropologist* 11 (1899): 297–318; Fillmore, "The Zuni Music as Translated by Mr. Benjamin Ives Gilman," *Music* 5 (1893): 39–46.

26. A. C. Fletcher, "Indian Songs and Music," *Journal of American Folk-Lore* 11 (1898): 89.

27. A. C. Fletcher, "The Study of Indian Music," *Proceedings of the National Academy of Sciences* 1 (1915): 231–35.

28. John C. Fillmore, "A Study of the Structural Peculiarities of the Music," in Fletcher, "A Study of Omaha Indian Music," 304.

29. Ibid.

30. Gilman, "Zuni Melodies," 89.

31. Benjamin Ives Gilman, "Hopi Songs," *Journal of American Archaeology and Ethnology* 5 (1908): 12.

32. Hewitt Pantaleoni, "A Few of Densmore's Dakota Rhythms Reconsidered," MS, 1985, 47n.

33. Karl Stumpf, *Die Anfange der Musik* (Leipzig: J. A. Barth, 1911), 7.

34. Fillmore to Fletcher, May 27, 1894, Fletcher Papers. Wead's paper is Charles Kasson Wead, "Contributions to the History of Musical Scales," *Annual Report of the U.S. National Museum* (1900), 421–62.

35. Fletcher to Putnam, Dec. 6, 1891, Peabody Museum Papers. See also Fletcher to Putnam, June 7, 1891, F. W. Putnam Papers, and Aug. 6, 1891, Peabody Museum Papers.

36. Putnam to Fletcher, July 25, 1891, Fletcher Papers, quoted in Welch, "Alice Cunningham Fletcher," 165.

CHAPTER SEVENTEEN

1. Fletcher to Isabel Barrows, n.d., 1892, Barrows Papers.

2. *Official Catalog*, World's Columbian Exposition, Part XII, Department M (Chicago: W. B. Conkey Publisher, 1893). "The Fair's Strange Faces: The People of the Midway and Whence They Came," *Daily Evening Telegraph*, Philadelphia, Jan. 20, 1894, clipping in F. W. Putnam, *Journal Scrapbook: World's Fair*, Tozzer Library, Peabody Museum.

3. Gilman's cylinders are probably the earliest extant recordings of indigenous music from these countries. De Vale, "Benjamin Ives Gilman," in Sadie, ed., *New Grove Dictionary*, 382.

4. Gilman, "Hopi Songs," 66.

5. Fletcher to Putnam, July 13, 1891, F. W. Putnam Papers.

6. A. C. Fletcher, "Music as Found in Certain North American Indian Tribes," *Music* 4 (1893): 457–67, also in *Music Review* 2 (August 1893): 534–38.

7. Personal communication from Dell Hymes.

8. John C. Fillmore, "Scales and Harmonies of Indian Music," *Music* 4 (1893): 478–89.

9. Alice C. Fletcher, "Love Songs among the Omaha Indians," in *Memoirs, International Congress of Anthropologists*, ed. C. S. Wake (Chicago: Schulte, 1894), 153–57; John C. Fillmore, "Primitive Scales and Rhythms," ibid., 158–75.

10. "Casual," and "Music of the Vancouver Indians," editorial comment in *Music* 4 (1893): 491. Notes from F. H. Cushing's diaries, courtesy of Jesse Green.

11. Fletcher Diary, Aug. 30, 1893, Fletcher Papers.

12. Fletcher to Isabel Barrows, Sept. 12, 1893, Barrows Papers.

13. Fletcher to Jane Smith, Sept. 11, 1893, Peabody Museum Papers.

14. Alice C. Fletcher, "The Religion of the North American Indians," in *The World's Congress of Religions. The Addresses and Papers and an Abstract of the Congress*, ed. John W. Hanson (Chicago: W. B. Conkey, 1894), 545.

15. Alice Fletcher Diary, Sept. 25, 1893, Fletcher Papers.

16. Fletcher to Putnam, Nov. 7, 1893, F. W. Putnam Papers.

17. F. W. Putnam, Editorial Note, in Fletcher, "A Study of Omaha Indian Music."

18. Margaret Rossiter documents this in *Women Scientists in America: Struggles and Strategies to 1940* (Baltimore: Johns Hopkins University Press, 1982).

19. As quoted in John H. Barrows, ed., *The World's Parliament of Religions*, 11 (Chicago: Parliament Publishing Company, 1893), 1567.

20. Curtis M. Hinsley, Jr., and Bill Holm, "A Cannibal in the National Museum: The Early Career of Franz Boas in America," *American Anthropologist* 78 (1976): 306–16.

21. Fletcher to Isabel Barrows, Oct. 1, 1893, Barrows Papers.

22. Fletcher to Putnam, July 24, 1894, Peabody Museum Papers; Fletcher to Dall, Nov. 12, 1894, Dall Papers.

23. Fletcher to Putnam, Oct. 19, 1894, Peabody Museum Papers.

24. Fletcher to Putnam, Feb. 13, 1895, Peabody Museum Papers.

25. Fletcher to Isabel Barrows, Sept. 11, 1894, Barrows Papers.

26. Fletcher to Isabel Barrows, Nov. 10, 1894, Barrows Papers.

27. Fletcher to Miss Mead, March 9, 1896, F. W. Putnam Papers. The young man was George A. Dorsey.

CHAPTER EIGHTEEN

1. Fletcher to Putnam, April 9, 1895, Peabody Museum Papers.

2. Fletcher to Isabel Barrows, Easter morning, 1895, Barrows Papers.

3. Fletcher to Rosalie Farley, June 27, 1896, La Flesche Family Papers.

4. Fletcher to Isabel Barrows, Feb. 2, 1896, Barrows Papers.

5. Fletcher to Jane Gay, Sept. 21, Sept. 26, 1898, Fletcher Papers.

6. Fletcher to "Lassie" (Jane Gay), Oct. 11, Oct. 18, 1898, Fletcher Papers.

7. Fletcher to Miss Mead, Feb. 11, 1899, Peabody Museum Papers.

8. Fletcher to Isabel Barrows, Dec. 20, 1893, Barrows Papers.

9. Alice Fletcher Diary, 1901, Fletcher Papers.

10. Fletcher to Putnam, July 18, 1895, Peabody Museum Papers.

11. Fletcher to Putnam, Nov. 29, 1895, F. W. Putnam Papers.

12. Fletcher to Putnam, Feb. 13, 1895, Peabody Museum Papers.

13. Members of the AAAS had only to be nominated by two persons, but fellows were elected by a standing committee after having been nominated by their section as "professionally engaged in science or by their labor having advanced science." *Proceedings of the American Association for the Advancement of Science* 29 (1890): xxxvii.

14. Fletcher to Putnam, Nov. 29, 1895, F. W. Putnam Papers.

15. Fletcher to Putnam, June 17, 1896, F. W. Putnam Papers.

16. A. C. Fletcher, "The Emblematic Use of the Tree in the Dakotan Group," *Proceedings of the American Association for the Advancement of Science* 45 (1897): 191–209.

17. Clipping, n.d., Fletcher Papers.

18. Alice Fletcher Diary, Sept. 18, 1896, Fletcher Papers.

19. "Life with Poor Lo," *Buffalo Courier*, Aug. 31, 1896, clipping, Fletcher Papers.

20. A. C. Fletcher, "The Import of the Totem," *Science* 7 (1898): 296–304.

21. Franz Boas's "The Origin of Totemism," *Race, Language, and Culture* (New York: Macmillan, 1940), 316–23, is an expansion of his earlier statements

dating back to 1896, 1897, 1898, and 1916. In 1940 Boas dissociated himself from this "American theory" of totemism, writing that no single psychic process produced the wide variety of phenomena lumped together as "totemism." But Alice Fletcher had never claimed to be giving an explanation of all totemic phenomena. She was simply concerned with showing that J. G. Frazer's theory was based on erroneous data. He had used a quotation from J. O. Dorsey that was a misrepresentation of the Omaha saying and that made it seem that the Omahas believed themselves to be descended from the totem animal when in fact they did not. For a European view of American ethnological work in music see Richard Wallaschek in *Music* 9 (1895): 168–95.

22. Fletcher to Putnam, Sept. 29, 1897, Peabody Museum Papers.

23. Anita Newcomb McGee, "The Women's Anthropological Society of America," *Science* 13 (1889): 240–42; Jane C. Croly, *The History of the Woman's Club Movement in America* (New York: J. J. Little, 1898), 348.

24. A. Maurice Low, "Washington: The City of Leisure," *Atlantic Monthly* 86 (1900): 767–78.

25. Elden E. Billings, "Social and Economic Life in Washington in the 1890s," *Records of the Columbia Historical Society, 1966–1968* (Washington, D.C., 1969), 169.

26. *Washington Wife: Journal of Ellen Maury Slayden from 1897–1919* (New York: Harper and Row, 1962), 27.

27. Ibid., 62.

28. Ibid., 154.

29. Jane Gay Dodge to Elizabeth B. Borden, Dec. 4, 1951, Schlesinger Library.

30. De Hegermann-Lindencrone, *The Sunny Side of Diplomatic Life*, 16.

31. J. Kirkpatrick Flack, *Desideratum in Washington: The Intellectual Community in the Capital City, 1870–1900* (Cambridge, Mass.: Schenkman Pub., 1975), 42; Frances Carpenter Huntington, "Ladies of 'The Literary,'" *Records of the Columbia Historical Society, 1966–1968* (Washington, D.C., 1969), 205–15.

32. Fletcher to Putnam, Jan. 21, 1903, F. W. Putnam Papers.

33. Constance McLaughlin Green, *Washington, Capital City, 1879–1950*, (Princeton: Princeton University Press, 1963), 194.

34. Fletcher to Putnam, March 27, 1895, Peabody Museum Papers.

35. Fletcher to Putnam, Nov. 6, 1895, Peabody Museum Papers.

36. Fletcher to Putnam, Jan. 22, 1896, F. W. Putnam Papers.

37. Fletcher Diary, June 22, 1896, Fletcher Papers.

38. Fletcher to Putnam, March 1, 1897, F. W. Putnam Papers.

39. Fletcher to Putnam, July 31, 1897, F. W. Putnam Papers.

40. Fletcher to Putnam, May 1, 1897, Peabody Museum Papers.

41. Fletcher to Putnam, Feb. 3, 1898, Peabody Museum Papers.

CHAPTER NINETEEN

1. Fletcher to A. S. Smiley, Oct. 12, 1897, Quaker Collection, Haverford College Library, Haverford, Pennsylvania.

2. Fletcher to A. S. Smiley, Oct. 10, 1896, Quaker Collection.

3. Francis La Flesche to George Vaux, Jr., Oct. 16, 1916, Fletcher Papers.

4. Olson, *History of Nebraska*, 255; Robert Rydell, *All the World's a Fair: America's International Expositions, 1876–1916* (Chicago: University of Chicago Press, 1983).

5. James Mooney, "The Indian Congress at Omaha," *American Anthropologist* 11 (1899): 128–29; Kenneth G. Alfers, "Triumph of the West: The Trans-Mississippi Exposition," *Nebraska History* 53 (1972): 324; L. G. Moses, *The Indian Man: A Biography of James Mooney* (Urbana: University of Illinois Press, 1984).

6. Fletcher to Miss Mead, June 2, 1898, F. W. Putnam Papers.

7. Alice C. Fletcher, "The Indian at the Trans-Mississippi Exposition," *Southern Workman* 27 (November 1898): 217.

8. Alice F. Fletcher, "Flotsam and Jetsam from Aboriginal America," *Southern Workman* 28 (January 1899): 12–14.

9. Fletcher to A. S. Smiley, Oct. 18, 1905, Quaker Collection. The years in which Fletcher accepted and then declined the invitation are 1897, 1899, 1905, 1914, and 1916, and the collection of letters is incomplete, with no records for 1908, 1911, and 1915.

10. Hoxie, *A Final Promise*.

11. Allen F. Davis, *American Heroine: The Life and Legend of Jane Addams* (New York: Oxford University Press, 1973), 200.

12. Fillmore to Fletcher, March 30, 1898, Fletcher Papers.

13. Fletcher to Putnam, March 30, 1898, F. W. Putnam Papers.

14. Fletcher to Putnam, May 13, 1884, Peabody Museum Papers.

15. Fletcher to Miss Mead, July 27, 1898, Peabody Museum Papers.

16. Fletcher to Walter McClintock, June 6, 1898, Walter McClintock Papers, Beinicke Library, Yale University, New Haven, Connecticut.

17. Fletcher to Miss Mead, July 27, 1898, Peabody Museum Papers.

18. *Proceedings of the American Association for the Advancement of Science,* 1900, p. 315. The paper was not printed and apparently has not survived.

19. Fletcher to Francis La Flesche, Aug. 14, 1899, Fletcher Papers.

20. Fletcher to Putnam, July 6, 1897, Peabody Museum Papers.

21. Fletcher to Putnam, Nov. 26, 1898, x-files, Peabody Museum.

22. Fletcher to Putnam, July 28, 1884, Peabody Museum Papers.

23. John C. Fillmore was killed in an accident on his way to the AAAS meeting in August 1898. Although Fletcher mourned the death of her music collaborator and paid warm tribute to him (see "Note" to Fillmore, "The Harmonic Structure of Indian Music," 297–318), his death freed her from

having to defend his work and his theories. In her later work (a hundred Pawnee songs and several hundred Osage songs), she transcribed the songs simply with a melody line and rhythmic accents, text, and translation. Unfortunately this later—and much superior—work is buried in monographs with titles (*The Hako: A Pawnee Ceremony* and *The Osage Tribe*) that give no hint that they contain music. Alice Fletcher's reputation as an ethnomusicologist still suffers because her best-known works are "A Study of Omaha Indian Music" and the slight and popular *Indian Story and Song from North America* and *Indian Games and Dances*. While she used some of Fillmore's four-part harmonizations of Omaha songs in these last, she baldly labelled them "harmonized by John C. Fillmore for interpretation on the piano." An excellent contemporary evaluation of Fillmore's work and his overblown reputation is Hewitt Pantaleoni, "A Reconsideration of Fillmore Reconsidered," *American Music* 3 (1985): 217–28.

Fillmore's death left Alice Fletcher the unchallenged American expert on Indian music. The next generation of American ethnomusicologists and composers who used Indian themes (Arthur Farwell, Charles W. Cadman, Natalie Curtis, and Frances Densmore) were all her protégés. They generally sought her out after having read "A Study of Omaha Indian Music." Arthur Farwell founded the Wa-Wan Press (named for the Omaha calumet ceremony). Charles Wakefield Cadman dedicated "Four American Indian Songs" to Alice Fletcher and with Francis La Flesche wrote an opera "Da-o-ma." Natalie Curtis conferred with Alice Fletcher in Washington before setting out to make the transcriptions published in *The Indian's Book* (1907). Frances Densmore asked Fletcher's support for her initial request for research funds from the Bureau of American Ethnology in 1907. Densmore brought one of her early graphophone cylinders to 214, complaining that it sounded "simply horrible." But Alice Fletcher, listening, detected through the noisy machine and the singer, who was "yelling at the top of his lungs," a very good song. Frances Densmore looked at her in astonishment when she said so, but they listened to it over and over, and finally Densmore too mastered the song and agreed that it was a good one. (Fletcher to Francis La Flesche, April 30, 1911, Fletcher Papers.) Fletcher eventually turned over to Densmore her recordings of Winnebago music (information from Nancy Lurie). Densmore published thirteen monographs and well over a hundred other articles, books, and reports on North American Indian music during the course of her fifty-year career.

24. Fletcher Diary, Aug. 4, 1899, Fletcher Papers.

25. Ibid., Aug. 13, 1899.

26. A. C. Fletcher, "Star Cult among the Pawnee," *American Anthropologist* 4 (1902): 730–36; Fletcher, "Pawnee Star Lore," *Journal of American Folk-Lore* 16 (1903): 10–15.

27. Fletcher to Putnam, Dec. 1901, F. W. Putnam Papers.

28. Fletcher, "Star Cult among the Pawnee," 730.

29. Murie to Fletcher, telegram, April 29, 1902, Fletcher Papers.

30. Murie to Fletcher, Oct. 25, 1901, George Dorsey to Fletcher, May 2, 1902, Murie to Fletcher, May 2, 1902, Fletcher Papers.

31. James R. Murie, *The Ceremonies of the Pawnee*, ed. Douglas R. Parks (Washington: Smithsonian Institution Press, 1981); Douglas R. Parks, "James R. Murie, Pawnee, 1862–1921," in *American Indian Intellectuals*, ed. Margot Liberty (St. Paul: West, 1978), 76.

32. Fletcher to Mrs. Dawes, Feb. 3, 1901, Dawes Papers.

CHAPTER TWENTY

1. Alice C. Fletcher, "Frank Hamilton Cushing," *American Anthropologist* 2 (1900): 367–70.

2. Fletcher to Putnam, May 13, 1896, and Jan. 28, 1897, F. W. Putnam Papers.

3. Fletcher to Putnam, May 23, 1899, F.W. Putnam Papers.

4. Fletcher to Putnam, July 1, 1896, F. W. Putnam Papers.

5. Percy C. Madeira, Jr., *Men in Search of Man: The First Seventy-Five Years of the University Museum of the University of Pennsylvania* (Philadelphia: University of Pennsylvania Press, 1964), 21.

6. Zelia Nuttall to Phoebe Hearst, May 27, 1901, Phoebe Apperson Hearst Papers, Bancroft Library, University of California, Berkeley.

7. Zelia Nuttall to Phoebe Hearst, Nov. 6, 1902, Hearst Papers.

8. Fletcher Diary, April 4, 1901, Fletcher Papers.

9. Zelia Nuttall to Phoebe Hearst, May 19, 1901, enclosing Boas's letter, Hearst Papers. The full text of the letter is reproduced in Ross Parmenter, "Glimpses of a Friendship," in *Pioneers of American Anthropology: The Uses of Biography*, ed. June Helm (Seattle: University of Washington Press, 1966), 98–101.

10. Fletcher to W J McGee, Aug. 6, 1901, Fletcher Papers.

11. Fletcher to Putnam, Aug. 23, 1901, F. W. Putnam Papers.

12. Dodge, "Brief Biography of E. Jane Gay," MS, Schlesinger Library.

13. Fletcher Diary, Aug. 10, 1901, Fletcher Papers.

14. *35th Annual Report of the Peabody Museum* (1901) 271; *Science* (Oct. 18, 1901), clipping, Fletcher Papers.

15. Fletcher Diary, June 26, 1902, Fletcher Papers.

16. Ibid., Aug. 1, 1902.

17. Fletcher to Mrs. Putnam, Sept. 9, 1902, F. W. Putnam Papers. Fletcher's letter to Putnam on Sept. 2, 1902, mentioned in her diary, is not to be found in either the F. W. Putnam Papers or the Peabody Museum Papers.

18. Fletcher to Putnam, Oct. 2, 1902, F. W. Putnam Papers.

19. Invitation, Sept. 18, 1902, Fletcher Papers.

20. Fletcher to Putnam, Oct. 2, 1902, F. W. Putnam Papers. On McGee and the Bureau of American Ethnology see Curtis M. Hinsley, Jr., *Savages and Scien-*

tists: *The Smithsonian Institution and the Development of American Anthropology, 1846–1910* (Washington, D.C.: Smithsonian Institution Press, 1981), 231–61.

21. Zelia Nuttall to Phoebe Hearst, Nov. 6, 1902, Hearst Papers.

22. *Register*, University of California, 1902–1903 (1903), 159–60.

23. Fletcher to Mrs. Putnam, June 27, 1904, F. W. Putnam Papers.

24. Collection of Fletcher letters in Hearst Papers.

25. Winifred Black Bonfils, *The Life and Personality of Phoebe Apperson Hearst* (Privately printed, 1928).

26. Fletcher to Putnam, Oct. 15, 1902, F. W. Putnam Papers.

27. Fletcher to Isabel Barrows, Jan. 22, 1905, Barrows Papers.

28. Fletcher to Putnam, Jan. 10, 1903, F. W. Putnam Papers.

29. Fletcher to Phoebe Hearst, March 30, 1903, Hearst Papers.

30. "The AAA," *American Anthropologist* 5 (1903): 178–92.

31. Fletcher to Isabel Barrows, Jan. 22, 1905, Barrows Papers.

32. Adela C. Breton to Putnam, March 30, 1905, Peabody Museum Papers.

33. Fletcher to Phoebe Hearst, April 19, 1905, Hearst Papers.

34. Fletcher to Isabel Barrows, April 20, 1905, Barrows Papers.

35. Fletcher Diary, April 3, 1905, Fletcher Papers.

36. Fletcher to A. Smiley, Oct. 12, 1905, Quaker Collection.

37. Fletcher to Putnam, Nov. 11, 1905, F. W. Putnam Papers.

38. Ibid., Dec. 19, 1905.

39. Fletcher to Phoebe Hearst, Jan. 6, 1906, Hearst Papers.

40. Fletcher to Dall, Dec. 8, 1900, Dall Papers. Thanking Dall for her book of memoirs, *Alongside*, Fletcher wrote, "I read it again aloud to the family and we all enjoyed it."

41. Fletcher Diary, April 21, 1904, Fletcher Papers.

42. Ibid., April 24, 1904.

43. Ibid., June 28 and June 30, 1905.

44. Fletcher to Isabel Barrows, July 1, 1905, Barrows Papers.

45. Fletcher Diary, Oct. 1905, Fletcher Papers.

46. Ibid., March 5, 1906.

47. Ibid., March 15, 1906.

48. Ibid., March 29, 1906.

49. Ibid., April 6, 1906.

50. Fletcher to Phoebe Hearst, June 6, 1906, Hearst Papers.

51. Fletcher Diary, May 13, 1906, Fletcher Papers.

52. Jane Gay to Francis La Flesche, May 27, 1890, Fletcher Papers.

53. Fletcher Diary, May 27, 1906, Fletcher Papers.

CHAPTER TWENTY-ONE

1. Ross Parmenter, "Zelia Maria Magdalena Nuttall," in *Notable American Women*, vol. 2, ed. Edward T. James, Janet Wilson James, and Paul Boyer (Cambridge: Harvard University Press, 1971), 640–42; Parmenter, "Glimpses of a Friendship"; and Nancy Oestreich Lurie, "Women in Early American Anthropology," in *Pioneers of American Anthropology: The Uses of Biography*, ed. June Helm (Seattle: University of Washington Press, 1966).

2. Alfred M. Tozzer, "Zelia Nuttall," *American Anthropologist* 35 (1933): 476–77.

3. The stipend was $1,500 per year for research plus $500 for traveling expenses. Zelia Nuttall to Phoebe Hearst, Nov. 19, 1902, Hearst Papers.

4. Fletcher to F. W. Hodge, Nov. 10, 1906, F. W. Hodge Papers, Southwest Museum, Los Angeles, California.

5. Zelia Nuttall to Phoebe Hearst, March 29, 1903, Hearst Papers. The amount was $3,000.

6. Fletcher to Putnam, Aug. 11, 1906, F. W. Putnam Papers.

7. *Eleventh Annual Report of the AIA*, 1890, p. 53.

8. "Nineteenth Annual Report of the AIA," *American Journal of Archaeology*, 2d ser., 2 (1898): 475.

9. Alfred M. Tozzer, "Charles Pickering Bowditch," *American Anthropologist* 23 (1921): 354; "Twentieth Annual Report of the Archaeological Institute of America," *American Journal of Archaeology*, 2d ser., 3 (1899): 665.

10. Fletcher to Putnam, Oct. 1899, F. W. Putnam Papers.

11. Franz Boas, "Some Problems in North American Archaeology," *American Journal of Archaeology*, 2d ser., 6 (1902): 1–6.

12. Carey McWilliams, *Southern California Country: An Island on the Land* (1946; reprint, Santa Barbara: Peregrine Smith, 1973).

13. Hoxie, *A Final Promise*.

14. "Twenty-fourth Annual Report of the AIA," *American Journal of Archaeology*, 2d ser., 7 (1903), Supplement, 6.

15. "Twenty-sixth Annual Report of the AIA," *American Journal of Archaeology*, 2d ser., 9 (1905), Supplement, 4.

16. Lummis to Charles Eliot Norton, Dec. 9, 1906, copy in C. P. Bowditch Papers, Peabody Museum.

17. "Virum Monumentum Priorum," *Out West* 20 (1904): 173.

18. "Twenty-fifth Annual Report of the AIA," *American Journal of Archaeology*, 2d ser., 8 (1904), Supplement, 5; "Twenty-sixth Annual Report of the AIA," *American Journal of Archaeology*, 2d ser., 9 (1905), Supplement, 5.

19. Dudley C. Gordon, "Lummis and the Lacey Act," *Masterkey* 42 (1968): 17–19.

20. Boas to Putnam, Feb. 26, 1904, March 7, 1904, and Putnam to Boas, April 6, 1904, Franz Boas Papers, American Philosophical Society Library, Philadelphia, Pennsylvania.

21. Charles P. Bowditch, "First Report of the Committee on American Archaeology," *American Journal of Archaeology*, 2d ser., 9 (1905): 41–44.

22. Memorandum of Meeting, Oct. 25, 1905, Edgar L. Hewett Papers, Museum of New Mexico, Historical Section, Santa Fe, New Mexico.

23. Edgar L. Hewett to Putnam, Aug. 1, 1903, Peabody Museum Papers.

24. Boas to Putnam, Feb. 7, 1906, Franz Boas Papers.

25. Fletcher to Putnam, Aug. 29, 1906, F. W. Putnam Papers.

26. Fletcher to Putnam, Oct. 30, 1906, F. W. Putnam Papers.

27. Fletcher to Putnam, Nov. 4, 1906, F. W. Putnam Papers.

28. Charles P. Bowditch, "The Work of the Institute in American Archaeology," *American Journal of Archaeology* 11 (1907): 47, quoting from Fletcher's report.

29. Fletcher Diary, Sept. 23, 1906, Fletcher Papers.

30. Fletcher to W. H. Holmes, Feb. 2, 1907, Fletcher Papers.

CHAPTER TWENTY-TWO

1. Rosa Bourassa to Gen. Pratt, April 10, 1921, Richard Henry Pratt Papers, Beinicke Library, Yale University.

2. Fletcher Diary, Dec. 22, 1906, Fletcher Papers. See also Francis La Flesche Diary, July 13, Oct. 3, Nov. and Dec. 1906, Fletcher Papers.

3. Barnes, *Two Crows Denies It*, 236; Green, *Iron Eye's Family*, 177.

4. Fletcher to Isabel Barrows, Feb. 10, 1907, Barrows Papers.

5. Hewett to Fletcher, Feb. 2, 1910, Fletcher Papers.

6. Fletcher Diary, Feb. 13, 1907, Fletcher Papers.

7. Dodge, "Brief Biography of E. Jane Gay," MS, Scheslinger Library.

8. Fletcher Diary, May 25, 1907, Fletcher Papers.

9. Ibid., Feb. 1907.

10. Ibid., Feb. 13, 1907.

11. Francis La Flesche Diary, May 14, 1907, Fletcher Papers.

12. Rosa Bourassa to Francis La Flesche, in La Flesche Papers, quoted in Green, *Iron Eye's Family*, 181.

13. Fletcher Diary, June 6, 1907, Fletcher Papers.

14. Ibid., April 4, 11, 12, 1907.

15. Fletcher to Miss Mead, June 8, 1907, Peabody Museum Papers.

16. Fletcher to Putnam, Aug. 20, 1907, F. W. Putnam Papers.

17. Isabel C. Barrows, *A Sunny Life: The Biography of Samuel June Barrows* (Boston: Little, Brown, 1913), 198.

18. Fletcher to Ida Conant, Aug. 9, 1907, Fletcher Papers.

19. Barrows, *A Sunny Life*, 195.

20. A. C. Fletcher, "A Visit to Tolstoy," 1907, MS, Fletcher Papers.

21. Fletcher to Count Tolstoy, March 21, 1908, Fletcher Papers. Tolstoy's eighty-page essay was published by the Free Press, Christchurch, and Everett and Co., London, n.d.

22. Fletcher Diary, Aug. 10, 1907, Fletcher Papers.

23. Fletcher to Putnam, Oct. 10, 1907, Putnam Papers; Barrows, *A Sunny Life,* 202.

24. Fletcher Diary, Sept. 24, 1907, Fletcher Papers.

25. Ibid., Sept. 30, 1907.

26. Ibid., 1907 and after; letter from Emlyn Hodge to Joan Mark, June 1981.

27. Cushing letters to Phoebe Hearst, Hearst Papers.

28. Fletcher Diary, Nov. 9, 1909, Fletcher Papers.

29. Ibid., Nov. 27, 1907.

30. Ibid., April 24, 1908; also Green, *Iron Eye's Family,* 180, based on Report of the Supreme Court of the District of Columbia, No. 27, 167, Equity Docket 60.

31. Checkbook stubs, 1927, Box 13, Fletcher Papers.

32. *Quarterly Journal, The Society of the American Indians* 2 (1914): 179.

33. Green, *Iron Eye's Family,* 221n.

34. Hazel W. Hertzberg, *The Search for an American Indian Identity: Modern Pan-Indian Movements* (Syracuse, N.Y.: Syracuse University Press, 1971), 84. Francis La Flesche's invitation apparently came through Charles Cadman, with whom he had worked on Omaha music. Green, *Iron Eye's Children,* 182.

35. *Quarterly Journal, The Society of the American Indians* 2 (1914): 85, 176.

36. Leicester Knickerbacker Davis, "Thomas L. Sloan, American Indian," *American Indian Magazine* 7 (1920): 39–40; W. Teller to commissioner of Indian affairs, June 1, 1883, Omaha Tribe to commissioner of Indian affairs, 1886 (letter 13786), Fletcher to commissioner of Indian affairs, April 28, 1884, all in Records of the Bureau of Indian Affairs. Sloan's grandmother would have to have been one-quarter Omaha for Thomas Sloan to be 1/16th Omaha. For resolution of the Sloan case see Records of the Bureau of Indian Affairs, letters 81781, 81782 (1904) and letter 2411 (1905).

37. Francis La Flesche to Fletcher, April 9, 1919, Fletcher Papers.

38. Fletcher Diary, Jan. 14, 1908, Fletcher Papers.

39. *New York Times,* Jan. 18, 1908, p. 5.

40. Fletcher Diary, Jan. 17, 1908, Fletcher Papers.

41. Fletcher to Cora Folsom, Jan. 18, 1908, Alice Fletcher Papers, Hampton University Archives, Hampton, Virginia.

42. Fletcher to Putnam, Oct. 10, 1907, F. W. Putnam Papers.

43. Ibid.

44. Thomas Seymour to Fletcher, Nov. 26, 1907, Hewett Papers.

45. Boas to Putnam, Jan. 8, 1908, Franz Boas Papers. For the work of the International Archaeological School in Mexico see Franz Boas, "Summary of the Work of the International School of American Archaeology and Ethnology in Mexico, 1910–1914," *American Anthropologist* 17 (1915): 384–91, and Ricardo Godoy, "Franz Boas and His Plans for an International School of American Archaeology and Ethnology in Mexico," *Journal of the History of the Behavioral Sciences* 13 (1977), 228–42.

46. Minutes of the Committee on American Archaeology, AIA, meeting of Nov. 14, 1908, Franz Boas Papers; Fletcher to members of the Committee on American Archaeology, Dec. 19, 1908, Franz Boas Papers.

47. Fletcher to Putnam, Dec. 30, 1908, F. W. Putnam Papers.

48. Fletcher to Putnam, Dec. 28, 1908, F. W. Putnam Papers.

49. Kelsey to Dean A. F. West, March 21, 1909, Hewett Papers.

50. Ralph W. Dexter, "Guess Who's Not Coming to Dinner: Frederic Ward Putnam and the Support of Women in Anthropology," *History of Anthropology Newsletter* 5 (1978): 5–6, quotes a letter from Fletcher to Putnam in which she wrote: "I am glad to know why I was left out of the dinner. I forgot I was a woman. I only remembered I was a friend and student." Although this letter implies that Fletcher was not invited to what apparently was an all-male dinner, the Boas-Fletcher correspondence in the Franz Boas Papers reveals that Boas wrote to Fletcher ahead of time telling her about the dinner and that she replied she would not be able to attend because she would be away on the AIA lecture tour. She was invited to contribute to the *Putnam Anniversary Volume*, edited by Franz Boas and presented to Putnam at the dinner, and did so with a paper on "Tribal Structure: A Study of the Omaha and Cognate Tribes" (New York: G. Stechert, 1909), 254–67.

51. Kroeber to Fletcher, April 23, 1909, Hewett Papers.

52. Fletcher to Kroeber, May 11, 1909, Hewett Papers.

53. Fletcher Diary, Sept. 6, 1909, Fletcher Papers.

54. Boas to C. P. Bowditch, Nov. 19, 1909; Putnam to Bowditch, Dec. 20, 1909; text of Bowditch's remarks at the AIA meeting Dec. 1909; memoranda "My Reasons for Distrusting Dr. Edgar L. Hewett" and "My Reasons for No Longer Trusting Miss Alice C. Fletcher" and *Correspondence between Edgar L. Hewett and Franz Boas* (privately printed, 1910); all in C. P. Bowditch Papers.

55. Fletcher Diary, Dec. 31, 1909, Fletcher Papers.

56. Kroeber to Fletcher, April 23, 1909, Hewett Papers, and Kroeber to Boas, same date, Franz Boas Papers.

CHAPTER TWENTY-THREE

1. Fletcher to Miss Mead, July 12, 1910, Peabody Museum Papers.

2. Fletcher Diary, Jan. 2, 1910, Fletcher Papers.

3. Fletcher to La Flesche, July 22, 1910, Fletcher Papers.

4. Ibid., July 25, 1910.

5. Ibid., Aug. 16, 1910.

6. Ibid., July 29, 1910.

7. Ibid., Aug. 11, 1910.

8. Ibid., Sept.13, 1910.

9. Ibid.; Fletcher to F. W. Kelsey, Sept. 6, 1910, AIA Archives, courtesy of Curtis Hinsley.

10. Fletcher to La Flesche, Aug. 16, 1910, Fletcher Papers.

11. Ibid., Sept. 16, 1910.

12. Ibid., Sept. 4, 1910.

13. Ibid., Sept. 18, 1910.

14. Ibid., Oct. 4, 1910.

15. Fletcher Diary, Nov. 2, 1910, and Fletcher to La Flesche, Dec. 6, 1910, Fletcher Papers.

16. Fletcher Diary, Dec. 31, 1910, Fletcher Papers.

17. Fletcher to La Flesche, Jan. 4, 1911, Fletcher Papers.

18. Ibid.

19. Fletcher to La Flesche, Jan. 9, 1911, Fletcher Papers.

20. Ibid., Jan. 5, 1911.

21. Ibid., Jan. 9, 1911.

22. Ibid., Jan. 11, 1911.

23. Ibid., Jan. 12, 1911.

24. Fletcher Diary, Feb. 7, 1911, Fletcher Papers.

25. Fletcher to La Flesche, Feb. 13, 1911, Fletcher Papers.

26. Ibid., Feb. 20, 1911.

27. Ibid., March 9, 1911.

28. Ibid., March 27, 1911.

29. Ibid., March 1, 1911.

30. Francis La Flesche to Fletcher, May 8, 1911, Fletcher and La Flesche Papers.

31. Ibid., April 15, 1911.

32. Ibid., April 23, 1911.

33. Fletcher Diary, June 30, 1911, Fletcher Papers.

CHAPTER TWENTY-FOUR

1. Fletcher to Miss Mead, July 20, 1911, Peabody Museum Papers.

2. Fletcher to Putnam, Aug. 18, 1911, F. W. Putnam Papers.

3. Fletcher Diary, Aug. 25, 1911, Fletcher Papers; Beatrice Chauvenet, *Hewett*

and Friends: A Biography of Santa Fe's Vibrant Era (Santa Fe: Museum of New Mexico Press, 1983), 72.

4. "Second Annual Report of the Managing Committee of the School of American Research," *Bulletin of the Archaeological Institute of America* 1 (1909–10): 175.

5. Flyer in Hewett Papers.

6. Robert William Rydell II, "All the World's A Fair: America's International Expositions, 1876–1916," (Ph.D. diss., University of California, Los Angeles, 1980), 424.

7. Fletcher to Hewett, Nov. 15, 1911, F. W. Kelsey to Fletcher, Nov. 21, 1911, Hewett Papers.

8. Fletcher to Hewett, Nov. 11, 1911, Hewett Papers.

9. Hewett to Fletcher, Nov. 19, 1911, Hewett Papers.

10. Kelsey to Fletcher, Dec. 3, 1911, Hewett Papers.

11. Hodge to Fletcher, Jan. 26, 1912, Hewett Papers.

12. Kelsey to Fletcher, Jan. 25, 1912, quoting a Mr. Harris, Hewett Papers.

13. Fletcher to Putnam, Jan. 29, 1912, F. W. Putnam Papers.

14. Mitchell Carroll to Fletcher, Oct. 22, 1912, Hewett Papers.

15. Fletcher to Putnam, Nov. 29, 1911, F. W. Putnam Papers.

16. Judd, *The Bureau of American Ethnology*, 52.

17. Paul Radin, "The Ritual and Significance of the Winnebago Medicine Dance," *Journal of American Folk-Lore* 24 (1911).

18. As quoted in Lurie, "Women in Early American Anthropology," in Helm, ed., *Pioneers of American Anthropology*, 45 n. 291; Hodge to Radin, Oct. 13, 1911, Fletcher Papers.

19. Alice C. Fletcher and Francis La Flesche, *The Omaha Tribe*, Smithsonian Institution, Bureau of American Ethnology, 27th Annual Report, 1905–1906 (Washington, D.C., 1911), 30.

20. Robert H. Lowie, "The Omaha Tribe," *Science* 37 (1913): 910–15.

21. Fletcher Diary, June 13–15, 1913, Fletcher Papers.

22. Francis La Flesche, "The Omaha Tribe," *Science* 37 (1913): 982–83.

23. "Review of *The Omaha Tribe*," *American Historical Review* 17 (1912): 634–36.

24. Alice C. Fletcher and Francis La Flesche, "Communication," *American Historical Review* 17 (1912): 885–86.

25. Fletcher Diary, March 29, 1913, Fletcher Papers.

26. A. C. Haddon, "The Significance of Life to the Omaha," *Nature* 90 (Oct. 24, 1912): 234.

27. Marcel Mauss, "Review of *The Omaha Tribe*," *L'Année sociologique* 12 (1909–12): 104–11, 105.

28. Emile Durkheim, "Review of *The Omaha Tribe*," *L'Année sociologique* 13 (1913): 366–71.

29.   A. C. Fletcher, "Brief History of the International Congress of Americanists," *American Anthropologist* 15 (1913): 529–34.

30.   Fletcher to Putnam, March 18, 1913, Peabody Museum Papers.

31.   Fletcher to Miss Mead, July 12, 1913, F. W. Putnam Papers.

32.   Fletcher Diary, Aug. 5, 1913, Fletcher Papers.

33.   Elizabeth Sturge, *Reminiscenses of My Life and Some Account of the Children of William and Charlotte Sturge and the Sturge Family of Bristol* (Privately printed, 1928), 142–48. The architect was Sir George Oatley. For a look at the architect's plans for Kamiah and a tour of the interior, I am indebted to the kindness of its present occupants, Paul and Jo Forrest, Rowington, Sidcot, Winscombe.

34.   Fletcher to Francis La Flesche, Oct. 26, 1913, Fletcher Papers.

35.   Fletcher to Putnam, June 6, 1914, and Fletcher Diary, May 20, 1914, Fletcher Papers.

36.   Chauvenet, *Hewett and Friends*, 27; Arrel Morgan Gibson, *The Santa Fe and Taos Colonies: Age of the Muses, 1900–1942* (Norman: University of Oklahoma Press, 1983), 31, 34.

37.   Hewett, "Report on the School of American Research for 1918," *Bulletin of the Archaeological Institute of America* 9 (1918): 33.

38.   Ibid., 43. Nor was Hewett willing to limit his activities to Santa Fe. From 1922 to 1927 he taught anthropology at the San Diego Teacher's College while still serving as director of the San Diego Museum. He resigned from the latter in 1928 and became head of the department of archaeology and anthropology at the University of New Mexico in Albuquerque.

39.   Francis La Flesche to Fletcher, Nov. 21, 1912, Fletcher Papers.

40.   Ibid., Jan. 15, 16, and 31, 1917.

41.   Ibid., May 2, 1919.

42.   Fletcher letter to Mabel Barrows, n.d., Barrows Papers; conversation with Emlyn Hodge, June 1981.

43.   A. C. Fletcher, "Indian Characteristics," *Southern Workman* 29 (1900): 203.

44.   Franz Boas, "History and Science in Anthropology: A Reply," in *Race, Language, and Culture*. Boas's article was "The Significance of Esoteric Doctrines," *Science*, n.s., 16 (1902): 872–74.

45.   Carobeth Laird, *Encounter with an Angry God: Recollections of My Life with John Peabody Harrington* (Banning, Calif.: Malki Museum Press, Morongo Indian Reservation, 1975), 83.

46.   Ibid.; Judd, *The Bureau of American Ethnology*, 54.

47.   Francis La Flesche to Marguerite Conn, April 20, 1923, La Flesche Family Papers.

48.   Francis La Flesche to Emma Gay, Feb. 21, 1923, Dodge Papers; obituary, *Washington Star*, Sunday, April 8, 1923.

49.   M. C. Thaw to Emma Gay, March 22, 1923, Dodge Papers.

50.   Francis La Flesche Diary, April 6, 1923, Fletcher Papers.

51. Francis La Flesche to Emma Gay, April 20, 1923, Dodge Papers.

52. Green, *Iron Eye's Family*, 35; Francis La Flesche to Emma Gay, Sept. 10, 1923, Dodge Papers; *Washington Star*, Sept. 13, 1923; other Dodge Papers.

53. Green, *Iron Eye's Family*, 198.

54. "Alice Cunningham Fletcher," *Southern Workman* 52 (May 1923): 213.

55. "An Interpreter of Indian Life," *Omaha Bee*, April 9, 1923, clipping, Fletcher Papers.

56. Hartley B. Alexander, "Dedication of Fletcher Memorial Tablet," *El Palacio* 16 (1926): 59–72, 67–69.

57. Lummis, "In Memoriam: Alice C. Fletcher," 75–76.

58. Francis La Flesche, *The Osage Tribe* (Part One), Smithsonian Institution, Bureau of American Ethnology, 36th Annual Report (Washington, D.C.: 1921), 45.

59. Fletcher to Putnam, May 3, 1911, F. W. Putnam Papers.

60. Rodney Needham, ed., *Right and Left* (Chicago: University of Chicago Press, 1973), 32–42.

61. Francis La Flesche, "The Symbolic Man of the Osage Tribe," *Art and Archaeology* 9 (1920): 68.

62. Fletcher to Miss Mead, July 20, 1911, Peabody Museum Papers.

63. Francis La Flesche, "Rite of the Wa-xo'-be," *The Osage Tribe* (Part Four), Smithsonian Institution, Bureau of American Ethnology, 45th Annual Report, 1927–28, (Washington, D.C.: 1930), 529–835, 532, 537.

64. Ronald Walcott, "Francis La Flesche: American Indian Scholar," *Folklife Center News* 4 (January 1981): 1, 10.

65. Hartley B. Alexander, "Francis La Flesche," *American Anthropologist* 35 (1933): 329–30; Margot Liberty, "Francis La Flesche: The Osage Odyssey," in *American Indian Intellectuals*, ed. Margot Liberty (St. Paul: West, 1978), 46–59.

66. As quoted in Green, *Iron Eye's Family*, 203, 196.

67. Obituary, Dr. Francis La Flesche, *Walthill* [Nebraska] *Times*, Sept. 15, 1932, clipping, La Flesche Family Papers; Green, *Iron Eye's Family*, 207.

68. Green, *Iron Eye's Family*, 206–7; also clipping, *Nebraska State Journal*, Sept. 16, 1932, p. 11, La Flesche Family Papers, gives La Flesche's estate as $60,000; Alice C. Fletcher will and depositions in Fletcher Papers.

69. Green, *Iron Eye's Family*, 169.

70. Personal communication from Dennis Hastings, August 1984.

71. Fletcher, *Indian Games and Dances*, v–vi.

72. Parkman, *Heroines of Service*, 230.

Bibliography of Works
by Alice Fletcher
and Francis La Flesche

Alice Fletcher

"Feminine Idleness." *Woman's Journal* 4 (Sept. 13, 1873): 291.

"Women's Clubs." *Woman's Journal* 9 (Oct. 19, 1878): 333.

"Among the Omahas." *Woman's Journal* 13 (Feb. 11, 1882): 46–47.

"Extract from Miss Fletcher's Letter." *Morning Star* 3 (October 1882): 1,4.

"Indian Home Building." *Publications of the Women's National Indian Association*. Paris, 1883.

"The Omahas." *Morning Star* 3 (April 1883).

"On Indian Education and Self-Support." *Century Magazine* 26 (1883): 312–15.

"Sun Dance of the Ogalalla Sioux." *Proceedings of the American Association for the Advancement of Science* 30 (1883): 580–84.

"Five Indian Ceremonies." *16th Annual Report of the Peabody Museum* 3 (1884): 260–333.

"Observations on the Laws and Privileges of the Gens in Indian Society." (Abstract) *Proceedings of the American Association for the Advancement of Science* 32 (1884): 395–96; also in *Science* 2 (1883): 367.

"Proofs of Indian Capacity for Citizenship." *Second Annual Lake Mohonk Conference of the Friends of the Indian*, 1884, pp. 5–6.

"Symbolic Earth Formations of the Winnebagoes." (Abstract) *Proceedings of the American Association for the Advancement of Science* 32 (1884): 396–97; also in *Science* 2 (1883): 367–68.

"An Average Day in Camp among the Sioux." *Science* 6 (1885): 285–87.

"An Evening in Camp among the Omahas." *Science* 6 (1885): 88–90.

"Historical Sketch of the Omaha Tribe of Indians in Nebraska." Washington, D.C.: Bureau of Indian Affairs, 1885.

"The Indian Bureau at the New Orleans Exposition." Report to the commissioner of Indian affairs, May 6, 1885. Carlisle, Penn.: Carlisle Indian School Print, 1885.

"Land and Education for the Indian." *Southern Workman* 14 (1885): 6.

"Lands in Severalty to Indians; Illustrated by Experiences with the Omaha Tribe." *Proceedings of the American Association for the Advancement of Science* 33 (1885): 654–65.

"A Letter from the World's Industrial Exposition at New Orleans to the Various Indian Tribes Who are Interested in Education." Carlisle, Penn.: Indian School Print, 1885.

"The New Orleans Exposition." *Southern Workman* 14 (1885): 79.

"Observations upon the Usage, Symbolism and Influence of the Sacred Pipes of Friendship among the Omahas." (Abstract) *Proceedings of the American Association for the Advancement of Science* 33 (1885): 615–17.

"Between the Lines." *Lend a Hand* 1 (July 1886): 429–31.

"Composite Portraits of American Indians." *Science* 7 (1886): 408–9.

"Economy of Justice." *Lend a Hand* 1 (July 1886): 528–30.

"The Problem of the Omahas." *Southern Workman* 15 (1886): 55.

"Tribute to H. H. Jackson." *Third Annual Lake Mohonk Conference of the Friends of the Indian*, 1885, p. 71.

"Brave Words of Miss Fletcher to Our Students at Their Sunday Evening Service, Feb. 20th." *Morning Star* 7 (February 1887): 5.

"The Crowning Act." *Morning Star* 7 (March 1887): 1.

"Letter from A. C. Fletcher from Winnebago Agency, Nebraska, Sept. 23, 1887," *Fifth Annual Lake Mohonk Conference of the Friends of the Indian*, 1887 pp. 14–17.

"Letter from Miss Fletcher." *Morning Star* 7 (June 1887): 1–2.

"The Supernatural among the Omaha Tribe of Indians." *Proceedings of the American Society of Psychical Research* 1 (1887): 3–18.

"Glimpses of Child-Life among the Omaha Tribe of Indians." *Journal of American Folk-Lore* 1 (1888): 115–23.

"The Indian and the Prisoner." *Southern Workman* 17 (1888): 45.

Indian Education and Civilization. Special Report, U.S. Bureau of Education, Department of the Interior, Washington, D.C., 1888. 693 pp.

"Joseph La Flesche." *Bancroft* [Nebraska] *Journal*, September 1888.

"Letter from the Winnebago Agency." *Sixth Annual Lake Mohonk Conference of the Friends of the Indian*, 1888, pp. 7, 78–79.

"Miss Fletcher's Letter from Winnebago Agency." *Red Man* 8 (February 1888): 1–2; also in *Southern Workman* 18 (1888): 19.

"On the Preservation of Archaeologic Monuments." *Proceedings of the American Association for the Advancement of Science* 36 (1888): 317.

"Among the Nez Perces." *Red Man* 9 (September 1889):1.

"Joseph La Flesche." *Journal of American Folk-Lore* 2 (1889): 11.

"Leaves from my Omaha Note-book." *Journal of American Folk-Lore* 2 (1889): 219–26.

"Letter from Miss Alice C. Fletcher." *Seventh Annual Lake Mohonk Conference of the Friends of the Indian*, 1889, pp. 13–15.

"Report of the Committee on the Preservation of Archaeologic Remains on the Public Lands." *Proceedings of the American Association for the Advancement of Science* 37 (1889): 35–37.

"Extracts from Letter from Alice C. Fletcher." *Eighth Annual Lake Mohonk Conference of the Friends of the Indian*, 1890, p. 152.

"The Phonetic Alphabet of the Winnebago Indians." *Proceedings of the American Association for the Advancement of Science* 38 (1890): 354–57; also in *Journal of American Folk-Lore* 3 (1890): 299–301.

"The Indian Messiah." *Journal of American Folk-Lore* 4 (1891): 57–60.

"Why Indians Need Higher Education." *Southern Workman* 20 (1891): 140.

"Experiences in Allotting Land." *Tenth Annual Lake Mohonk Conference of the Friends of the Indian*, 1892, p. 10.

"Hal-thu-ska Society of the Omaha Tribe." *Journal of American Folk-Lore* 5 (1892): 135–44.

"Nez Perce Country." (Abstract) *Proceedings of the American Association for the Advancement of Science* 40 (1892): 357.

"The Preparation of the Indian for Citizenship." *Lend a Hand* 9 (1892): 190.

"How Indian Songs are Borrowed." *American Anthropologist* 6 (1893): 376.

"Music as Found in Certain North American Indian Tribes." *Music Review* 2 (August 1893): 534–38; also in *Music* 4 (1893): 457–67.

"Personal Studies of Indian Life: Politics and 'Pipe-Dancing.'" *Century Magazine* 45 (1893): 441–45.

"A Study of Omaha Indian Music." Aided by Francis La Flesche and John C. Fillmore. *Archaeological and Ethnological Papers*, Peabody Museum of Archaeology and Ethnology, 1 (1893): 237–87.

"The Wa-wan, or Pipe Dance of the Omahas." *Music* 4 (1893): 468.

"Indian Music." *Music* 6 (1894): 188–99.

"Indian Songs: Personal Studies of Indian Life." *Century Magazine* 47 (January 1894): 421–31.

"Love Songs among the Omaha Indians." *Memoirs, International Congress of Anthropologists*, ed. C. S. Wake. (Chicago: Schulte, 1894), 153–57.

"The Religion of the North American Indians." *The World's Congress of Religions*, The Addresses and Papers and an Abstract of the Congress, ed. John W. Hanson (Chicago: W. B. Conkey, 1894), 541–45.

"Some Aspects of Indian Music and its Study." *Archaeologist* 2 (1894): 195–234.

"Hunting Customs of the Omahas." *Century Magazine* 47 (September 1895): 691–702.

"Indian Songs and Music." *Proceedings of the American Association for the Advancement of Science* 44 (1896): 281–84.

"Notes on Certain Beliefs concerning Will Power among the Siouan Tribes." *Proceedings of the American Association for the Advancement of Science* 44 (1896): 1-4.

Review of D. G. Brinton, "The Myths of the New World." *Science* 4 (1896): 798–99.

"Sacred Pole of the Omaha Tribe." *Proceedings of the American Association for the Advancement of Science* 44 (1896): 270–80; also in *American Antiquarian* 17 (1895): 257–68.

"Tribal Life among the Omahas." *Century Magazine* 51 (January 1896): 450–61.

"The Emblematic Use of the Tree in the Dakotan Group." *Proceedings of the American Association for the Advancement of Science* 45 (1897): 191–209.

"Notes on Certain Early Forms of Ceremonial Expressiveness" and "Ceremonial Hair Cutting among the Omahas." (Abstracts) *Science* 5 (1897): 215.

Review of Washington Matthews, "Navaho Legends." *Science* 6 (1897): 525–28.

"Flotsam and Jetsam from Aboriginal America." *Southern Workman* 28 (1898): 12–14.

"The Import of the Totem." *Science* 7 (1898): 296–304; also in *Annual Report*, Smithsonian Institution, 1897: 577–86, and in *Proceedings of the American Association for the Advancement of Science* 46 (1898): 325–34.

"The Indian at the Trans-Mississippi Exposition." *Southern Workman* 27 (1898): 216–17.

"Indian Songs and Music." *Journal of American Folk-Lore* 11 (1898): 85–104.

"The Significance of the Garment." *Proceedings of the American Association for the Advancement of Science* 47 (1898): 471–72.

"The Significance of the scalp-lock: A study of Omaha Ritual." *The Journal of the Anthropological Institute of Great Britain and Ireland* 27 (1898): 436–450.

"Indian Speech." *Southern Workman* 28 (1899): 426–28.

"The Indian Woman and Her Problem." *Southern Workman* 28 (1899): 172–76.

"A Pawnee Ritual Used When Changing a Man's Name." *American Anthropologist* 1 (1899): 82–97.

"Frank Hamilton Cushing." *American Anthropologist* 2 (1900): 367–70.

"Giving Thanks: A Pawnee Ceremony." *Journal of American Folk-Lore* 13 (1900): 261–66.

"Indian Characteristics." *Southern Workman* 29 (1900): 202–5.

Indian Story and Song From North America. Boston: Small, Maynard, 1900.

"The Old Man's Love Song: an Indian Story." *Music* 18 (1900): 137.

"The Osage Indians in France." *American Anthropologist* 2 (1900): 395–400.

"The Registration of Indian Families." *Eighteenth Annual Lake Mohonk Conference of the Friends of the Indian,* 1900, pp. 73–76.

"The 'Lazyman' in Indian Folklore." *Journal of American Folk-Lore* 14 (1901): 100–104.

"Star Cult among the Pawnee." *American Anthropologist* 4 (1902): 730–36.

"Pawnee Star Lore." *Journal of American Folk-Lore* 16 (1903): 10–15.

"The Preparation of the Indians for Citizenship." *Twenty-first Annual Lake Mohonk Conference of the Friends of the Indian,* 1903, pp. 67–70.

"The Significance of Dress." (Abstract) *American Journal of Archaeology* 7 (1903): 84–85.

The Hako: A Pawnee Ceremony. With James R. Murie. Smithsonian Institution, Bureau of American Ethnology, 22nd Annual Report. Washington, D.C., 1904. 372 pp.

"Indian Names." *Proceedings of the Congress of Indian Educators, St. Louis, June 25–July 1, 1904.* Reprinted in *Report of the Super. of Ind. Schools for 1904.*

"Indian Traditions." *Proceedings, National Educational Association* 1904, 425–26.

"Adornment," "Buffalo," "Dreams," "Feasts and Fasting," "Land Tenure," "Music and Musical Instruments," "Oratory," "Poetry," "Property and Property Rights," "Totemism," "Wakondagi," *et al.* In F. W. Hodge, *Handbook of the American Indians North of Mexico.* Smithsonian Institution, Bureau of American Ethnology, Bulletin no. 30. Washington, D.C., 1907, 1910.

"The Indian and Nature." *American Anthropologist* 9 (1907): 440–43.

"Remarks of Miss Alice C. Fletcher." *Twenty-fifth Annual Lake Mohonk Conference of the Friends of the Indian,* 1907, pp. 178–79.

Preface to *The Nez Perces Since Lewis and Clark,* by Kate McBeth. New York: Fleming H. Revell, 1908.

"Dr. Spofford as a Member of the Literary Society." *Ainsworth Rand Spofford: A Memorial Meeting at the Library of Congress,* Nov. 12, 1908. New York: Webster, 1909, pp. 40–45.

"Standing Bear." *Southern Workman* 38 (1909): 75–78.

"Tribal Structure: A Study of the Omaha and Cognate Tribes." *Putnam Anniversary Volume,* ed. Franz Boas, 245–67. New York: Stechert, 1909.

The Omaha Tribe. With Francis La Flesche. Smithsonian Institution, Bureau of American Ethnology, 27th Annual Report, 1905–1906 Washington, D.C., 1911. 672 pp.

"The Problems of Unity or Plurality and the Probable Place of Origin of the American Aborigines: Some Ethnological Aspects of the Problem." *American Anthropologist* 14 (1912): 37–39.

"Wakondagi." *American Anthropologist* 14 (1912), 106–8.

"Brief History of the International Congress of Americanists." *American Anthropologist* 15 (1913): 529–34.

Review of F. Densmore, "Chippewa Music." *Science* 39 (1914): 393.

"The Child and the Tribe." *Proceedings of the National Academy of Sciences* 1 (1915): 569–74.

Indian Games and Dances with Native Songs Arranged from American Indian Ceremonials and Sports. Boston: C. C. Birchard, 1915.

"The Study of Indian Music." *Proceedings of the National Academy of Sciences* 1 (1915): 231–35.

"A Birthday Wish from Native America." *Holmes Anniversary Volume.* Washington, D.C.: James Wilson Bryan, 1916, pp. 118–22.

"The Indian and Nature: The Basis of His Tribal Organization and Rites."
Red Man 8 (1916): 185–88.

Introduction to E. L. Hewett, "The School of American Archaeology." *Art
and Archaeology* 4 (1916): 319.

"Nature and the Indian Tribe." *Art and Archaeology* 4 (1916): 291.

"Prayers Voiced in Ancient America." *Art and Archaeology* 9 (1920): 73–75.

"A Study of Indian Music." *American Anthropologist* 36 (1934): 487–88.

Francis La Flesche

"The Sacred Pipes of Friendship." *Proceedings of the American Association for
the Advancement of Science* 33 (1885): 613–15.

"Omaha Games." *Journal of American Folk-Lore* 1 (1888): 118–19.

"Death and Funeral Customs among the Omahas." *Journal of American Folk-
Lore* 2 (1889): 3–11.

"The Omaha Buffalo Medicine-Men: An Account of Their Method of Practice." *Journal of American Folk-Lore* 3 (1890): 215–21.

"The Ceremonies of the Sacred Pole of the Omaha Tribe." *Proceedings of the
American Association for the Advancement of Science* 47 (1898): 480.

"An Indian Allotment." *Independent* 52 (1900): 2686–88.

"The Laughing Bird, the Wren." *Southern Workman* 29 (1900): 554–56.

The Middle Five: Indian Boys at School. 1900. Reprint. Madison: University
of Wisconsin Press, 1963

"The Shell Society among the Omahas." (Abstract) *Proceedings of the
American Association for the Advancement of Science* 49 (1900): 315.

"The Story of a Vision." *Southern Workman* 30 (1901): 106–9.

"Who was the Medicine Man?" *Annual Report, Fairmont Park Art Association*
32 (1904): 3–13; also in *Journal of American Folk-Lore* 18 (1905):
269–75.

"The Past Life of the Plains Indians." *Southern Workman* 34 (1905):
587–94.

The Omaha Tribe. With Alice Fletcher. Smithsonian Institution, Bureau of
American Ethnology, 27th Annual Report, 1905–1906. Washington,
1911. 672 pp.

"Osage Marriage Customs." *American Anthropologist* 14 (1912): 127–30.

"Wakondagi." *American Anthropologist* 14 (1912): 106–8.

The Osage Tribe. Part One: "Rite of the Chiefs; Sayings of the Ancient Men."
Smithsonian Institution, Bureau of American Ethnology, 36th Annual
Report, 1914–15. Washington, D.C., 1921, pp. 43–597.

"Protection of Indian Lands." *33rd Annual Lake Mohonk Conference of the Friends of the Indian*, 1915, pp. 70–72.

"Right and Left in Osage Ceremonies." *Holmes Anniversary Volume*. Washington, D.C.: James Wilson Bryan, 1916, pp. 278–87. Reprinted in Rodney Needham, ed., *Right and Left*. Chicago: University of Chicago Press, 1973, pp. 32–42.

"Omaha and Osage Traditions of Separation." *Proceedings, International Congress of Americanists* 19 (1917): 459–62.

The Osage Tribe. Part Two: "The Rite of Vigil." Smithsonian Institution, Bureau of American Ethnology, 39th Annual Report, 1917–18. Washington, D.C., 1925, pp. 37–630.

"The Symbolic Man of the Osage Tribe." *Art and Archaeology* 9 (1920): 68–72.

"The Scientific Work of Miss Alice C. Fletcher." *Science* 57 (1923): 115–16.

"Omaha Bow and Arrow Makers." *Proceedings, International Congress of Americanists* 20 (1924): 111–16; also in *Annual Report*, Smithsonian Institution, 1926 (1927): 487–94.

The Osage Tribe. Part Three: "Two Versions of the Child-Naming Rite." Smithsonian Institution, Bureau of American Ethnology, 43rd Annual Report, 1925–26. Washington, D.C., 1928, pp. 29–820.

The Osage Tribe. Part Four: "Rite of the Wa-xo'-be and Shrine Degree." Smithsonian Institution, Bureau of American Ethnology, 45th Annual Report, 1927–28. Washington, D.C., 1930, pp. 529–833.

"The Omahas were skillful in bow and arrow making." *American Indian* 3 (1929): 14–16.

A Dictionary of the Osage Language. Smithsonian Institution, Bureau of American Ethnology, Bulletin no. 109. Washington, D.C., 1932.

"War Ceremony and Peace Ceremony of the Osage Indians." Smithsonian Institution, Bureau of American Ethnology, Bulletin no. 101, Washington, D.C., 1939.

Selected Bibliography

Manuscript Collections

American Philosophical Society Library, Philadelphia, Pennsylvania
    Franz Boas Papers
Hampton University Archives, Hampton, Virginia
    Alice Fletcher Papers
Harvard University Archives, Cambridge, Massachusetts
    Peabody Museum Papers
    F. W. Putnam Papers
Haverford College Library, Haverford, Pennsylvania
    Quaker Collection
Houghton Library, Harvard University, Cambridge, Massachusetts
    Samuel J. and Isabel Barrows Papers
Library of Congress, Washington, D.C.
    Henry L. Dawes Papers
    Anita Newcomb McGee Papers
Maria Mitchell Library, Nantucket, Massachusetts
    Maria Mitchell Memorabilia
Massachusetts Historical Society, Boston, Massachusetts
    Carolin H. Dall Papers
    Horace Mann Papers
Museum of Mew Mexico, Historical Section, Santa Fe, New Mexico
    Edgar L. Hewett Papers
National Anthropological Archives, Smithsonian Institution, Washington, D.C.
    Alice C. Fletcher and Francis La Flesche Papers
National Archives, Washington, D.C.
    Records of the Bureau of Indian Affairs
Nebraska State Historical Society, Lincoln, Nebraska
    La Flesche Family Papers
New York Historical Society Library, New York, New York

Peabody Museum of Archaeology and Ethnology, Cambridge,
Massachusetts
C. P. Bowditch Papers
Alice C. Fletcher Papers
Presbyterian Historical Society, Philadelphia, Pennsylvania
Sheldon Jackson Collection
Schlesinger Library, Radcliffe College, Cambridge, Massachusetts
Jane Gay Dodge Papers
Saturday Morning Club Papers
Smith College Library, Sophia Smith Collection, Northampton,
Massachusetts
Sorosis Papers
Southwest Museum, Los Angeles, California
F. W. Hodge Papers
University of California, Berkeley, the Bancroft Library
Phoebe Apperson Hearst Papers
University of Rochester, Rush Rhees Library, Rochester, New York
Lewis Henry Morgan Papers
Yale University, Beinicke Library, New Haven, Connecticut
Richard Henry Pratt Papers
Walter McClintock Papers

Published Sources

Adler, Cyrus. "Samuel Pierpont Langley." *Bulletin of the Philosophical Society of Washington* 15 (1907): 1–26.

Alexander, Hartley B. "Francis La Flesche." *American Anthropologist* 35 (1933): 328–31.

Alfers, Kenneth G. "Triumph of the West: The Trans-Mississippi Exposition." *Nebraska History* 53 (1972): 313–29.

Baker, Theodore. *The Music of the North American Indians*, trans. Anne Buckley. 1882. Reprint. Buren, The Netherlands: Fritz Knuf, 1976.

Barnes, R. H. *Two Crows Denies It: A History of Controversy in Omaha Sociology*. Lincoln: University of Nebraska Press, 1984.

Barrows, Isabel C. *A Sunny Life: The Biography of Samuel June Barrows*. Boston: Little, Brown, 1913.

Billings, Elden E. "Social and Economic Life in Washington in the 1890s."

Records of the Columbia Historical Society, 1966–68 (Washington, D.C., 1969), 167–81.

Bland, T. A. *Life of Alfred B. Meacham.* Washington, D.C.: T. A. and M. C. Bland, Publishers, 1883.

Bles, Geoffrey. *The Trial of Harry Thaw.* London: n.p., n.d.

Boas, Franz. *Race, Language, and Culture.* New York: Macmillan, 1940.

———. Review of "A Study of Omaha Indian Music." *Journal of American Folk-Lore* 7 (1894): 169–71.

———. "Summary of the Work of the International School of American Archaeology and Ethnology in Mexico, 1910–1914," *American Anthropologist* 17 (1915): 384–91.

Bonfils, Winifred Black. *The Life and Personality of Phoebe Apperson Hearst.* Privately printed, 1928.

Browne, William B. *Genealogy of the Jenks Family of America.* Concord, N.H.: Rumford Press, 1952.

Buck, Paul. "Harvard Attitudes Toward Radcliffe in the Early Years." *Proceedings of the Massachusetts Historical Society* 74 (May 1962): 33–50.

Chambers-Schiller, Lee Virginia. *Liberty, A Better Husband. Single Women in America: The Generation of 1780–1840.* New Haven: Yale University Press, 1984.

Chauvenet, Beatrice. *Hewett and Friends: A Biography of Santa Fe's Vibrant Era.* Santa Fe: Museum of New Mexico Press, 1983.

Clark, Stanley. "Ponca Publicity." *Mississippi Valley Review* 29 (1943): 495–516.

Clifford, Deborah. *Mine Eyes Have Seen the Glory: A Biography of Julia Ward Howe.* Boston: Little, Brown; Atlantic Monthly, 1979.

Coleman, Michael C. "The Mission Education of Francis La Flesche." *American Studies in Scandinavia* 18 (1986): 67–82.

Conant, Frederick Odell. *A History and Genealogy of the Conant Family in England and America.* Portland, Maine: privately printed, 1887.

Croly, Jane C. *The History of the Woman's Club Movement in America.* New York: J. J. Little, 1898.

———. *Sorosis: Its Origin and History.* New York: J. J. Little, 1886.

Davis, Allen F. *American Heroine: The Life and Legend of Jane Addams.* New York: Oxford University Press, 1973.

Davis, Leicester Knickerbacker. "Thomas L. Sloan, American Indian." *American Indian Magazine* 7 (1920): 39–40.

Dawson, Lillian W., comp. *Jane Gay Photograph Collection Catalog*. Boise, Idaho: Idaho State Historical Society, 1980.

de Hegermann-Lindencrone, L. *The Sunny Side of Diplomatic Life, 1875–1912*. New York: Harper and Bros., 1914.

Densmore, Frances. "The Study of Indian Music in the Nineteenth Century." *American Anthropologist* 29 (1927): 77–86.

Dorsey, James Owen. *Omaha and Ponka Letters*. Smithsonian Institution, Bureau of Ethnology, Bulletin no. 11. Washington, D.C., 1891.

―――. *Omaha Sociology*. Smithsonian Insitution, Bureau of Ethnology, 3rd Annual Report. Washington, D.C., 1884.

―――. *The Degiha Language: Myths, Stories, and Letters*. Smithsonian Institution, Bureau of Ethnology, Contributions to North American Ethnology, VI. Washington, D.C., 1890.

Douglas Wood, Ann. "The War Within a War: Women Nurses in the Union Army." *Civil War History* 18 (September 1972): 197–212.

Durkheim, Emile. "Review of *The Omaha Tribe*." *L'Année sociologique* 13 (1913): 366–71.

Ehrlich, David Henry. "Problems Arising from Shifts of the Missouri River on the Eastern Border of Nebraska." *Nebraska History* 54 (1973): 341–63.

Fillmore, John C. "The Harmonic Structure of Indian Music." *American Anthropologist* 11 (1899): 297–318.

―――. "Primitive Scales and Rhythms." In *Memoirs. International Congress of Anthropologists*, ed. C. S. Wake, 158–75. Chicago: Schulte, 1894.

―――. "Scales and Harmonies of Indian Music." *Music* 4 (1893): 478–89.

―――. "A Study of Indian Music." *Century Magazine* 47 (1894): 616–23.

―――. "What do Indians mean to do when they sing." *Journal of American Folk-Lore* 8 (1895): 138–42.

―――. "The Zuni Music as Translated by Mr. Benjamin Ives Gilman." *Music* 5 (1893): 39–46.

Flack, J. Kirkpatrick. *Desideratum in Washington: The Intellectual Community in the Capital City, 1870–1900*. Cambridge, Mass.: Schenkman Publishers, 1975.

Fletcher, Edward H. *The Descendants of Robert Fletcher of Concord, Mass*. New York: Rand, Avery, and Co., 1881.

Fontana, Bernard L. "Meanwhile, Back at the Rancheria." *Indian Historian* 8 (1975): 13–18.

Fritz, Henry E. *The Movement for Indian Assimilation, 1860–1890.* Philadelphia: University of Pennsylvania Press, 1963.

Galton, Francis. *Inquiries into Human Faculty and Its Development.* London: Macmillan, 1883.

Gay, E. Jane. *With the Nez Perces: Alice Fletcher in the Field, 1889–1892.* ed. Frederick E. Hoxie and Joan T. Mark. Lincoln: University of Nebraska Press, 1981.

Gibson, Arrel Morgan. *The Santa Fe and Taos Colonies: Age of the Muses, 1900–1942.* Norman: University of Oklahoma Press, 1983.

Giffen, Fannie Reed. *Oo-Ma-Ha Ta-Wa-tha.* Lincoln: privately printed, 1898.

Gilman, Benjamin Ives. "Hopi Songs." *Journal of American Archaeology and Ethnology* 5 (1908): 1–226.

———. "Zuni Melodies." *Journal of American Archaeology and Ethnology* 1 (1891): 63–91.

Godoy, Ricardo. "Franz Boas and His Plans for an International School of American Archaeology and Ethnology in Mexico." *Journal of the History of the Behavioral Sciences* 13 (1977): 228–42.

Gordon, Dudley. *Charles F. Lummis: Crusader in Corduroy.* N.p.: Cultural Assets Press, 1972.

Green, Constance McLaughlin. *Washington, Capital City, 1879–1950.* Princeton: Princeton University Press, 1963.

Green, Norma Kidd. *Iron Eye's Family: The Children of Joseph La Flesche.* Lincoln, Neb.: Johnsen Publishing Co., 1969.

Gruening, Ernest. *The Story of Alaska.* New York: Random House, 1954.

Hagan, William T. "Civil Service Commissioner Theodore Roosevelt and the Indian Rights Association." *Pacific Historical Review* 44 (1975): 187–200.

Hall, G. Stanley. *Adolescence: Its Psychology and Its Relation to Physiology, Anthropology, Sociology, Sex, Crime, Religion, and Education,* 2 vols. New York: D. Appleton & Co., 1904.

Hanaford, Phebe A. *Daughters of America; or, Women of the Century.* Boston: B. B. Russell, 1883.

Haskell, Thomas L. *The Emergence of Professional Social Science: The American Social Science Association and the Nineteenth Century Crisis of Authority.* Urbana: University of Illinois Press, 1977.

Helm, June, ed. *Pioneers of American Anthropology: The Uses of Biography.* Seattle: University of Washington Press, 1966.

Herman, Judith Lewis. *Father-Daughter Incest.* Cambridge: Harvard University Press, 1981.

Hertzberg, Hazel W. "Nationality, Anthropology, and Pan-Indianism in the Life of Arthur C. Parker (Seneca)." *Proceedings of the American Philosophical Society* 123 (1979): 47–72.

———. *The Search for an American Indian Identity: Modern Pan-Indian Movements.* Syracuse, N.Y.: Syracuse University Press, 1971.

Hetherington, Mary Grant. "Private Woman, Public Person: An Account of the Life of Julia Ward Howe from 1819 to 1868." Ph.D. diss., George Washington University, 1982.

Hinsley, Curtis M., Jr. *Savages and Scientists: The Smithsonian Institution and the Development of American Anthropology, 1846–1910.* Washington, D.C.: Smithsonian Institution Press, 1981.

Hinsley, Curtis M., Jr., and Bill Holm. "A Cannibal in the National Museum: The Early Career of Franz Boas in America." *American Anthropologist* 78 (1976): 306–16.

Hough, Walter. "Alice Cunningham Fletcher." *American Anthropologist* 25 (1923): 254–58.

Howe, Julia Ward. *Reminiscences, 1819–1910.* Boston: Houghton Mifflin, 1900.

Hoxie, Frederick E. *A Final Promise: The Campaign to Assimilate the Indians, 1880–1920.* Lincoln: University of Nebraska Press, 1984.

Huntington, Frances Carpenter. "Ladies of 'The Literary.'" *Records of the Columbia Historical Society,* 1966–1968. (Washington, D.C., 1969), 205–15.

Jackson, Helen Hunt. *A Century of Dishonor.* New York: Harper, 1881.

James, Henry. *The Art of Travel.* Edited by Morton Dauwen Zabel. Garden City, N.Y.: Doubleday Anchor, 1962.

Jensen, Robert E., ed. "Commissioner Theodore Roosevelt Visits Indian Reservations, 1892." *Nebraska History* 61 (Spring 1981): 85–106.

Josephy, Alvin M., Jr. *The Nez Perce Indians and the Opening of the Northwest.* New Haven: Yale University Press, 1965.

Judd, Neil M. *The Bureau of American Ethnology: A Partial History.* Norman: University of Oklahoma Press, 1967.

Keller, Dorothy J. "Maria Mitchell, An Early Woman Academician." Ed.D. diss., University of Rochester, 1974.

Kohlstedt, Sally Gregory. "Maria Mitchell and the Advancement of Women in Science." *New England Quarterly* 51 (1978): 39–63.

Laird, Carobeth. *Encounter with an Angry God: Recollections of My Life with John Peabody Harrington*. Banning, Calif.: Malki Museum Press, Morongo Indian Reservation, 1975.

Landford, Gerald. *The Murder of Stanford White*. Indianapolis: Bobbs-Merrill, 1962.

Lanier, Sidney. *Letters, 1869–1873*. Vol. 8. Edited by Charles R. Anderson and Aubrey H. Starke. Baltimore: Johns Hopkins University Press, 1945.

———. *Letters of Sidney Lanier: Selections from His Correspondence, 1866–1881*. New York: Charles Scribner's Sons, 1899.

Lazell, J. Arthur. *Alaskan Apostle: The Life of Sheldon Jackson*. New York: Harper, 1960.

Lee, Dorothy Sara, and Maria La Vigna, eds. *Omaha Indian Music: Historical Recordings from the Fletcher/La Flesche Collection*. Washington, D.C.: Library of Congress, 1985.

Liberty, Margot. "Francis La Flesche: The Osage Odyssey." In *American Indian Intellectuals*, ed. Margot Liberty, 44–59. St Paul: West, 1978.

———. "Native American Informants: The Contribution of Francis La Flesche." In *American Anthropology: The Early Years*. ed. John V. Murra, 99–110. St. Paul: West, 1978.

Livermore, Mary A. *The Story of My Life; or, The Sunshine and Shadow of Seventy Years*. Hartford, Conn.: A. D. Worthington, 1897.

Logan, Mrs. John A. *Thirty Years in Washington; or, Life and Scenes in Our National Capital*. Washington, D.C.: A. D. Worthington, 1902.

Low, A. Maurice. "Washington: The City of Leisure." *Atlantic Monthly* 86 (1900): 767–78.

Lummis, Charles F. "In Memoriam: Alice C. Fletcher." *Art and Archaeology* 16 (1923): 75–76.

Lurie, Nancy O. "Winnebago." *Handbook of North American Indians*, 15. Washington, D.C.: Smithsonian Institution Press, 1978, pp. 690–707.

———. "Women in Early American Anthropology." In *Pioneers of American Anthropology: The Uses of Biography*, ed. June Helm, 29–82. Seattle: University of Washington Press, 1966.

McBeth, Kate. *The Nez Perces Since Lewis and Clark*. New York: Fleming H. Revell, 1908.

McGee, Anita Newcomb. "The Women's Anthropological Society of America." *Science* 13 (1889): 240–42.

McGillycuddy, Julia. *McGillycuddy Agent*. Palo Alto: Stanford University Press, 1941.

McWilliams, Carey. *Southern California Country: An Island on the Land.* 1946. Reprint. Santa Barbara: Peregrine Smith, 1973.

Madeira, Percy C., Jr. *Men in Search of Man: The First Seventy-Five Years of the University Museum of the University of Pennsylvania*. Philadelphia: University of Pennsylvania Press, 1964.

Mark, Joan. *Four Anthropologists: An American Science in Its Early Years.* New York: Neale Watson Science History Publications, 1980.

―――. "Francis La Flesche: The American Indian as Anthropologist." *Isis* 73 (1982): 497–510.

―――. "The Impact of Freud on American Cultural Anthropology, 1909–1945." Ph.D. diss., Harvard University, 1968.

Mauss, Marcel. "Review of *The Omaha Tribe.*" *L'Année sociologique* 12 (1909–12): 104–11.

Mead, Margaret. *The Changing Culture of an Indian Tribe*. New York: Columbia University Press, 1932.

Mitchell, Henry. "Biographical notice of Maria Mitchell." *Proceedings of the American Academy of Arts and Sciences* 25 (1890): 331–43.

Mitchell, Maria. *Life, Letters, and Journals*. Comp. Phebe Mitchell Kendall. Boston: Lee and Shepard, 1896.

Mooney, James. *The Ghost Dance Religion and the Sioux Outbreak of 1890.* Smithsonian Institution, Bureau of American Ethnology, 14th Annual Report. Washington, D.C., 1896.

―――. "The Indian Congress at Omaha." *American Anthropologist* 11 (1899): 128–29.

Mooney, Michael Macdonald. *Evelyn Nesbit and Stanford White: Love and Death in the Gilded Age*. New York: William Morrow, 1976.

Morantz-Sanchez, Regina Markell. *Sympathy and Science: Women Physicians in American Medicine*. New York: Oxford University Press, 1985.

Morgan, Lewis Henry. *The American Beaver and His Works*. Philadelphia: J. B. Lippincott and Co., 1868.

―――. *Ancient Society; or, Researches in the Lines of Human Progress from Savagery through Barbarism to Civilization*. New York: Holt, 1877.

―――. "Factory Systems on Indian Reservations." *Nation* 23 (1876): 58–59.

―――. "The Hue and Cry Against the Indians." *Nation* 23 (1876): 40–41.

―――. "The Indian Question." *Nation* 27 (1878): 332.

Morison, Samuel Eliot. *Three Centuries of Harvard, 1636–1936*. Cambridge: Harvard University Press, 1946.

Morrill, Allen C., and Eleanor D. Morrill. *Out of the Blanket: The Story of Sue and Kate McBeth, Missionaries to the Nez Perces*. Moscow: University Press of Idaho, 1978.

Moses, L. G. *The Indian Man: A Biography of James Mooney*. Urbana: University of Illinois Press, 1984.

Moses, L. G., and Raymond Wilson, eds. *Indian Lives: Essays on Nineteenth and Twentieth-Century Native American Leaders*. Albuquerque: University of New Mexico Press, 1985.

Murie, James R. *The Ceremonies of the Pawnee*. Edited by Douglas R. Parks. Washington: Smithsonian Institution Press, 1981.

Myers, Susan H. "Capitol Hill, 1870–1900: The People and Their Homes." *Records of the Columbia Historical Society*, 1973–74 (Washington, D.C., 1976), 276–99.

Needham, Rodney, ed. *Right and Left*. Chicago: University of Chicago Press, 1973.

Neihardt, John G. *Patterns and Coincidences: A Sequel to All Is But A Beginning*. Columbia: University of Missouri Press, 1978.

Nichols, Jeannette Paddock. *Alaska: A History of Its Administration, Exploitation, and Industrial Development During Its First Half Century Under the Rule of the United States*. Cleveland: Arthur H. Clark, 1924.

Nickerson, Marjorie L. *A Long Way Forward: The First Hundred Years of the Packer Collegiate Institute*. Brooklyn, N.Y.: Packer Collegiate Institute, 1945.

Odell, Ruth. *Helen Hunt Jackson*. New York: D. Appleton-Century, 1939.

Oles, Carolyn. *Night Watches: Inventions on the life of Maria Mitchell*. Cambridge, Mass.: alice james books, 1985.

Olson, James C. *History of Nebraska*. Lincoln: University of Nebraska Press, 1955.

Ostrander, Stephen M. *A History of Brooklyn and King's County*, 2 vols. Brooklyn, N. Y.: privately printed, 1894.

Otis, D. S. *The Dawes Act and the Allotment of Indian Lands*, ed. Francis Paul Prucha. Norman: University of Oklahoma Press, 1973.

Pantaleoni, Hewitt. "A Few of Densmore's Dakota Rhythms Reconsidered." MS, 1985.

———. "A Reconsideration of Fillmore Reconsidered." *American Music* 3 (1985): 217–28.

Parkman, Mary R. *Heroines of Service*. New York: Century Company, 1918.

Parks, Douglas R. "James R. Murie, Pawnee, 1862–1921." In *American Indian Intellectuals*, ed. Margot Liberty, 75–89. St Paul: West, 1978.

Parmenter, Ross. "Glimpses of a Friendship." In *Pioneers of American Anthropology: The Uses of Biography*, ed. June Helm. Seattle: University of Washington Press, 1966.

——. "Zelia Maria Magdalena Nuttall." In *Notable American Women*, ed. Edward T. James, Janet Wilson James, and Paul Boyer. Cambridge: Harvard University Press, 1971.

Perry, Helen Swick. *Psychiatrist of America: The Life of Harry Stack Sullivan*. Cambridge: Harvard University Press, 1982.

Priest, Loring Benson. *Uncle Sam's Stepchildren: The Reformation of United States Indian Policy, 1865–1887*. New Brunswick, N.J.: Rutgers University Press, 1942.

Prucha, Francis Paul. "Thomas Jefferson Morgan (1889–93)." In *The Commissioners of Indian Affairs, 1824–1977*, ed. Robert M. Kvasnicka and Herman J. Viola, 193–203. Lincoln: University of Nebraska Press, 1979.

Putnam, F. W. "The Serpent Mound of Ohio." *Century Magazine* 39 (April 1890): 871–88.

Richards, Laura E., and Maud Howe Elliott. *Julia Ward Howe, 1819–1910*. 2 vols. Boston: Houghton Mifflin, 1916.

Rideout, Henry Miller. *William Jones: Indian, Cowboy, American Scholar, and Anthropologist in the Field*. New York: Frederick A. Stokes, 1912.

Rogin, Michael Paul. *Fathers and Children: Andrew Jackson and the Subjection of the American Indians*. New York: Knopf, 1975.

Rosenberg, Rosalind. *Beyond Separate Spheres: Intellectual Roots of Modern Feminism*. New Haven: Yale University Press, 1982.

Rossiter, Margaret W. *Women Scientists in America: Struggles and Strategies to 1940*. Baltimore: Johns Hopkins University Press, 1982.

Rydell, Robert. *All the World's a Fair: America's International Expositions, 1876–1916*. Chicago: University of Chicago Press, 1983.

Seagle, William. "The Murder of Spotted Tail." *Indian Historian* 3 (1970): 10–22.

Sherwood, Morgan B. *Exploration of Alaska, 1865–1900*. New Haven: Yale University Press, 1965.

Sicherman, Barbara. "The Uses of Diagnosis: Doctors, Patients, and Neurasthenia." *Journal of the History of Medicine and Allied Sciences* 32 (1977): 33–54.

[Slayden, Ellen Maury] *Washington Wife: Journal of Ellen Maury Slayden from 1897–1919.* New York: Harper and Row, 1962.

Slickpoo, Allen P., Sr. *Noon-Nee-Me-Poo (We, the Nez Perces)* Privately published, 1973.

Smith, Hubert. "Notes on Omaha Ethnohistory, 1763–1820." *Plains Anthropologist* 18 (1973): 257–70.

Smith, Jane F., and Robert M. Kvasnicka, eds. *Indian-White Relations: A Persistent Paradox.* Washington, D.C.: Howard University Press, 1976.

Smith-Rosenberg, Carroll. *Disorderly Conduct: Visions of Gender in Victorian America.* New York: A. Knopf, 1985.

Solomon, Barbara Miller. *In the Company of Educated Women: A History of Women in Higher Education in America.* New Haven: Yale University Press, 1985.

Starr, Kevin. *Inventing the Dream: California through the Progressive Era.* New York: Oxford University Press, 1985.

Stein, Gertrude. *The Autobiography of Alice B. Toklas.* New York: Harcourt, Brace, 1933.

———. *Everybody's Autobiography.* New York: Random House, 1937.

———. *The Geographical History of America.* New York: Random House, 1936.

———. *The Making of Americans.* 1925. Reprint. New York: Something Else Press, 1966.

———. *Three Lives.* 1909. Reprint. New York: Vintage, 1936.

———. *Writings and Lectures, 1909–1945.* Edited by Patricia Meyerowitz. 1967. Reprint. London: Penguin Books, 1971.

Stevenson, Robert. "Written Sources for Indian Music until 1882." *Ethnomusicology* 17 (1973): 1–40.

Stocking, George W., Jr., ed. *The History of Anthropology Newsletter,* 1973–.

Storrs, Charles. *The Storrs Family, Genealogical and Other Memoranda.* New York: privately printed, 1886.

Stumpf, Carl. *Die Anfange der Musik.* Leipzig: J. A. Barth, 1911.

Sturge, Elizabeth. *Reminiscences of My Life and Some Account of the Children of William and Charlotte Sturge and the Sturge Family of Bristol.* Privately printed, 1928.

Sullivan, Harry Stack. *The Fusion of Psychiatry and Social Science.* New York: W. W. Norton, 1964.

Tibbles, Thomas Henry. *Buckskin and Blanket Days: Memories of a Friend of the Indians.* Garden City, N.Y.: Doubleday and Co., 1957.

———. "The Indian Emancipation Act." *Lend a Hand* 1 (1886): 285.

————. *Ploughed Under: The Story of an Indian Chief.* New York: Fords, Howard, and Hurlbert, 1881.

————. *The Ponca Chiefs: An Account of the Trial of Standing Bear.* 1880. Edited by Kay Graber. Reprint. Lincoln: University of Nebraska Press, 1972.

Vennum, Thomas, Jr. "Frances Theresa Densmore." In *Notable American Women*, ed. Edward T. James, Janet Wilson James, and Paul Boyer. Cambridge: Harvard University Press, 1980.

Walker, Deward E., Jr. *Conflict and Schism in Nez Perce Acculturation: A Study of Religion and Politics.* Pullman: Washington State University Press, 1968.

Waller, Altina L. *Reverend Beecher and Mrs. Tilton: Sex and Class in Victorian America.* Amherst: University of Massachusetts Press, 1982.

Warner, Deborah. "Science Education for Women in Antebellum America." *Isis* 69 (1978): 58–67.

Wead, Charles Kasson. "Contributions to the History of Musical Scales." *Annual Report of the U.S. National Museum* (1900), 421–62.

Welch, Rebecca Hancock. "Alice Cunningham Fletcher, Anthropologist and Indian Rights Reformer." Ph.D. diss., George Washington University, 1980.

Whitehill, Walter Muir. *Boston: A Topographical History.* Cambridge: Harvard University Press, 1959.

Wiebe, Robert. *The Search for Order, 1877–1920.* New York: Hill and Wang, 1967.

Wilkins, Thurman. "Alice Cunningham Fletcher." In *Notable American Women*, ed. Edward T. James, Janet Wilson James, and Paul Boyer. Cambridge: Harvard University Press, 1971.

Willard, Frances E., and Mary A. Livermore, eds. *A Woman of the Century: 1470 Biographical Sketches.* Buffalo: C. W. Moulton, 1893.

Wilson, Dorothy Clarke. *Bright Eyes: The Story of Susette La Flesche, An Omaha Indian.* New York: McGraw-Hill, 1974.

Wood, W. Raymond, and Margot Liberty, eds. *Anthropology on the Great Plains.* Lincoln: University of Nebraska Press, 1980.

Wright, Helen. *Sweeper in the Sky: The Life of Maria Mitchell.* 1949. Reprint. Nantucket, Mass.: Nantucket Maria Mitchell Association, 1959.

Index